Recht und Verfassung in Afrika –
Law and Constitution in Africa

Volume 50

Oliver C. Ruppel | Harald Ginzky [eds.]

# Legislating for the Future

## The Pan-African Model Law for Sustainable Soil Management

Nomos

**The Deutsche Nationalbibliothek** lists this publication in the Deutsche Nationalbibliografie; detailed bibliographic data are available on the Internet at http://dnb.d-nb.de

1st Edition 2026



Published by
Nomos Verlagsgesellschaft mbH & Co. KG
Waldseestraße 3–5 | 76530 Baden-Baden
www.nomos.de

Production of the printed version:
Nomos Verlagsgesellschaft mbH & Co. KG
Waldseestraße 3–5 | 76530 Baden-Baden

ISBN 978-3-7560-3274-7 (Print)
ISBN 9978-3-7489-6660-9 (ePDF)
DOI https://doi.org/10.5771/9783748966609

Onlineversion
Nomos eLibrary

Table of contents

## Preface by the editors

Healthy soils are of great importance for human survival. Without healthy soils, people in Africa cannot be provided with sufficient nutrition, prosperity cannot be achieved, and the culture, traditions, and respect among humans and towards nature may be lost.

The adoption of the Model Law on Soil Management in Africa by the Pan-African Parliament on 6 November 2025 marked the end of a long, extensive, and successful process.[1] Hopefully, it will be a turning point towards real changes in the daily realities of people in Africa.

Based on the outcomes of two workshops in Kampala, Uganda, and Nairobi, Kenya, held in 2017[2] and 2018,[3] an initial analysis was conducted to map out options for a model law on soil management in Africa.[4] After a break due to the COVID-19 pandemic, considering the findings of this analysis, the Pan-African Parliament decided in 2022 to work towards such a model law.[5] From 2023 onwards, a draft of the model law was prepared by a team of legal and soil experts for further consideration and refinement by the Parliament.[6] The two previous publications, *African Soil*

---

1 See https://pap.au.int/en/news/press-releases/2025-11-06/african-parliamentarians-adopt-continents-first-model-law, accessed 19 March 2026; https://www.fao.org/partnerships/parliamentary-alliances/news/news-article/en/c/1754895/, accessed 19 March 2026; https://www.su.ac.za/en/news/pan-african-parliament-adopts-continents-first-model-law-sustainable-soil-management, accessed 19 March 2026.

2 See https://www.umweltbundesamt.de/system/files/medien/421/dokumente/kampala_workshop_program.pdf, accessed 23 March 2026; https://www.umweltbundesamt.de/system/files/medien/421/dokumente/kampala_outcome_document_301117.pdf, accessed 23 March 2026.

3 See https://www.umweltbundesamt.de/system/files/medien/2875/dokumente/nairobi_program_final_13_august_2018.pdf, accessed 23 March 2026; https://www.umweltbundesamt.de/system/files/medien/2875/dokumente/nairobi_outcome_document.pdf, accessed 23 March 2026.

4 See https://www.africanparliamentarynews.com/2020/03/pap-maps-first-steps-for-model.html?m=1, accessed 19 March 2026.

5 Republic of Namibia (2022), *Report of the First Ordinary Session of the Sixth Parliament of the Pan-African Parliament (PAP)*, Midrand, Johannesburg, South Africa, from 24 October to 12 November 2022, available at https://www.parliament.na/wp-content/uploads/2023/02/Report-of-the-First-Ordinary-Session-of-the-6th-Paliament-of-PAP.pdf, accessed 14 April 2026. The report noted that the Model Law for Sustainable Soil Management in Africa was presented and adopted during the session (page 16); Republic of The Gambia (2022), *Report of the National Assembly delegation to the Pan-African Parliament*, Sixth Parliament, First Ordinary Session, Midrand, South Africa, October–November 2022, available at https://www.assembly.gm/wp-content/uploads/2023/03/Report-on-the-First-Ordinary-Session-of-the-Sixth-Pan-African-Parliament.pdf, accessed 14 April 2026. The report records that, in his presentation of the draft report on the project to develop a model law on soil management, Hon. Assane Marou dit Koubou (Niger) pointed out that Kenya, Cameroon, and Zambia were the pilot countries for studying African soils, and further indicated that the study was conducted under the auspices of Stellenbosch University, South Africa (pages 23–24).

6 See https://pap.au.int/en/news/press-releases/2025-09-26/pap-analyses-draft-model-law-sustainable-soil-management-africa, accessed 19 March 2026; https://pap.au.int/en/news/press-releases/2025-10-19/consultations-central-northern-and-western-african-regions-model-la, accessed 19 March 2026.

*Protection Law* (2021)[7] and *Legal Pathways to Sustainable Soil Management in Africa* (2025),[8] were essential in providing the analytical foundation for the Model Law.

Now, the new book *Legislating for the Future: The Pan-African Model Law for Sustainable Soil Management*, the third in the series of publications, intends first to conclude the process and, second, enable the national domestication of the Model Law. To these ends, it makes the Model Law and the so-called Commentaries on regulatory options for specific topics of soil governance publicly accessible. The characteristics of the Model Law are critically analysed to assess whether, and to what extent, it can serve as a benchmark, blueprint, or practical toolbox for African countries and, potentially, other regions globally. The volume further includes a dedicated chapter on the colonial legacy of soil governance and explores pathways towards the decolonisation of African soils. In addition, the role of digital technologies in sustainable soil management is addressed, highlighting both emerging opportunities and associated challenges, particularly those related to artificial intelligence. Finally, the book features a chapter on soil governance and digital transformation within the African Union, offering a comparative legal analysis from a European Union perspective.

It was our honour to coordinate this unique and somewhat historic project over the years. It was a pleasure and a privilege to support the Pan-African Parliament in its noble task. The adoption of the Model Law could only be achieved through the collaborative spirit of the Committee on Rural Economy, Agriculture, Natural Resources, and Environment of the Pan-African Parliament. Moreover, continuous support has been provided by several international organisations, such as the United Nations Environment Programme (UNEP), the Food and Agriculture Organization (FAO), the United Nations Convention to Combat Desertification (UNCCD), the African Soil Partnership, and the African Ministerial Conference on the Environment (AMCEN).[9]

We would also like to cordially thank the team of African legal experts for their hard work and commitment to this project over the years. Without all their inputs, the Model Law could not have been materialised. Finally, it is highlighted that the financial support of the German government made the whole endeavour possible. While the workshops held in Kampala, Uganda, and Nairobi, Kenya in 2017 and 2018, were jointly funded by the Konrad Adenauer Foundation's Climate Policy and Energy

7 See https://www.nomos-shop.de/en/p/african-soil-protection-law-gr-978-3-8487-6693-2, accessed 23 March 2026.

8 See https://www.nomos-shop.de/en/p/legal-pathways-to-sustainable-soil-management-in-africa-gr-978-3-7560-0210-8, accessed 23 March 2026.

9 This collaboration was further formalised through Memoranda of Understanding between the United Nations Environment Programme (UNEP), the German Environment Agency, and Stellenbosch University's Development and Rule of Law Programme (DROP) (2021–2023; 2024–2027), which, *inter alia*, supported the development of the Model Law, capacity-building workshops, and knowledge production on soil governance. Additional institutional backing was reflected in Letters of Intent issued by the African Soil Partnership (ASP) and the Food and Agriculture Organization (FAO) (25 February 2022), as well as the African Ministerial Conference on the Environment (AMCEN) (8 July 2022).

Security Programme for Sub-Saharan Africa, the German Environment Agency (UBA), and the German Gesellschaft für Internationale Zusammenarbeit (GIZ), the first project phase (2018-2020) was funded by GIZ and the second project phase (2023-2025) was funded by the German Ministry for Economic Cooperation and Development (BMZ). Regarding the project's administration, we cordially thank the professional staff of the Development and Rule of Law Programme (DROP), which is affiliated with both the Faculty of Law and the School for Climate Studies at Stellenbosch University (SU) in South Africa.

Ultimately, we need to thank all the partners, legislators, parliamentarians, diplomats, traditional leaders, soil scientists, government officials, members of civil society, religious leaders, students, women and men, both at the grassroots level and in the cities, where we held consultations over the years. With this Model Law, Africa takes a decisive step towards ensuring that the continent's soils, one of its most fundamental natural resources, remain alive, productive, and protected for generations to come. Its reality represents a historic step towards harmonised soil governance across Africa and affirms the Pan-African Parliament's growing legislative maturity and leadership in environmental and agricultural policy.

The protection of soil is not merely an environmental issue—it is an act of justice, a moral duty, and an investment in Africa's future. More still needs to be done: In particular, the national transposition of the Model Law will require will, determination and commitment. More so, its implementation on the ground. Yet we are convinced that it was and will be worth every effort. Time is of essence in the interest of the people. Therefore, the work needs to be continued.

*Oliver C. Ruppel* — *Harald Ginzky*

Stellenbosch (South Africa) — Dessau (Germany)

April 2026

# Preface by the Pan-African Parliament

The process of developing a standard, whether legislative or otherwise, is subject to certain criteria for its adoption. These criteria determine its effectiveness and efficiency.

Some authors believe that the adoption of a successful standard must necessarily address social needs and integrate social practices.[1] In general, certain dimensions are often required for a standard to be valid: it must be adopted in strict compliance with the procedures laid down for this purpose; it must meet the criteria of legitimacy by not only conforming to social values but also being in line with customs and taking into account the plurality of social beliefs; and it must be effectively applied by the social actors who have internalised it.

In general, the adoption of the standard must result from a process involving several stakeholders, particularly through consultation and participation.

Africa is a reservoir of arable land, representing 60% of the world's unexploited land. It is home to a significant share of the world's biodiversity and stores a large proportion of the world's carbon, helping regulate the climate and purify water. In Africa, given its multifunctionality, soil is one of the main tools for reducing poverty.

However, Africa is facing accelerated soil degradation and depletion. Sustainable soil management is therefore a priority for the development and survival of its people. This explains the growing interest of African legislators.

A group of experts working at a research centre called the Development and Rule of Law Programme (DROP) at Stellenbosch University, one of the universities in an African Union member country, namely South Africa, conducted extensive research on soil management in Africa over several years. Researchers from several African universities took part in this study, which covered countries in all sub-regions, including:

- In East Africa: Kenya, Uganda
- In Southern Africa: South Africa, Zambia, Namibia, Mozambique
- In Central Africa: Cameroon
- In West Africa: Ghana, Burkina Faso
- In North Africa: Morocco
- Island countries: Madagascar

Following this study, the group of experts noted disparities in legislative standards for soil management across African countries. To this end, they suggested drafting a model law on soil management.

The Pan-African Parliament (PAP) is one of the organs of the African Union (AU). Its role, among others, is to draft model laws. These laws are not binding.

---

1 Jean (1976); Ost & Van de Kerchove (2002).

Following meetings between the DROP expert group and members of the Standing Committee on Rural Economy, Agriculture, Natural Resources, and Environment between 2020 and 2022, the PAP adopted the decision to draft a preliminary model law on soil management.

This adoption was made effective by the adoption in 2022 of Resolution PAP.6/PLN/RES/19/NOV.22 of the Pan-African Parliament on the development of a model law on sustainable soil management, which, among other things, instructs the Committee on Rural Economy, Agriculture, Natural Resources, and Environment to lead the development of a model law on soil management, taking into account the diverse legal traditions of the African continent, and to submit the model law to the plenary of the Pan-African Parliament for consideration.

Following this resolution, the relevant Committee held technical meetings to exchange and share ideas with the drafters of the preliminary draft, first in Midrand, South Africa (November 2024), then in Nairobi, Kenya (December 2024), with a view to preparing a draft for the Committee's plenary session.

On 27 February 2025 in Midrand, the draft bill was presented and adopted at the Commission's plenary session. To this end, the Commission's plenary session recommended holding a consultative meeting to finalise the model law. This meeting was held on 28 and 29 April 2025 in Stellenbosch.

On 30 July 2025, the draft model law was presented to the PAP plenary by the Chair of the Commission, followed by comments from the DROP experts. By its resolution PAP.6/PLN/CREANRE/RES/08/JUL.25 of 31 July 2025, the PAP plenary voted on the first reading of the Model Law on Soil Management, and by the same resolution, the plenary requested the Committee on Rural Economy, Agriculture, Natural Resources, and Environment to conduct further consultations across the continent with all relevant stakeholders, with a view to incorporating their views into the Model Law before its final adoption by the PAP plenary. Two major regional consultations were organised in Africa:

- In Midrand, on 25 and 26 September 2025 (for Southern and Eastern Africa); and
- in Cairo, Egypt, on 15 and 16 October 2025 (for Northern, Western, and Central Africa).

For each consultation, several stakeholders from different backgrounds, including academics, the Food and Agriculture Organization (FAO), the African Union Development Agency-NEPAD (AUDA-NEPAD), the Southern African Development Community (SADC), Pan-African Climate Justice Alliance (PACJA), Alliance for Food Sovereignty in Africa (AFSA), Seed and Knowledge Initiative (SKI), and civil society, actively participated in and contributed to the text.

The draft model law was resubmitted to the plenary session on 6 November 2025 for general debate and article-by-article voting. Thus, on 6 November 2025, the PAP plenary adopted the Model Law on Soil Management.[2]

Following the Pan-African Parliament's adoption of the Model Law, the resolution adopting it is forwarded to the AU Assembly of Heads of State and Government for final approval. The law approved by the AU is then sent to and disseminated among national parliaments and the public. As indicated in the resolution of 6 November 2025, the role of the PAP will be to follow up with states to assess the status of implementation.

The Model Law on Soil Management in Africa complied with all the adoption procedures set out in the AU Constitutive Act, its Protocol on the PAP, and the PAP Rules of Procedure. The technical and public consultations were conducted to the great satisfaction of the participants and the general public. It is hoped that its integration into national laws and its implementation will be satisfactory.

*Prof Garry Sakata Tawab*
Professor at the University of Kinshasa (Democratic Republic of the Congo)
Member of the PAP and Chair of the Committee for Rural Economy, Agriculture, Natural Resources, and Environment

Kinshasa (Democratic Republic of the Congo), March 2026

2 See https://pap.au.int/en/news/press-releases/2025-11-06/african-parliamentarians-adopt-continents-first-model-law, accessed 19 March 2026; https://www.fao.org/partnerships/parliamentary-alliances/news/news-article/en/c/1754895/, accessed 19 March 2026; https://www.su.ac.za/en/news/pan-african-parliament-adopts-continents-first-model-law-sustainable-soil-management, accessed 19 March 2026.

# Foreword by the BMZ

The adoption of the "Model Law on Soil Management in Africa" by the Pan-African Parliament (PAP) on 6 November 2025 marks a significant milestone.[1] The adoption underscores the essential role of healthy soils in addressing the core challenges of the people of Africa. Healthy soils are central to eradicating hunger and poverty, enabling sustainable economic development, strengthening climate resilience, and securing a safe future for Africa's population. In addition, the adoption emphasises that political leaders must take responsibility for establishing a framework to protect and sustainably manage soils through legislative decisions, capable administrative institutions, awareness-raising mechanisms, and sufficient funding.

The Model Law is the result of an exemplary development cooperation project, a partnership between African and German institutions in the common interest. A key enabler was the scientific analysis using a participatory, bottom-up approach, involving African and German experts, African political leaders, civil society and communities on the ground, and, in particular, cooperation with the PAP and the responsible Committee on Rural Economy, Agriculture, Environment, and Natural Resources. All of this makes the whole process a real success story for Africa, the PAP, and cooperation between Africa and Germany.

The process started in 2017 and 2018, when two conferences on the sustainable management of soils in Africa were held in Kampala, Uganda, and Nairobi, Kenya, involving African experts, international organisations such as FAO and UNCCD, and international experts. This laid the foundation for the Model Law, which is based on scientific analysis, as documented in the two published books: "African Soil Protection Law" (2021) and "Legal Pathways to Sustainable Soil Management in Africa" (2025).

The Federal Ministry for Economic Cooperation and Development in Germany (BMZ) has promoted this endeavour from the very beginning through funding, as well as political and technical support, to leverage sustainable soil management to strengthen food security, rural development, and resilience in Africa. In doing so, BMZ advances strategic partnerships and promotes implementation in partner countries, in line with BMZ's 2023 Africa strategy, "Shaping the Future with Africa," and the German government's 2025 Africa Policy Guidelines, "Shaping Partnerships Together in a Changing World".

The Model Law on Soil Management adopted by the PAP is a pioneering sign for Africa's efforts to reconcile environmental sustainability, tenure rights, digitalisation, gender equality, and foreign investment rules. It includes modern mechanisms, such

---

1 See https://pap.au.int/en/news/press-releases/2025-11-06/african-parliamentarians-adopt-continents-first-model-law, accessed 19 March 2026; https://www.fao.org/partnerships/parliamentary-alliances/news/news-article/en/c/1754895/, accessed 19 March 2026; https://www.su.ac.za/en/news/pan-african-parliament-adopts-continents-first-model-law-sustainable-soil-management, accessed 19 March 2026.

as soil impact assessments, compensation for degradation, and zoning approaches. It emphasises proper implementation and enforcement tools. This makes it a benchmark for modern soil governance worldwide.

Therefore, we welcome this book, "Legislating for the Future: The Pan-African Model Law for Sustainable Soil Management," which includes the Model Law on Soil Management, as well as the Commentaries and helpful explanatory chapters, all of which are accessible to a wider audience. Much remains to be done, especially the domestication of the Model Law now in all African states. BMZ remains committed to working with its partners to advance ambitious action for sustainable soil management.

We extend our sincere appreciation to all actors involved in the process, in particular to the PAP Committee on Rural Economy, Agriculture, Environment, and Natural Resources for its leadership throughout the formulation of the Model Law, as well as to the German Environment Agency (UBA), and to the Development and Rule of Law Programme (DROP) of Stellenbosch University, South Africa for the joint coordination of the project since 2019.

*Dr Ariane Hildebrandt*
Federal Ministry for Economic Cooperation and Development in Germany (BMZ)
Director General for Global Health, Equality of Opportunities, Digital Technologies, and Food Security

Bonn (Germany), 4 February 2026

## Foreword by the UNCCD

The United Nations Convention to Combat Desertification (UNCCD) is the Rio Convention that operates as "the global voice for land" and has a particular origin, identity, and historical connection with Africa. Within the Convention's mandates, healthy land is the foundation of resilient and prosperous economies, communities, and societies.

There is no healthy land without healthy soils. Soil is the natural medium that connects groundwater and plants on the land's surface. Soil is a living entity and, when healthy, hosts rich biodiversity, acts as the largest natural reservoir of water, and provides nutritious food. Without healthy soils, UNCCD cannot accomplish its mandate and mission.

For this reason, the adoption of the "Model Law on Soil Management in Africa" by the Pan-African Parliament on 6 November 2025 is a landmark moment.[1] This Model Law will be instrumental in improving living conditions across Africa and enabling food and water security, resilience, and prosperity.

The Model Law takes a holistic approach, incorporating modern governance instruments and provisions to facilitate effective implementation and enforcement. It also addresses critical issues such as land tenure, gender equality and equity, and the need for foreign investments. All of those are essential to ensure that soils are sustainably managed in the interests of present and future generations.

In 2015, the world community adopted the 2030 Agenda for Sustainable Development, including the important objective in SDG 15 to strive towards Land Degradation Neutrality (LDN). According to UNCCD, 1.5 billion hectares of land globally will need to be restored by 2030 to achieve this target. Through this Model Law, Africa is demonstrating global leadership by showing how to develop effective instruments to protect, restore, and manage its land, particularly agricultural land, which is recognised as a critical asset for generating jobs, nutritious food, and thriving investments and inclusive growth.

UNCCD extends its deep appreciation and gratitude to the Pan-African Parliament for its visionary leadership and commitment on the matter. Sincere thanks also go to the two coordinating institutions, the German Environment Agency (UBA) and the Development and Rule of Law Programme (DROP) of Stellenbosch University, South Africa, as well as to the many African experts and stakeholders who contributed their expertise and insights, and to the German Federal Ministry for Economic Cooperation and Development (BMZ) for its continued technical and financial support.

---

1 See https://pap.au.int/en/news/press-releases/2025-11-06/african-parliamentarians-adopt-continents-first-model-law, accessed 19 March 2026; https://www.fao.org/partnerships/parliamentary-alliances/news/news-article/en/c/1754895/, accessed 19 March 2026; https://www.su.ac.za/en/news/pan-african-parliament-adopts-continents-first-model-law-sustainable-soil-management, accessed 19 March 2026.

Together we can work to ensure that healthy land and soils become the foundation for prosperous, resilient, and inclusive African economies and societies.

*Yasmine Fouad*
Under-Secretary-General to the United Nations & Executive Secretary of the United Nations Convention to Combat Desertification (UNCCD)

Bonn (Germany), 27 February 2026

## Foreword by the FAO

Healthy soils are fundamental to life on this planet. They underpin food and nutrition security, agricultural productivity, climate resilience, and the natural systems that sustain plant, animal, and human life. Yet soil is a finite and fragile resource. Across regions, including in Africa, soil degradation continues to threaten livelihoods, ecosystems, and the long-term sustainability of agrifood systems. Recognising the central role of soils, the Food and Agriculture Organization of the United Nations (FAO) places sustainable soil management at the heart of its Strategic Framework 2022–2031 and its vision of achieving the *Four Betters*: better production, better nutrition, a better environment, and a better life for all. Healthy soils are indispensable to each of these objectives. They support productive, resilient agriculture, safe, nutritious food, environmental sustainability, and people's resilience and livelihoods.

While knowledge on sustainable soil management continues to grow, experience shows that lasting progress depends on how this knowledge is reflected in laws, institutions, and policies. Legal and policy frameworks translate knowledge into rights and responsibilities, shape land-use decisions, and ensure accountability over time. For this reason, FAO, through its Legal Office's Development Law Service, supports members in strengthening the legal foundations for sustainable natural resource management, including soils, by assisting them in developing national measures that take into account their respective legal traditions and institutional frameworks. In this context, the PAP Model Law on Soil Management outlines key elements identified by FAO as essential building blocks for effective legislative and policy frameworks to support sustainable soil management.

Over the years, FAO has developed several resources to assist countries in reinforcing their legal frameworks in this critical area. The Voluntary Guidelines for Sustainable Soil Management (VGSSM) were developed through an inclusive process under the Global Soil Partnership as an internationally agreed reference for sustainable soil management. They are complemented by FAO's legal knowledge platforms, notably FAOLEX and SoiLEX, which provide access to national legal and policy instruments related to soil protection and soil degradation, and enhance legal understanding of sustainable soil management. FAO will continue to work closely with members and regional institutions to support inclusive and informed law-making. This engagement reflects FAO's conviction in the vital role of coherent, effective, and context-appropriate legal responses in promoting sustainable soil management as a cornerstone of sustainable development and the foundation of the well-being of present and future generations.

*Donata Rugarabamu* Rome (Italy), 27 February 2026
Assistant Director-General / Legal Counsel
Food and Agriculture Organization of the United Nations

## About the authors and editors

**Dr Emma CHITSOVE (lead author)**
A qualified lawyer and a registered attorney in Zimbabwe and Botswana, with a career spanning thirteen years. Over the past five years, she has focused on natural resource management in Botswana, specialising in sustainable wildlife management and community-based natural resource practices. Since 2016, she has been a lecturer in law at the University of Botswana. She is an accomplished legal researcher, having published a monograph and numerous articles in academic journals on environmental protection and other areas of law. Dr Chitsove is an active member of the Law Society of Botswana and the Association of Environmental Law Lecturers in African Universities, contributing significantly to the development and dissemination of environmental legal knowledge in Africa.

**Ines DEHAENE (author)**
A student pursuing a Master of Laws (LLM) degree at KU Leuven, Belgium, including a double degree in collaboration with Stellenbosch University, South Africa. As part of this double degree, she completed an LLM in International Trade Law at Stellenbosch University, where she worked as an assistant for the Development and Rule of Law Programme (DROP) under the supervision of Professor OC Ruppel. Her involvement in developing the Model Law on Soil Management inspired her master's thesis, which focused on the legal framework governing the use of digitalisation, particularly artificial intelligence, in soil monitoring and protection.

**Prof Riyad FAKHRI (lead author)**
A Professor of Law and Director of the Business Law Research Laboratory at Hassan First University, Morocco. He is an expert consultant-evaluator for the Moroccan National Centre for Scientific and Technical Research and a co-editor of Biodiversity and Nature Conservation Law and Policy in the Middle East and North Africa Region. He has also contributed to works on water resource protection in North Africa and institutional responses to climate change in the MENA region, published in Climate Change Law and Policy in the Middle East and North Africa Region. Additionally, he serves as Vice President of the Association of Environmental Law Lecturers at Middle Eastern and North African Universities.

**Dr Harald GINZKY (editor and coordinating lead author)**
Lawyer with 30 years of expertise in environmental law. He has authored over 120 scientific papers covering a diverse range of environmental law topics. Since 2003, he has been affiliated with the German Environment Agency (UBA), contributing to German delegations to various international environmental treaties and organisations, including the International Seabed Authority, the International Maritime Organisation,

the UNCCD, OSPAR, HELCOM, FAO, and the Global Soil Partnership. Additionally, he has extensive experience in technical cooperation, particularly in Africa. Dr Ginzky serves as the editor-in-chief of the International Yearbook of Soil Law and Policy (Springer) and has overseen two special issues on "Soil Governance" in the journal Soil Security (Elsevier).

**Dr Delwendé Innocent KIBA (lead author)**
A Soil Scientist at the National Centre for Scientific and Technological Research in Burkina Faso. He currently serves as the President of the Soil Science Society of Burkina Faso and is a former Minister of Agriculture. As a co-author of numerous publications on soil fertility management, he has made significant contributions to the advancement of soil science. He has also mentored and trained many students in the field. In recognition of his expertise, Dr Kiba has been affiliated with the African Academy of Sciences for the 2021-2025 term.

**Eng. Laban Kipkorir KIPLAGAT (lead author)**
Registered engineer with a Bachelor's in Agricultural Engineering from Egerton University and a master's in project planning and management from the University of Nairobi. Kiplagat has served as Director of Agriculture, Land, and Environment Management at the Ministry of Agriculture and Livestock Development and is the Chairman of the Steering Committee of the Inter-Sectoral Forum on Agroecology and Agrobiodiversity (ISFAA). He is also a member of the Engineers' Board and the Institution of Engineers of Kenya.

**Dr Ruda MURRAY (author)**
A qualified lawyer and Postdoctoral Research Fellow at the Faculty of Law, Stellenbosch University, South Africa. She is also a researcher for the Development and Rule of Law Programme (DROP) at Stellenbosch University. She earned her Bachelor of Laws (LLB) from Stellenbosch University. Dr Murray pursued further studies at the University of Cape Town, where she received her Master of Laws (LLM) in Marine and Environmental Law. She completed her Doctor of Laws (LLD) at Stellenbosch University under the supervision of Prof OC Ruppel. Her research focuses on environmental law, natural resource governance, and the intersection of international law, sustainable development, and ecological protection.

**Félicie RALALAHARIMIADANA (lead author)**
CEO of Tontolo Maharitra Research and Consultancy Cabinet, she is a legal consultant and project leader with extensive expertise in sustainable development. She has completed 16 major studies and contributed to drafting laws on tourism, biosafety, urban planning, and land use. She holds advanced degrees in law, public administration, urban management, sustainable tourism, and environmental law. Her career includes

roles as Director of Tourism, Environment, and Regional Development, as well as Advisor to ministers in justice, environment, and urban planning. She has consulted for organisations such as the World Bank, UNICEF, and UNDP, focusing on protected areas, tourism codes, urban planning, and biosafety.

**Prof Oliver C. RUPPEL (editor and coordinating lead author)**
Professor of Law, Faculty of Law, Stellenbosch University, South Africa and Director, Development and Rule of Law Programme (DROP), School for Climate Studies, Stellenbosch University. Director, Research Centre for Climate Law (ClimLaw: Graz), University of Graz, Austria. Professor Extraordinaire, University of Central Africa (UCAC), Yaoundé, Cameroon; Strathmore Law School, Nairobi, Kenya; China-Africa Institute for Business and Law, Xiangtan University, China; and European Faculty of Law, Nova University, Slovenia. Founding Director, Climate Policy and Energy Security Programme for sub-Saharan Africa, Konrad-Adenauer-Stiftung, Germany; founding WTO Chair-holder, World Trade Organisation (WTO) and University of Namibia. Co-editor of the International Yearbook of Soil Law and Policy (Springer) and member of the editorial board of the journal Soil Security (Elsevier).

**Dr Pamela Towela SAMBO (lead author)**
Holds a PhD in Environmental Law from the University of Manchester, a Master of Laws in Environmental Law from the University of KwaZulu-Natal, and a Bachelor of Laws from the University of Zambia. With 24 years of extensive experience in legal practice and policy research, she is a licensed lawyer specialising in environmental law. Her research focuses on critical issues, including legislating for sustainable soil management in Africa, the nexus between soils and climate change, climate justice, and human rights. Dr Sambo collaborates with the Centre for International Sustainable Development Law, a global think tank advancing law and governance for sustainable development and climate change. In addition to her research contributions, she serves as Chairperson of the Zambia Human Rights Commission and lectures in law at the University of Zambia.

**Prof Christopher Funwie TAMASANG (lead author)**
Holds a PhD in Environmental Law from the University of Yaoundé II in Cameroon and is a Professor of Law in its Faculty of Laws and Political Science. He is the first Vice Dean of the Faculty, responsible for Programming and Academic Activities, and coordinates the Master's two programs in English Law. Additionally, he directs the university's Interdisciplinary Research Laboratory on Environment, Natural Resources, and Sustainable Development Law. As a senior international legal consultant specialising in environmental and natural resource issues, he has authored numerous scholarly publications in Environmental and Natural Resource Law. He belongs to several international learned societies, notably the Academy of Environmental Law

and the World Commission on Environmental Law. Furthermore, he is the Vice Chair-person of the Association of Environmental Law Lecturers from African Universities (ASSELLAU).

# The Model Law on Soil Management in Africa: explanatory notes

*Harald Ginzky & Oliver C. Ruppel*

## 1. Introduction

During its plenary session held on 6 November 2025, the Pan-African Parliament (PAP) officially adopted the Model Law on Soil Management in Africa.[1] The PAP is one of the organs of the African Union. The Model Law on Soil Management was developed over an extended period, beginning with a comprehensive and representative legal study of existing soil legislation across African states.[2] The process involved soil experts, politicians, and representatives from academia, public administration, and civil society, and included numerous consultations across the continent.[3] The PAP, through its Committee on Rural Economy, Agriculture, Natural Resources, and Environment, coordinated the consultation process within the institution, including regular Committee deliberations and regional consultation meetings.[4] The draft Model Law was debated twice in the PAP plenary and was continuously amended and refined throughout the process. The adoption of this Model Law by the PAP[5] was historic in several respects:

- Healthy soils are formally recognised as a precondition for sustainable development.
- A legal framework for soil management has been established.
- The framework is designed to be applicable not only to a single state but across an entire continent.

Shortly thereafter, another continent-wide legal framework addressing soil governance was adopted. Following extensive negotiations, the European Union (EU) Directive on Soil Monitoring and Resilience entered into force on 16 December 2025.[6]

The following aims to determine whether and to what extent the Model Law on Soil Management could serve as a benchmark, a toolbox, or even a blueprint for other continents, regions, or states. To this end, the summary begins by explaining the importance of soils for the prosperity and sustainability of societies. The next section

1 See https://pap.au.int/en/news/press-releases/2025-11-06/african-parliamentarians-adopt-continents-first-model-law, accessed 11 March 2026, https://www.africanparliamentarynews.com/2025/11/pan-african-parliament-adopts-landmark_7.html, accessed 11 March 2026; Mutingwende (2025a and b).

2 See Ruppel & Ginzky (2021); Ruppel et al. (2025).

3 See Preface to the Model Law, Nr. 3 and Pan-African Parliament (2025a, b and c).

4 See https://pap.au.int/en/news/press-releases/2025-09-26/pap-analyses-draft-model-law-sustainable-soil-management-africa, accessed 11 March 2026.

5 See FAO (2025b and c).

6 Available at https://eur-lex.europa.eu/legal-content/EN/TXT/PDF/?uri=OJ:L_202502360, accessed 11 March 2026.

outlines the key characteristics and specific features of the Model Law on Soil Management, both in its substantive provisions and in its legal design. Subsequently, the core elements of the EU Directive on Soil Monitoring and Resilience will be examined to understand its approach, including its strengths and weaknesses, and to assess its potential relevance for other regions.

## 2. Importance of fertile/healthy soils for Africa

Soil is the silent, crumbling foundation of global food security and ecological stability. It is as fundamental to the natural environment as plants, animals, rivers, or the climate itself. Soil provides habitat for countless organisms, regulates the flow of water and nutrients, and serves as a reservoir for gases such as oxygen and carbon dioxide. It also functions as a cultural archive, bearing the imprint of human history—from agricultural practices to archaeological remains. In addition, soils represent the second-largest reservoir of carbon after the oceans and are therefore critical for climate mitigation and adaptation. At the same time, soils are increasingly affected by changing weather patterns associated with climate change, including flooding, intense rainfall, and water scarcity. As hosts to immense biodiversity, they are also indispensable to addressing biodiversity loss. In short, soils are both ecological foundations and cultural legacies, forming an intricately balanced system more complex than any machine humankind has ever created.

Healthy soils are also essential for human health and well-being. Soil health is directly linked to human well-being through food production, water filtration, air quality regulation, and its role in adapting to changing climatic patterns. Degraded soils may reduce the nutritional value of crops, limit access to clean water, and increase exposure to contaminants. In addition, healthy soils provide the foundation for green spaces in urban areas, which can improve residents' mental well-being and foster social cohesion. Protecting soil health is therefore not only about preserving nature, but also about safeguarding the well-being of present and future generations.[7]

Soil is equally central to economic prosperity. Healthy soils underpin agricultural productivity, with agriculture accounting for approximately 20% of Africa's per capita gross domestic product (GDP) and employing around 60% of the continent's workforce. Sustainable soil management is thus not only an environmental necessity but also an economic imperative. Well-managed soils can strengthen national economies, enhance agricultural exports, and ensure that economic benefits reach local farmers and rural communities.

At the same time, this finite resource faces unprecedented threats.[8] To feed a projected global population, food production must increase by 35–56% by 2050—a target

7 Ginzky & Ruppel (2025b).
8 Hou et al. (2025: 1).

that is increasingly jeopardised by widespread soil degradation.[9] Meeting this demand on already degraded soils is placing the livelihoods of approximately 1.3 billion people worldwide at risk.[10] According to the Food and Agriculture Organization of the United Nations (FAO), up to 90% of the world's soils may be at risk by mid-century due to erosion, the excessive use of fertilisers and pesticides, industrial pollution, and climate change.[11]

An estimated one-third of the world's soils are already degraded, resulting in the loss of approximately 75 billion tonnes of arable soil annually and roughly USD 400 billion in lost agricultural production.[12] These figures illustrate not only an ecological crisis but also a profound economic and human development challenge. A significant proportion of the world's irrigated land is already affected by salinity—estimates range from one-fifth to nearly half—particularly in arid and semi-arid regions.[13] In northern India, salinisation has severely reduced wheat and rice yields.[14] Soil acidification represents another growing threat, particularly in Asia, Europe, and North America, driven by acid rain, the excessive use of nitrogen fertilisers, and intensive agricultural practices.[15] In Europe, inefficient nitrogen management has exacerbated acidification, forcing costly lime applications that provide only temporary stabilisation.[16] Armed conflict has further aggravated soil degradation. Russia's war of aggression against Ukraine has contaminated an estimated one-third of the country's farmland, while the use of white phosphorus munitions has poisoned agricultural soils in southern Lebanon.[17] More broadly, Europe reports that approximately 61% of its soils are unhealthy, primarily due to carbon loss, biodiversity decline, and peatland deterioration.[18]

## 3. The characteristics of the Model Law on Soil Management in Africa

The following section examines the characteristics of the Model Law on Soil Management in Africa, focusing on its substantive features, the categories of provisions it contains, its legal nature, and its genesis and development.

---

9 Ibid.
10 Ibid.
11 Ibid.
12 See https://eu.boell.org/en/SoilAtlas-soil-degradation, accessed 29 September 2025.
13 Heinrich-Böll-Stiftung (2024).
14 Ibid.
15 Ibid.
16 Ibid.
17 Ibid.: 13.
18 Ibid.

## 3.1. Substantial characteristics of the Model Law on Soil Management in Africa

This subsection outlines the key substantive characteristics of the Model Law on Soil Management in Africa.

### 3.1.1. Substantial elements

From a substantive perspective, the Model Law on Soil Management in Africa is characterised by five core features.

#### 3.1.1.1. Inclusive governance perspective

The adopted Model Law takes an inclusive approach, addressing the multiple dimensions of soil governance. Traditionally, soil governance focuses primarily on maintaining, restoring, and enhancing soils and their qualities. This is usually achieved through regulating potentially harmful activities, establishing restoration and rehabilitation measures for degraded soils, and creating planning instruments and administrative structures to oversee soil protection.[19] The Model Law on Soil Management in Africa adopts a broader perspective. It addresses additional and often overlooked dimensions of soil governance, including land tenure rights and the role of traditional leaders; the impacts of transnational trade and foreign investment; the use of digital technologies—including artificial intelligence (AI); gender equality; and the importance of indigenous knowledge.[20]

For instance, Article 8 provides that land laws should be implemented with due consideration of the Model Law. Article 28 highlights the central role of traditional leaders as custodians of sustainable soil management and emphasises the importance of close cooperation between competent authorities and traditional leadership structures. The interaction between sustainable soil management and international trade and investment is addressed in Articles 12 and 13. These provisions stipulate, *inter alia,* that international trade should not negatively affect soil properties, that foreign investors must comply with national legislation, and that foreign investments must not undermine soil health or local land rights. The Model Law also recognises the role of emerging technologies. Article 21 requires the national competent authority to coordinate the effective use of digital tools, including AI, in a manner consistent with guiding principles such as non-discriminatory access. Article 28 further emphasises that indigenous knowledge is a valuable source of information for sustainable soil management

19 Ginzky (2022).
20 Ginzky & Ruppel (2025a and b).

and calls for mechanisms to collect and make it accessible. In addition, Article 29 establishes that women and men shall enjoy "equal rights in access to, use, and management" of soils, and that gender-specific considerations should be recognised in decision-making processes.

This inclusive approach reflects the broader sustainability principle, which integrates ecological, social, and economic dimensions. By adopting such a perspective, the Model Law underscores the fundamental importance of soils for sustainable development. While addressing the environmental aspects of soil protection and management, the Model Law also emphasises the need to safeguard soils in the interest of human well-being and societal development. In doing so, it promotes economic prosperity, social justice, and equity. By explicitly recognising these social dimensions, the Model Law also strengthen public trust in legal and political institutions to address complex environmental challenges.

The holistic approach adopted by the Model Law on Soil Management in Africa is, therefore, particularly appropriate. Rather than focusing on a single aspect of soil governance, it encompasses the full range of relevant dimensions. Given that the Model Law is intended to guide national legislation in comprehensively organising sustainable soil management, this inclusive approach appears both suitable, practical, and instrumental. It empowers national legislators to address the diverse aspects of soil governance in a coherent, integrated manner, guided by the Model Law's provisions.

#### 3.1.1.2. Modern understanding of the legal nature of soil

A second characteristic of the Model Law on Soil Management in Africa is its grounding in a modern understanding of soil's legal nature. Despite the fundamental importance of soils for sustainable development, soil has remained something of a legal orphan in many African jurisdictions. It is frequently subsumed under broader "land" or "environmental" legislation, resulting in fragmented regulatory approaches and often ineffective protection. Given that soils regenerate only over geological timescales, the need for coherent, enforceable governance frameworks grounded in a contemporary understanding of soil is particularly pressing.[21]

Article 5 constitutes the central provision in this regard. Paragraph 1 explicitly states that soil is "a limited and fragile natural resource". The emphasis on soil as a "natural resource" is significant, as soil has often been treated primarily as an "economic commodity" under the broader legal concept of "land". By contrast, the Model Law recognises soils as a direct environmental resource that requires dedicated protection. To this end, Article 5(1) provides that soils must be "conserved, maintained and protected against all forms of degradation" to "preserve their ecological,

21 Bodle (2022).

economic, social and cultural services". This formulation underscores that all forms of soil degradation must be accounted for. Protection, therefore, extends beyond contamination, which has traditionally been the primary focus of soil-related legislation,[22] to include other forms of degradation such as erosion, compaction, salinisation, and the loss of organic matter. Article 5(1) further highlights that soils provide multiple services to humans and society, identifying four categories: ecological, economic, social, and cultural services. These categories are further elaborated in the subsequent paragraphs of Article 5. Notably, the inclusion of social services is relatively exceptional in soil-related legislation and reflects a broader recognition of the importance of social justice and equity in achieving sustainable development in Africa.

Finally, Article 5(1) emphasises that the preservation of soil services must be undertaken in the interest of "present and future generations". This reflects the modern principle of intergenerational equity, highlighting the need to safeguard soil resources for the long-term benefit of both current and future generations.[23]

#### 3.1.1.3. Linkage to international strategies, agreements, and processes

The Model Law on Soil Management in Africa is closely connected to a range of international strategies, agreements, and policy processes. In doing so, it clearly demonstrates that it does not operate in isolation but instead takes into account the international obligations and commitments of African states.

The recitals refer, *inter alia*, to the 2015 development agenda, the "Soil Initiative for Africa", and the "Africa Fertiliser and Soil Health Action Plan". They also acknowledge the work of international institutions and frameworks[24] such as the United Nations Convention to Combat Desertification (UNCCD), the Food and Agriculture Organization of the United Nations (FAO), and the United Nations Environment Programme (UNEP). In addition, the Model Law references key political commitments, including the Maputo Declaration on Agriculture and Food Security (2024) and the Nairobi Declaration on African Fertiliser and Soil Health (2024).

Article 2, entitled "Purpose and Objective of the Law", identifies achieving "Land Degradation Neutrality" (LDN) as one of its central objectives, reflecting a key target of the 2015 Sustainable Development Agenda.[25] As the concept of LDN encompasses both quantitative and qualitative dimensions of land degradation, Article 2 requires states to ensure a neutral balance between ongoing degrading and restoration and/or rehabilitation measures.[26] This objective is particularly ambitious, as it essentially

22 Ginzky (2021 and 2022).
23 Rawls (1999: 260); Araújo & Kössler (2021).
24 Ruppel (2022a).
25 Ginzky (2023).
26 Ehlers (2016).

requires maintaining—or improving—the overall condition of soils despite ongoing pressures.

Furthermore, several specific provisions of the Model Law require that relevant international standards and obligations be taken into account or complied with. For example, Article 10(7), which addresses "Soil, Sustainable Agriculture, and Food and Nutrition Security", emphasises the importance of aligning national measures with relevant international frameworks.

In sum, the Model Law on Soil Management in Africa situates itself within a broader landscape of international strategies, agreements, and policy processes. By doing so, it provides a mechanism through which states may help fulfil their international commitments, whether by implementing or domesticating the Model Law.

#### 3.1.1.4. Modern and innovative regulatory mechanisms and instruments

A third characteristic of the Model Law on Soil Management in Africa is the introduction of modern, innovative regulatory mechanisms and instruments to govern, manage, and promote sustainable soil management.

To begin with, Article 3 establishes an extensive list of legal definitions for terms used throughout the Model Law. This approach, now widely regarded as good legislative practice, enhances legal certainty by clarifying the scope, objectives, and regulatory ambitions of the provisions. Article 6 further sets out a catalogue of "guiding principles" intended to inform the application and interpretation of the Model Law. The provision identifies twelve principles, including accountability, effective participation, precaution, prevention, proportionality, sustainability, and transparency.

Notably, the Model Law places particular emphasis on equity and justice. Two of the guiding principles explicitly address "gender equity and equality" and "non-discrimination and social justice". In addition, the "Degradation Responsibility Principle" provides that individuals or entities responsible for, or benefiting from, soil degradation should bear the costs of its management and remediation. The principle of "subsidiarity" further requires that decision-making be exercised, where appropriate, at the lowest effective administrative level, while ensuring cooperation between higher levels of administration, including ministries, as well as local communities, traditional authorities, and local governments.

Articles 14 and 15, read together with Article 29(2), establish an important regulatory mechanism to ensure that negative impacts on soils are either prevented, effectively managed, or compensated through soil restoration measures where impacts are unavoidable. To ensure effective implementation, "any use of soil that may pose a risk of significant degradation" requires prior authorisation from the competent authority. Such authorisation may only be granted where "negative impacts on the soil are minimised", and unavoidable impacts are "equally compensated". This mechanism directly contributes to implementing the objective of land degradation neutrality set out in Article 1(2).

To support informed decision-making, Article 23 requires the establishment of "environmental quality standards" addressing all forms of soil degradation. These standards should serve as benchmarks for assessing soil impacts and determining the necessary mitigation or compensation measures.

In particular, the obligation to offset unavoidable impacts through restoration or compensation measures represents an innovative regulatory tool aimed at achieving LDN. The Model Law also introduces two additional mechanisms within the authorisation process that are both novel and significant. First, Article 15 requires the preparation of a specific "Soil Impact Assessment" (SIA) as part of the broader "Environmental Impact Assessment" (EIA) process. This requirement is intended to ensure that the impacts on soils are addressed through a dedicated analytical framework, as experience has shown that soils are often insufficiently considered within conventional EIA procedures.[27] The SIA should also recommend case-specific soil management and mitigation measures.

Secondly, Article 29(2) requires competent authorities to assess the implications of proposed activities for gender equality and other forms of vulnerability. The inclusion of such a gender-sensitive assessment represents an important and innovative feature within soil governance frameworks.

Beyond these regulatory procedures governing specific activities or projects, the Model Law on Soil Management in Africa introduces several planning and management instruments to support long-term, strategic soil governance. One such instrument is the "zoning of uses of soils", provided for in Article 18. This provision allows competent authorities to "divide land into different zones according to the value" of the soil services they provide. Such zoning enables the coordination of soil use with soil quality and ecological value. For example, highly fertile soils should not be permanently sealed for industrial development where alternative land uses are available. A related planning instrument is set out in Article 19, which allows for the establishment of spatial protection mechanisms, including protected areas for soils of particularly high ecological or productive value. These instruments empower public authorities to manage soil resources in a coordinated and long-term manner. Furthermore, the Model Law requires the identification and dissemination of "good practices for sustainable uses of soil". These practices are to be compiled and made publicly accessible by publication in a "national soil information system", thereby promoting knowledge sharing and capacity building.

Finally, the Model Law adopts a sector-specific regulatory approach to address the cross-cutting nature of soil governance. It introduces tailored requirements and obligations for sectors such as agriculture and food security (Article 10), climate mitigation

27 See the country studies in Ruppel et al. (2025).

and adaptation (Article 11), mining (Article 17), and urban development (Article 20). By integrating soil protection considerations into these key sectors, the Model Law provides a comprehensive regulatory framework to address the complex, interconnected challenges of sustainable soil management.

### 3.1.1.5. Focus on ensuring effective implementation and enforcement

Another important characteristic of the Model Law on Soil Management in Africa is its strong focus on enabling African states to establish effective mechanisms for implementing and enforcing its substantive provisions. This emphasis reflects a widely recognised challenge in many jurisdictions: while environmental legislation is often well designed in substantive terms, implementation and enforcement frequently remain weak.[28] Without effective implementation, even the most carefully crafted legal provisions remain largely symbolic, failing to translate into tangible improvements on the ground or to benefit affected people and communities.[29]

Effective environmental administration depends fundamentally on reliable data and information. As the well-known principle suggests: "What you do not measure, you cannot regulate." Article 21, therefore, establishes a comprehensive framework for data management and monitoring. The provision identifies three key processes: the collection of soil data, the assessment and analysis of such data, and its dissemination. Article 21(3) further clarifies that soil data should include information on soil quality, soil use, and tenure rights. The provision also delineates the responsibilities of different administrative levels for these processes. Transparency and public access to information are important components of this framework. It is widely recognised that soil data should be publicly accessible. Accordingly, Articles 25 and 26 require public authorities to ensure effective public participation in decision-making processes and to undertake measures to raise awareness and sensitise the public to soil-related issues.

Parts VI and VII of the Model Law further establish the organisational and institutional framework necessary for effective soil governance, as well as mechanisms for dispute resolution within administrative and judicial proceedings. Pursuant to Article 31(1), a National Soil Management Authority should be established, which is obliged to cooperate closely with regional and local entities. The Model Law explicitly assigns certain responsibilities to this national authority, including the establishment of a national soil database (Article 21(1)), the collection of indigenous knowledge (Article 27(2)), and the submission of draft soil quality standards to the relevant ministry for adoption (Article 23(3)). Where the Model Law refers to the "competent authority", responsibility should generally lie with regional or local administrative bodies. In addition, Article 31(2) allows the establishment of a Sustainable Soil Management

28 Ginzky & Ruppel (2025b).
29 Ginzky (2022).

Coordination Mechanism, conceived as an intersectoral, multi-stakeholder platform that may perform advisory, consultative, or decision-making functions. Such a mechanism may play an important role in facilitating coordination between different sectors and levels of governance. The specific scope of its responsibilities is to be determined at the national level.

Articles 32 and 33 provide further provisions on monitoring and surveillance, as well as on transnational cooperation within Africa. Monitoring and surveillance mechanisms are essential to ensure compliance with the Model Law and with decisions taken by competent authorities under its framework.

Taken together, these provisions are intended to enable African states to establish effective administrative systems capable of implementing and enforcing sustainable soil management in practice.

### 3.1.2. The Model Law on Soil Management in Africa and the Commentaries[30]

Another innovative feature of the Model Law is that it is accompanied by sixteen guidance Commentaries that provide detailed explanations and practical implementation guidance. The legal status of these Commentaries is clarified in the preface of the Model Law, which states: "The Commentaries do not, in themselves, constitute part of this Model Law, but may be of guidance in facilitating its understanding, use, and transposition into domestic legislation."[31] Accordingly, the Commentaries do not constitute binding legal provisions but serve as interpretative and practical tools to support the application and domestication of the Model Law. The Commentaries address the following non-conclusive list of topics:

- Awareness Raising and Capacity Building;
- Sustainable Soil Management Practices for Food Production;
- Dispute Settlement;
- Data Management;
- Fertilisers;
- Foreign Investment;
- Gender;
- Implementation and Enforcement;
- Industry, Infrastructure, and Energy Transition;
- Mining;
- Migration;
- Pesticides;
- Pastoralism;
- Urbanisation;

30 See the Commentaries in this book.
31 Preface to the Model Law, Nr. 5.

- Tenure Rights; and
- Traditional Leaders.

The Commentaries, therefore, address soil governance in considerably greater detail, whereas the Model Law itself sets out the core principles and provisions in a more general and normative manner. All Commentaries follow a consistent structure. First, the policy challenges associated with the respective topic are outlined. This is followed by an overview of policy options to address these challenges through legislative and administrative measures. Finally, each Commentary provides concrete drafting suggestions or text proposals.

Some Commentaries are directly linked to specific provisions of the Model Law. These include, for example, Commentaries on Article 8 ("Relation to Land Laws"), Article 13 ("Foreign Investments"), Article 17 ("Mining"), and Article 20 ("Soils in Urban Areas"). Other Commentaries address key thematic areas that intersect with soil governance but are only briefly covered in the Model Law itself. This is particularly the case for Commentaries on "Sustainable Soil Management Practices for Food Production", "Fertilisers", "Pastoralism", and "Pesticides", which address the critical interface between soil health, agriculture, and food security—issues of particular relevance for Africa that are otherwise primarily addressed in Article 10 ("Soil, Sustainable Agriculture, and Food and Nutrition Security"). A further group of Commentaries adopts a more cross-cutting perspective, addressing broader socio-economic and policy dimensions relevant to soil governance. These include, for example, Commentaries on "Industry, Infrastructure, and Energy Transition" and on "Migration".

Taken together, the Commentaries constitute an extensive toolbox of soil governance options to support national domestication of the Model Law. A distinctive feature of this approach is that the policy options presented in the Commentaries are directly linked to the Model Law's provisions. They therefore do not constitute purely academic reflections but are closely integrated with the legal framework established by the Model Law. Their common structure further facilitates their practical use by policymakers and legislators. By explicitly emphasising their non-binding character, the Commentaries also clarify the distinction between the Model Law's legal authority and their explanatory and supportive nature.

Overall, the Commentaries provide a legally integrated "menu" of governance options that may assist states in better understanding the rationale behind the Model Law's provisions and in selecting context-specific approaches for domestication with regard to topic-specific challenges.

### 3.2. Different categories of provisions

From the perspective of national domestication, the Model Law's provisions can be grouped into four categories. Recognising these distinctions can assist national legislators in organising the domestication process efficiently and in a structured manner. It also illustrates how the Model Law strikes a balance between providing clear regulatory guidance and allowing flexibility and adaptability across different national legal systems.

### 3.2.1. Category 1: Self-executing, directly implementable

The first category comprises provisions that may be considered self-executing. These provisions could be incorporated directly into national legislation without requiring significant legal refinement or additional regulatory instruments. Once transposed into domestic law, they can be applied immediately. This appears to be the case, *inter alia*, for the following provisions:

- Article 4 – Definitions
- Article 5 – Services of Soils
- Article 6 – Guiding Principles
- Article 7 – Interface with other Sectoral Provisions
- Article 8 – Relation to Land Laws
- Article 14 – Obligation to Minimise and Compensate Detrimental Effects on Soil
- Article 15 – Soil Impact Assessment (SIA) as part of Environmental or Strategic Impact Assessment
- Article 18 – Zoning of Land
- Article 19 – Protection of Particularly Valuable Soil by Spatial Measures
- Article 21 – Data Management and Monitoring
- Article 35 – Criminal Offences, Penalties and Sanctions
- Article 36 – Administrative Offences

Additional provisions may also fall within this category depending on the structure of the respective national legal system and the extent to which supplementary regulations are required.

### 3.2.2. Category 2: Provisions which need to be contextualised with sectoral provisions

The second category consists of provisions that require contextualisation within existing sectoral legal frameworks. Given that soil governance is inherently cross-cutting, such integration is both necessary and expected.[32] The following provisions illustrate this category:

32 Ginzky (2022).

- Article 10 – Soil, Sustainable Agriculture, and Food and Nutrition Security
- Article 11 – Soil and Climate Mitigation and Adaptation
- Article 17 – Mining
- Article 20 – Soil in Urban Areas
- Article 28 – Role of Traditional Leaders
- Article 29 – Gender Equity and Equality

These provisions intersect with policy areas typically regulated by specialised legislation. For instance, Article 10 addresses matters such as fertiliser and pesticide regulation and requires that all agricultural practices be conducted in accordance with sustainable soil management practices (Article 10(8)). In such cases, the effective implementation of the Model Law requires the review and, where necessary, amendment of existing sectoral legislation on fertilisers and/or pesticides. Simply transposing the Model Law's provisions into national legislation would therefore not be sufficient to achieve its objectives. The accompanying Commentaries provide further guidance and policy options to assist legislators in developing appropriate legislative responses within these sectors.

#### 3.2.3. Category 3: The need to undertake administrative actions for its implementation

A third category consists of provisions whose implementation depends primarily on specific administrative actions. Although all legislative provisions ultimately require administrative structures for their implementation, some provisions explicitly require preparatory actions before they can become operational. Examples include:

- Article 23 – Development of Soil Quality Standards
- Article 24 – Good Practices
- Article 27 – Indigenous Knowledge
- Article 32 – Monitoring and Surveillance
- Article 33 – Transnational Cooperation

These provisions require activities such as collecting information, developing standards or guidelines, establishing monitoring systems, or initiating cooperation mechanisms with neighbouring states. Without these preparatory administrative measures, the provisions cannot be effectively implemented.

#### 3.2.4. Category 4: Strategic provisions

The fourth category comprises provisions that require strategic planning, typically through the adoption of long-term strategies, programmes, or comparable policy instruments. Such provisions cannot be implemented solely through legislative transposition. Examples include:

- Article 22 – Digitalisation and Sustainable Soil Management
- Article 26 – Public Sensitisation and Awareness Raising
- Article 29 – Gender Equity and Equality

These provisions require the development of strategic frameworks that define priorities, timelines, and institutional responsibilities. They may also overlap with the previous categories, as their implementation may require the release of new sectoral legislation, their amendments or the establishment of specific administrative measures.

The Commentaries accompanying the Model Law provide further guidance on these issues and may assist policymakers and legislators in designing appropriate strategic planning instruments.

### 3.3. Legal nature of the Model Law on Soil Management in Africa

The following subsection examines the legal nature of the Model Law on Soil Management in Africa. Three aspects are addressed. First, the mandate of the PAP is analysed, as it determines the level of legal obligation, if any, of AU member states to domesticate the Model Law. Second, the subsection explains how the Model Law provides sufficient flexibility to allow African states to address their specific legal, institutional, and socio-economic circumstances. Finally, it considers whether and to what extent the Model Law could serve as a basis for developing an international soil treaty at the regional or even global level.

#### 3.3.1. Legal mandate of PAP for issuing a model law and its legal nature

The mandate of the PAP to discuss and adopt model laws derives from three principal legal instruments:

- The Constitutive Act of the African Union, signed by 53 African states and entered into force in May 2001;[33]
- the Protocol to the Treaty Establishing the African Economic Community relating to the Pan-African Parliament of March 2001, which entered into force in December 2003;[34] and

33 Available at https://au.int/sites/default/files/pages/34873-file-constitutiveact_en.pdf, accessed 11 March 2026.

34 Available at https://au.int/sites/default/files/treaties/36301-treaty-0022_-_protocol_to_the_treaty_establishing_the_african_economic_community_relating_to_the_pan-african_parliament_e.pdf, accessed 11 March 2026.

- the Rules of Procedures of the Pan-African Parliament, as amended in November 2022.

The Constitutive Act recognises the PAP as one of the organs of the AU. Article 17(1) of the Act states that the PAP shall be established "in order to ensure the full participation of African peoples in the development and economic integration of the continent". The PAP is therefore conceived as a mechanism to enhance democratic participation in decision-making processes at the continental level. The reference to "development and economic integration" is broad, encompassing a wide range of political, economic, and social policy areas.

Article 17(2) of the Constitutive Act further provides that the organisation and functions of the PAP shall be defined in a subsequent protocol. This instrument is the "Protocol to the Treaty Establishing the African Economic Community relating to the Pan-African Parliament" (PAP-Protocol), which builds upon the broader objectives of the "Treaty establishing the African Economic Community."[35] Article 14 of that Treaty contains language similar[36] to Article 17 of the Constitutive Act regarding the Parliament's participatory role.

Article 2 of the PAP Protocol expressly states that the PAP currently exercises only consultative and advisory functions, although "the ultimate aim of the Pan-African Parliament shall be to evolve into an institution with full legislative powers".

Article 3 of the PAP Protocol further outlines the institution's objectives. Among other tasks, the PAP is mandated to "facilitate the effective implementation of the policies and objectives (…) of the African Union", to "encourage good governance, transparency and accountability in the Member States", and to "contribute to a more prosperous future for the people in Africa by promoting collective self-reliance and economic recovery". The functions and powers of the PAP are elaborated in Article 11 of the Protocol. The Parliament is empowered to examine, discuss, and express opinions on matters relating to the African Union, and to make recommendations on issues such as promoting good governance and the rule of law. Importantly, Article 11(3) assigns the PAP a role in working towards the harmonisation or coordination of the laws of member states.

The Rules of Procedure of the PAP further elaborate these functions. Rules 4 and 5 specify that the PAP shall facilitate the implementation of the AU's policies, objectives, and programmes and contribute to the harmonisation and coordination of the member states' legislation. To fulfil these functions, the Parliament may oversee the

35 Available at https://africanlii.org/en/akn/aa-au/act/treaty/1991/african-economic-community/eng@1991-06-03#chp_III, accessed 11 March 2026. The Treaty was signed in June 1991 and entered into force in July 1994.

36 Para 1 reads as follows: "In order to ensure that the peoples of Africa are fully involved in the economic development and integration of the Continent, there shall be established a Pan-African Parliament."

implementation of policies, adopt resolutions, and make recommendations on matters relating to the African Union.

None of the relevant legal instruments explicitly refers to the adoption of model laws. However, the mandate to develop such instruments can be derived from the PAP's consultative and advisory role, as well as from its function of promoting the harmonisation and coordination of member states' legislation. In this context, model laws represent one practical mechanism through which the Parliament may formulate policy guidance and support legislative convergence across the continent.

The PAP is currently considering revisions to its founding Protocol that would explicitly recognise the power to propose and adopt model laws. This revised draft emphasises that even under the existing institutional framework, the PAP's advisory mandate is sufficiently broad to enable it to propose and formulate model laws.[37]

Given the "consultative and advisory" nature of the Parliament's mandate, model laws adopted by the PAP are not legally binding on member states. African member states, therefore, retain discretion regarding whether and how they domesticate a model law, and to what extent they adapt its provisions to their national legal systems.[38] Model laws should instead be understood as normative guidance instruments designed to support good governance and to encourage the harmonisation or coordination of national legislation.

The revised Protocol provides a clear definition of this concept, stating that: "Model law refers to uniform legislation proposed for adaptation by a legislative body. The purpose of a model law is to establish a useful framework that enables legislative bodies to have some uniformity in their governance, organisation, and management. It helps institutions to conduct their functions smoothly and effectively discharge their responsibilities."[39] In other words, a model law provides a legislative template that national authorities may adapt to their own legal and institutional contexts. The purpose and objectives of the Model Law on Soil Management in Africa are articulated in the instrument itself. Article 2(1) provides that: "The purpose of this Law is to guide and inspire AU Member States in the governance of soil through sustainable soil management." Article 1(2) further specifies its objectives, which include to "[P]rovide rules and mechanisms for the sustainable management of soil to foster sustainable development" and to "[P]rovide a basis or tool for policy guidance of all stakeholders to ensure harmonisation of regulations, policies, and administrative practice for effective and sustainable soil management."

Taken together, these provisions confirm that the Model Law is intended to serve as a guiding framework for national legislation on sustainable soil management. At the same time, it explicitly recognises that member states should take into account their specific national circumstances, institutional capacities, and policy priorities when

37 See https://pap.au.int/en/legislation, accessed 11 March 2026.
38 Murray & Ruppel (2025).
39 See https://pap.au.int/en/legislation, accessed 11 March 2026.

considering the domestication of its provisions.

### 3.3.2. Flexible and adaptable for national and local circumstances

The AU comprises five regions and more than fifty member states, each characterised by significant diversity in terms of ecological conditions—particularly soils—levels of economic development, cultural contexts, political systems, legal traditions, and governance challenges. The Model Law on Soil Management in Africa takes this diversity into account by striking a balance between providing clear guidance on key issues that should be considered in the domestication process and allowing sufficient flexibility for national adaptation. More specifically, the Model Law first offers recommendations on core issues that member states should address when developing national soil governance frameworks. Second, it introduces modern and innovative regulatory mechanisms. Third, it proposes institutional arrangements to ensure implementation and enforcement. At the same time, the Model Law preserves sufficient flexibility for each African state to determine which elements are most appropriate in light of its specific legal system, socio-economic context, and policy priorities.

From the outset, it was recognised that the domestication of the Model Law could not be understood as a purely technocratic exercise of legislative transposition. Rather, it is inherently a political process requiring normative decisions about policy priorities and institutional arrangements. Ideally, such decisions should be informed by inclusive, participatory processes that involve a broad range of societal stakeholders.

The Model Law accommodates this need for flexibility in several ways. First, as explained above, it is not legally binding on member states. Second, its provisions are drafted to allow for adaptation across different national legal frameworks and under distinct legal traditions. Finally, the accompanying Commentaries provide policy options and implementation guidance to facilitate context-specific domestication.

### 3.3.3. The Model Law on Soil Management in Africa: International law at the regional or global level?

In general terms, the Model Law is intended to address soil governance across all African states. In this sense, it may be viewed as a normative instrument operating at the continental level and thus sharing certain characteristics with regional international law. However, the Model Law does not, *per se*, constitute an international treaty or agreement between states. It was prepared, debated, and adopted by the PAP, which comprises parliamentarians from the national parliaments of AU member states.[40]

40 Art 4 of the PAP Protocol.

Consequently, the Model Law represents an initiative of the legislative branch within the AU framework rather than a treaty negotiated and concluded by states.

Furthermore, the Model Law lacks several elements typically associated with international agreements, such as provisions concerning treaty organs, decision-making procedures, ratification and accession mechanisms, or subsidiary rule-making processes.

Nevertheless, the absence of these features does not *ab initio* preclude the possibility that elements of the Model Law could eventually form part of a regional or global international agreement.[41] As demonstrated above, the Model Law addresses the full range of key issues relevant to soil governance and incorporates a variety of innovative regulatory mechanisms and policy instruments. If there were sufficient political will, the substantive provisions of the Model Law could serve as a basis for developing an international treaty on soil governance. Such an instrument would, of course, require the addition of institutional provisions concerning governance structures, decision-making processes, and implementation mechanisms. In this sense, the Model Law on Soil Management in Africa may be regarded as a valuable starting point for the future development of an international legal framework on soil governance.[42]

## 4. Characteristics of the drafting process of the Model Law on Soil Management in Africa

The drafting process of the Model Law on Soil Management also exhibits several distinctive characteristics. First, the structure and substantive elements of the Model Law are grounded in extensive legal expertise and a comprehensive analysis of the realities of soil governance across Africa. In 2017 and 2018, two international and interdisciplinary workshops were organised in cooperation with the Regional Programme on Climate Policy and Energy Security of the Konrad Adenauer Foundation, the German Environment Agency, several African universities, and GIZ. These workshops were held in Kampala, Uganda, and Nairobi, Kenya, and focused on soil governance challenges in Africa.[43] Building on the outcomes of these two workshops,[44] the German government funded an exploratory project entitled "Mapping Out Options for a Model Law for Sustainable Soil Management in Africa". The project included detailed

---

41 Boer et al. (2016).

42 The International Union for the Conservation of Nature (IUCN) in 2025 adopted a "motion" to work towards an international instrument on soil protection. See https://iucncongress2025.org/assembly/motions/motion/007, accessed 11 March 2026; Ruppel & Murray (2025); Ruppel (2024).

43 See https://www.umweltbundesamt.de/en/international-workshop-kampala-uganda-september, accessed 11 March 2026; https://www.umweltbundesamt.de/en/node/71702, accessed 11 March 2026.

44 Outcome documents of the two workshops are documented in the following webpages: https://www.umweltbundesamt.de/en/international-workshop-kampala-uganda-september, accessed 11 March 2026; https://www.umweltbundesamt.de/en/node/71702, accessed 11 March 2026.

country studies in Cameroon, Kenya, and Zambia, conducted by teams of African experts. These studies analysed the strengths and weaknesses of existing national legislation and identified potential options for developing a model law on sustainable soil management.[45] The findings were subsequently presented to the Committee on Rural Economy, Agriculture, Natural Resources and Environment of the PAP. Based on this work, the PAP in 2023 decided to initiate the development of a model law on soil management.[46] By the end of 2024, eleven additional country studies had been prepared or updated to ensure broad regional representation across the continental north, south, east, and west, as well as the central part, and one island state. New studies were conducted for Burkina Faso, Botswana, Madagascar, Morocco, Mozambique, Namibia, Uganda, and South Africa, while the earlier studies for Cameroon, Kenya, and Zambia were updated.[47] These analyses, together with scientific insights from the seven volumes of the "International Yearbook of Soil Law and Policy",[48] formed, among others,[49] an intellectual foundation for the drafting of the Model Law.

Second, the drafting process followed a strongly interdisciplinary, consultative, and participatory approach. The African Soil Partnership closely followed the process and contributed expertise from a soil science perspective. Additional soil experts were involved throughout the drafting process. International organisations such as FAO, UNCCD, and UNEP supported the initiative, provided technical input, and monitored its development.[50] Several civil society consultations and meetings with high-level representatives of national governments were organised to better understand local challenges and policy priorities, and to gather feedback on proposed regulatory

45 Ruppel & Ginzky (2021); Ruppel et al. (2025).

46 Pan-African Parliament, Resolution on the Development of a Model Legislation on Sustainable Soil Management in Africa, 2023.

47 Ruppel et al. (2025). The German government again funded this process.

48 See Ginzky, H., I.L. Heuser, T. Qin, O.C. Ruppel & P. Wegerdt (eds), 2017, *International Yearbook of Soil Law and Policy 2016*. Cham: Springer International Publishing; Ginzky, H., E. Dooley, I.L. Heuser, E. Kasimbazi, T. Markus & T. Qin (eds), 2018, *International Yearbook of Soil Law and Policy 2017*. Cham: Springer International Publishing; Ginzky, H., E. Dooley, I.L. Heuser, E. Kasimbazi, T. Markus & T. Qin (eds), 2019, *International Yearbook of Soil Law and Policy 2018*. Cham: Springer International Publishing; Ginzky, H., E. Dooley, I.L. Heuser, E. Kasimbazi, R. Kibugi, T. Markus, T. Qin & O.C. Ruppel (eds), 2021, *International Yearbook of Soil Law and Policy 2019*. Cham: Springer International Publishing; Ginzky, H., E. Dooley, I.L. Heuser, P. Kameri-Mbote, R. Kibugi, T. Markus & O.C. Ruppel (eds), 2022, *International Yearbook of Soil Law and Policy 2020/2021*. Cham: Springer International Publishing; Ginzky, H., F. De Andrade Corrêa, E. Dooley, I.L. Heuser, P. Kameri-Mbote, R. Kibugi & O.C. Ruppel (eds), 2024, *International Yearbook of Soil Law and Policy 2022*. Cham: Springer International Publishing; Ginzky, H., D. Grinlinton, I.L. Heuser, P. Kameri-Mbote, A. Khatibi, N. Rodriguez-Eugenio & O.C. Ruppel (eds), 2026, *International Yearbook of Soil Law and Policy 2025*. Cham: Springer International Publishing.

49 Such as the Journal for Soil Security, cf. https://www.sciencedirect.com/journal/soil-security, accessed 11 March 2026.

50 These international organisations provided letters of intent to express their support for the project. Their continuous support is also documented by respective forewords in this book.

concepts.[51] Through this iterative and participatory process, the draft Model Law was progressively refined and aligned with practical realities on the ground.

Third, the PAP itself served as the central "driving force" throughout the process. The Parliament regularly requested information on the progress of the drafting work and issued recommendations concerning the design and focus of the analytical studies following its decision to pursue the development of the Model Law. The PAP also concluded a "Memorandum of Understanding" with the two institutions responsible for drafting the Model Law: The Development and Rule of Law Programme (DROP) at Stellenbosch University, South Africa and the German Environment Agency.[52] Furthermore, the PAP—through its Committee on Rural Economy, Agriculture, Natural Resources, and Environment—co-organised two regional consultations with DROP following the Parliament's endorsement of the first draft of the Model Law in June 2025.[53] These consultations took place in Midrand, South Africa, in July and September 2025 and in Cairo, Egypt, in October 2025. The Committee subsequently submitted the final draft to the PAP, which formally adopted the Model Law on 6 November 2025.[54]

Four factors appear to have been central to the Model Law's successful adoption. First, the strong sense of "ownership" exercised by the Committee on Rural Economy, Agriculture, Natural Resources, and Environment throughout the entire process. Second, the rigorous scientific analysis of soil governance challenges and of existing legal frameworks across Africa, including a detailed assessment of the strengths and weaknesses of national legislation. Third, the highly consultative and participatory nature of the drafting process, which ensured that diverse perspectives and expertise were incorporated into the final instrument.[55] Fourth, the close partnership among the leading institutions and, particularly, their competent representatives.[56]

## 5. Core elements of the EU-Soil Monitoring and Resilience Directive

The EU also adopted legislation addressing soil governance by the end of 2025. The legal nature of this legislation, as well as its core elements, must be examined to enable meaningful comparison between the two legislative approaches.

---

51 Ruppel et al. (2025).

52 Memorandum of Understanding of 2020.

53 See https://spikedmedia.co.zw/pan-african-parliament-committee-discusses-model-law-on-soil-a-milestone-for-climate-and-agricultural-justice/, accessed 11 March 2026.

54 Cf. https://pap.au.int/en/news/press-releases/2025-11-06/african-parliamentarians-adopt-continents-first-model-law, accessed 11 March 2026.

55 Cf. also https://www.fao.org/policy-support/news/detail/pan-african-parliament-breaks-new-ground-with-landmark-soil-and-gender-laws/en, accessed 11 March 2026.

56 See https://spikedmedia.co.zw/pap-adoption-of-model-law-on-sustainable-soil-management-step-toward-food-security-and-climate-resilience/, accessed 11 March 2026.

The EU's soil legislation emerged from a similarly extended policy process.[57] On 17 November 2021, the EU Commission published the "Soil Strategy"[58] as one of the essential pillars of the EU Biodiversity Strategy.[59] The core ambition of the Soil Strategy is to achieve "healthy soils" across the EU by 2050. The strategy also envisaged adopting a legislative instrument as one of the key mechanisms to achieve this objective. Subsequently, on 5 July 2023, the EU Commission published the "Proposal for a Directive of the European Parliament and of the Council on Soil Monitoring and Resilience".[60] Following extensive discussions amongst the Commission, the Council and the European Parliament, the Soil Monitoring and Resilience Directive[61] entered into force on 16 December 2025.[62]

Under Article 191 et seq. of the Treaty on the Functioning of the European Union (TFEU),[63] the EU possesses competence to adopt legislation in the field of environmental protection. Article 288 of the TFEU distinguishes between different categories of legislative instruments. While a regulation is binding in "its entity" and "directly applicable in all Member States", a directive is binding only with regard to the objectives to be achieved, leaving member states discretion regarding the "form and methods" used to achieve those objectives. Consequently, directives must be transposed into the domestic legal system of member states.[64] Each directive specifies its own transposition deadline. Article 26(1) of the Soil Monitoring Directive provides that "Member States shall bring into force the laws, regulations and administrative provisions necessary to comply with this Directive by 17 December 2028." If a member state fails to fulfil these obligations, the European Commission may initiate "treaty

57 Ginzky & Pieper (2025); Heuser & Itey (2021).

58 EU Soil Strategy for 2030 – Reaping the Benefits of Healthy Soils for People, Food, Nature and Climate. Communication from the Commission to the European Parliament, the Council, the European Economic and Social Committee and the Committee of the Regions. COM/2021/699 Final. Available at https://eur-lex.europa.eu/legal-content/EN/TXT/?uri=CELEX%3A52021DC0699, accessed 11 March 2026.

59 EU Biodiversity Strategy for 2030 – Bringing Nature Back into Our Lives. Communication from the Commission to the European Parliament, the Council, the European Economic and Social Committee and the Committee of the Regions. COM/2020/380 Final. Available at https://data.europa.eu/doi/10.2779/677548, accessed 11 March 2026.

60 Proposal for a Directive of the European Parliament and of the Council on Soil Monitoring and Resilience (Soil Monitoring Law). COM/2023/416 Final. 5.7.2023. Available at https://eur-lex.europa.eu/legal-content/EN/TXT/?uri=CELEX:52023PC0416, accessed 11 March 2026.

61 Directive 2025/2360 of the European Union and the Council of 12 November 2025 on Soil Monitoring and Resilience - (Soil Monitoring Law). Available at https://eur-lex.europa.eu/legal-content/EN/TXT/HTML/?uri=OJ:L_202502360, accessed 11 March 2026.

62 See https://www.europeansoilpartnership.org/news-page/european-parliament-adopts-first-ever-soil-monitoring-law, accessed 11 March 2026.

63 Available at https://eur-lex.europa.eu/resource.html?uri=cellar:2bf140bf-a3f8-4ab2-b506-fd71826e6da6.0023.02/DOC_2&format=PDF, accessed 11 March 2026.

64 Ginzky (2021).

violation proceedings" before the European Court of Justice, which may ultimately lead to financial penalties.[65] Article 1 of the Directive outlines its central objectives:

> The objectives of this Directive are to establish a solid and coherent soil monitoring framework for all soils across the Union, to reduce soil contamination to levels no longer considered harmful to human health and the environment, to continuously improve soil health in the Union, to maintain soils in a healthy condition and to prevent and address all aspects of soil degradation, with a view to achieving healthy soils by 2050 so that they can provide multiple ecosystem services on a scale sufficient to meet environmental, societal and economic needs, prevent and mitigate the impacts of climate change and biodiversity loss, and increase resilience against natural disasters and in terms of food security.

In essence, the Directive pursues three principal objectives:

- The establishment of a comprehensive monitoring and assessment framework for soils across the EU;
- the implementation of measures to improve soil resilience; and
- the management of contaminated sites.

The overarching aim is to achieve "healthy soils by 2025", enabling soils to provide ecosystem services necessary to meet environmental, social, and economic needs. The recitals of the Directive, which provide the legislative justification and interpretive context for EU acts, make clear that the instrument's primary focus is on establishing a monitoring and assessment framework.[66] In this regard, the Directive prioritises the systematic collection and evaluation of information on soil conditions across the Union. Importantly, the Directive does not impose direct obligations on landowners or land users to undertake remediation or resilience measures. Instead, Articles 11 and 12 primarily require member states to provide information and guidance to landowners and land users on measures that may improve soil resilience, and to promote further research and knowledge development.[67]

Part IV of the Directive establishes a structured framework for managing contaminated sites. The approach consists of several stages: identification of potentially contaminated sites; investigation of these sites; site-specific risk assessment; and implementation of appropriate management measures. Many EU member states already apply similar regulatory approaches. The Directive seeks to harmonise these practices across the Union. However, Part IV addresses only one specific form of soil degradation: contamination. Other forms of soil degradation—such as erosion, compaction, salinisation, or loss of organic matter—are not directly regulated through this part of the Directive. An important procedural innovation is the introduction of formal requirements for public participation. Throughout the process—from the identification of potentially contaminated sites to their final management—member states must ensure public consultation and participation (Article 13(3)–(4)).For the purposes hereof, particular attention must be given to the Directive's conceptual approach to monitoring

65 Kassner & Ruppel (2025).

66 Part 2 of the Directive.

67 Ginzky & Pieper (2025).

and assessing soil health, as these elements may offer valuable benchmarks for soil governance in other regions. Part II of the Directive contains the core provisions on monitoring and assessment. Member states are required to establish soil districts and soil units, which serve as the spatial reference framework for monitoring activities (Article 4).

The Directive provides detailed methodological guidance for the monitoring process. Monitoring and assessment must be based on soil descriptors, indicators used to assess soil conditions. Notably, these soil descriptors address all major forms of soil degradation, as listed in Annex I. In this respect, the Directive adopts a modern and comprehensive approach, as it avoids focusing exclusively on a single form of soil degradation, unlike in Germany, for example.[68] Instead, monitoring systems must capture the full range of soil degradation processes.[69] Article 6(3) introduces two important categories of reference values for assessing soil health, namely non-binding sustainable target values and operational trigger values.

For certain soil descriptors, non-binding sustainable target values are already specified in Annex 1, Part A. For other descriptors listed in Annex 1, Part B, as well as for operational trigger values, member states are responsible for establishing appropriate thresholds. According to Article 10(5), soils are considered to be in a healthy condition if the non-binding sustainable target values are not exceeded. Operational trigger values are intended to signal situations in which soil conditions are at moderate or poor levels and therefore require intervention. These operational trigger values are designed to guide the implementation of measures to improve soil resilience under Articles 11 and 12.

The Commission's proposal for the Soil Monitoring Law in July 2023 was widely criticised for failing to impose stronger obligations on member states to implement the measures necessary to achieve healthy soils.[70] Compared with other EU environmental instruments—such as the Water Framework Directive (2000)—the Soil Monitoring Directive is considered relatively weak in terms of binding regulatory requirements.[71] However, the Directive includes a review clause after 6 years that allows the Commission to revise the instrument in light of data collected through the monitoring system and to consider additional mechanisms to improve the soil quality. The political context in which the Directive was adopted must also be taken into account.[72] Achieving consensus among EU Member States on soil governance has historically been difficult.

Despite these limitations, the Directive nevertheless represents an important advancement in soil governance in two respects. First, by addressing all major forms of soil degradation, the monitoring framework adopts a comprehensive, holistic approach

68 Ginzky (2024).
69 Ginzky & Pieper (2025); Kassner & Ruppel (2025).
70 Ginzky & Pieper (2025); Heuser & Itey (2021).
71 Ginzky & Pieper (2025).
72 See, for example: https://www.martin-haeusling.eu/images/Briefing_RL_Boden%C3%BCberwachung_und_resilienz_Martin_H%C3%A4usling.2pdf_en-GB.pdf, accessed 11 March 2026.

to collecting soil data and assessing soil health across the EU. Second, the introduction of non-binding sustainable target values and operational trigger values constitutes a significant governance innovation. Although these are not legally binding, they will carry considerable normative authority. They are expected to be developed through scientifically informed, consultative processes, using agreed methodologies and adopted by legitimate governmental institutions. Once established, these values will serve as benchmarks for assessing soil health and identifying the need for measures to improve soil resilience. In this way, the Directive may indirectly stimulate stronger soil governance in practice, even though its formal regulatory obligations remain limited.[73]

## 6. Lessons learnt

Having analysed the key characteristics of the Model Law on Soil Management in Africa, outlined the drafting process, and examined the conceptual approach of the European Soil Monitoring and Resilience Directive, the following section assesses whether, and to what extent, the African Model Law could serve as a blueprint, a benchmark or a toolbox for other states, regions, or continents. As a starting point, it is necessary to consider whether soil governance poses a challenge comparable to that faced by other regions of the world.[74]

### 6.1. Soil governance – a global challenge

Healthy soils are a precondition for sustainable development, as shown above. The following describes the soil conditions in Latin America and South America, as well as in India, to underscore the urgency of effective soil governance.

#### 6.1.1. Latin and South America

Healthy soils are central to reconciling food security, climate change mitigation and adaptation, and human health. In Latin America and the Caribbean (LAC), this linkage is especially urgent: soil degradation is driven by unsustainable land use and management, deforestation and forest disturbance (including logging and fires), biodiversity loss, erosion, and high vulnerability to climate change.[75] Erosion alone threatens nearly 20% of the region's soils, with Argentina (25 million hectares), Mexico (19% of its

73 Heuser & Itey (2021).
74 Ruppel & Murray (2025). Rodi et al. (2025); Ruppel (2025); Schnedl et al. (2024).
75 Poppiel et al. (2025).

territory), El Salvador (75%), Cuba (43%), Ecuador (50%), and Uruguay (30%) facing particularly acute pressures.[76] Desertification compounds these risks, affecting 12% of Guatemala, 17% of Colombia, 28% of Ecuador, and up to 62% of Chile.[77] Across the region, desertification affects 35% of the land—approximately 6.9 million km²—while in humid zones, deforestation is the dominant driver, already impacting 1.3 million km² (6.5% of the territory).[78] Almost half of LAC's land (49%) is vulnerable to water erosion, and more than half (56%) is affected by chemical degradation, including acidity and salinity.[79]

Climate change intensifies these pressures by reshaping agriculture itself: expanding pest and disease risks, altering water availability, shifting cropping cycles, and disrupting prevailing farm models. Climate shocks are already deepening poverty and inequality in rural areas, with disproportionate impacts on women. In an average year, poor rural households lose about 5% of their total income due to heat stress and 4.4% due to floods relative to better-off households.[80] These shocks also widen structural inequalities: floods increase the income gap between poor and non-poor households by approximately USD 21 billion annually, while heat stress contributes over USD 20 billion.[81] Gender disparities are particularly pronounced. Female-headed households experience income losses that are 8% higher from heat stress and 3% higher from floods compared to male-headed households.[82] In aggregate terms, this translates into annual income losses of about USD 37 billion due to heat and USD 16 billion due to floods for women in low- and middle-income countries. Looking ahead, climate change is expected to further exacerbate these inequalities: a 1°C increase in long-term average temperatures is associated with a 34% greater reduction in total incomes for female-headed households relative to male-headed households.[83] The stakes are both ecological and economic: 93% of LAC's economic activities depend directly on soils, three-quarters of which are already degraded, resulting in annual production losses of around USD 60 billion.[84]

### 6.1.2. India

Healthy soils are central to reconciling food security with climate change mitigation and adaptation, and to supporting rural livelihoods. In India, this linkage is especially

76 Montaño-Lopez et al. (2021: 615).
77 Ibid.
78 Ibid.: 617.
79 Ibid.
80 FAO (2024: 21).
81 Ibid.: 23.
82 Ibid.: 27.
83 Ibid.: 30.
84 See https://www.fao.org/americas/news/news-detail/suelos-en-riesgo/en, accessed 4 April 2026.

acute: the country supports nearly 18% of the world's population with just 2.4% of global land area.[85] Soil degradation—particularly water erosion—threatens the foundation of its agrarian economy.[86] The annual soil loss rate is estimated at 15.35 tonnes per hectare per year, stripping 5.37-8.4 million tonnes of nutrients, reducing crop productivity and contributing to floods, droughts, biodiversity loss, and a 1–2% decline in reservoir capacity annually. Major rainfed crops alone suffer an annual production loss of 13.4 million tonnes, valued at ₹205.32 billion. The ecological consequences are equally severe: nutrient-laden runoff pollutes rivers and groundwater, undermines freshwater biodiversity, and accelerates the release of carbon dioxide from decomposed organic matter, thereby aggravating climate change.

Land degradation in India spans 53 to 188 million hectares, depending on the definition, with erosion and vegetation loss as the primary drivers. Small and marginal farmers, who are most vulnerable to climate shocks and insecure tenure, bear the brunt of these impacts. Climate change will intensify pressures: projections suggest that by 2050, a 10% increase in rainfall intensity could lead to a 20% increase in rainfall erosivity, while soil loss from croplands could rise by 1.5% for every 1% increase in rainfall intensity.[87] These dynamics will deepen food, livelihood, and environmental insecurity in an already land-hungry agrarian economy.

### 6.1.3. Conclusion

Similar conclusions could be drawn for most regions of the world.[88] Globally, societies urgently require stronger and more effective soil governance to maintain—and, where possible, enhance—the services that soils provide for humanity, both now and in the future. Given this urgent need for improved soil governance frameworks, the question arises: whether and how the Model Law on Soil Management in Africa could serve as a blueprint, benchmark, or toolbox for other states, regions, or continents. Although the Model Law contains many innovative conceptual approaches, it should not be regarded as a blueprint for soil governance to be literally transposed into national legislation elsewhere. First, the Model Law was never intended to be directly implemented. Rather, it functions as a model framework and a compilation of regulatory options. Even within Africa, its provisions must be adapted to national conditions, institutional structures, and policy priorities. Second, the Model Law is grounded in a detailed analysis of African legal frameworks and governance challenges. Conditions, institutional capacities, and legal traditions in other regions may differ significantly.

85 Desai (2023: 3).
86 Bhattacharyya et al. (2015).
87 Bhattacharyya et al. (2023).
88 Ruppel et al. (2025); Ruppel & Ginzky (2021); Ginzky (2022); Schnedl (2025); Kameoka & Takahashi (2025).

Nevertheless, the Model Law can serve as both a benchmark and a toolbox for developing soil governance frameworks elsewhere.

As discussed above, the Model Law adopts a comprehensive and inclusive approach to soil governance. It addresses not only the maintenance and enhancement of soil quality but also related issues, including land tenure systems, foreign investment, international trade, gender equality, digitalisation,[89] and the role of indigenous knowledge. In this respect, the Model Law may serve as a benchmark by illustrating the wide range of policy areas to consider when designing national legislation on soil governance. Another important benchmark is the Model Law's modern understanding of soil as a natural resource that provides multiple services to society, including ecological, economic, social, and cultural services. Using this conceptual framework as the starting point for soil legislation may help policymakers and societies to recognise the fundamental importance of soils for sustainable development.

The approach of the African Model Law—designed as a framework applicable across an entire continent—may also be relevant to large federal states or regions comprising multiple jurisdictions, where overarching legislative frameworks must accommodate substantial internal diversity.

The Model Law may also serve as a toolbox of regulatory instruments. Several of its mechanisms could be adapted and incorporated into soil governance frameworks elsewhere. These include, *inter alia*: soil impact assessment procedures; obligations to minimise and compensate detrimental effects on soils; gender impact assessment; the integration of the principle of land degradation neutrality; zoning approaches for soil uses; and spatial planning mechanisms for the protection of particularly valuable soils.

Similarly, the provisions concerning the establishment of effective administrative structures—such as national soil information systems and coordinated mechanisms—provide a useful conceptual foundation for ensuring effective implementation and enforcement.

In addition to its substantive provisions, the Model Law also offers three important procedural benchmarks:

- First, the drafting process was based on rigorous legal analysis and extensive stakeholder consultations, involving experts from multiple disciplines and ensuring broad regional representation.
- Second, the process was guided throughout by a politically legitimate institution— the Pan-African Parliament—which provided institutional leadership and oversight.
- Third, the Model Law is accompanied by extensive Commentaries, which provide contextual explanations and additional regulatory options. These Commentaries facilitate the interpretation and adaptation of the Model Law and may serve as a valuable tool for legislators and policymakers. Such

89 Ginzky & Ruppel (2025a).

accompanying explanatory materials could be particularly useful when developing framework legislation for regions or continents.

The Model Law shall also be made available in four official languages of the AU: English, French, Arabic, and Portuguese, thereby facilitating its accessibility and potential use across a wide range of countries.

Taken together, the Model Law represents a significant contribution to global soil governance. It functions not as binding legislation but as a non-prescriptive template that can guide national and regional soil governance initiatives. Where states wish to domesticate elements of the Model Law, a stepwise approach may be particularly effective and could include the following components:

- Conducting a diagnostic assessment of national soil governance gaps through comparative legal analysis and multi-stakeholder consultations involving farmers, customary authorities or indigenous peoples, local governments, industry representatives, and scientists;
- developing a core legislative framework anchored in key law principles, such as those entailed in Article 6 of the Model Law, *inter alia*, prevention, precaution, and the polluter-pays principle, while adapting relevant policy options from the Model Law's Commentaries;
- establishing institutional arrangements for implementation, including clearly defined mandates across ministries, a national soil information system, and transparent monitoring and reporting mechanisms;
- ensuring effective enforcement through a coordinating authority working in cooperation with traditional and indigenous governance structures, supported by accessible dispute-resolution mechanisms and proportionate sanctions.

Different modes of uptake are possible. Some countries may adopt specific regulatory mechanisms—such as soil impact assessments or restoration obligations—while others may focus on broader policy areas, such as gender equality, mining governance, or soil data management. In addition, the co-production process used to develop the Model Law—characterised by scientific research, stakeholder participation, and institutional leadership—may serve as a replicable model for other regions. In this sense, the Model Law may function as both a benchmark and a toolbox, not only in terms of its substantive provisions but also in its participatory and interdisciplinary drafting process.

With respect to the development of a future international instrument on soil governance—such as a treaty, convention, or protocol—the Model Law may even be regarded as a potential blueprint. Apart from additional provisions concerning institutional arrangements, subsidiary rulemaking, compliance mechanisms, and dispute settlement, the Model Law already addresses the principal dimensions of soil governance and provides detailed regulatory mechanisms. Its provisions could therefore serve as a starting point for translating soil governance concepts, mechanisms, and instruments into the structure of an international legal instrument, either at the regional or at the global level.[90]

## 6.2. What may need to be added?

Two elements are particularly critical for effective soil governance. The first is the systematic gathering of soil data and assessment of soil health, including chemical, physical, and biological indicators. The second is the development of environmental quality standards that provide benchmarks for determining acceptable soil conditions and identifying the need for management measures. Both aspects are addressed in the African Model Law, notably in Articles 21 ("Data Management and Monitoring") and 23 ("Development of Soil Quality Standards").

However, the EU Soil Monitoring and Resilience Directive provides a more detailed and operational framework in this regard. The Directive specifies, *inter alia*, the establishment of spatial reference units for monitoring; clearly defined soil descriptors and indicators for soil health across all forms of soil degradation; and detailed methodologies for sampling, including the locations, numbers, and frequencies of measurements. Similarly, the Directive provides a more structured approach to soil quality standards by introducing two categories of reference values: sustainable target values, which indicate healthy soil conditions; and operational trigger values, which indicate the need for management measures to improve soil quality. The Directive also specifies the indicators to be used for assessing different forms of soil degradation.

Given the importance of these elements for effective soil governance, other states, regions, or continents may consider the EU Soil Monitoring Directive as an additional benchmark or tool in the toolbox, complementing the broader governance framework offered by the African Model Law.

# 7. Summary and outlook

It has been demonstrated that the Model Law on Soil Management in Africa can serve as a highly relevant benchmark and toolbox for developing soil governance frameworks across other continents, regions, and states. In particular, regarding the collection of soil data, the assessment of soil health, and the development of soil quality standards, the EU Soil Monitoring and Resilience Directive offers additional insights that may complement the Model Law's broader governance approach.

However, neither the African Model Law nor the EU Soil Monitoring Directive should be regarded as a blueprint for soil governance. Local adaptation will, in any

90 See Ruppel & Murray (2025).

case, be necessary and must begin with a thorough analysis of existing legislation, institutional capacities, and the specific challenges faced at the national or regional level.

The domestication of the Model Law will take place within African states. It will therefore be important to document and assess the experience emerging from these domestication processes. Such assessments may generate two valuable outcomes. First, they could serve as the basis for developing a generic guidance framework on the domestication of the Model Law for Soil Management in Africa. Second, they may provide insights that could inform future refinements and adjustments of the Model Law itself.

The adoption of the Model Law represented a significant milestone in the development of global soil governance and may even be considered a historic step. However, its true impact will depend on the success of its domestication and implementation. Effective national adaptation will be essential to translate the Model Law's principles into tangible on-the-ground improvements and to enhance the well-being of communities that depend on healthy soils. While the initial focus of domestication will necessarily be in Africa, the Model Law's conceptual foundations and regulatory innovations may also offer valuable insights for the broader international community. Soil governance must never be viewed through a "one-size-fits-all lens" but rather understood as an evolving process of learning, adaptation, and continuous improvement.

# The Model Law on Soil Management in Africa

## 1. Preface to the Model Law on Soil Management in Africa

### 1.1. Introduction

A Model Law is a comprehensive legal instrument comprising detailed provisions that reflect internationally recognised and recommended standards on a specific subject matter. It is designed to serve as a template or guide for developing, reforming, or harmonising national legislation. As a supra-national normative tool, a Model Law may be adopted in its entirety or adapted to suit the specific legal, social, and institutional contexts of individual Member States.

The African Union (AU), through its various organs, has established a strong tradition of developing Model Laws on issues of continental significance. Pursuant to its mandate under Article 11 (3) and (7) of the Protocol to the Treaty Establishing the African Economic Community relating to the Pan-African Parliament (PAP Protocol), and in accordance with Rules 4 (d) and 4 (e) of the PAP Rules of Procedure, the Pan-African Parliament (PAP) has itself developed several Model Laws across diverse thematic areas, including the Model Law on Food and Nutrition Security in Africa.

### 1.2. Justification for a Model Law on Soil Management in Africa

One of the core objectives of establishing the Organisation of African Unity (OAU) was to promote the unity and solidarity of African states and to improve the well-being of their peoples. Article 2 (1)(b) of the 1963 OAU Charter affirms the commitment of Member States "to co-ordinate and intensify their co-operation and efforts to achieve a better life for the peoples of Africa." Furthermore, Article 2 (2) calls on Member States to harmonise their general policies, particularly in the fields of nutrition, science, and technical cooperation, all of which are closely linked to the sustainable use and protection of Africa's soil resources.

Following the attainment of political independence, African nations redirected their collective efforts toward inclusive development and environmental sustainability. This mission is reaffirmed in the Constitutive Act of the AU (2000), particularly Article 3, which sets out the Union's objectives, including the promotion of sustainable development at the economic, social, and environmental levels.

A unified and coordinated approach is essential to ensure that AU policies and programmes translate into tangible improvements in the lives of African people. Among the most pressing priorities is the sustainable management of Africa's soil, which is the foundation of food systems, water regulation, biodiversity, climate adaptation, and livelihoods. Yet soil across the continent faces mounting pressures from degradation, overuse, pollution, and the impacts of climate change.

In response, the AU has initiated key continental frameworks, including the Soil Initiative for Africa (2020) and the Africa Fertiliser and Soil Health Action Plan (2023–2033), which was officially endorsed at the Africa Fertiliser and Soil Health Summit held in May 2024. These initiatives reflect a growing recognition that healthy soil is central to achieving the vision of Agenda 2063, particularly:

- Aspiration 1: A prosperous Africa based on inclusive growth and sustainable development, including healthy and well-nourished citizens, modern agriculture for increased productivity and production, and environmentally sustainable, climate-resilient economies and communities; and
- Aspiration 6: An Africa whose development is people-driven, relying on the potential of its citizens, especially women and youth.

Despite growing awareness, many African states are still developing comprehensive legal frameworks to enforce sustainable soil use, prevent degradation, and promote restoration. Effective soil governance requires coordinated legal, institutional, and financial mechanisms, alongside inclusive participation from all sectors of society. In this regard, the meaningful involvement of women, youth, and marginalised communities remains essential, not as a standalone solution, but as a necessary element of a broader, systemic approach that ensures equitable access to soil resources and decision-making processes. In this context, the Model Law on Soil Management in Africa, developed under the auspices of the PAP, provides normative guidance to AU Member States for adopting or updating national legislation. It draws on African legal traditions, scientific knowledge, and traditional knowledge systems, as well as the shared continental commitment to sustainability, equity, and long-term prosperity.

### 1.3. The Process of Developing the Model Law

In developing this Model Law, the drafters drew inspiration from a range of continental and international instruments, including the AU Policy Framework for Pastoralism in Africa (2010), the AU Declaration on Land Issues and Challenges (2009), and the African Charter on Human and Peoples' Rights (1981). The Malabo Declaration on Accelerated Agricultural Growth and Transformation for Shared Prosperity and Improved Livelihoods (2014) and the aspirations of Agenda 2063—particularly those related to sustainable development, environmental stewardship, and inclusive governance—also provided critical guidance for shaping the legal and normative direction of this text.

In addition, the drafters drew from the 10-year Comprehensive Africa Agriculture Development Programme (CAADP) Strategy and Action Plan for 2026–2035, which aims to transform Africa's agrifood systems and achieve food and nutrition security, as well as the Kampala CAADP Declaration, adopted in January 2025, which outlines a continental vision for sustainable agrifood transformation. These frameworks emphasise the promotion of sustainable land management, integrated soil fertility management, sustainable grazing practices, reforestation, and afforestation—all of which contribute to reducing erosion, enhancing soil health and agricultural productivity, sequestering carbon, and restoring degraded lands.

Further normative grounding was drawn from the revised version of the African Convention on the Conservation of Nature and Natural Resources (2003). The Convention obliges State Parties to take effective measures to prevent land degradation by adopting long-term, integrated strategies for the sustainable management of land resources, including soil, vegetation, and hydrological processes. It calls for the conservation and improvement of soil to combat erosion, misuse, and the deterioration of its physical, chemical, biological, or economic properties.

Moreover, this Model Law is informed by existing AU Model Laws and policy instruments, including the Model Law on Food and Nutrition Security in Africa (2022), as well as national legislation and regional best practices on soil management, land use, and environmental protection. It also draws on the extensive research and comparative legal analysis presented in "Legal Pathways to Sustainable Soil Management in Africa" (2025) and "African Soil Protection Law: Mapping out Options for a Model Legislation for Improved Sustainable Soil Management in Africa" (2021). Both publications—co-authored by the drafters of this Model Law together with leading experts—contain in-depth African country studies and underscore the importance of sustainable natural resource governance, food and nutrition security, climate resilience, and human rights, reinforcing the vital role of healthy soil in achieving Africa's development vision.

In addition, a review of scholarly literature, institutional reports, and lessons from implementation experiences across Member States enriched the drafting process with critical insights, legal innovations, and context-sensitive recommendations.

### 1.4. Scope and Purpose of the Model Law

This Model Law on Soil Management in Africa provides a framework to facilitate Member States in developing and enhancing their national legislation and policies related to soil management.

The purpose of this Model Law is twofold:

(1) to establish a framework that promotes the sustainable management of soil, recognising its critical role in ensuring food and nutrition security and resilience against climate change; and

(2) to facilitate strategies for soil conservation, restoration, and enhancement of soil fertility and productivity, aimed at combating degradation, as well as an effective Land Degradation Neutrality (LDN) implementation.

Effective administration of soil governance is paramount; thus, this Model Law emphasises the necessity for robust implementation, continuous monitoring, and appropriate sanctioning mechanisms to ensure compliance and accountability, utilising effective data management, soil information systems, and other digital means, including Artificial Intelligence (AI).

This Model Law is cognisant of Africa's unique context, recognising the value of local knowledge, traditional practices, and the critical role of traditional leaders in sustainable soil management. It embraces the continent's diverse legal traditions and cultural specificities, fostering a collaborative approach integrating modern scientific knowledge with indigenous practices to achieve sustainable outcomes.

## 1.5. Use and Interpretation of the Model Law

Given the complexity of soil science and the intricacies of sustainable soil management, Commentaries were developed for possible inclusive and participatory consultation and use by national and regional parliaments and other relevant stakeholders through a process of progressive realisation, to facilitate their understanding, interpretation, domestication, and application of the Model Law.

The Commentaries do not, in themselves, constitute part of this Model Law, but may be of guidance in facilitating its understanding, use, and transposition into domestic legislation.

The Commentaries address the following subjects:

- Commentary I — Awareness Raising and Capacity Building;
- Commentary II — Sustainable Soil Management Practices for Food Production;
- Commentary III — Dispute Settlement;
- Commentary IV — Data Management;
- Commentary V — Fertilisers;
- Commentary VI — Foreign Investment;
- Commentary VII — Gender;
- Commentary VIII — Implementation and Enforcement;
- Commentary IX — Industry, Infrastructure, and Energy Transition;
- Commentary X — Mining;
- Commentary XI — Migration;
- Commentary XII — Pesticides;
- Commentary XIII — Pastoralism;

- Commentary XIV — Urbanisation;
- Commentary XV — Tenure Rights; and
- Commentary XVI — Traditional Leaders.

## 1.6. Conclusion

Soil is among Africa's most valuable, yet vulnerable, and at times neglected resources. Soil is fundamental to food and nutrition security, climate resilience, and the health of ecosystems. Healthy soil is, furthermore, the indispensable bedrock for sustainable livelihoods, particularly for rural populations and smallholder farmers, and a precondition for long-term prosperity and welfare. Healthy soil contributes to inclusive development by sustaining agricultural productivity, supporting biodiversity, and mitigating the impacts of climate change. However, the full potential of soil can only be realised within a supportive legal and institutional environment that protects it from degradation and promotes its sustainable use.

To this end, effective legislation should go beyond acknowledging the importance of soil. It should provide clear rights, responsibilities, standards, and enforcement mechanisms that empower communities, farmers, and institutions to protect and restore this essential resource. This Model Law on Soil Management in Africa is intended to serve as a normative framework that supports AU Member States in developing or reforming national legislation. It reflects Africa's legal diversity, integrates scientific and traditional knowledge systems, and affirms that soil is a shared and living foundation for sustainable development.

By enabling coherent, inclusive, and forward-looking soil governance, this Model Law aims to ensure that Africa's soil continues to serve present and future generations while making a meaningful contribution to the realisation of the AU's development vision under Agenda 2063.

## 2. Model Law on Soil Management in Africa[1]

### PREAMBLE

**THE PAN-AFRICAN PARLIAMENT,**

**CONSIDERING** that Article 17 of the Constitutive Act of the African Union (AU) establishes the Pan-African Parliament (PAP) to ensure the "full participation of the African people in developing and integrating the continent";

**NOTING** that Article 3 of the Protocol to the Treaty Establishing the African Economic Community Relating to the Pan-African Parliament (PAP Protocol) and Rule 4 (a) of the Rules of Procedure of the PAP empower the PAP to facilitate regional cooperation, development, and promotion of "collective self-reliance", as well as the "implementation of the policies, objectives and programmes" of the AU;

**CONSIDERING** further that Article 11 (3) of the PAP Protocol and Rules 4 and 5 of the PAP Rules of Procedure empower the PAP to work towards harmonising or coordinating the laws of Member States;

**RECOGNISING** that the soil in Africa is a vital and limited natural resource that sustains the continent's food systems, livelihoods, ecosystems, and social cohesion, serving as a foundation for peace and stability, and recognising the pressing need for a comprehensive and coherent legal framework to address the challenges of soil degradation, drought, desertification, and its impact on food and nutrition security, climate mitigation, and adaptation;

**RECALLING** the Sustainable Development Agenda of 2015 of the United Nations and, in particular, the objective of Land Degradation Neutrality (LDN) pursuant to the Sustainable Development Goal (SDG) 15.3 and the leadership of "United Nations Convention to Combat Desertification in those countries experiencing serious drought and/or desertification, particularly in Africa" (UNCCD) to support LDN implementation at the national level;

**RECALLING FURTHER** the Soil Initiative for Africa of 2020, through which the AU launched a call for a long-term, continent-wide effort to systematically enhance the health and productivity of Africa's soil, notably by scaling up proven, locally adapted technologies, including the balanced and efficient application of both

---

1 Notwithstanding its adoption, for the purposes of this publication, the legislative proposal of the Model Law on Soil Management in Africa, which was tabled at the Plenary Session of the Sixth Parliament of the Pan-African Parliament (PAP) on 6 November 2025, shall be utilised. See https://pap.au.int/en/news/press-releases/2025-11-06/african-parliamentarians-adopt-continents-first-model-law, accessed 19 March 2026; https://www.fao.org/partnerships/parliamentary-alliances/news/news-article/en/c/1754895/, accessed 19 March 2026; https://www.su.ac.za/en/news/pan-african-parliament-adopts-continents-first-model-law-sustainable-soil-management, accessed 19 March 2026.

inorganic and organic fertilisers; and the adoption of the Africa Fertiliser and Soil Health Action Plan, a ten-year initiative (2023–2033) designed to address Africa's most pressing soil fertility and fertiliser management challenges, which was officially endorsed at the Africa Fertiliser and Soil Health Summit held in May 2024;

**RECALLING FURTHER** the work of international institutions, such as the United Nation's Convention on Climate Change (UNFCCC), the Food and Agriculture Organization (FAO) and the United Nation's Environment Programme (UNEP), as well as the adoption of the Maputo Declaration on Agriculture and Food Security of 2003, and the Nairobi Declaration on Africa Fertiliser and Soil Health of 2024, which underscores the critical importance of improving soil health and enhancing the use of fertilisers to achieve sustainable agricultural growth and food and nutrition security across the continent;

**NOTING** that land use is distinct from land ownership or access rights and **RECOGNISING** that secure land tenure is essential for sustainable soil management, which allows communities to invest in sustainable practices that improve soil health for future generations;

**RECALLING** Resolution PAP.6/PLN/RES/19/NOV.22 of the Pan-African Parliament on the Development of a Model Law on Soil Management, which, among others, the Committee on Rural Economy, Agriculture, Natural Resources and Environment and the PAP Alliance on SDGs to lead the formulation of a Model Legislation on Sustainable Soil Management, taking into account the diverse legal traditions within the African continent, and to present the said Model Legislation for consideration by the Plenary of the PAP;

**CONVINCED** that a Model Legislation on Sustainable Soil Management in Africa by the Pan-African Parliament can significantly contribute to improving and protecting soil in the continent, as well as advancing the realisation of the Agenda 2063 aspirations and the "land degradation neutrality" objective of the Sustainable Development Goals;

**CONVINCED FURTHER** that a Model Law on Soil Management can also be an effective tool for harmonising laws and policies governing soil health and management among the AU Member States, taking into account the cross-cutting and multi-sectoral nature of soil, and the diverse legal traditions of African states;

**IN ACCORDANCE WITH** Rule 5 (b), (c), and (d) of the Rules of Procedure of the PAP, empowering it to, *inter alia*, make recommendations and resolutions on matters relating to the AU and its organs, Regional Economic Communities (RECs), Member States, and their respective institutions.

**HEREBY ADOPTS THE FOLLOWING**

**MODEL LAW ON SOIL MANAGEMENT IN AFRICA:**

## Part I: Preliminary Provisions

### Article 1 — Title of the Law

This Law may be cited as the "Law on Soil Management in Africa."

### Article 2 — Purpose and Objectives of the Law

(1) The purpose of this Law is to guide and inspire AU Member States in the governance of soil through sustainable soil management, preserving and enhancing its ecological, economic, social, and cultural services, particularly food and nutrition security, and achieving the objective of LDN.

(2) To this end, the objectives of this Law shall be to:
   (a) Provide rules and mechanisms for the sustainable management of soil to foster sustainable development.
   (b) Provide a basis or tool for policy guidance of all stakeholders to ensure harmonisation of regulations, policies, and administrative practice for effective and sustainable soil management.

### Article 3 — Scope of Application of the Law

This Law shall apply to all forms of soil degradation and to all activities that have, or may have, detrimental effects on soil, as well as to activities undertaken to conserve, maintain, enhance, restore, or otherwise promote soil health and services.

### Article 4 — Definitions

In this Law, unless the context otherwise requires:

(1) '**Artisanal Mining**' — Means traditional and customary mining operations, using mainly rudimentary methods and manual tools to mine minerals available on the surface and at shallow depths.

(2) '**Competent Authority**' — Means the authority determined to be responsible for specific tasks under this Law.

(3) '**Environmental Impact Assessment**' — Means a process to identify, evaluate, and communicate the potential environmental impacts, *inter alia* on soil, water, air, biodiversity, and ecosystems, of a proposed activity to inform decision-making.

(4) '**Food and Nutrition Security**' — Means a situation that exists when all

people at all times have physical, social and economic access to food, which is safe and consumed in sufficient quantity and quality to meet their dietary needs and food preferences and is supported by an environment of adequate sanitation, health services and care, allowing for a healthy and active life.

(5) '**Industrial Mining**' — Means mining by industrial means and techniques.

(6) '**Land**' — Means, as per the relevant international instrument, the terrestrial bio-productive system that comprises soil, vegetation, and other biota, and the ecological and hydrological processes that operate within the system.

(7) '**Land Degradation Neutrality**' — Means, as per the relevant international instrument, a state whereby the amount and quality of land resources necessary to support ecosystem services and services to enhance food and nutrition security remain stable, or increase, within specified temporal and spatial scales and ecosystems.

(8) '**Land Grabbing**' — Means the control (whether through ownership, lease, concession, contracts, quotas, or general power) of larger than locally typical amounts of land by any persons or entities (public or private, foreign or domestic) by any means ('legal' or 'illegal') for purposes of speculation, extraction, resource control or commodification at the expense of agroecology, land stewardship, food sovereignty and human rights, as per the definition formulated by the Food and Agriculture Organization of the United Nations.

(9) '**Land Take**' — Means the conversion of natural land into land used as a platform for constructions and infrastructure or as a direct source of raw material.

(10) '**Risk of Significant Degradation**' — Means the likelihood or potential that soil quality, structure, or services may be adversely affected by, among others, erosion, contamination, compaction, loss of organic matter, salinisation, sealing, or biodiversity loss.

(11) '**Soil Contamination**' — Means the occurrence of pollutants in soil above a certain level, causing a deterioration or loss of one or more soil services.

(12) '**Soil Degradation**' — Means the deterioration of soil quality, resulting in the failure of the soil to provide essential services effectively. It encompasses a range of physical, chemical, and biological impairments, including, but not limited to, erosion, contamination, compaction, salinisation, desertification, and the depletion of biodiversity.

(13) '**Soil Health**' — Means the continued capacity of soil to function as a vital living ecosystem that sustains plants, animals, and humans.

(14) '**Soil Impact Assessment**' — Means a structured evaluation process that identifies and analyses the potential effects of proposed activities on soil health, structure, and services. It includes the assessment of direct and indirect impacts across environmental, social, cultural, and economic dimensions. It incorporates the comparison of alternative options, co-benefits, trade-offs, and

mitigation or adaptation measures. SIAs may be conducted independently or as part of broader environmental impact assessments.

(15) '**Soil Management**' — Means the application of operations, practices, treatments, and processes to protect, maintain, and enhance soil and its services. It includes soil conservation, protection, soil amendment, and restoration.

(16) '**Soil Quality Standards**' — Means the maximum capacities of negative impact on the soil with regard to the various forms of soil degradation. The soil quality standards shall be legally binding.

(17) '**Soil Rehabilitation Measures**' — Means undertaking measures to restore soil health and their services to achieve a healthy status of soil.

(18) '**Soil Sealing**' — Means the covering of the soil surface with impervious materials.

(19) '**Soil**' — Means the upper layer of the earth's crust, extending from the surface to the bedrock, composed of mineral particles, organic matter, water, air, and living organisms. Soil is a basic and non-renewable natural resource that provides essential ecological, economic, social, and cultural services, including food and biomass production, water regulation, climate moderation, carbon storage, biodiversity conservation, and a physical platform for human activity.

(20) '**Spatial Instruments**' — Means land-use planning and regulatory tools established under national legislation to designate, manage, or restrict the use of soil, particularly in areas of environmental, agricultural, or cultural value. These instruments aim to coordinate the spatial impacts of sectoral policies, ensure the sustainable provision of soil services and fertility, and promote a rational, equitable, and integrated approach to land use and territorial development.

(21) '**Sustainable Development**' — Means, as per the relevant international instrument, development that meets the needs of the present without compromising the ability of future generations to meet their own needs.

(22) '**Sustainable Soil Management**' — Means the responsible use and management of soil, their functions, and services in a manner that ensures their long-term capacity to support human well-being, environmental health, and economic development. It aims to maintain and enhance soil services for current and future generations.

(23) '**Use of Soil**' — Means any activity that is conducted by means or utilisation of soil or elements thereof, whether or not such activity may have a positive or negative impact on soil.

**Article 5 — Services of Soil**

(1) Soil is a limited and fragile natural resource that shall be conserved, maintained,

and protected against all forms of degradation to preserve its ecological, economic, social, and cultural services for present and future generations.

(2) Within the meaning of this Law, ecological soil services are:
   (a) the basis of life and habitat for humans, animals, plants, and soil organisms, as well as the basis of soil biodiversity;
   (b) a medium for decomposition and compensation due to its filtering, buffering, and material conversion properties, especially for the protection of groundwater;
   (c) a sink for greenhouse gases as a vital tool to counteract climate change, and promote economic and social resilience of ecosystems and economies; and
   (d) establishing areas for promoting climate adaptation, including in urban areas.

(3) Within the meaning of this Law, economic soil services include, among others, the provision of food, fibre, fuel, construction materials, minerals, and the use of land as a foundation for human buildings and infrastructure.

(4) Within the meaning of this Law, social soil services refer to the role of soil in supporting human well-being, livelihoods, and social cohesion, including through food production, promotion of human health, employment, equitable access to resources, and the resilience of communities and society.

(5) Within the meaning of this Law, cultural soil services provide numerous material and non-material benefits, including the preservation of cultural heritage, traditional practices, sacred sites, and archaeological remains embedded in or associated with soil.

**Article 6 — Guiding Principles**

(1) Sustainable soil management, as regulated under this Law, shall be guided by the following principles:
   (a) **Accountability** — Ensure responsibility of authorities, societal actors, stakeholders, and individuals for their respective actions and activities.
   (b) **Effective Participation** — Ensure the free, fair, informed, full, and effective participation of stakeholders, including women, men, elders, youth, persons with disabilities, and vulnerable groups, in decision-making, implementation, and monitoring processes related to sustainable soil management.
   (c) **Gender Equity and Equality** — Ensure equal and equitable rights for women and men concerning the use of soil.
   (d) **Non-discrimination and Social Justice** — Ensure that soil is used non-discriminately and foster social justice.
   (e) **Precaution** — Apply a precautionary approach to all soil uses to prevent unnecessary detrimental effects and consider and manage risks even if no

complete evidence can be provided.

(f) **Prevention** — Avoid any unnecessary harm to or impairment of soil or the services of soil.

(g) **Proportionality** — The measures taken to address soil degradation shall be proportionate to the severity of the harm caused, the scale of the degradation, and the available resources.

(h) **Protection of Soil Biodiversity** — Measures shall be taken to conserve the biodiversity of soil ecosystems, including organisms that contribute to soil health, structure, and productivity, and fauna dependent on soil habitats.

(i) **Degradation Responsibility Principle** — The individual or entity causing, contributing to, or benefiting from pollution or soil degradation shall bear the costs of managing such impacts, including the expenses associated with preventing, mitigating, or remedying the damage. This includes the responsibility for financing soil rehabilitation efforts.

(j) **Subsidiarity** — Decisions concerning sustainable soil management shall be taken at the lowest competent and effective level, ensuring that local and sub-national actors, including communities, traditional authorities, and local governments, have the opportunity to participate meaningfully. Higher-level authorities shall make decisions, if necessary, at this level and provide support, coordination, and oversight where necessary, particularly in cases requiring broader technical capacity, financing, or cross-regional integration.

(k) **Sustainability** — Consider all dimensions of sustainability, economic, ecological, social, and cultural, ensuring maximum benefits for current and future generations while minimising risks for human beings and the environment.

(l) **Transparency** — Ensure that the process and outcome of decision-making at every stage concerning soil management are clearly defined, and adopt a context-sensitive strategy for communication with all stakeholders.

(2) In interpreting and applying this Law, competent authorities may have regard to other relevant, widely recognised principles of international law that may further its purpose.

**Article 7 — Interface with other Sectoral Provisions**

(1) Insofar as other national sectoral provisions regulate the use of soil, the requirements of this Law shall be complied with.

(2) In cases of overlap or conflict, the requirements of this Law shall prevail over other sectoral laws, unless the other sectoral laws provide higher protection standards.

**Article 8 — Relation to Land Laws**

(1) Land laws shall be implemented with due consideration for the provisions of this Law to foster sustainable soil management and sustainable development in the national territory.
(2) Land laws shall also be designed to provide equal and non-discriminatory access to, and use of, soil, land, and associated rights.

**Article 9 — Interpretation Clause**

(1) When interpreting this Law, due consideration shall be given to the principles and purpose of this Law, and consideration may be given to relevant international, regional, and constitutional instruments as interpretive guidance, where appropriate.
(2) In so doing, the rights and obligations in this Law shall be interpreted, so far as possible, in the manner that best furthers its purpose.

## Part II: Linkages to Sustainable Development

**Article 10 — Soil, Sustainable Agriculture, and Food and Nutrition Security**

(1) Soil shall be protected, maintained, and enhanced as the basis for sustainable agriculture and food and nutrition security. A policy on soil, sustainable agriculture, and food and nutrition security should be established and aligned with the provisions and recommendations of relevant AU Model Laws, allowing for increased agricultural production.
(2) Preference shall be given to natural, organic, and biological methods for maintaining soil fertility and managing pests.
(3) Fertilisers and pesticides shall be used in a manner that avoids harm to living organisms that live in, depend on, or interact with the soil, and that ensures the protection, maintenance, and enhancement of all soil services. Pesticides shall only be applied when necessary.
(4) The National Soil Management Authority, pursuant to Article 31 (1), shall establish and regularly update a list of fertilisers and pesticides, which may have detrimental effects on soil health, human health, and water resources.
(5) Fertilisers and pesticides may only be used if the competent authority has granted permission.
(6) Seed autonomy shall be promoted to enhance sustainable agriculture and the sustainable management of soil. A precautionary approach shall be applied to the use and introduction of genetically modified organisms (GMOs), ensuring that their potential impacts on soil health, biodiversity, and traditional seed systems are carefully assessed and regulated.

(7) All forms of agricultural practices, such as crop cultivation, forestry, livestock, and pastoralism, shall be carried out according to good soil use practices, taking into account guidance provided by relevant international bodies.
(8) When implementing sectoral provisions concerning agricultural practices and food and nutrition security, the provisions of this Law, in particular Articles 14, 15, 18, and 19, shall be complied with.

### Article 11 — Soil and Climate Mitigation and Adaptation

(1) Soil shall be recognised as an essential tool in addressing climate change mitigation and as a critical enabler of climate adaptation.
(2) Its services as a sink for greenhouse gases shall be preserved and enhanced through sustainable soil management practices in accordance with relevant international instruments.
(3) The competent authority shall take measures to protect, maintain, and enhance soil services in climate adaptation, including through the protection of biodiversity, the improvement of water retention, and the regulation of temperature, to strengthen ecosystem resilience under climate variability.
(4) Natural marshes, swamps, wetlands, and peatlands shall be protected and maintained as reservoirs and sinks for greenhouse gases.
(5) Degraded marshes, swamps, wetlands, and peatlands shall be managed to avoid further greenhouse gas emissions, particularly through rewetting programmes and activities.

### Article 12 — International Trade

The National Soil Management Authority, pursuant to Article 31 (1), shall ensure that transnational trade in commodities, goods, equipment, or services promotes sustainable soil management and does not have a detrimental impact on the soil.

### Article 13 — Foreign Investment

(1) Foreign investors shall comply with national legislation, in particular with the obligations pursuant to this Law. Respective sanctions shall be implemented for violations of soil use.
(2) The competent authority shall take appropriate measures to ensure that large-scale land acquisitions, including land grabbing, or utilisations by foreign investors do not undermine soil health or local land rights.
(3) In consultation with the competent authority, foreign investors shall consider the interests of local communities.

## Part III: Soil Use Regulation and Planning

### Article 14 — Obligation to Minimise and Compensate Detrimental Effects on Soil

(1) Soil shall be used in such a manner as to avoid, to the extent possible, any impairment of the services outlined in Article 5. In case of unavoidable impairments of those services, they have to be equally compensated by soil restoration measures in accordance with the principle of proportionality.

(2) Any use of soil that may pose a risk of significant degradation requires permission from the competent authority. Permission can only be granted if the operator of the soil use demonstrates that negative impacts on the soil are minimised, taking into account the standards of Article 23, and that adverse effects that cannot be avoided are equally compensated by soil restoration measures.

(3) Where restoration is impossible, financial compensation shall be paid to the competent authority. The monetary income is to be used to restore soil in other locations.

(4) Pursuant to paragraph (3), in cases where smallholder farmers or vulnerable communities are unable to bear the costs of soil restoration or compensation for degradation, the competent authority shall provide support, including financial assistance or technical aid, to ensure that these groups are not unduly burdened. This support shall be proportionate to the scale of their operations and the degree of degradation, aiming to protect their livelihoods while promoting sustainable soil management practices.

(5) The National Soil Management Authority, pursuant to Article 31 (1), shall determine the specific soil uses for which permission is required, as outlined in paragraph (2) of this Article.

### Article 15 — Soil Impact Assessment (SIA) as part of Environmental or Strategic Impact Assessment

(1) A Soil Impact Assessment (SIA) shall be conducted as part of an Environmental Impact Assessment (EIA) whenever a proposed activity poses a risk of significant detrimental effect on soil, and where necessary, before granting permission to use the soil.

(2) The SIA shall be carried out by a body determined by the National Soil Management Authority.

(3) The SIA shall examine the extent to which there may be negative impacts on soil and its services, as set out in Article 5 (2) and (4). The SIA shall recommend measures to mitigate the potential adverse effects, taking into account the soil quality standards outlined in Article 23.

(4) National regulation concerning the responsibilities to undertake and finance the

EIA shall also apply to SIA.

(5) Where there is no national provision, the applicant for a specific use of soil shall be responsible for undertaking and financing the SIA.

**Article 16 — Obligation to Reduce Land Take and Soil Sealing**

(1) Any person and entity shall avoid land take and soil sealing. The National Soil Management Authority, pursuant to Article 31 (1), shall develop national strategies to reduce land take and soil sealing.

(2) To achieve land degradation neutrality, the following shall apply:

(a) Reduction of further land take and soil sealing as much as possible; and

(b) Offsetting unavoidable land take and soil sealing by restoration measures in another place, considering the quality and quantity of the land take and the soil sealing.

**Article 17 — Mining**

(1) Any person or company who intends to carry on any artisanal or industrial mining, small-scale mining, or large-scale mining shall apply to the National Soil Management Authority, pursuant to Article 31 (1), for an appropriate mining licence in the prescribed manner and form upon payment of a prescribed fee.

(2) Before commencing mining operations following issuance of a license under paragraph (1), a person or company shall first apply for and receive the permission referred to under Articles 14 (2) and 15.

(3) Any prospecting or mining operation must be conducted in accordance with good international mining industry practice.

(4) The holder of a small-scale or large-scale mining licence shall assist in the development of mining communities affected by its operations to promote sustainable development, enhance the general welfare and the quality of life of the inhabitants, and shall recognise and respect the rights, customs, traditions, and religion of local communities.

(5) A mining licence holder shall maintain records of all geological information obtained by, or on behalf of, the holder, including data on soil properties.

(6) The holder of a mining licence shall ensure that their mining area is well maintained and rehabilitated from time to time and ultimately reclaimed, so far as is practicable, in a manner acceptable to the competent authority.

**Article 18 — Zoning of Uses of Soil**

(1) The competent authority may divide land into different zones according to the value of its soil with respect to the services provided and its need for

protection to implement sustainable soil management and maintain and enhance soil services.

(2) The competent authority may determine prohibited activities in specific zones.

(3) Stakeholders shall be consulted before a decision is taken on defining the zones and regulating soil uses.

**Article 19 — Protection of Particularly Valuable Soil by Spatial Measures**

(1) Soil that is particularly valuable for its services, *inter alia*, the fertility of soil, shall be protected by spatial instruments.

(2) Such spatial instruments shall be established through legally binding mechanisms pursuant to national legislation. These legal mechanisms shall determine the prohibited or regulated soil uses within these areas.

(3) Stakeholders shall be consulted before establishing spatial instruments, pursuant to paragraph (1) of this Article.

**Article 20 — Soil in Urban Areas**

(1) The competent authority shall take measures to maintain and develop healthy soil in urban and peri-urban areas, support climate adaptation, enhance ecosystem functions such as cooling, and improve the well-being of the population. Public participation shall be ensured in the planning and implementation of such measures.

(2) Urban planning shall be implemented to avoid unnecessary soil sealing for infrastructure and buildings, ensure the maintenance and development of green spaces in urban areas, and identify options for de-sealing projects.

## Part IV: Soil Data, Monitoring, and Innovation

**Article 21 — Data Management and Monitoring**

(1) The National Soil Management Authority, pursuant to Article 31 (1), shall establish a national soil database (soil information system) to collect data concerning the soil's physical, chemical, and biological properties to analyse its environmental quality.

(2) Soil data management entails three processes:

(a) Soil data gathering, including *in situ* measurements;

(b) Assessment and synthesis of the soil data; and

(c) Disseminating soil information, including making it publicly accessible.

(3) Soil data is defined as it entails the following data and information:

(a) Data on the chemical, physical, and biological properties of soil in a specific location;

(b) Information on the current soil use; and
(c) Information on tenure rights on the relevant land.

(4) The purposes of soil data management are as follows:
(a) Determination of the status quo of soil in a specific location regarding the chemical, physical, and biological properties;
(b) Development and determination of soil quality standards concerning all forms of soil degradation pursuant to Article 23;
(c) Use of the soil data for zoning approaches, pursuant to Article 18; and
(d) The establishment of a soil-protected area, pursuant to Article 19.

(5) The soil data and information entailed shall be accessible to all competent authorities implementing soil-related provisions.

(6) The landowner or the person or entity with a right to land must allow the competent authority to undertake *in situ* measurements of soil on the respective land or mandate a third party to do so.

(7) The collected data, pursuant to paragraph (1) of this Article, shall be assessed with regard to the general health of the soil, the risks and levels of degradation, as well as the risks it generates for its services laid out in Article 5 (2) and (4) of this Law.

(8) Soil information shall be made publicly accessible, ensuring transparency and availability for all relevant stakeholders. Confidential or private data shall be protected and inaccessible to the general public.

(9) Pursuant to paragraph (8), the soil information shall be updated regularly. The National Soil Management Authority, pursuant to Article 31 (1), is obliged to regularly publish a soil protection report online or through other appropriate means of communication. The report includes the results of soil quality monitoring, an analysis of the risks of contamination or degradation, an assessment of preventive and improvement measures and their costs, and the nation's soil maps in the respective country.

(10) The National Soil Management Authority, pursuant to Article 31 (1), shall take the necessary measures to promote scientific and technical research into the monitoring, protection, and sustainable environmental management of soil.

(11) The National Soil Management Authority, pursuant to Article 31 (1), shall establish a system of extension services for farmers and other users of soil in close cooperation with the responsible authorities at regional and local levels.

**Article 22 — Digitalisation and Sustainable Soil Management**

(1) The National Soil Management Authority, pursuant to Article 31 (1), shall take measures to coordinate the effective use of digital means, including artificial intelligence (AI), with regard to sustainable soil management, taking into account the following principles:
(a) Ensuring non-discriminatory access to digital means, in particular for

women;
(b) Ensuring the privacy of data;
(c) Enable local communities and small-scale farmers to make use of the digital means; and
(d) Inform and enable extension services to be facilitators for the use of digital means.

(2) The policies shall align with the AU's digitalisation and AI strategies.
(3) The National Soil Management Authority, pursuant to Article 31 (1), shall promote the use of digital means in sustainable soil management.

**Article 23 — Development of Soil Quality Standards**

(1) Based on the data obtained in accordance with Article 21, soil quality standards for all forms of soil degradation should be developed in a reasonable time.
(2) The soil quality standards may be defined for the various zones pursuant to Article 18, as appropriate.
(3) The National Soil Management Authority, pursuant to Article 31 (1), shall submit a draft of the standards to the relevant ministry, which shall then approve and publish them.

**Article 24 — Good Practices**

(1) The National Soil Management Authority, pursuant to Article 31 (1), shall compile good practices for sustainable uses of soil, taking into account relevant international guidance.
(2) The compilation shall be published in the national soil information system, pursuant to Article 21 (1). It should be regularly revised and updated.
(3) The National Soil Management Authority, pursuant to Article 31 (1), should inform the national extension services regularly with regard to good practices for the agricultural sector.

## Part V: Public Participation and Knowledge Systems

**Article 25 — Public Participation**

(1) The competent authority shall ensure the free, fair, informed, and effective participation of stakeholders, including women, men, elders, youth, indigenous peoples, persons with disabilities, farmers, and other vulnerable or marginalised groups, in soil-related governance.
(2) The participation referred to in paragraph (1) includes, but is not limited to, the development, implementation, monitoring, and evaluation of laws,

policies, programmes, and decisions relating to the sustainable use, protection, and rehabilitation of soil.

(3) Participation processes shall be inclusive, transparent, and accessible, taking into account local languages, customary practices, and traditional knowledge systems, supported by adequate information, consultation mechanisms, and feedback procedures.

## Article 26 — Public Sensitisation and Awareness Raising

The National Soil Management Authority, pursuant to Article 31 (1), shall undertake to:

(1) Develop and implement public education and sensitisation programmes to promote understanding of the value of soil and the importance of its sustainable use, protection, and restoration across all sectors of society.

(2) Raise awareness on the responsibilities of all persons in relation to sustainable soil management.

(3) Determine the structure and modalities of cooperation with the private sector, local communities, and civil society.

(4) Design and disseminate information on sustainable soil practices in accessible formats and local languages, ensuring that, among others, farmers, rural communities, and vulnerable groups can participate meaningfully in soil conservation efforts.

(5) Promote inclusive participation of women, youth, indigenous peoples, and marginalised communities in soil-related programmes and initiatives, recognising their traditional knowledge.

(6) Support soil science, including indigenous knowledge, in national education systems, vocational training, and agricultural extension services to build long-term capacity in sustainable land management.

(7) Encourage media, non-state actors, including civil society, and research institutions to contribute to public discourse on soil degradation and restoration.

(8) Strengthen institutional and human capacity for sustainable soil management through appropriate measures, which may include, *inter alia*, training, technical support, and facilitation of knowledge exchange and research collaboration among relevant authorities, extension services, and local community structures.

(9) Recognise efforts by individuals, communities, or organisations that contribute to soil protection and rehabilitation.

## Article 27 — Indigenous Knowledge

(1) Indigenous knowledge shall be regarded as a valuable source of information for guiding sustainable soil management, particularly in the respective local communities.

(2) The National Soil Management Authority, pursuant to Article 31 (1), is responsible for regularly collecting indigenous knowledge and disseminating it to the local communities and other relevant authorities and entities. It shall also publish the information in the soil information system, pursuant to Article 21 (1).
(3) Local research centres shall be funded to identify and validate indigenous knowledge and develop innovative, context-specific solutions for sustainable soil use and management.
(4) In cases where foreign investors intend to use indigenous knowledge, an appropriate payment system shall be established.
   (a) The income due to the payment system shall be made available for the respective local communities.
   (b) International regulations have to be respected, particularly those concerning benefit sharing under the relevant international instrument.

**Article 28 — Role of Traditional Leaders**

(1) Where applicable, traditional leaders shall be acknowledged as custodians of sustainable soil management, serving as vital representatives for their communities.
(2) Traditional leaders shall be encouraged to promote sustainable practices, disseminate information, and advocate for soil conservation efforts locally.
(3) Traditional leaders shall collaborate closely with competent authorities at regional and local levels to implement this Law, participating in joint initiatives and regular consultations to enhance community engagement in soil management.
(4) Traditional leaders shall be involved in establishing educational programmes for sustainable soil management, local soil governance, and conflict resolution. These programmes shall cover essential topics such as soil conservation techniques, community mobilisation strategies, negotiation skills, and community internal conflict-solving mechanisms to address local soil-related challenges effectively.
(5) Local community representatives, including traditional leaders, shall be effectively involved and consulted in relevant decision-making procedures.

**Article 29 — Gender Equity and Equality**

(1) The National Soil Management Authority, pursuant to Article 31 (1), shall ensure that women and men enjoy equal rights in access to, use, and management of soil and soil-related resources. Measures related to soil governance shall recognise gender-specific barriers and take steps to promote equitable participation, decision-making, and benefit-sharing.

(2) Before permission is granted pursuant to Article 14, the competent authority shall undertake an assessment of the implications for gender and other vulnerabilities.

## Part VI: Rehabilitation and Administrative Governance

### Article 30 — Rehabilitation of Current Soil Degradations: Responsibilities, Requirements, Costs, and Competent Authorities

(1) The National Soil Management Authority, pursuant to Article 31 (1), shall identify existing soil degradation.
(2) The person or entity responsible for the degradation or the owner of the property from which the degradation originates is accountable for rehabilitating soil contamination or soil degradation that has occurred.
(3) The National Soil Management Authority, pursuant to Article 31 (1), shall determine the level of soil rehabilitation to be achieved by the person or entity responsible according to paragraph (2) of this Article, considering the principle of proportionality.
(4) If the person or entity responsible for the degradation or the owner of the property from which the degradation originates fails to undertake the required rehabilitation, they shall bear the costs of rehabilitation by third parties.

### Article 31 — Institutional Supervision, Monitoring, and Enforcement

(1) A National Soil Management Authority responsible for sustainable soil management is to be established, which shall closely cooperate with the competent authorities at the regional and local levels.
(2) The National Soil Management Authority, pursuant to paragraph (1), may establish a Sustainable Soil Management Coordination Mechanism as an inter-sectoral and multi-stakeholder platform with advisory, consultative, and/or decision-making responsibilities to promote effective coordination of sustainable soil management.
(3) Competent authorities may be established at the regional and local levels, as appropriate, to enforce the provisions of this Law.
(4) The National Soil Management Authority, as well as regional and local competent authorities, shall receive adequate resources, facilities, and training to improve their effectiveness and integrity in enforcing the provisions of this Law.

### Article 32 — Monitoring and Surveillance

(1) The National Soil Management Authority, pursuant to Article 31 (1), shall

ensure an effective monitoring and surveillance by its services, including the regional and local competent authorities, on the compliance with the obligations of this Law.

(2) In pursuance of the monitoring and surveillance provided for under Paragraph (1) of this Article, the National Soil Management Authority shall, within three months of the promulgation of this Law, issue regulations that define criteria and mechanisms for effective soil monitoring and surveillance.

(3) The National Soil Management Authority and the competent authority at the local and regional level, where applicable, shall regularly monitor and survey the compliance with the obligations of this Law in their respective areas, taking into account the criteria and mechanisms mentioned in paragraph (2).

(4) Where required, a renewed SIA, pursuant to Article 15, shall be undertaken to evaluate ongoing or modified activities that may affect the health of the soil, particularly where monitoring and surveillance reveal significant changes in the condition of the soil or compliance with this Law.

**Article 33 — Transnational Cooperation in Africa**

(1) Without prejudice to the responsibilities of the relevant Government Ministry, the National Soil Management Authority, pursuant to Article 31 (1), shall provide technical and policy support to the state authority in charge of international cooperation with other respective authorities in Africa.

(2) The transnational cooperation shall focus on, *inter alia:*
   (a) Exchange of soil data;
   (b) Dissemination of good practices;
   (c) Joint endeavour concerning capacity building; and
   (d) Transboundary soil projects.

(3) Any transboundary soil dispute should, as far as possible, be settled amicably through negotiations, conciliation, or mediation.

(5) Mutually agreed solutions shall be made publicly available. However, the version disclosed to the public may not contain any information that a disputing party has designated as confidential.

(6) Reports specifying progress on sustainable soil management, any gaps in implementation, and necessary adjustments shall be submitted to the relevant AU organs.

**Article 34 — Programmes and Measures to Promote Sustainable Soil Management**

The National Soil Management Authority, pursuant to Article 31 (1), in consultation with local and regional authorities, shall provide programmes and measures of incentives that promote sustainable soil management by those using the land and soil.

These programmes and measures shall be regularly submitted to the relevant ministry for adoption.

## Part VII: Offences, Penalties, Sanctions, and Dispute Settlement

### Article 35 — Criminal Offences, Penalties, and Sanctions

(1) The following conduct shall be considered criminal offences under this Law and shall be subject to appropriate penalties and sanctions under national law:
   (a) **Deliberate or negligent contamination of soil:** The unauthorised release or discharge of substances that lead to the deterioration of soil quality or its services.
   (b) **Use of prohibited fertilisers or pesticides:** The production, sale, or application of substances listed by the competent authority, pursuant to Article 10 (4), as detrimental to soil health.
   (c) **Unauthorised land take or soil sealing:** Converting land or sealing soil surfaces in contravention of national zoning regulations, pursuant to Articles 18 and 19, or without permission required under this Law.
   (d) **Non-compliance with soil protection or rehabilitation orders:** Failure to undertake legally mandated measures to restore or prevent further degradation of soil.
   (e) **Destruction or alteration of protected soil areas:** Engaging in prohibited activities within areas designated under spatial instruments, pursuant to Article 19, or other legal mechanisms for soil conservation.
   (f) **Falsification, concealment, or obstruction of soil data:** Deliberately providing false information or obstructing soil assessments, monitoring, or inspections carried out under this Law.
   (g) **Failure to conduct required SIAs:** Commencing or continuing soil use activities that require prior assessment, pursuant to Article 15, without having undergone the required process.
   (h) **Illegal mining or prospecting activities:** Conducting, authorising, or participating in artisanal or industrial, small-scale, or large-scale mining operations without a valid licence or permission pursuant to Article 17 (1) and (2), or in contravention of conditions established by the competent authority, including failure to rehabilitate or reclaim affected soil areas as required under Article 17 (6).
   (i) **Non-compliance by foreign investors:** Engaging in soil-related activities or large-scale land acquisitions (land grabbing) that violate the provisions of Article 13 on foreign investment, including failure to comply with obligations under this Law, neglecting the rights and interests of local communities, or undertaking investments that undermine soil health or local

land rights.

(j) **Violation of procedural or substantive requirements:** Failure to comply with, or deliberate breach of, any procedural or substantive obligations established under this Law, including omissions or actions contrary to prescribed processes.

(2) The National Soil Management Authority, pursuant to Article 31 (1), may determine penalties and sanctions for the offences listed in paragraph (1) in accordance with their national legal frameworks. In doing so, they shall ensure that such measures are effective, proportionate, and dissuasive, taking into account the nature of the offence, the harm caused to the soil, and any relevant aggravating or mitigating factors.

### Article 36 — Administrative Offences

(1) In addition to the criminal offences set out under Article 35, the National Soil Management Authority, pursuant to Article 31 (1), shall determine conduct which shall constitute administrative offences under this Law and shall be subject to appropriate administrative penalties under national law, including but not limited to warnings, fines, suspension of authorisations, or nullification of approvals.

(2) Where such administrative offences materially undermine the rights of affected communities or the integrity of decision-making processes, the competent authority may suspend or revoke the related permit, authorisation, or decision as per national law.

### Article 37 — Dispute Settlement

(1) Existing administrative or non-judicial bodies shall be utilised, or new ones established where necessary, to settle disputes concerning the application of this Law.

(2) Where applicable, traditional leaders and local communities shall be invited to participate in the settlement of soil management disputes by the administrative or non-judicial bodies referred to in paragraph (1) of this Article.

(3) For such participation as referred to in paragraph (2) of this Article, clear procedural roles and responsibilities shall be established.

(4) Specialised courts or tribunals in existing court structures may be established for disputes concerning the use of soil.

(5) People(s) and communities affected by soil degradation shall have unhindered access to such procedures, courts, or tribunals.

(6) Judges, administrators, and extrajudicial officers shall be trained in the scientific background of sustainable soil management and its legal provisions.

(7) Nothing in this Article shall preclude the utilisation or establishment of other

appropriate means of dispute settlement, consistent with national law and the objectives of this Law.

(8) A mechanism for public compliance control may be established to which all persons and entities shall be entitled to raise issues of compliance.

## Part VIII: Miscellaneous Provisions

### Article 38 — Regulations

(1) The competent authority may, by statutory instruments, make regulations to prescribe anything required under this Law and for the effective implementation of the provisions of this Law.

(2) The National Soil Management Authority, pursuant to Article 31 (1), may submit to the competent authority proposals for regulations or other policy measures, as may be required under this Law, and for the effective implementation of the provisions of this Law.

### Article 39 — Revision or Amendment of the Law

(1) This Law may be amended or revised in accordance with applicable legislative procedures.

(2) Where this Law is repealed, it shall be without prejudice to the legal status of all acts carried out under the repealed Law.

(3) Any amendments to this Law may not be retrogressive and affect acquired rights.

### Article 40 — Safeguard Clause

(1) No provision in this Law shall be construed as derogating from the principles and values contained in other relevant instruments for the realisation of the sustainable management of soil.

(2) In the event of a contradiction between two or more provisions of this Law, the interpretation that favours the sustainable management of soil shall prevail.

### Article 41 — Entry into Force

This Law shall enter into force at such time as the national authority responsible shall determine.

### Article 42 — Authentic Texts

(1) This Law shall be translated into the relevant national official languages.

(2) In the event of a conflict of interpretation, the English version of the Pan-African

Parliament's Model Law on Soil Management shall be used as the authoritative reference.

(3) This Law shall also, as soon as practicable, be translated into the languages most understood and used by persons with disabilities.

---

**END OF TEXT**

# Commentaries to the Model Law on Soil Management in Africa

*Harald Ginzky, Oliver C. Ruppel, Emma Chitsove, Riyad Fakhri, Christopher Funwie Tamasang, Delwendé Innocent Kiba, Laban Kipkorir Kiplagat, Ruda Murray, Félicie Ralalaharimiadana, and Pamela Towela Sambo*[1]

## 1. Introduction

Soil is the silent foundation of Africa's food security, ecological resilience, and sustainable development. Yet across the continent, soils face mounting pressures from unsustainable land use, climate change, urban expansion, and competing economic interests. These challenges threaten not only agricultural productivity and food security but also the broader goals of poverty reduction, environmental sustainability, and human well-being. Recognising this, the Pan-African Parliament (PAP) has developed the Model Law on Soil Management. The following detailed Commentaries complement the Model Law by providing interpretive guidance, policy options, and draft legislative provisions.

The Commentaries collected here neither aim to be comprehensive in nature nor do they form part of the Model Law, but rather shall serve as a practical toolbox for policymakers, legislators, practitioners, and civil society. Each Commentary addresses a critical theme of soil governance—ranging from awareness-raising, crop cultivation, and dispute settlement to data management, fertilisers, foreign investment, gender equity, mining, migration, pesticides, pastoralism, urbanisation, tenure rights, and the role of traditional leaders. Together, these contributions bridge the gap between broad legal principles and the concrete realities of African governance systems, offering context-sensitive strategies, mechanisms and instruments for implementation and enforcement.

By combining comparative research, legal analysis, and practical recommendations, the Commentaries aim to ensure that the Model Law is not merely an abstract framework but an actionable tool for strengthening national soil governance. They also highlight the interconnections between soil health and Africa's

1 The authors and editors also wish to express their sincere gratitude to the Pan-African Parliament (PAP) delegation that attended the Write-Shop and Consultative Meeting on the Finalisation of the Model Law on Soil Management in Africa, held at Lanzerac Estate, Stellenbosch, South Africa, from 28–29 April 2025. The delegation's valuable insights, guidance, and constructive engagement significantly contributed to the refinement of the Commentaries. Special thanks are extended to Phebe Clement Mavungu (Legal Counsel, PAP); Hon. Sulayman Saho (The Gambia), Member of the Pan-African Parliament; Hon. Garry Sakata (DRC), Chairperson of the PAP Committee on Rural Economy, Agriculture, Natural Resources, and Environment; Hon. Abdallah Barakat Ibrahim (Djibouti), Vice-Chairperson of the same Committee; Hon. Awatef Cheniti (Tunisia), Member of the same Committee; and Dr Ndidi Abanno (Senior Committee Clerk, PAP).

broader developmental priorities, including food security, climate mitigation and adaptation, biodiversity conservation, economic prosperity, and social equity.

In this way, the Commentaries underscore that protecting Africa's soils is not simply an environmental imperative. It is a legal, economic, and moral responsibility—one that requires inclusive governance, innovative policy design, and sustained commitment at all levels of society.

All Commentaries follow the same structure. First, the challenges of the specific policy topic are explained, followed by policy options to address them through legislative and administrative means. Finally, each Commentary entails concrete text proposals.

## 2. Commentary I: Awareness raising and capacity building

While most African countries have established legal and policy frameworks that incorporate environmental education and public awareness initiatives, this Commentary highlights a significant gap in public understanding and engagement, particularly regarding the crucial role of soil in sustaining life. The far-reaching impacts of soil degradation on both present and future generations remain poorly recognised. This Commentary highlights specific governance mechanisms to address the challenges of limited awareness and capacity-building for sustainable soil management in Africa.

By increasing awareness and education, African countries can enhance public support for soil sustainability and foster a long-term commitment to more responsible soil management. The interrelationships between soils and socio-economic issues, such as agriculture, food security and safety, sustainability, climate change, carbon sequestration, greenhouse gas emissions, soil degradation through erosion, and loss of organic matter and nutrients, need to be simplified and consistently communicated through educational awareness programs to all stakeholders.

### 2.1. Description of challenges

Most African nations have legal frameworks that address environmental protection and indirectly support soil conservation and sustainable land management. These African laws and policies largely acknowledge the importance of environmental and soil information, as well as public participation; however, weak implementation remains a significant challenge. Additionally, these laws often lack the specificity needed to address soil health comprehensively.

Further, a lack of awareness and education among key stakeholders about soil conservation hampers effective mitigation. Smallholder farmers face numerous challenges, including low soil fertility, limited access to equipment, and insufficient income. Additionally, they often struggle to access climate information and lack basic agricultural knowledge.

Access to accurate and up-to-date soil-related information is essential for effective awareness-raising and capacity-building efforts. However, across much of Africa, inadequate investment in research and innovation continues to impede the development of modern soil conservation technologies. Compounding this challenge are fragmented land management systems that often favour immediate economic returns over long-term soil health. Consequently, soil data across the continent is frequently outdated, insufficient, and rarely supported by geospatial referencing. This lack of reliable information contributes to limited public awareness about the scale and severity of soil degradation. The problem is particularly acute within agricultural extension services, where access to timely soil health information is vital but remains largely unavailable in many regions.

Most African countries are also ill-prepared for climate risks, with indigenous knowledge of soil conservation often overlooked. Uncoordinated research and information generation related to soil also compounds the existing challenges.

Women play a vital role in land and soil management, particularly in rural areas across Africa. They head nearly one-third of rural households and contribute up to 70% of household food production. Despite their central role in sustaining agricultural livelihoods, women are frequently excluded from decision-making processes related to sustainable soil management due to entrenched cultural, religious, and institutional biases.

To succeed in raising awareness of soil, "an up-to-date and effective definition of soil that directly focuses the public's attention on its economic value"[2] is needed. This will require promoting awareness of the soil's critical role in shaping sustainable soil governance, agriculture, food security, climate change mitigation and adaptation, freshwater availability, and biodiversity conservation.

## 2.2. Options of legal governance mechanisms

Increasing women's participation in soil research, policy development, and decision-making is essential to advancing sustainable soil management across Africa. To support this, women, particularly in rural areas, must have improved access to land, credit, and other essential resources and services. Empowering women in this way strengthens both environmental stewardship and community resilience.

Civil society organisations (CSOs) play a crucial role in collecting, publishing, and disseminating environmental data, as well as raising awareness of environmental

2 Dazzi & Papa (2022).

issues. CSOs and the media must partner more closely on soil-related awareness campaigns and information dissemination to enhance capacity, promote transparency, and foster public engagement.

Strengthening institutional capacity and raising public awareness about the importance of soil data transparency are critical steps toward sustainable soil management. This requires improving both the accessibility and quality of soil data through collaborative efforts between governments, civil society, and local communities.

In most African countries, agricultural extension programs are well-established and play a crucial role in raising awareness among farmers and local communities about sound soil management practices, including conservation, erosion control, and sustainable farming techniques. To maximise their impact, these efforts must be complemented by specialised training and broader awareness campaigns delivered through media platforms, community events, and public forums.

Traditional leaders hold a position of deep respect within their communities and are recognised as influential actors within many African governance systems. As such, they serve as a key institution for promoting awareness and delivering educational initiatives on soil and environmental stewardship. Their moral authority and strong communication networks position them well to promote environmentally responsible behaviours, particularly by transmitting indigenous knowledge and sustainable land and soil management practices. However, the effectiveness of their role depends on several factors, including meaningful collaboration with government authorities and the active engagement of local communities.

Traditional knowledge and community participation are vital components of effective soil governance. Integrating indigenous soil management practices with modern scientific approaches can offer context-specific solutions to soil degradation across the continent. In many African societies, the deep cultural and emotional connection to land fosters a strong sense of responsibility and motivation for sustainable practices. When harnessed effectively, these connections can empower traditional leaders and communities to take an active role in soil protection efforts.

Equally important is the need for clear, focused messaging and sustained public awareness campaigns to build support for soil protection policies. These campaigns should address locally relevant concerns and resonate with diverse audiences by blending traditional knowledge with contemporary scientific insights. Leveraging both digital platforms and grassroots initiatives presents a powerful means to educate, engage, and mobilise communities in support of sustainable soil management.

Strengthening legal and policy frameworks, decentralising natural resource management, enhancing political will, increasing local authority involvement, and integrating environmental considerations into all development sectors would help achieve sustainable soil governance in Africa.

Raising awareness among young people about the importance of soil conservation is essential, not only to promote sustainable practices but also to challenge historical and cultural barriers that have hindered broad-based engagement. Integrating sustainable soil management into school curricula is crucial for fostering environmental stewardship from an early age. By educating children about the importance of soil health and its central role in food security, climate resilience, and ecosystem sustainability, African countries can cultivate a generation committed to protecting the soil. Early exposure to these concepts encourages responsible behaviour and advocacy, with positive ripple effects across families and communities. This approach ensures the long-term preservation of soil as a vital resource and empowers young people to contribute actively to environmental sustainability and local development.

Equally important is the establishment of robust national soil information systems and centralised institutional frameworks to guide evidence-based decision-making. Improved coordination across sectors, including agriculture, environment, land, and mining, is essential for data sharing, research, and the implementation of sustainable soil management practices. Collaboration between research institutions and civil society organisations can play a key role in raising public awareness, generating knowledge, and driving legal and policy reforms. Creating platforms for cross-sectoral cooperation and stakeholder coordination would be instrumental in this regard.

Another strategic priority is establishing specialised educational and training institutions focused on soil conservation and management. These institutions would equip professionals with the technical and interdisciplinary skills needed to address soil degradation while also enhancing communication among scientific, legal, and policy communities. Such capacity building would contribute meaningfully to the development of coherent soil governance frameworks and more effective public policy.

## 2.3. Concrete text for legal provisions

### 2.3.1. Soil awareness strategy

Promoting awareness and building capacity in sustainable soil management requires a multi-faceted approach that engages stakeholders at all levels. Some of the strategies to consider are:

- Develop an enabling policy and legislative environment to promote and encourage awareness raising and capacity building on sustainable soil governance.
- Align public policies with local development plans to support sustainable practices and incentivise community participation.

- Finance or raise funds to support programmes to promote or facilitate sustainable soil governance.
- Collaborate with government agencies, research institutions, civil society, local communities, and the private sector to create a unified vision for sustainable soil management. Possible partnerships include cooperation, coordination, multisector collaboration, or networking.
- Establish networks and working groups that facilitate the exchange of information, ideas, and experiences.
- Launch targeted media campaigns, community events, and workshops highlighting the importance of healthy soils.
- Integrate indigenous knowledge systems with modern systems to communicate the benefits of sustainable soil practices.
- Integrate soil management topics into school curricula and vocational training programs to raise early awareness among future generations.
- Develop specialised training programs, workshops, and certification courses for professionals and local community leaders.
- Develop awareness-raising toolkits for the appropriate stakeholders.
- Establish or support educational institutions focused on soil conservation and management.
- Leverage online learning platforms, interactive websites, and mobile applications to disseminate best practices and up-to-date research findings on soil health.
- Promote community projects that showcase sustainable soil management techniques.
- Establish and fund events that promote soil conservation, such as contests on select soil topics, and award prizes and recognition to outstanding participants.

### 2.3.2. Legal implementation

- The competent authority shall publish any information on the protection, conservation, management, and utilisation of the soil resource as it considers necessary for public education and awareness.
- The competent authority shall establish and operate a Central Soil Information System to store any findings, data, and statistics generated by both public and private bodies during soil preservation and management.
- The competent authority shall, in consultation with all other competent authorities, particularly those at local and regional levels, take measures to integrate soil preservation and management matters in schools, colleges, and institutions of higher learning.

- The competent authority shall facilitate greater public awareness of the cultural, economic, and social benefits of conserving and increasing sustainable soil management by developing programmes in training, research, and public education.
- The competent authority may enhance its employees' skills, knowledge, and effectiveness by providing, or assisting in providing, facilities for training, education, and research, including awarding scholarships for such training.
- The competent authority shall establish a Soil Conservation Fund or an equivalent, whose objectives include promoting awareness of the importance of protecting, developing, and sustainably using soil resources through public education and training.
- The competent authority shall determine the structure and modalities of cooperation with the private sector, local communities, and civil society.

## 3. Commentary II: Crop cultivation

Most soils in Sub-Saharan Africa have developed from highly weathered parent materials. These soils are generally old, heavily leached, and characterised by low natural fertility, including low organic matter content, limited cation exchange capacity, and low base saturation. To address these constraints and improve agricultural productivity, farmers have increasingly adopted soil management practices that enhance soil health and boost food production.

### 3.1. Challenges

Agriculture in Sub-Saharan Africa (SSA) is predominantly driven by smallholder farmers, whose production is primarily geared toward household food security, with limited semi-commercial and commercial operations. This structure contributes to persistently low productivity, widespread food insecurity, poverty, particularly among farming households, and ongoing environmental degradation. In a context where nearly half of the population is engaged in farming, both the production and consumption dimensions of food systems must be strengthened to achieve Sustainable Development Goals (SDGs) 1 and 2, which aim to eradicate poverty and achieve zero hunger.

Crop farmers in SSA face many challenges that undermine their productivity and food security. The following are some of the challenges:

- Inadequate soil health information to establish soil limitations and requirements: Stakeholders (from government agencies to farmers) must improve

data access, soil test information, and soil health management to make informed decisions in SSA's agricultural sector.
- Nutrient mining and imbalance: Africa loses between 30 and 60 kg of nutrients per hectare each year while using only one-tenth of the average application of fertiliser compared with the rest of the world.[3]
- Food and nutrition insecurity: The 2024 Nairobi Summit on Africa and Soil Health affirmed that the challenges of food and nutrition insecurity, malnutrition, and climate change remain persistent across the continent and require urgent and coordinated action.
- Increasing yield gaps: Currently, yields of major food crops in SSA are below 1.0 t $ha^{-1}$ compared to 5.0 t $ha^{-1}$ levels in other parts of the world.[4]
- Land degradation: The Nairobi 2024 Summit declared that building soil health and regenerating degraded soils are crucial for transforming sustainable food systems and are a prerequisite for the efficient and effective use of fertilisers.
- Declining soil fertility: Recent studies confirm that soil fertility decline remains widespread in sub-Saharan Africa.[5]
- Climate change and food production: Farmers experience severe droughts more frequently, especially in the dry semi-arid regions of the Sahel, which already experience low rainfall and variations in the length of the growing season.

Other challenges include:
- Inadequate knowledge of soil management and extension services.
- Financial constraints.
- Soil salinisation and acidity.
- Dependence on blanket fertilisation and imported fertilisers.
- Limited adoption of integrated soil fertility management (ISFM) technologies.
- Improved soil health approaches vary from one location to another (inconsistent application).
- Use of current soil data and advisory service to guide soil management.
- Use of soil amendments (e.g., liming when the soil is acidic or gypsum when the soil is alkaline).
- Controlling soil erosion by cover cropping, strip-cropping on slopes or terracing on the uplands, contour ploughing, tied ridging, etc. (whichever is appropriate for the location) for improved soil and water conservation.
- Always maintaining soil cover where practicable.
- Improving soil organic matter by applying organic manure and compost or incorporating organic residues and cover crops.

---

3 Batono & Wanswa (2011).
4 Ongoma et al. (2025).
5 FAO (2025c).

- Intercropping cereals with legumes (e.g., maize, sorghum, or soybean).
- Adoption of Integrated Soil Fertility Management Technologies (ISFM).
- Application of recommended inorganic fertiliser nutrients (N, P, K, Zn, etc.) at appropriate soil depth and at critical stages of crop growth (at the correct rate, right time, right type, and proper placement).
- Application of mulch to conserve moisture and minimise soil erosion.
- Adoption of agro-ecological approaches.
- Planting of leguminous trees to fix nitrogen and carbon (organic matter) in agroforestry systems.
- Prevention of wildfires to improve the accumulation of soil organic matter.

## 3.2. Options for legal governance mechanisms

### 3.2.1. Preconditions for effective legal governance

- Funding: For legal soil management governance to be effective, funding to acquire the necessary logistics for monitoring and enforcing the law is crucial. Many policies and laws remain on the books without being implemented due to inadequate enforcement capacity.
- Inadequate knowledge and skills; thus, training is required. There is a need to build the capacity of those using the soils and those responsible for enforcing laws on sustainable soil management. More extension workers should be trained in improved soil management technologies so they can share this knowledge with smallholder farmers who may be relying on outdated practices.
- Technological innovations: Smartphones and other digital devices, drones, and satellite images can contribute to soil governance and the enforcement of laws on soil degradation.
- Markets and value addition: Markets drive technology adoption. With improved markets and value-added farm produce, farmers could be better positioned to adopt and implement recommended soil management technologies. However, poverty and limited resources often hinder the adoption of recommended soil management practices.
- Monitoring and evaluation systems must be available to ensure effective monitoring of programmes and related initiatives.

### 3.2.2. Policies and strategy

Policy interventions:

- Support of farmers to purchase crop insurance;
- price stabilisation;
- subsidies on agricultural inputs (fertiliser, lime, seed, etc.);
- strategic grain reserves; and
- use of market-hedging instruments.

#### 3.2.2.1. Actions by individuals

- Individuals managing soils must act as stewards to ensure that soils are managed sustainably.
- Undertake sustainable soil management in the production of crops.

#### 3.2.2.2. Actions by groups and the science community

- Disseminate information and knowledge on sustainable soil management.

#### 3.2.2.3. Actions by the government

- Support a research programme that will provide sound scientific backing for developing and implementing sustainable soil management relevant to end users.
- Incorporate the principles and practices of sustainable soil management into policy guidance and legislation at all levels of government, ideally leading to the development of national soil policy.
- Explicitly consider the role of soil management practices in planning for adaptation to, and mitigation of, climate change and maintaining biodiversity.
- Establish and implement regulations to limit the accumulation of contaminants beyond established levels to safeguard human health and well-being and facilitate remediation of contaminated soils that exceed these levels where they pose a threat to humans, plants, and animals.
- Develop and maintain a national soil information system and contribute to the global soil information system.

#### 3.2.2.4. Actions by international organisations

- Coordinate efforts to develop an accurate, high-resolution national soil information system.
- Assist governments in establishing appropriate legislation, institutions, and processes to mount, implement, and monitor appropriate sustainable soil management practices.

### 3.3. Concrete legal text

The legislative provisions may be integrated into existing agricultural laws or other laws that concern agrarian resources. The legal text aims to promote sustainable soil management in crop cultivation. The matters covered therein are not exhaustive.

Definitions

(1) Sustainable Soil Management (SSM): [exact definition in the Model Law].
(2) Crop Cultivation means the agricultural production process involving the growing of crops for food, feed, fibre, fuel, or other uses.
(3) Fertilisers means any compound or natural substance applied to soils or plants to supply one or more essential nutrients, OR as defined in domestic laws.
(4) Pesticides means chemical, biological, or physical agents intended to manage pests, diseases, and weeds which impact crop production OR as defined in domestic laws.

Section 1. Sustainable Soil Management in Crop Cultivation

(1) The competent authority responsible for agriculture, in coordination with the competent authority responsible for soil, shall develop and promulgate guidelines for sustainable soil management in crop cultivation.
(2) The guidelines shall include, but are not limited to:
  (a) Soil preparation and conservation techniques;
  (b) Crop rotation and intercropping strategies; and
  (c) Organic and integrated nutrient management practices.
(3) These guidelines shall be updated regularly to reflect advances in research and local agro-ecological conditions.

Section 2. Dissemination of Information and Knowledge

(1) A comprehensive outreach and extension program shall be established by the competent authority to disseminate best practices in sustainable soil management to farmers, extension workers, and rural communities.

(2) The outreach and extension program shall utilise diverse platforms, including mobile units, digital media, printed materials, community workshops, and demonstration sites, to ensure broad accessibility and effectiveness.
(3) The competent authority shall partner with academic institutions, non-governmental organisations, and local agricultural cooperatives to enhance the reach and relevance of the outreach and extension program.

Section 3. Support for Scientific Research
(1) The competent authority shall establish a Fund to support innovation in soil management practices.
(2) This Fund shall provide financial grants, scholarships, and research awards to public and private entities engaged in studies related to soil health and sustainable crop production, including studies on the integration of traditional knowledge with modern soil science.

Section 4. Integration of Sustainable Soil Management Principles in Agricultural Policies
(1) The principles of sustainable soil management shall be embedded in all national and local agricultural policies, ensuring alignment with soil and environmental protection and food security objectives.
(2) All relevant agricultural, environmental, and land-use policies shall be reviewed and amended, as necessary, to incorporate sustainable soil management principles.
(3) A cross-sectoral policy committee shall be established to ensure consistency and coherence across government policies.

Section 5. Incentives to Farmers and Agricultural Stakeholders
(1) The government shall provide fiscal and technical incentives to promote the adoption of sustainable soil management practices among farmers.
(2) Incentives may include:
  (a) Tax relief and deductions;
  (b) Subsidised loans and grants; and
  (c) Other incentive programmes established by the government.
(3) Special funding mechanisms shall be established to support smallholder farmers and vulnerable communities in adopting soil conservation techniques.
(4) The criteria for accessing these incentives shall be developed transparently, ensuring they target small and marginalised farming communities while rewarding demonstrable improvements in soil health.

Section 6. Regulation on the Use of Fertilisers and Pesticides

(1) The competent authority shall formulate and enforce regulations concerning the selection, storage, application, and disposal of fertilisers and pesticides.
(2) All users must comply with prescribed application methods, timing, and dosage to minimise environmental harm and prevent soil degradation.
(3) Training and certification programs shall be mandated for agricultural professionals to ensure safe and calibrated use of these agro inputs.
(4) Violations of these regulations may result in penalties including fines, suspension of licences, or revocation of permits, or other sanctions as determined appropriate by regulatory authorities.

Section 7: Monitoring

(1) The competent authority shall establish a monitoring and evaluation framework to assess:
    (a) The implementation of sustainable soil management practices;
    (b) Compliance with fertiliser and pesticide regulations; and
    (c) The overall impact of the law on soil health and crop productivity.
(2) Annual reports detailing progress, challenges, and recommendations shall be submitted by the competent authority to the Parliament and shall be available for public inspection.

## 4. Commentary III: Dispute settlement

This Commentary examines the challenges of resolving soil disputes in Africa. It highlights the lack of specialised courts, the limitations of traditional dispute resolution mechanisms, and the difficulties in accessing justice. The Commentary proposes various policy options for addressing these challenges, including maintaining the *status quo*, enhancing the jurisdiction of existing land courts, and establishing specialised courts or divisions. It outlines legislative elements and text proposals that could be incorporated into national legal frameworks to improve dispute resolution processes, promote sustainable soil management, and ensure access to justice for all, including disadvantaged groups.

### 4.1. Description of challenges

Most soil disputes arise from land-related activities, including agriculture, urbanisation, industrialisation, and mining. All African states maintain mechanisms to resolve land disputes. Although soil is recognised as a separate natural resource in many national environmental laws, it is often treated as incidental in land and environmental disputes.

Furthermore, while most African states have various mechanisms to resolve land disputes, including courts, there is diversity in how these courts exercise jurisdiction. These include environmental courts, green chambers, designated green judges in general courts, independent tribunals, quasi-independent environmental tribunals, and captive tribunals. Kenya's Environment and Land Court (ELC) remains the most advanced type of environmental court in Africa, with expansive jurisdiction over land and environmental disputes. Due to this lack of specialisation and comprehensive laws dedicated to sustainable soil management, soil disputes are not effectively adjudicated.

In addition to courts of ordinary jurisdiction, most legislation provides administrative mechanisms to resolve disputes arising from the application of legal provisions. While some administrative bodies are effective, evidence suggests that others do not perform their statutory duties for various reasons, including a lack of resources and expertise.

Due to the dual nature of many African legal systems, most countries recognise traditional or customary law mechanisms to resolve disputes. However, in most instances, the jurisdiction of these customary courts is limited to matters of customary law, such as inheritance. Furthermore, most customary laws have not evolved to encompass all aspects of sustainable soil management. However, the case of Madagascar is different, as Malagasy law is still strongly influenced by custom, which remains a living source of law.

Access to courts or justice is another issue in land and soil disputes. This includes *locus standi*, access to legal aid for indigents, costs, and procedural rules. In some countries that recognise the right to a safe, clean, and healthy environment such as South Africa (Sections 24 and 38, Constitution of the Republic of South Africa); Kenya (Articles 22 (1) and 258 of the Constitution of the Republic of Kenya), Zimbabwe (Section 85 of the Constitution of the Republic of Zimbabwe), the rules on *locus standi* gives legal standing to persons to enforce environmental legislation in the public interest or the interest of the environment.

### 4.2. Sources and types of soil disputes

While land-based activities are fundamental to every economy, they can also lead to disputes. These conflicts may arise from the proposed or actual use of land resources. For instance, mineral extraction is often incompatible with agricultural activities, creating a natural source of tension. Most conflicts over soil resources stem from various factors, often involving land. Typically, one or more of the following key issues are at play: (1) disputes over land tenure/ownership; (2) disagreements over access to natural resources; (3) disputes over decisions or authorisations made by the competent authority over a particular resource; and (4) conflicts over distribution of resource revenue, benefits, and burdens. Some of the characteristics that influence the dynamics of conflicts over soil resources include:

- Availability, quality, and perceived value of soil resources.
- Numerous actors and stakeholders with diverse interests exist, including nation-states, local governments, ethnic groups, communities, civil society organisations, and private companies.
- Significant power imbalances and asymmetries between the parties (e.g., international corporations versus local communities, or lack of formal representation of a specific livelihood group in decision-making).
- Legal pluralism—a combination of customary and statutory institutions, or a hybrid political order.

## 4.3. Options of legal governance mechanisms

To ensure sustainable soil management, legislation must include provisions for resolving disputes over soil access and use. Numerous approaches exist for resolving disputes, including litigation/adjudication, Alternative Dispute Resolution (ADR) [i.e., mediation, arbitration, and conciliation], and administrative solutions.

### 4.3.1. Policy options

#### 4.3.1.1. Option A: maintenance of the status quo

This option involves utilising existing dispute resolution mechanisms. It is optimal for countries with advanced dispute resolution mechanisms, such as specialised environmental courts or tribunals that adjudicate environmental disputes across various forums. It is also optimum for countries that do not have a specialised environmental court or tribunal, but whose judicial systems are advanced. Some of the indicators are:

(1) independent judiciary;
(2) presence of specialised divisions in the ordinary court structure, i.e., environment law division;
(3) specialised human personnel on soil management or environmental management, or natural resources management;
(4) advanced/comprehensive laws on natural resources management, including soil management;
(5) easily accessible courts [including distance, rules on *locus standi* and costs]; and

(6) available and functional ADR mechanisms.

Therefore, where existing systems, whether courts, tribunals, or indigenous justice systems, are sufficiently equipped to deliver environmental justice and solve soil disputes, the *status quo* must be maintained. However, a country must consider reforms within the existing system, such as judicial training or refresher courses, the employment of more experienced judges, or improved access to the courts through mobile courts.

#### 4.3.1.2. Option B: enhancing land courts/tribunals

Option B is intended for countries without specialised environmental courts or tribunals; however, they do have land courts, tribunals, or other local dispute-resolution bodies. These land courts or bodies primarily determine land disputes and hear appeals and reviews of decisions made by public bodies concerning land. Land disputes are generally defined as disagreements between two or more parties over the ownership or use of a specific piece of land. Often, land rights directly affect the use of a particular area, making the inclusion of environmental considerations in decisions about these rights crucial. In some jurisdictions, such as Botswana, the Minister may withhold consent for the transfer of agricultural land if the transfer is likely to lower the standards of good husbandry on that land. A crucial component of good husbandry is farming sustainably, with a concern for the health of both soils and animals. Therefore, since considerations for refusing to grant certain land rights include environmental factors, it would be prudent to extend the jurisdiction of land courts or tribunals to cover environmental issues. This policy option is not novel in Africa; Kenya has an Environment and Land Court that addresses disputes over both land and environmental issues.

The principal advantage of this option lies in its use of established legal frameworks within existing jurisdictions, thereby facilitating cost-effectiveness. Furthermore, this approach promotes the integration of land use and environmental regulations, which are inherently interdependent. By augmenting the jurisdiction of specialised land courts, this option ensures consistency in decision-making and jurisprudence, mitigating the risks of divergent outcomes when different adjudicators address the same issues at different times.

#### 4.3.1.3. Option C: establishment of specialised courts or divisions

Establishing specialised courts and tribunals remains a contentious issue among judges, legislators, governmental officials, advocates from non-governmental organisations, academics, and members of civil society. Arguments favour specialised courts underscore the necessity of having decision-makers with expertise in environmental law, promoting consistency and efficiency within the judicial system, and establishing robust oversight and accountability mechanisms. Conversely, objections to specialised courts or divisions highlight the potential for fragmentation of the judicial system, which may isolate judges and relevant subject matter from the broader legal framework. Additionally, concerns arise regarding the significant costs associated with the establishment of specialised courts, the heightened risk of judicial "capture" by a small cohort of people or organisations, and the challenge of determining the appropriate jurisdiction for cases that involve cross-cutting environmental issues, thus complicating the decision-making process regarding whether such "mixed" cases should be adjudicated in specialised courts or general courts. These advantages and concerns are also relevant to Option B, which proposes enhancing the jurisdiction of land courts/tribunals.

### 4.3.2. Legislative elements

The following elements are to be reflected in legislation:

(1) The role, responsibilities, and powers of a court concerning the hearing and settlement of disputes over access to and use of soil.
(2) How individuals may obtain access to the court.
(3) The rules for a court to follow in adjudicating soil disputes.
(4) Disclosure and submissions, including protection of the confidentiality of sensitive information.
(5) Alternative dispute resolution mechanisms to resolve soil disputes.
(6) The appointment of adjudicators and mediators conversant with sustainable soil management or the environment.

In addition to these general elements, the legislation must also cater to disadvantaged groups within society. These are typically the primary users of soil for agricultural activities. They may have limited access to information, knowledge, opportunities, and services due to their socioeconomic status, ethnic background, or geographic location. These include people who live and farm traditionally, indigenous people, persons with disabilities, refugees, and women. As such, legislation should consist of procedures in soil legislation to:

(1) Outline the role and responsibilities of a court in relation to the special needs of the disadvantaged people and the sustainable use of soil.
(2) Enable ready access for disadvantaged people to a court of law in relation to disputes over the sustainable use of soil.
(3) Set out procedures to enable disadvantaged people to obtain legal aid.

(4) Establish a special mediation procedure [or other alternative methods] for disadvantaged people.
(5) Ensure fair and equitable discussions, disclosures, and submissions in relation to soil disputes.
(6) Enable the appointment of a mediator conversant with the special needs of disadvantaged people, particularly in relation to cultural and traditional manner and land use.

### 4.4. Text proposals

The proposed provisions enhance existing or future soil legislation by establishing essential elements for an effective soil dispute resolution mechanism. The court-proceedings provisions apply to all proposed policy options. In contrast, provisions on complaints and investigations empower the institution responsible for sustainable soil management to address stakeholder concerns before they escalate to litigation. Therefore, the proposals for resolving or settling soil disputes can be incorporated into the existing and/or prospective soil legislative framework.

Resolution or settlement of soil disputes—Interpretation
"Competent authority" means a body or institution responsible for the sustainable management of soil resources.
"Soil dispute" means a dispute that arises in relation to the access, use, control, and management of soil resources.

Part I - Complaints and investigations[6]

Lodging of complaints
(1) Any person may lodge a complaint with the competent authority against violations of the provisions of this Act.
(2) The competent authority shall assist the complainant, where necessary, in submitting a written complaint.

6 Part I provides an opportunity for the competent soil authority to remedy complaints filed by various stakeholders. The provisions herein are both preventative and reactive, particularly with respect to the authority granted to the competent soil authority to conduct investigations on its own motion. Section 2(1) provides for *locus standi*. "Any person" in this instance has to be construed liberally, therefore, giving legal standing to persons to enforce soil legislation in the public interest or the interest of the environment. Moreover, the provisions outlined in Section 6(2)–(4) enable parties to resolve their disputes through mutual consent; however, such consent is subject to confirmation by the competent authority. This requirement addresses potential power imbalances and the limited expertise or knowledge between the disputing parties.

(3) The competent authority shall conduct a preliminary analysis of a complaint and make a report containing recommendations on whether sufficient grounds exist to warrant investigations.
(4) In cases where the complainant alleges that adverse soil impacts are caused by activities originating from another country or countries, the competent authority shall seek consultation with the Minister.

Investigations
(1) The competent authority may, either on its own initiative or upon receipt of information or a complaint from any person, investigate any alleged violation of the Act and/or set of good standards or practices.
(2) Where the competent authority decides not to carry out an investigation, having received a complaint or a request to investigate any alleged violation of the Act and/or set of good standards or practices, the Authority shall, in writing, inform the complainant of the reasons for its decision.

Power to summon and question
(1) The competent authority may, before or during investigations, -
  (a) publish a notice in the [Government Gazette] and a newspaper circulating in any area to which the investigation or enquiry relates; and
  (b) shall, where practicable, cause any person whose material or pecuniary interests may or will, in the authority's opinion, be involved in, or affected as a result of, such investigation or enquiry to be notified thereof in writing and to be given a reasonable opportunity to make representations to the competent authority concerning the subject matter of such investigations or enquiry.
(2) The competent authority may summon any person who can furnish any information on the subject of an investigation to appear before the competent authority to be questioned or to produce such documentary evidence as, in its opinion, may assist it in such investigation or enquiry.
(3) A person summoned to appear before the competent authority may be assisted at the hearing by any person reasonably acquainted with the facts of the subject of the investigation.

Power to search and seize
The competent authority may, without warrant, enter upon any land or premises to investigate, gather information, take samples, seize, and if necessary, remove from the land or premises for examination and safeguarding, any document or article that has a bearing on the investigation and do all such acts thereon as are necessary for or incidental to the investigation and resolution of an alleged violation of the Act and/or set of good standards or practices.

Decision of the competent authority

(1) The competent authority shall, after conducting its investigations, report in writing its findings and render a decision to the parties.

(2) Without derogating from subsection (1), the competent authority may, at any time before the investigations conclude, conclude an arrangement or agreement for the remediation of the complained violations.

(3) Where the parties have made an arrangement or agreement, such arrangement or agreement shall be presented to the competent authority, which may –

(a) give or withhold its confirmation; or

(b) return the matter to the parties, indicating any changes required to the consent agreement or undertaking before the competent authority confirms it.

(4) If the consent agreement has been confirmed, it shall be considered as a final order or decision of the competent authority and shall not be subject to appeal and any person or supplier who does not comply with such order commits an offence and shall be liable, upon conviction, to a fine not exceeding [...], or to imprisonment for a term not exceeding [...] years, or to both.

PART II - Court proceedings

Institution of proceedings

(1) Any party aggrieved by the competent authority's decision may appeal within 30 days in accordance with the court's procedural rules.

(2) The parties shall adhere to the procedural rules for filing appeals as prescribed in the applicable laws of the competent court.

(3) In any proceedings to which this Act applies, the court shall act expeditiously, without undue regard to technicalities of procedure.

Representation[7]

(1) A party to the proceedings may act in person or be represented by a duly authorised representative.

(2) The court may appoint or make arrangements for the appointment of a qualified legal practitioner to assist the indigents in the proceedings.

### 4.5. Alternative dispute resolution

The competent court may, on its own motion, or upon the agreement or request of the parties, adopt and implement any appropriate alternative dispute resolution methods, including but not limited to conciliation, mediation, and traditional dispute resolution mechanisms.

This provision permits the use of alternative dispute resolution methods in lieu of litigation. While there are no rigid criteria for determining the appropriate alternative forum or mechanism, several factors may guide the selection of a forum, including: (1) the relationship of the disputants; (2) the nature and number of parties involved in the dispute; (3) the type of relief sought; (4) the financial stakes involved; (5) the significance of expeditiousness and cost-effectiveness; (6) the power dynamics between the parties; and (7) the desirability of establishing principles to govern the resolution of future disputes.

Generally, disputes that are predominantly legal in nature are best resolved through adjudication. Similarly, disputes that present novel or complex issues should be referred to a forum that provides sufficient opportunity to present evidence and arguments comprehensively. Conversely, disputes that centre on non-legal issues, such as cultural values and principles, and those that present more straightforward or routine matters, are more appropriately resolved through non-adjudicatory processes.

---

7 Since all countries have specialised or general courts, this provision grants the parties the option to select a court forum in accordance with applicable law. In this context, the term "competent courts" pertains to courts that exercise jurisdiction over natural resources, where applicable, or to courts of general jurisdiction. Further, the existing laws provide for various remedies or reliefs available through the courts, including: (1) interim or permanent preservation orders, including injunctions; (2) prerogative orders; (3) awards of damages; (4) compensation; (5) specific performance; (6) restitution; (7) declarations; and (8) costs. This provision grants access to the courts in person or through a representative, including legal counsel. Considering the costs of hiring lawyers, this provision allows litigants to obtain legal representation from any chosen entity, including non-governmental organisations (NGOs). The appointment of legal representation by the courts for indigent parties is enshrined in the legislative frameworks of most jurisdictions. However, a significant challenge arises because attorneys designated to aid often lack the requisite expertise or specialisation in critical areas such as natural resources management and environmental law. Such attorneys must rapidly familiarise themselves with novel legal concepts and procedural requirements, a process that can prove arduous and time-consuming. Consequently, it is essential to appoint legal counsel with the necessary skills and expertise in the relevant fields of law.

## 4.6. Transboundary disputes

- Any transboundary soil dispute should, as far as possible, be settled amicably through negotiations, conciliation, or mediation.
- Mutually agreed solutions shall be made publicly available. However, the version disclosed to the public may not contain any information that a disputing party has designated as confidential.
- Where a dispute has not been resolved in a manner as provided for under subsection (1), any disputing party may submit the dispute to any international adjudicating body.

## 4.7. Traditional institutions

- Subject to existing laws, traditional institutions may resolve a soil dispute arising in their community in accordance with relevant customary law.
- Where a dispute has not been resolved in a manner as provided for under subsection (1), any disputing party may appeal to the relevant court.
- In resolving a dispute under this section, regard shall be given to the relevant customary law and traditional practices of the community where the dispute has arisen.

Most African countries have traditional or customary dispute settlement mechanisms in place. However, the extent to which these mechanisms are used to resolve natural resource disputes varies. Consequently, this provision allows counties with existing traditional institutions to use them. Traditional leaders play a crucial role in preserving and promoting cultural values. Dispute resolution through traditional leaders in customary courts is often preferred due to its accessibility, affordability, and speed. Furthermore, the recognition of traditional institutions fosters the integration of indigenous knowledge.

# 5. Commentary IV: Data management

Knowledge regarding the condition of soils and landscapes in Africa, and how they are changing over time, is both incomplete and outdated. This data gap is particularly concerning given that Africa's population is projected to double over the next 25 to 30 years, placing immense pressure on the continent's agricultural systems.[8] Therefore, improving soil management, productivity, and sustainability in Africa should be a top priority. Achieving these goals requires the collection and application of accurate, up-

8 See http://www.prb.org, accessed 29 September 2025.

to-date soil and land data to enable evidence-based decision-making and support agricultural productivity, economic development, environmental sustainability, and climate resilience. As emphasised in the World Soil Charter, policymakers must ensure that national soil information systems are developed, maintained, and utilised effectively. Similarly, the 2024 Nairobi Summit on Fertilisers and Soil Health called for the development of standardised and context-specific tools to assess soil fertility, soil health, and soil management. It also urged the deployment of digital information systems to operationalise fertiliser–crop–climate decision support tools at national, regional, and continental levels.

### 5.1. Challenges

There are several deficiencies and challenges concerning soil data management and outreach. Among the most critical deficiencies that need to be resolved for effective and sustainable management of soils are:

- Many African states lack sufficient soil and land data management infrastructure, including inadequate soil testing laboratories for soil quality assessment and monitoring. As a result, soil data is often outdated or unavailable. If available, soil data frequently lack georeferencing.
- Several African states have established a soil information system (SIS). However, the data and information in these SIS are often incomplete and outdated.
- Only a few African states have developed and published soil maps documenting all the information, particularly for decision-making, including the necessary information for decision-making authorities and entities.
- Many African states lack sufficient human capital, not only in quantitative terms but also in knowledge, expertise, and experience. This applies to trained personnel for collecting, assessing, and disseminating laboratory data.
- Law implementation and enforcement in many African states remain weak, partly due to the lack of clearly defined legal mandates outlining the roles and responsibilities of relevant institutions. This challenge also extends to data management, where legal frameworks often fail to specify the distinct purposes, institutional responsibilities, funding mechanisms, and capacity-building requirements, particularly in relation to training, for effective and coordinated soil data governance.

Further challenges are as follows:

A common understanding of the scope, purposes, and steps of data management is currently lacking. Data management on soil and land consists mainly of three steps. The first step is gathering data, which includes taking local measurements that require extracting the soil and later analysing it. The information could then be used to determine the current state of the soil in a specific area. The information provided should consider the chemical, physical, and biological properties of soils and should, thereby, address all forms of soil degradation.

Soil data should also include information about current and past soil uses and current (agricultural) practices. Finally, soil data should include information on land tenure and foreign investment.

The second step of data management is the assessment and synthesis of data for different purposes. Skilled personnel are required for this task. The evaluation of soil data could be used for various purposes, *inter alia*:

- Soil health assessments should evaluate the chemical, physical, and biological properties of soil at specific locations to generate reliable, site-specific data.
- This information is essential for developing Environmental Quality Standards (EQS). EQS can define acceptable thresholds of soil degradation. Where such thresholds are exceeded, the level of impact would be deemed unacceptable, and land uses resulting in that exceedance should be legally restricted or prohibited.
- Assessed and synthesised soil data can also support zoning approaches. It enables the identification of high-value soils, guiding decisions on land-use planning and the siting of large-scale projects such as infrastructure developments (e.g., buildings, roads, or railways).
- Finally, this information can inform spatial protection measures, helping to designate particularly valuable soils for legal protection through instruments such as conservation zones or soil-protected areas established in land use or environmental planning frameworks.

The third step is disseminating the information to relevant actors, such as policymakers, competent authorities responsible for determining soil uses by granting permissions or deciding on soil zoning or protected areas, and/or farmers. The means of dissemination may vary. Extension services may be the most effective mechanism for informing farmers.

Furthermore, the data and information need to be made accessible to the public, particularly to civil society organisations. To this end, regularly updated soil reports or soil information systems, along with high-resolution soil maps, should be published online and through traditional channels. There are concerns regarding data sharing. Stakeholders regularly express hesitancy to share data due to concerns about how their data could be used and a lack of transparency about attribution. To this end, a legal framework is required. From the perspective of effective data management, competent authorities need the right to access private land to take local measurements.

Incentives for data producers.

Data collection is expensive, and funding is limited. Therefore, some compensation should be granted to those who gathered and provided the data. Data gathering also serves a purpose, and those using the data could make an economic contribution if this does not hinder access to it.

Ensuring confidentiality and privacy of data.
Confidentiality, data privacy, and data integrity are further challenges that must be considered. Responsibilities within the administration must be determined carefully and clearly. Determining responsibilities is key to establishing a well-functioning system. For various reasons, this determination is never a pure formality.[9]

- The attribution of responsibilities should be cost-effective, rational, and reasonable.
- The division of responsibilities must fit into the existing system of power attribution. Assigning numerous responsibilities to local entities within a centralised system would not be advisable, as they are likely unprepared to handle the tasks.
- The attribution of responsibilities typically corresponds with reputation, influence, and the endowment of human and financial resources. Therefore, the attribution of powers may also create conflicts of interest among various entities.

Generally, it seems rational to request that local authorities conduct the measurements and empower more centralised units to manage the assessment and dissemination process. However, this may vary from country to country.

Data management must be reasonably funded. The entire data management process is time-consuming and labour-intensive, requiring significant investment in modern, advanced equipment. Additionally, data management requires regular updates across data collection and information dissemination. In this context, a fee system needs to be established, again by legal provision, for the use of data by private individuals and entities. Some potential users, such as small-scale farmers, may not be able to afford access to soil and land data.

Use of modern digital means, including AI (Artificial Intelligence), needs to be developed. Digital means are already used broadly. However, modern techniques, including AI, could facilitate the implementation of all data management steps. Data gathering could benefit from modern methods in terms of time and frequency, and improved analytical methods and assessment precision could accelerate data analysis. For data dissemination, AI can be very instrumental, by, among other things, translating scientific information into everyday language, making the information readily available in local languages, and providing more interactive and, thus, more inclusive means of making the information accessible *via* the internet. Maps could be used to make the information more tangible.

9 Ginzky (2022).

Data that could then be published on the internet should include the following categories of information.

- Metadata: Include metadata with explicit data conversions (variables and components), indicating sources for user reference and ownership.
- Soil data: Information on the properties of the soil in a specific location.
- Tenure right information: Information on the rights, including information on foreign investments and their rights to the respective land.
- Multilingual support: Offer translations and audio options in multiple languages to enhance accessibility.
- Weather data integration: Link with weather data to inform agricultural decision-making.
- Fertiliser and pesticide recommendations: Enable data regarding which fertilisers and pesticides to use for specific soil types.
- Outreach, especially to farmers, needs to be improved.

Outreach systems to (small-scale) farmers exist in most African states. However, they are often understaffed and lack sufficient technical and logistical equipment. Outreach services need to be easily accessible to all farmers, including, if possible and appropriate, access via call centres for additional support (development and printing of extension materials; printing of handouts, posters, and production guides; and radio and TV talk shows).

### 5.2. Options for legal governance mechanisms

This section outlines the preconditions for legal governance mechanisms that extend beyond legal means and the need for specific policies as a foundation for these mechanisms, before analysing the options.

#### 5.2.1. Preconditions for an effective legal governance system for data management and outreach

Legal provisions can influence realities on the ground only if certain preconditions are met. This is particularly true for data management and outreach, as it depends on a capable and effective administration. To operationalise this, the following points need to materialise:

- Sufficient financial funding is required. Otherwise, responsible administrative entities will remain understaffed and lack sufficient technical resources.
- Skilled personnel are required, in terms of expertise but also in terms of number, to fulfil the work-intensive task of data management and outreach.
- Power services and IT infrastructure are needed.

- The use and application of modern digital means, including AI, must be fostered.

### 5.2.2. Policies and strategies

Nationally agreed policies and strategies should be developed for data management and outreach to jointly determine priorities, mechanisms, and the use of available funds.

- Develop a soil data governance policy, which will make clear what roles are needed for data ownership and management, and what their responsibilities will be. For example, are there existing data managers or stewards for Soil Information Systems (SIS), or is there scope for creating this role? Are there short-term and long-term budgets for these roles? This soil data governance policy should align with the general data governance policies or strategies of most African states. Such plans should also consider existing policies or strategies concerning digitalisation and AI.
- Develop capacity building/succession plans, which entail a concept for developing human capital capable of implementing soil data management and outreach.
- Develop a plan for regular training and awareness on each stakeholder's role in data governance, ensuring they understand their roles and responsibilities and are equipped with the knowledge to maintain high standards in data governance.

### 5.2.3. Legal governance

As national policies and legislation concerning soil management and outreach differ in content, levels of detail in the regulatory framework, natural and economic conditions, challenges, available resources, and priorities, the following can only provide some insights into aspects that should be clarified by national legislation. Through these clarifications in national law, it can be ensured that national priorities concerning soil data management and outreach are effectively implemented and enforced.

National legislation should clarify the following aspects to establish a reasonable and reliable legislative basis for soil data management and outreach.

- A legal definition of what is meant by "soil data management" is required. This should include the three steps of gathering soil data, assessment, synthesis, transformation, and dissemination of soil data. Furthermore, the legislation should clarify the specific purposes of data management in accordance with national needs. This is required to explain the purposes for which the soil data could and should be used. Finally, the term "soil data" should be legally defined. By these clarifications, resistance against sharing soil data would be delegitimised.

- The legislation should establish an obligation on the part of landowners and/or those who have rights to land to tolerate soil measurements on their land. This obligation is necessary for soil measurements, which are the basis of soil data management. It must also be valid for foreign investors.
- Most importantly, the legislation must clarify the responsibilities of the administrative entities. The specific division of powers depends on the national administrative system. Thus, the decision concerning the division of powers for soil data management can only be made considering the national specificities.

In general, it is advisable to mandate that local authorities collect soil data. In contrast, soil data assessment, synthesis, and dissemination should be attributed to more central administration entities. Furthermore, it is recommended that the responsibilities of the extension services be clearly defined.

- Legal provisions should also define the means of informing the public. Soil data and information shall be made publicly accessible, either through a soil report or by establishing a soil information system. The law needs to specify the time cycles during which the report and/or the SIS must be updated. Additionally, the law should require the publication and regular update of a soil map with an adequate resolution that includes relevant information in an interactive format.
- The law should also indicate the fees private persons or entities pay for using soil data and information and, if appropriate, determine exemptions from this obligation according to national circumstances. Small-scale farmers, for instance, should primarily be exempt from this obligation.

## 5.3. Text proposals

As national legal, economic, cultural, and environmental circumstances differ, only a few guidelines for drafting legal texts are presented here.

Definition of "soil data management"

(1) Soil data management entails three processes:
  (a) Soil data gathering, including *in situ* measurements;
  (b) Assessment and synthesis of the soil data; and
  (c) Dissemination of soil data, including making it publicly accessible.
(2) Soil data is defined as it entails the following data and information:

(a) Data on the chemical, physical, and biological properties of soils in a specific location;
(b) Information on the current soil use; and
(c) Information on tenure rights on the relevant land.

(3) The purposes of soil data management are as follows:
(a) Determination of the status quo of soils in a specific location regarding the chemical, physical, and biological properties;
(b) Development and Determination of Environmental quality standards concerning all forms of soil degradation;
(c) Establishment of a soil-protected area; and
(d) Use of the soil data for zoning approaches.

Obligation to tolerate *in situ* measurements
The owner of land or the person or entity that has a right on land has to allow the competent authority in charge to undertake *in situ* measurements of soils on the respective land or mandate a third party to do so.

Division of responsibilities
The responsibilities concerning soil data management pursuant to Section xy shall be as follows: (…)

Information for the general public
Two alternative versions:

Alternative A

(1) A soil report containing all soil data and information shall be published on an internet webpage. It shall be publicly accessible free of cost and updated every five years. Additionally, a high-resolution soil map should be published.
(2) Confidential or private information must not be published or made publicly accessible.

Alternative B

(1) A soil information system entailing a summary of all soil data and information shall be published on an internet webpage. The soil report shall be publicly accessible at no cost and updated every 5 years. Additionally, a high-resolution soil map should be published.
(2) Confidential or private information must not be published or made publicly accessible.

Finally, both options could also be combined:
Fee for use of soil data for private persons or entities

(1) The competent authority will collect fees for using soil data by private persons or entities.

(2) The fee system has to be developed and established by the national authority pursuant to Section 30 (1) of the Model Law.

## 6. Commentary V: Fertilisers

Efficient fertilisers are crucial for enhancing crop yields while promoting environmental sustainability, primarily by adopting sustainable soil management practices. However, accessibility, affordability, and regional disparities complicate the management of fertilisers across Africa. At the Africa Fertiliser and Soil Health Summit, held in Nairobi in May 2024,[10] the Declaration outlined African nations' significant commitment to addressing the pressing fertiliser issues, particularly facing smallholder farmers. It also outlined ambitious goals to triple domestic production and distribute certified organic and inorganic fertilisers by 2034.

According to the International Standard ISO 7851, inorganic fertilisers are defined as fertilisers containing declared nutrients in the form of inorganic salts obtained through extraction or industrial processes.[11] Organic fertilisers are residues from plants, animals, humans, and various industrial wastes. Key actions of the Nairobi Declaration include prioritising local production and blending of mineral fertilisers, revitalising the African Centre for Fertiliser Development in Harare, Zimbabwe, and promoting decentralised, low-carbon fertiliser production methods.

Additionally, the Summit aimed to provide targeted agronomic recommendations to 70% of smallholder farmers by 2034, leveraging digital tools for efficient soil management and nutrient stewardship. These efforts are set to enhance policy frameworks, improve fertiliser accessibility, and build institutional capacity across the continent for sustainable soil health management. This Commentary examines the complexities of fertiliser governance in Africa and outlines mechanisms to promote the responsible and sustainable use of fertilisers. It explores regulatory frameworks, enforcement policies, and complementary strategies. It aims to provide actionable recommendations to enhance fertiliser policies in Africa to support sustainable soil management.

### 6.1. Challenges

Multiple challenges hinder the effective and efficient use of fertilisers in Africa, hindering their potential to boost crop yields and ensure food security. Those

10 See https://au.int/en/AFSH-2024, accessed 29 September 2025.

11 See https://www.iso.org/standard/77570.html, accessed 29 September 2025.

challenges include limited access, affordability issues, low adoption rates, limited knowledge, environmental concerns, and poor governance.

### 6.1.1. Limited accessibility

#### 6.1.1.1. Inorganic fertilisers

Many African farmers, particularly smallholders, struggle to access inorganic fertilisers due to weak distribution networks, inadequate infrastructure, and inefficient supply chains. Rural areas often lack reliable transportation and storage facilities, leading to inconsistent availability of fertilisers.[12] Due to various reasons, including high import costs, poor economies of scale, and inefficient subsidy programs, fertiliser prices in Africa are among the highest globally.[13] Since many African countries depend on imported fertilisers, they face fluctuating international prices and high transportation costs. The limited local production capacity exacerbates this issue, making fertilisers unaffordable for smallholder farmers. Although governments provide fertiliser subsidies, these programs often suffer from inefficiencies, corruption, and poor targeting, leaving many farmers unable to benefit.

#### 6.1.1.2. Organic fertilisers

Although organic fertilisers can be produced locally, they may not be accessible to farmers due to various logistical, technical, and economic constraints, as well as ethical considerations. Establishing a national production system for organic fertilisers in Africa presents numerous challenges that hinder its widespread adoption and effectiveness. One major constraint is the limited availability of raw materials such as animal manure, crop residues, and compost, which are often used for other purposes, such as fuel or animal feed,[14] reducing their availability for fertiliser production. Additionally, high production costs pose a significant barrier, as processing organic fertilisers requires substantial investment in labour, infrastructure, and technology, which small-scale producers often lack. The lack of quality control standards and incentives discourages investment in the organic fertiliser industry. Weak supply chains and poor rural infrastructure further complicate access, making it challenging to distribute organic fertilisers efficiently from production sites to farmers. Technological gaps and limited research further hinder the optimisation of organic

12 Klutse et al. (2018).
13 Amankwah et al. (2024).
14 See https://www.ipcc.ch/srccl/, chapter 4.

fertiliser production, while market constraints, such as higher costs and unstable demand, make organic options less competitive.

### 6.1.2. Lack of knowledge

Many farmers lack knowledge about the proper application of inorganic fertilisers, leading to inefficient use and potential soil degradation. Extension services that provide training on best fertiliser practices are often inadequate or underfunded in many African countries.[15] Farmers may overuse, underuse, or misapply fertilisers without proper guidance, reducing their effectiveness and leading to economic losses and soil degradation. The lack of awareness and education among farmers about the benefits and applications of organic fertilisers results in their slow adoption, especially when they are perceived as less effective than synthetic fertilisers. Furthermore, there is a lack of soil testing and tailored fertiliser recommendations, resulting in farmers often using fertilisers that do not match their soil and crop needs, thereby limiting their benefits. The lack of knowledge and the effects of climate change, such as irregular rainfall and rising temperatures, may significantly impact fertiliser efficiency and agricultural outcomes.

### 6.1.3. Environmental concerns

Overusing or misusing chemical fertilisers can contribute to soil degradation, nutrient imbalances, and environmental pollution, particularly where proper soil testing and management practices are not followed. Excessive fertiliser application, whether inorganic or organic, can also lead to water pollution through runoff, which in turn affects aquatic ecosystems.[16] In contrast, underusing fertilisers can deplete soil nutrients, leading to declining soil fertility.[17] Sustainable fertiliser management practices, including integrated soil fertility management,[18] are not widely adopted due to insufficient awareness, limited policy support, and limited access to fertilisers, including organic fertilisers.

---

15 Agwu et al. (2023).
16 Craswell (2021).
17 Dimkpa (2023).
18 Vanlauwe et al. (2010); See https://www.ipcc.ch/srccl/chapter/chapter-4/, accessed 7 April 2026.

#### 6.1.4. Governance deficiencies

Weak regulatory frameworks and inconsistent policies for fertiliser production, importation, and distribution hinder market stability. Corruption, mismanagement of subsidy programs, and a lack of harmonised regulations among African nations further exacerbate the problem. Many countries lack strong enforcement mechanisms to ensure the quality of fertilisers sold in the market, leading to the proliferation of counterfeit and substandard products. Furthermore, regional trade barriers and inconsistent taxation policies increase costs and hinder the efficient cross-border distribution of fertilisers. Particularly for organic fertilisers, poor governance in waste management practices can also reduce the availability of raw materials. In contrast, government subsidies for synthetic fertilisers create an uneven playing field, favouring chemical options over organic alternatives. Furthermore, inadequate investment in research and development and limited collaboration among key stakeholders restrict innovation in the sector.

### 6.2. Options for legal governance mechanisms, including explanatory notes

Effective legal governance mechanisms are crucial for regulating the production, distribution, and use of fertilisers in Africa. A well-structured legal framework ensures that fertilisers are accessible, affordable, and used sustainably while minimising negative environmental and economic impacts. African governments can implement regulatory measures tailored to local specificities and Sustainable Development Goals (SDGs) to enhance fertiliser management. These policies could address key challenges in improving fertiliser management in Africa, including accessibility, affordability, quality control, and environmental impact.

#### 6.2.1. Improving accessibility and affordability

The key options for improving accessibility and affordability of fertilisers in Africa involve:

(1) Subsidy programs and financial incentives to reduce costs and improve purchasing power. A digital platform for transparency and efficiency can manage this.
(2) Private sector involvement in fertiliser production and distribution, and implementing public-private partnerships.
(3) Investment in infrastructure development to ensure widespread access to affordable fertilisers across African countries and the development of agro-dealer networks.

(4) Promote sustainable organic waste collection, including crop residues, animal manure, and food waste, while encouraging composting, vermiculture programs, and waste management policies that prioritise agricultural and biodegradable waste for organic fertiliser production at the national level.

Fertiliser accessibility is key to improving agricultural productivity, particularly for smallholder farmers who often face financial constraints. Subsidy programs and financial incentives help address this challenge by reducing costs and increasing farmers' purchasing power. Smart subsidies, such as direct input subsidies (where governments provide fertilisers at a reduced price) and voucher-based systems (where farmers receive vouchers to exchange for fertilisers at authorised suppliers), ensure that assistance reaches those in need while minimising inefficiencies and corruption. To maximise effectiveness, subsidy and incentive programs should be designed to avoid long-term dependency, foster private-sector participation, and align with national agricultural policies to ensure sustainable resource allocation.

Beyond government support, private sector involvement is essential in fertiliser production and distribution. However, regulatory frameworks must be in place to guarantee fair pricing, product quality, and environmental sustainability. Encouraging public-private partnerships can further support local fertiliser manufacturing.

Infrastructure development is crucial to ensuring efficient fertiliser distribution. Investments in transportation and storage facilities help reduce logistical costs, making fertilisers more affordable for farmers in rural areas. Developing agro-dealer networks also improves last-mile distribution, ensuring fertilisers are available when and where needed.

Promoting sustainable organic waste collection at the national level is crucial for developing an efficient organic fertiliser production system. This involves waste management policies that prioritise recycling biodegradable waste, support a circular economy, decrease reliance on synthetic fertilisers, and improve soil health. Effective implementation requires coordinated efforts from government agencies, private-sector actors, and local communities to establish collection networks, processing facilities, and quality standards, thereby contributing to sustainable and climate-smart agriculture.

### 6.2.2. Improving quality control

The following options can be considered for improving the quality control of fertilisers:

(1) Implementation of comprehensive legal frameworks governing fertiliser production.

(2) Compliance is enforced through certification processes and periodic inspections.
(3) Harmonising regulations through regional economic blocs to facilitate cross-border trade while preventing the proliferation of counterfeit fertilisers.

Fertiliser quality, safety, and availability are critical for agricultural productivity and food security. Without proper regulations, markets can be flooded with counterfeit or substandard products that harm soil health and reduce crop yields. Governments play a crucial role in establishing legal frameworks that ensure fertilisers meet national and international standards. Effective regulations should cover fertiliser production, importation, distribution, and usage. This includes licensing requirements for manufacturers and importers, marketing regulations to ensure transparency, and compliance measures to prevent market distortions.

Strong enforcement mechanisms, including regular inspections, penalties for violations, and collaboration with law enforcement agencies, are crucial for maintaining compliance. A robust certification system is necessary to guarantee that only high-quality fertilisers enter the market. Certified laboratories assess fertilisers for chemical composition, effectiveness, and environmental impact before approval.

Harmonised regulations across national and regional levels help streamline fertiliser trade and ensure uniform quality standards. Regional economic blocs, such as the Economic Community of West African States (ECOWAS) and the Common Market for Eastern and Southern Africa (COMESA), facilitate cross-border trade by reducing regulatory discrepancies among member states. This enhances market efficiency and prevents counterfeit fertilisers from being circulated across borders.

### 6.2.3. Reducing environmental impacts

Several options are possible to reduce the environmental impacts of fertilisers. The following options are possible:
(1) Implementing legal, governance, monitoring, and evaluation mechanisms ensures policy effectiveness.
(2) Encourage scientific research to refine fertiliser recommendations based on empirical data.

A strong legal and governance structure is essential for regulating fertiliser production, distribution, and use while balancing agricultural productivity with environmental protection. Governments must establish clear laws and policies to ensure the responsible management of fertilisers. Laws should mandate soil testing before fertiliser application to prevent overuse and degradation. Policies promoting Integrated Soil Fertility Management, which combines organic and inorganic fertilisers, ensure efficient nutrient use and soil conservation. A decentralised governance system allows local authorities to tailor policies to their needs. Regulations should enforce buffer zones near water bodies to prevent runoff, limit excessive fertiliser application, and penalise non-compliance. These measures protect ecosystems and maintain soil health. Regular audits, compliance reporting, and field surveys ensure fertiliser policies achieve their objectives.

Scientific research supports evidence-based policymaking, refining recommendations based on real-world data. This allows governments to adjust regulations to improve efficiency and minimise negative impacts. It helps create customised fertiliser recommendations tailored to specific soil and crop needs. This reduces environmental risks and promotes efficient fertiliser use, preventing nutrient imbalances that can harm soil and water resources. Research evidence is also needed for organic fertilisers, precision agriculture, and ISFM, which can optimise fertiliser efficiency and minimise environmental impact.

## 6.3. Concrete text for legal provisions

This proposal is intended as a point for consideration and must be tailored to the country's national needs and legislative framework. It outlines a potential approach to formulating a law that regulates the core elements of fertiliser governance.

### General Provisions

#### Objective

This law regulates the production, distribution, and use of fertilisers to enhance agricultural productivity while ensuring environmental sustainability, maintaining soil health, and protecting farmers.

#### Scope

This law applies to all entities that manufacture, import, distribute, sell, and use fertilisers within the national territory.

#### Definitions:

"Fertiliser" refers to any substance containing one or more recognised plant nutrients used to promote plant growth;

"Integrated Soil Fertility Management (ISFM)" refers to the combined use of mineral fertilisers, organic inputs, and soil conservation practices to optimise agricultural productivity sustainably;

"Certification Authority" refers to the designated national body responsible for fertiliser quality control and compliance enforcement.

Accessibility and Affordability

(1) The government shall implement targeted subsidy programs to support smallholder farmers, ensuring affordability and access through transparent mechanisms such as digital vouchers and direct input subsidies. The competent authority shall oversee distribution and conduct periodic reviews.

(2) The state shall encourage private sector participation in local fertiliser production through investment incentives and regulatory support. Public-private partnerships shall be established to enhance domestic manufacturing and distribution while ensuring transparent pricing and compliance with environmental regulations.

(3) The government shall invest in transportation and storage infrastructure to improve distribution efficiency and promote agro-dealer networks for last-mile accessibility. A monitoring system shall track fertiliser availability to prevent supply chain disruptions.

(4) The government shall establish a national framework for systematically collecting, processing, and recycling biodegradable waste in collaboration with private sector stakeholders and local communities to support organic fertiliser production.

Quality Control and Standards

(1) All fertiliser manufacturers and importers must obtain a licence from the Certification Authority before commercial operations. Imported fertilisers must meet national and international quality standards and undergo mandatory laboratory testing. Counterfeit and substandard fertilisers are prohibited.

(2) All fertilisers must undergo quality certification before market introduction. National regulatory agencies shall conduct periodic inspections, and testing laboratories shall assess fertilisers for composition, effectiveness, and environmental impact.

(3) The government shall collaborate with regional economic blocs to harmonise fertiliser quality standards and ensure mutual recognition of cross-border trade requirements.

Environmental Protection and Sustainability

(1) Runoff and Pollution Control. Fertiliser application must adhere to environmental guidelines to minimise soil and water pollution. Buffer zones shall be maintained near water bodies, and violations shall result in fines, suspension of business licences, or criminal liability.

(2) Farmers must conduct soil testing before applying fertilisers. The competent authority shall provide crop- and region-specific recommendations, and extension services shall train farmers on best practices.

(3) The government shall promote organic fertilisers and precision agriculture while supporting ISFM. Research institutions should develop innovative and environmentally friendly fertiliser solutions.

Monitoring, Enforcement, and Penalties

(1) A national system shall track fertiliser production, distribution, and usage. Annual reports will assess policy impact, and stakeholder engagement will ensure regulatory improvements.
(2) Entities distributing counterfeit or substandard fertilisers shall face fines and/or imprisonment. Environmental violations, excessive fertiliser use, and pollution shall result in penalties, including the suspension of business operations and mandatory remediation. Repeat offenders may face increased fines and licence revocation.
(3) Farmers and consumers may report grievances to the Certification Authority. Disputes shall be resolved through arbitration before legal proceedings. A Fertiliser Regulatory Tribunal shall handle disputes and ensure fair enforcement of regulations.

## 7. Commentary VI: Foreign investment

Foreign Direct Investment (FDI) plays a crucial role in supporting economic development across Africa, prompting many countries to actively promote it. However, this must be carefully balanced against the host state's sovereign right to regulate its natural resources, including land and soil. The legal framework governing investment and soil protection is complex, shaped by a patchwork of national laws, inconsistencies in implementation, and growing international influence. This complexity is further compounded by the involvement of numerous stakeholders—governments, NGOs, private investors, and global organisations—leading to significant coordination challenges. In many cases, soil degradation is linked to agricultural investments that lack specific legal or regulatory safeguards for soil health. To address this, the legal framework for FDI must be revised to promote responsible investment practices that align with sustainable soil management objectives.

African states regulate investor conduct through both civil and criminal law frameworks, covering areas such as taxation, licensing, and environmental impact assessments. However, the broader legal landscape governing FDI is highly fragmented, comprising international, transnational, national, and contractual rules. Many older Bilateral Investment Treaties (BITs) disproportionately emphasise investor protection, often at the expense of imposing clear obligations, particularly regarding environmental and soil protection. In response, several African states are now revising their investment treaties to better balance investors' rights with their corresponding duties. In addition to treaty reforms, national investment laws and state–investor contracts also play a critical role in shaping investor responsibilities and ensuring alignment with sustainable development objectives.

This Commentary examines the legal texts governing the relationship between investors and host states, focusing on investors' obligations regarding environmental protection and soil conservation.

## 7.1. Description of the challenges of foreign investment and soil protection in Africa

A key challenge in addressing the environmental and soil-related impacts of foreign investment in Africa lies in the diversity of the legal landscape, which draws from both domestic and international sources. National laws can play a critical role by designating strategic sectors and mandating investor conduct in line with the Sustainable Development Goals (SDGs). Investment codes and sector-specific legislation increasingly impose direct obligations or conditions on investors. For example, Mozambique's 2018 investment law requires compliance with national standards on taxation, labour safety, and environmental protection. Egypt permits investors to contribute voluntarily to social development initiatives, while Ethiopia's legal framework encourages socially and environmentally responsible investment. Similarly, Morocco's new investment charter explicitly highlights sustainable development as a guiding principle.

African legal systems are diverse and influenced by civil law, common law, Islamic law, or a mix of these. Customary law also plays a significant role, particularly in land access, as seen in Zambia, where traditional chiefs administer most of the land. Land access for foreign investors is often restricted, requiring local partnerships (Nigeria), leases (Ethiopia), or limited private leases (South Sudan).

International legal instruments, particularly BITs, also play a significant role in regulating foreign investment. These treaties establish binding international obligations, meaning that government actions lawful under domestic law may still constitute a breach of treaty commitments. Liberia adopts a different approach, relying primarily on investment contracts rather than BITs to govern its foreign investment relationships.

Contracts allow host states to achieve specific objectives in sectors such as infrastructure and mining. Still, investors often prefer alternative jurisdictions or stabilisation clauses due to perceived instability in host state laws.

African nations are developing a new model for investment promotion and development agreements, emphasising balance and responsible investment. The 2016 Nigeria-Morocco treaty, for instance, has been commended for its focus on sustainable development.

Africa's regional investment landscape is shaped by a range of bilateral and regional treaties, reflecting the continent's legal and institutional diversity. These include:

- The 1990 Arab Maghreb Union Investment Agreement, which is still not yet in force.
- The 2007 Common Market for Eastern and Southern Africa (COMESA) Investment Agreement (COMESA Protocol), intended to be replaced by the revised COMESA Common Investment Area (CCIA) Agreement, which is also not yet in force.
- The 2018 Economic Community of West African States (ECOWAS) Supplementary Act on the Common Investment Code, which is in force and complements the 2008 ECOWAS Competition Rules.
- The 2006 Southern African Development Community (SADC) Protocol on Finance and Investment, as amended by the 2016 Agreement, which is currently in force.

Additionally, African states participate in broader regional initiatives:

- The 1980 and 2013 Unified Agreements for Arab Capital Investment (Arab League).
- The 1981 Agreement on Promotion, Protection and Guarantee of Investments amongst the Member States of the Organisation of the Islamic Conference (OIC).

Despite these efforts, the African investment regime remains fragmented. Key points to consider include:

- South Africa has reformed its investment policy, terminating several BITs.
- Liberia favours investment contracts over international treaties, which can pose risks for investors due to the application of host state law.

In summary, while there is a push for more balanced and sustainable investment agreements, the African investment framework remains complex and fragmented, characterised by regional and bilateral agreements and differing national approaches.

Unlike regional treaties, intra-African BITs often lack a strong focus on sustainable development. While approximately 20 African countries are parties to two regional African investment treaties, eight are parties to only one, and Libya is a party to four. Notably, five countries—Equatorial Guinea, the Central African Republic, the Republic of Congo, São Tomé and Principe, and South Sudan—are not party to such agreements.

Two key legal instruments stand out for their provisions on environmental protection and sustainable development: the AfCFTA Investment Protocol and the ECOWAS Investment Code. It is essential to note that the AfCFTA Investment Protocol has not yet entered into force because the African Union (AU) has not adopted its annexes.

The AfCFTA Investment Protocol has the potential to reshape investment rules across the continent, prioritising sustainable development alongside investment protection. It covers all 55 AU member states and acknowledges the host state's right to regulate services and to introduce new regulations for legitimate policy objectives, including environmental protection and sustainable development. Article 3 explicitly promotes sustainable development in line with the SDGs. The AfCFTA's protocols, such as the Protocol on Trade in Goods, also include environmental safeguards, allowing states to adopt measures for human, animal, and plant health, as reinforced by Article 26.

The ECOWAS Investment Code dedicates Chapter 6 (Articles 21-29) to provisions related to environmental and sustainable development. Article 21 outlines general provisions for environmental protection. It reaffirms member states' commitment to promoting sustainable investment policies that advance environmental protection, encourage high environmental protection standards, facilitate the effective implementation of national environmental laws, and enhance member states' capacity to address investment-related environmental issues through regional cooperation.

The code defines "environmental legislation" as any member state law or provision whose primary objective is to protect the environment or prevent harm to human, animal, or plant life or health, through:

- Preventing, reducing, or controlling the release of pollutants.
- Controlling hazardous chemicals and waste.
- Protecting wildlife and natural habitats.
- Implementing relevant environmental agreements.

It also emphasises that encouraging investment by relaxing national health, safety, or environmental measures is illegal.

Article 22 of the ECOWAS Investment Code recognises the importance of coherent investment, trade, and environmental policies in enhancing environmental protection and promoting sustainable economic development. It affirms the sovereign right of member states to establish their own environmental protection levels and policies, while also committing them to maintaining and improving high environmental protection standards.

Article 27 of the ECOWAS Investment Code outlines the environmental obligations of investors, requiring them to:

- Conduct business in strict accordance with national environmental laws, regulations, administrative practices, and applicable multilateral agreements.
- Perform mandatory environmental and social impact assessments before undertaking business activities and investments.
- Apply the precautionary principle in environmental and social impact assessments and investment decisions.
- Make environmental and social impact assessments publicly accessible to affected communities and stakeholders.

- Restore environmental damage using appropriate technologies and provide compensation to affected parties.
- Provide relevant environmental information to national environmental authorities.
- Implement waste production and disposal standards equivalent to or stricter than those in their home countries.

Furthermore, Article 29 of the Code introduces innovative obligations, requiring investors to take measures to:

- Increase resource efficiency, including recycling and waste reduction.
- Develop and implement methodologies for integrating environmental costs into accounting and pricing mechanisms.
- Adopt global sustainable development policies and ensure environmentally sound technologies are accessible to subsidiaries within member states, including using environmental audits.
- Establish partnerships with SMEs to facilitate knowledge exchange in management skills, market development, and technological expertise.
- Increase national and global research and development in environmentally sound technologies and environmental management systems.
- Ensure responsible and ethical product and process management, considering environmental aspects.
- Adopt and implement production and hazardous waste disposal standards equivalent to or stricter than those in their home countries, including impact assessments on local resources and health risks.
- Prepare emergency plans for environmental damage prevention and mitigation.

The ECOWAS Investment Code and the AfCFTA Investment Protocol promote responsible investment and impose significant obligations on member states and investors. However, the effective implementation of these obligations remains a separate and crucial challenge, since most African countries' systems adopt a dualistic approach, which implies the juxtaposition of the international and domestic legal orders. Consequently, international treaties and conventions may apply in the state's legal order only from their transposition into domestic legislation, in accordance with the procedure laid down for that purpose in that legislation, which may differ from one country to another. For example, the Moroccan Constitution provides in its preamble that it grants international conventions duly ratified and published by the state primacy over the domestic law of the country, and that the state must harmonise the relevant provisions of its national legislation; nevertheless, these conventions and agreements must respect the immutable national identity of the state. In most African countries, the provisions of international agreements must be transposed to be applied.

## 7.2. Governance

It is crucial to distinguish between investment governance within a state's domestic legal order and that under bilateral or multilateral agreements governing foreign investment.

Regarding domestic law, foreign investment is a cross-cutting issue that involves multiple institutions and administrations. Therefore, a coordinating body for public policy in this sector that engages all stakeholders is essential. In Morocco, for instance, the Moroccan Agency for Investment and Export Development (AMDIE), established in 2017, fulfils this role. AMDIE, a public entity with legal personality and financial autonomy, implements the national strategy to develop, incentivise, and promote domestic and foreign investments and exports. AMDIE's responsibilities include:

- Proposing and analysing strategies to achieve government investment and export development objectives and evaluating results.
- Providing opinions on investment and export promotion matters.
- Serving as the secretariat for the National Investment Commission (CNI).

In addition to AMDIE's national role, Regional Investment Centres (CRIs) support foreign investment at the regional level. These centres support regional investors and serve as the initial point of contact for investment projects. CRIs, under the supervision of the Head of Government (delegating some authority to the MICEPP), are public entities across Morocco's twelve regions, offering services such as:

- Information and guidance on regional investment opportunities and administrative procedures.
- Personalised support for project development, from planning to implementation.
- Post-investment support for business startups and growth.
- Acting as a mediator for investor-administration disputes.

The governance of bilateral or multilateral agreements (such as FTAs, BITs, and IPAs) typically includes governance mechanisms within their provisions. For example, Article 9 of the AfCFTA establishes an institutional framework for its implementation, including bodies for administration, facilitation, implementation, and monitoring. The AfCFTA's governance structure comprises:

- The Conference;
- The Council of Ministers;
- The Committee of Senior Trade Officials; and
- The Secretariat.

Title Three of the AfCFTA Agreement outlines the administration and organisation of the Free Trade Area. The Conference of the Member States provides oversight and strategic guidance on the AfCFTA's operations, including the action plan to boost intra-African trade. All decisions must be made by consensus, establishing a hierarchical structure among the bodies. Specifically, the Committee of Senior Trade Officials refers issues that lack attainable consensus to the Council of Ministers for review. The Council of Ministers, in turn, refers unresolved matters to the Conference (Article 14 of the Agreement). Article 11 of the Agreement details the composition and functions of the Council of Ministers, while Article 12 specifies the composition and functions of the Committee of Senior Trade Officials.

## 7.3. Options for legal governance mechanisms

A multifaceted approach to legal governance is essential for addressing the challenges of soil protection in Africa in the context of foreign investment. The following are options for legal governance mechanisms that can be implemented:

Integration of soil protection into investment laws and policies:

- Mechanism: Amend or develop national investment codes and policies to explicitly incorporate soil protection standards and requirements.
- Purpose: Ensure that soil health is a fundamental consideration in all foreign investment projects.
- Implementation: Requires collaboration between investment promotion agencies, environmental authorities, and legal experts.

Strengthening Environmental Impact Assessment (EIA) frameworks:

- Mechanism: Enact or reinforce laws mandating comprehensive EIAs, including detailed soil impact assessments for all relevant foreign investment projects.
- Purpose: Identify, evaluate, and mitigate potential soil degradation risks from investment activities.
- Implementation: Establish clear EIA guidelines, competent assessment bodies, and public participation mechanisms.

Land use planning and zoning regulations:

- Mechanism: Develop and enforce land use planning and zoning regulations that designate areas for specific investment activities, considering soil sensitivity and ecological vulnerability.
- Purpose: Prevent incompatible land uses, control urban sprawl, and protect fertile agricultural lands.
- Implementation: Strong local government capacity, spatial planning expertise, and community involvement are required.

Contractual agreements and investment treaties:

- Mechanism: Incorporate soil protection clauses into investment contracts and bilateral/multilateral treaties (BITs/MITs).
- Purpose: Set clear environmental obligations for foreign investors and establish dispute resolution mechanisms for soil-related issues.
- Implementation: Requires careful drafting of contract terms and negotiation of treaty provisions that balance investor rights with environmental responsibilities.

Regulatory frameworks for specific sectors:

- Mechanism: Develop sector-specific regulations for agriculture, mining, and infrastructure development, with detailed provisions for soil conservation and rehabilitation.
- Purpose: Address the unique soil degradation risks associated with each sector.
- Implementation: Requires technical expertise, stakeholder consultation, and effective monitoring and enforcement.

Community participation and empowerment:

- Mechanism: Establish legal mechanisms for community participation in land use planning, environmental monitoring, and enforcement of soil protection laws.
- Purpose: Enhance local ownership, promote sustainable land management practices, and ensure environmental policies reflect community needs and priorities.
- Implementation: Requires capacity building for community organisations and access to information.

## 7.4. Proposed legal framework modifications

Significant legal reforms are necessary to ensure sustainable foreign investment that respects the environment and protects soil integrity. These reforms should target domestic African legislation related to foreign investment, as well as international instruments, particularly BITs/MITs. The latter presents a greater challenge, as negotiations often prioritise economic interests over ecological concerns.

To safeguard the host state's environment, African nations must revise their existing BITs to better balance investor rights and obligations. New BITs should incorporate the following elements:

- The contribution of foreign investment to sustainable development.
- The host state's right to regulate in the public interest.

- Updated definitions for key terms such as investment, investor, fair and equitable treatment, expropriation (including indirect), national treatment, and most-favoured-nation treatment.
- The imposition of specific obligations on foreign investors operating within the host state.
- Facilitating investment through joint committees for agreement implementation and national focal points for investor communication.

These updated BITs should promote economic cooperation centred on sustainable investment, encompassing economic, social, and environmental dimensions. They should explicitly define investor obligations regarding social and environmental responsibility, including contributions to the host state's sustainable development through responsible practices, as well as compliance with human rights, labour standards, responsible business conduct, and environmental protection.

The following are concrete examples of legal provisions that could be included in legislation or investment treaties to address the challenges of soil protection associated with foreign investment in Africa. These provisions aim to strike a balance between investment promotion and environmental sustainability.

Environmental Impact Assessments (EIAs) and due diligence:

(1) All foreign investments exceeding [specified threshold] in sectors impacting land use, including but not limited to agriculture, mining, and infrastructure development, shall be subject to a mandatory, comprehensive, and publicly accessible Environmental and Social Impact Assessment (ESIA) before project commencement. The ESIA shall include a detailed soil impact assessment, outlining mitigation measures for potential degradation.

(2) Foreign investors shall conduct thorough environmental due diligence, encompassing soil health assessments, before acquiring land or commencing operations. This due diligence shall be documented and submitted to the relevant environmental authority for review.

Soil conservation and sustainable land management:

(1) Foreign investors in agricultural projects shall implement sustainable land management practices, including but not limited to minimum tillage, crop rotation, and integrated nutrient management, to prevent soil erosion and maintain soil fertility. A soil management plan shall be integrated into the project's operational plan.

(2) Mining operations by foreign investors shall include mandatory soil restoration and rehabilitation plans, ensuring the restoration of topsoil and vegetation to pre-mining conditions. Financial guarantees shall be provided to ensure compliance.

(3) Foreign investment projects that will lead to deforestation must have a clear reforestation program and ensure that the soil quality of the reforested land is monitored for at least ten (10) years.

Investor obligations and environmental responsibility:

(1) Foreign investors shall adhere to the host state's environmental laws and regulations, including those related to soil protection, waste management, and water resources. Any deviation from these laws shall result in penalties, including fines and project suspension.
(2) Foreign investors shall adopt and implement best environmental practices and technologies, including soil conservation measures, to minimise their environmental footprint. They shall also provide regular environmental performance reports to the relevant authorities.
(3) Foreign investors are obligated to contribute to local community development, including restoring environmental damages that their activities caused. They are also obligated to provide environmental training for the local workers.

Transparency and public participation:

(1) All environmental impact assessments, soil management plans, and environmental performance reports related to foreign investment projects shall be publicly available. Public consultations shall be conducted to gather input from affected communities.
(2) Local communities shall have the right to monitor and report environmental violations by foreign investors. A transparent and accessible complaints mechanism shall be established.

Dispute resolution and environmental safeguards:

(1) Investment treaties shall include provisions that explicitly recognise the host state's right to regulate in the public interest, including protecting soil and land resources. Dispute resolution mechanisms shall consider the environmental impacts of investment projects.
(2) Any dispute relating to environmental damages, or soil degradation caused by a foreign investor, will be handled by the host state's courts, and according to the host state's environmental law.

Incentives for sustainable investment:

(1) Foreign investors who implement sustainable land management practices and invest in soil restoration technologies shall be eligible for tax incentives and other benefits.

(2) Priority shall be given to foreign investment projects demonstrating a commitment to environmental protection and contributing to the host state's sustainable development goals.

These provisions aim to create a legal framework that promotes responsible foreign investment while safeguarding Africa's valuable soil resources.

## 8. Commentary VII: Gender equality and equity

Many African countries have undertaken legal reforms to promote gender equality and create a more enabling environment for women's effective participation in national economies. Within the African human rights framework, the Protocol to the African Charter on Human and Peoples' Rights on the Rights of Women in Africa (Maputo Protocol) affirms women's rights to land and environmental resources. Article 15 explicitly links the right to land with the right to food security, highlighting the fundamental importance of soil resources to agriculture in Africa. Article 19 further obliges State Parties to promote women's access to and control over productive resources, including land, and to guarantee their property rights.

Similarly, the New Partnership for Africa's Development (NEPAD) Environment Action Plan recognises the critical role of women in environmental management and calls for their full participation in environmental decision-making processes. Despite these policy and legal advancements, however, gender disparities remain entrenched. Women continue to face disproportionate vulnerability to the impacts of climate change and land degradation, and to exclusion from decision-making processes in Sustainable Soil Management (SSM). Although women are central to soil-dependent livelihoods, many SSM initiatives fail to incorporate gender parity, thereby undermining both equity and environmental sustainability. This Commentary explores these persistent gaps and considers their implications for more inclusive and effective soil governance across Africa.

### 8.1. Description of challenges

Some of the challenges that impede women's effective participation in SSM include:

- Laws, policies, and decision-making processes often overlook gender issues and women's rights, particularly in matters related to poverty eradication, environmental degradation, soil management, market access, and economic development. Even in countries with gender-sensitive laws, weak implementation remains a significant challenge.

- Women in African countries generally lack access to, control over, and ownership of land and environmental resources, which are closely linked, such as soil, food, fuel, timber, water, and genetic resources. The roles of traditional authorities in allocating land resources within communal land complicate efforts to enforce equity and gender equality in land distribution. Due to insecure land access, women are frequently relegated to marginal, lower-quality, and remote areas, where sustaining healthy soils and ensuring ecosystem services remain particularly difficult.
- Additionally, women farmers lack access to cash and/or credit facilities, technical support, and information to enable them to implement sustainable soil health practices. Gender-neutral laws (laws using 'they/them' to refer to both men and women) on land and environmental resources have not led to an increase in women owning these resources due to structural barriers, such as limited access to credit, and the prevalence of the myth that women are not entitled to own land.[19]
- Despite women's significant involvement in agriculture and food security initiatives across Africa, they remain underrepresented in institutions managing land and environmental issues. Women are significantly underrepresented in policy formulation and decision-making processes related to natural resource management, conservation, protection, and rehabilitation. In patriarchal systems, this exclusion extends to family-level decisions on land use and soil management, where women's knowledge and interests are often overlooked in development planning.
- Soil erosion and environmental degradation have severe impacts on the African populace, but more so on the lives and roles of women and girls. As a result, economic stress within households and dependency on scarce resources are compounded.
- In most countries in Africa, women's roles and contributions to agriculture and soil-related activities are identified according to the limited soil data available, thereby making it difficult to fully capture the exact role, contribution, and challenges faced by women in SSM.
- In conclusion, women in many African countries face a range of interconnected obstacles that hinder their effective participation in SSM. These include limited and insecure land rights, restricted access to land and natural resources, often of lower quality or smaller size, and exclusion from decision-making processes at local and national levels. Women also frequently lack the financial capital needed to access production inputs and are denied access to soil-related knowledge and training, mainly due to patriarchal norms and socially imposed roles that confine them to caregiving responsibilities

19 Kameri-Mbote (2007).

within their communities. Addressing these systemic barriers is essential to achieving equitable, effective, and sustainable soil governance in Africa.

### 8.2. Options for legal governance mechanisms

To effectively address these challenges, women and girls must be recognised and included as key stakeholders in gender-responsive interventions, whether projects, programmes, policies, or strategies, that are tailored to the specific needs and priorities of both women and men. Their active participation is essential to ensuring equitable engagement, influence, and benefit-sharing across all SSM initiatives.

Furthermore, identifying effective governance options to advance gender equality while promoting soil health requires an in-depth analysis of the complex interlinkages between SSM and gender dynamics. These relationships are influenced by a diverse array of economic, social, cultural, educational, and political factors that vary significantly across national and local contexts. Some of the proposed options include:

- Design or improve national soil management and supportive agricultural and environmental legal frameworks to be more gender sensitive.
- Design and implement inclusive and gender-responsive education and extension programmes. This can be achieved by strengthening the linkages among women's land rights, development, and sustainability, which are often neglected across much of Africa.
- Ensure inclusion of men in gender training programmes to ensure that they develop a willingness to work with and implement women's ideas and innovations. This would foster a culture of managing soil and soil-related resources based on collective, rather than patriarchal, decisions.
- Adopt a gender specific approach in soil-related decisions and policymaking processes.
- Apply gender sensitive tools in the dissemination of soil information. Gender equality and enhanced women's empowerment in SSM require working with both women and men, bringing them to an equal level of knowledge, knowledge sharing, and access to natural resources. This avoids the misconception that gender equality will simply target women without understanding and addressing gender roles, norms, and relationships peculiar to SSM.
- Design and apply gender mainstreaming tools and gender responsive and gender transformative approaches in sustainable soil management practices.
- Address gender issues and monitor gender-related impacts of the normative legal and policy frameworks governing soil resources.

- Create an enabling environment, such as quota systems, to facilitate equal access for women and men to land and other productive resources, services, local institutions, and organisations.
- Embed into law and policy the recognition of the critical role women play in agriculture, and more specifically, towards soil health and SSM.
- Promote and implement "women-friendly" rules and regulations and revise existing local and national regulatory frameworks and cultural barriers that perpetuate gender inequality. For instance, gender discrimination limits women's access to (agricultural) resources, education, extension, financial services, and labour markets, thereby impacting negatively on SSM in Africa.
- Mainstream gender parity in land tenure and soil management frameworks, which include gender equality as a definite goal, with clear and identifiable targets. In this vein, the plight of women in rural Africa may require more nuanced gender policies to integrate the needs of rural women in agriculture and other soil-related projects and activities.
- Identify gender-specific needs in all soil and soil-related activities, namely climate adaptation, agricultural land, water, forest, and other natural resources; and incorporation of gender-sensitive processes.
- Strengthen public support for soil sustainability and ensure long-term commitment to more responsible soil management by increasing awareness and education on women's involvement. The inter-relationships between soils and social issues, such as agriculture, food security and safety, sustainability, climate change, soil carbon sequestration,[20] greenhouse gas emissions, erosion-driven degradation, and loss of organic matter and nutrients, need to be simplified and consistently packaged into educational awareness programs for all stakeholders, without exception.
- Adopt legal provisions on procedural rights, which are critical in relation to the role of women in soil and environmental management. These procedural rights include the right to access soil information, participation in soil-related decision-making processes, freedom of association, and other related rights of access.
- Increasing women's participation in soil research, policy development, and decision-making would be instrumental in promoting SSM across Africa.
- Build the capacity of universities and research institutes to conduct gender-responsive soil research that informs national programmes and policy, improves collaboration with diverse land users, and ensures women and men can restore, steward, and benefit from soils' ecosystem services.
- Support investments and positive incentives aimed at promoting SSM and gender equality.

20 Fawad (2025).

- Invest in women's leadership and technical skills in SSM.

## 8.3. Concrete text for legal provisions

These legislative texts may be incorporated into the SSM law or laws that specifically address gender.

Interpretation

Gendered soil sensitisation: The process of educating, engaging, and integrating gender perspectives into sustainable soil and land management practices.

Section 1: Gendered soil sensitisation

(1) The competent authority, in collaboration with the relevant government department, shall design and implement educational and public awareness programs tailored explicitly to gendered soil sensitisation.

(2) These programs will include modules that illustrate the distinct roles, contributions, and challenges experienced by different genders in soil management.

(3) The initiatives shall be integrated into broader sustainable soil management strategies and evaluated regularly through gender-disaggregated data to measure their impact on community awareness and engagement.

(4) The competent authority shall facilitate partnerships with local governments, non-governmental organisations, academic institutions, and community groups to ensure a coordinated and inclusive approach to soil management education.

Section 2: Women's land tenure security

(1) The competent authority shall ensure that policies and laws are reviewed to guarantee equal access to, use of, and control over land for women.

(2) Subject to constitutional limitations and other written laws, discriminatory practices that limit women's ability to own, inherit, lease, or otherwise secure land shall be prohibited.

(3) The relevant competent authority shall establish a transparent registration and dispute resolution process, ensuring efficient and speedy redress for any infringement of women's land rights.

Section 3: Women's participation and empowerment

(1) To ensure robust representation in decision-making, women shall be provided with a minimum quota of [X]% participation in all advisory boards,

committees, and policy-making bodies related to soil management and environmental conservation.

(2) The government will establish empowerment programs, including capacity-building workshops, leadership training, and access to financial services, tailored specifically for women engaged in agriculture and soil conservation initiatives.

(3) Funding shall also be allocated for grassroots projects led by women with promising sustainable soil management practices.

Section 4: Gender-specific needs and vulnerabilities assessment

(1) The relevant competent authority shall conduct periodic assessments to identify and address the gender-specific needs, vulnerabilities, and risks related to soil degradation and unsustainable land use practices.

(2) These assessments shall be participatory in nature, engaging community stakeholders and disaggregating data by gender to inform adaptive policy measures and targeted support programs.

(3) The competent authority shall ensure that results from these assessments are used to prioritise interventions and resource allocations that mitigate the adverse impacts on the most vulnerable groups.

Section 5: Integration of gendered indigenous and local knowledge

Recognition of the value of indigenous and local knowledge systems in sustainable soil management is encouraged, particularly those practices developed and sustained by women and other gender minorities over generations and all necessary measures shall be taken to protect such knowledge and promote its integration in existing training curricula, policy and legislative frameworks to foster a more inclusive and culturally sensitive approach to soil management.

Section 6: Funding, incentives, monitoring, and evaluation

(1) The competent authority shall ensure that the annual budget is allocated to support the implementation of this law, including the development of educational materials, legal support mechanisms, and empowerment projects.

(2) Incentives, including tax benefits and subsidies, may be provided to organisations, cooperatives, and community projects that demonstrably integrate gender-inclusive practices in soil conservation and management.

(3) The competent authority shall establish regular monitoring and evaluation mechanisms, incorporating gender-disaggregated indicators to measure the progress and impact of gender laws in promoting sustainable soil management.

(4) The competent authority shall submit an annual report detailing the progress, challenges, and outcomes associated with these initiatives, with recommendations for ongoing improvements.

(5) Reports shall include metrics such as gender-disaggregated participation rates in training programs, outreach effectiveness, and measurable improvements in sustainable soil practices.

Section 7: Implementation
The provisions of this law shall be implemented by relevant governmental agencies in coordination with local authorities, civil society organisations, and traditional community leaders.

## 9. Commentary VIII: Implementation and enforcement

This Commentary examines the challenges associated with enforcing and implementing laws for sustainable soil management in Africa. It focuses on the institutional and administrative challenges involved in establishing effective systems to implement and enforce national legislation aligned with the Model Law.

### 9.1. Challenges

The core challenge lies in the persistent gap between legal development and practical enforcement. While many African states have made progress in drafting soil-related legal provisions, implementation and enforcement remain weak and insufficient. Without effective implementation, legislation has little real-world impact and remains largely symbolic. Therefore, strengthening the mechanisms for implementing and enforcing soil-related laws is a critical precondition for achieving tangible improvements in soil health and land management across the continent.

The main challenges towards an effective administrative implementation and enforcement system are:

#### 9.1.1. Responsibilities within administration are not sufficiently clarified by law

In many cases, responsibilities among ministries and administrative bodies are not clearly defined, resulting in conflicts over competencies and institutional authority. This lack of clarity can lead to inactivity, as it becomes difficult to determine which entity is accountable for implementation outcomes or to duplication of efforts, with overlapping or even contradictory approaches. Such inefficiencies not only delay progress but also consume time and resources that could be saved through clear attribution of mandates. Moreover, disputes over institutional roles can significantly slow critical decision-making, undermining the timely implementation of sustainable soil management policies.

### 9.1.2. Insufficient financial resources

Insufficient financial resources within government institutions, including administrative bodies, remain a widespread reality in many African countries. This includes limited access to adequate office infrastructure, digital and communication equipment, transport facilities, and basic operational resources such as electricity and fuel. Such resource constraints significantly hinder the effective implementation and enforcement of legal provisions, including those related to sustainable soil management. Without adequate institutional support, even well-drafted laws struggle to translate into meaningful action on the ground.

### 9.1.3. Insufficient personnel with adequate expertise and experience

Among other challenges, the lack of financial resources means that many administrative bodies in African countries are understaffed and unable to fulfil their mandates effectively. In addition, existing personnel often lack the necessary expertise and experience required to implement and enforce sustainable soil management laws and policies.

### 9.1.4. Digitalisation

Emerging digital technologies, including artificial intelligence (AI), offer significant opportunities to enhance the implementation and enforcement of soil-related provisions. However, most African administrative bodies are poorly equipped—or not equipped at all—to adopt and effectively utilise these technologies, limiting their potential impact.

### 9.1.5. Interplay between modern administration and traditional governance systems

In many African countries, particularly in rural areas, traditional governance systems continue to play a vital role in land and resource management. However, the relationship between modern administrative structures and traditional authorities is often poorly defined, leading to overlapping mandates, contradictory decision-making, and unclear lines of accountability. This lack of coordination can hinder effective implementation and enforcement of soil-related policies and undermine efforts to establish coherent governance frameworks.

## 9.2. Main tasks for implementation and enforcement

A wide range of tasks must be implemented and enforced to support sustainable soil management. While the following list is not exhaustive, it illustrates the diversity and complexity of the responsibilities involved. Importantly, clearly attributing these tasks to specific institutions or actors is essential to ensure effective and well-organised implementation. The various tasks are described in the following.

### 9.2.1. Data management

Data management in the context of soil governance typically involves three main steps: first, the collection of field data on soil qualities, land use, and tenure rights; second, the analysis and interpretation of the collected data; and third, the dissemination of the results to relevant stakeholders, including farmers, competent authorities, and policymakers.

### 9.2.2. Determination of environmental quality standards

To effectively implement soil-related legal provisions, competent authorities require clear environmental quality standards (EQS). These standards can be developed to address various forms of soil degradation, including erosion, compaction, salinisation, and contamination. The development of EQS typically involves both scientific assessments and normative decision-making. It should be carried out in consultation with relevant stakeholders to ensure legitimacy, contextual relevance, and practical applicability.

### 9.2.3. Permission procedure concerning potentially detrimental soil uses

According to the Model Law, "Any use of soil that may pose a risk of significant degradation" requires permission by the competent authority (Article 13(2)). The Environmental Impact Assessment should include a specific "soil impact assessment".

#### 9.2.4. Urban planning

The Model Law also requires urban planning to avoid unnecessary soil sealing and to protect valuable soils, and to "identify options for de-sealing projects" (Article 19(2)).

#### 9.2.5. Zoning mechanisms, including soil-protected areas

The Model Law also foresees zoning mechanisms being undertaken by the competent authority to utilise soil qualities most effectively and to ensure the provision of soil services. To this end, soil-protected areas shall be established (Articles 17 and 18 of the Model Law).

#### 9.2.6. Public participation processes and awareness raising

The Model Law requires that the administration effectively engage the public and relevant stakeholders in decision-making processes, including urban planning, zoning, and the establishment of protected soil areas. The administration should also work towards raising public and political awareness on soil issues.

#### 9.2.7. Monitoring and surveillance

Another key responsibility of the administration is to ensure that relevant societal actors comply with soil-related legal provisions. To achieve this, it is essential to establish an effective system of monitoring and enforcement, which may include on-the-ground inspections, oversight of land-use practices, and other relevant control measures. Digital technologies, such as remote sensing and geographic information systems (GIS), can play a vital role in enhancing the efficiency and accuracy of monitoring efforts.

### 9.3. Options/recommendations

Given the significant diversity in governmental and administrative systems across African states, a one-size-fits-all solution is neither practical nor appropriate. Accordingly, the following discussion highlights selected dimensions to consider when designing effective systems for implementing and enforcing soil-related legal provisions. It is essential that legislation clearly defines the allocation of powers, competences, and responsibilities, enabling these to be identified, assigned, and exercised in a structured manner. Importantly, clarifying such roles is often contentious, as they are typically linked to the distribution of resources, institutional authority, and political influence.

### 9.3.1. Clarification of the responsibilities of ministries

At the highest level of government, it is essential to determine which ministry should assume primary responsibility for implementation and enforcement, and how other relevant ministries should be involved. These decisions should be guided by the nature of the tasks and the specific expertise required for each. Additionally, it must be clearly established whether participating ministries should have veto powers over some issues, particularly where their mandates intersect or where specialised input is critical to decision-making.

### 9.3.2. Clarification of the responsible level of administration – central, regional, local, community level

Most African administrative systems recognise competence across multiple levels of governance, including federal, regional, and local authorities. It is, therefore, essential, both legally and practically, to clearly define which tasks are to be performed at which level. For example, the collection of field data may be most effectively carried out by local or regional entities with proximity to the land and communities, while the analysis of such data and the development of environmental quality standards may be more appropriately handled at the federal or national level, where greater technical and institutional capacity is available. Ultimately, the allocation of responsibilities should be tailored to each country's specific administrative structure and designed to integrate seamlessly with existing governance systems.

### 9.3.3. Clarification of science/administration/policy interface

Scientific advice is essential for the effective development and implementation of sustainable soil management policies. To support this, a dedicated scientific entity focused on soil issues should be established at the national or regional level. The mandate and competences of such an entity, particularly its role in decision-making processes such as permit approvals, urban planning, and the designation of protected soil areas, should be clearly defined by law. This legal clarity will help ensure that scientific expertise is systematically integrated into governance processes affecting soil health.

#### 9.3.4. Clarification of cooperation with traditional leaders

Finally, the cooperation between modern administrative institutions and traditional governance systems, which remain prevalent in most African states, particularly in rural areas, should be clearly defined by law. While this process may be politically and socially sensitive, legal clarity regarding the roles and competencies of each governance actor is essential. Such clarification can help prevent duplication of effort, reduce the risk of conflicting decisions, and promote more efficient, coordinated use of resources in implementing sustainable soil management policies.

### 9.4. Benefits

Establishing an effective administrative system to implement and enforce soil-related legal provisions is crucial to achieving sustainable soil management and delivering long-term benefits to the population. From this perspective, such a system is not optional but imperative.

Beyond its foundational necessity, an effective administrative system can yield several additional benefits: First, it enables more efficient use of limited resources. By reducing duplication and improving coordination, fewer inputs are required to achieve the same or better outcomes, which is especially important for resource-constrained societies. The savings generated can be redirected to meet other pressing needs. Second, it fosters accountability, reliability, and transparency—hallmarks of a modern, functional, and prosperous state. Third, from the citizens' perspective, such a system enhances public trust and reinforces the legitimacy of political institutions. Fourth, it helps establish a level playing field for all actors, including foreign investors. Reducing mismanagement, abuse of power, and corruption strengthens the rule of law and improves the overall governance environment.

Ultimately, an effective administrative system enhances the state's reputation, both domestically and internationally, as a credible and reliable partner. This, in turn, attracts long-term investment from domestic and foreign economic actors, enabling sustainable economic development that benefits both investors and society.

## 10. Commentary IX: Industry, infrastructure and projects, and energy transition

Soil degradation in Africa is primarily, but not uniquely, driven by agriculture, mining, industrialisation, infrastructure, and rapid urbanisation. This Commentary focuses on the soil impacts of industrial facilities and infrastructure projects, addressing: 1) the adverse effects of industrial waste and soil sealing, and 2) the impact of renewable energy infrastructure on soil management. It examines governance measures, including zoning, permits, and soil restoration and remediation mechanisms.

Africa is a rising renewable energy powerhouse, crucial for its industrialisation. With vast resources and growing demand, it is driving significant technological and infrastructural advancements. Abundant solar, wind, geothermal, and hydropower potential could add hundreds of gigawatts of capacity by 2030, especially through large-scale projects. However, this infrastructure build-up poses environmental challenges, particularly to the soil.

## 10.1. Description of soil-related challenges

### 10.1.1. Challenges in the construction of industrial facilities

Industrial development remains limited in several African countries. While many governments acknowledge the importance of industrialisation for economic growth and improved livelihoods, the establishment of key industrial zones often proceeds with insufficient attention to soil and environmental management. This imbalance has resulted in widespread environmental degradation. For example, in Nigeria's Niger Delta and along oil pipeline corridors in Angola, frequent oil spills continue to pollute soil and water resources, underscoring the serious consequences of inadequate environmental oversight and regulatory enforcement.

Most industries in African countries lack international environmental certifications, such as ISO 14001, which promotes the development of effective environmental management systems and accountability for environmental impacts. In the absence of such standards, many industries discharge pollutants that contribute significantly to soil degradation and broader ecological harm. Furthermore, refinery operations across the continent are significant sources of soil and marine pollution, particularly due to the indiscriminate disposal of sludge and other hazardous by-products. The weak enforcement of environmental laws and regulations exacerbates these challenges.

Soil conservation is not prioritised in development planning, even as Africa's growing population, rapid urbanisation, and infrastructure development continue. Legal measures have not evolved to address these challenges, often sidelining soil conservation in favour of production/construction goals. Zoning approaches are not sufficiently implemented to protect valuable soil compartments.

Infrastructure development is often associated with massive land clearing, deforestation, soil compaction, sealing, and alteration of natural drainage patterns, leading to soil degradation and loss of fertility.

Industrial development must be aligned with food production to ensure sustainable growth. Building industrial facilities and infrastructural projects on agricultural land should be avoided.

### 10.1.2. Challenges in renewable energy and industrial facilities

In response to the immense continental potential, increasing energy demand, and global climate commitments, many African countries are implementing policies to accelerate the adoption of renewable energy sources. Some countries are revising their energy frameworks to incentivise clean energy investments and infrastructure through tax incentives, feed-in tariffs, and streamlined permitting processes.[21] These policy shifts pave the way for a more favourable investment climate, increasing demand for technological innovations, and boosting infrastructure. This, in turn, creates a significant demand for land and, consequently, negatively impacts soil and other natural resources. Emerging technologies, such as advanced energy storage systems and smart grid solutions, are enhancing the reliability and integration of renewable energy sources.[22] Innovations in micro-grid and off-grid solutions significantly extend electricity access to remote and underserved communities, driving inclusive economic growth.

Despite these promising trends, most African countries face several challenges in their transition to renewable energy, including infrastructure limitations. In many regions, outdated or insufficient grid infrastructure is hampering the integration of renewable energy projects. Investments in modernising transmission networks are crucial to ensure that newly generated renewable power reaches consumers reliably.

While the energy transition presents opportunities, it also requires significant investment in infrastructure and technology. Africa's urbanisation has concentrated demand for household building materials and services. This presents a novel opportunity for African countries to advance climate-resilient manufacturing and industrialisation by developing low-carbon regional value chains that meet this demand.

Developing robust energy infrastructure is more than just constructing power stations. It involves a complex system of interconnected components, including long-distance transmission lines that distribute electricity across entire countries, pipeline networks that transport oil and natural gas, sophisticated refineries that process raw materials into usable fuels, and a diverse transportation system encompassing maritime and rail logistics. This infrastructure is the foundation for powering our homes, businesses, and industries. Africa's development is at a critical juncture. Therefore, rapid and substantial investment in essential public services, such as schools and

21 GIZ (2020).
22 Kataray et al. (2023).

hospitals, as well as in all economic sectors, is necessary to accelerate this process to drive meaningful progress.

The establishment of green energy systems is often funded by foreign investments, which may lead to high energy exports to foreign countries. This could be detrimental to the domestic population and seen as neocolonialism.

Industrial infrastructure construction often involves land conversion and clearing, resulting in the loss of fertile soil and land degradation. Agricultural expansion, urbanisation, infrastructure development, mining, and unsustainable logging practices are the main drivers of deforestation and soil degradation.

Sustainability in infrastructure is critical across multiple sectors, particularly in the design, construction, engineering, and operation of electric grids, oil and gas facilities, hydrogen infrastructure, and buildings. Integrating environmental, social, and governance (ESG) principles into these systems ensures that development meets present needs without compromising the ability of future generations to meet their own needs. Sustainable infrastructure practices enhance resource efficiency, reduce environmental impacts, and contribute to climate resilience and long-term economic viability.

Climate change remains a significant threat impeding the pathway to sustainable development for many African countries. Extreme climatic conditions have impacted key economic sectors, including agriculture, infrastructure, energy, and forestry. Given the prevailing climatic conditions, agricultural production is expected to decline. Other African countries are also facing climate-related challenges, such as drought, which is negatively impacting energy production and exacerbating food insecurity.

Industry and infrastructure are governed by various laws and regulations to mitigate adverse impacts on land and the environment. Environmental legislation requires infrastructure and industry developers to conduct EIAs to assess the potential effects on land, natural resources, and local communities. An environmental permit must be obtained before any industrial or infrastructure project begins, stipulating the conditions necessary to minimise environmental impacts.

Spatial planning requires that industrial and infrastructure projects align with established land use and urban development plans. This includes the clear designation of industrial zones, protected areas, and environmentally sensitive sites. To minimise adverse impacts on land resources, such projects must comply with construction and waste management standards. This entails adopting sustainable construction techniques, responsible siting, and implementing efficient, environmentally sound waste management practices.

Government authorities must actively monitor and regulate industrial and construction activities to ensure full compliance with environmental laws and policies. Regular inspections should be conducted to identify violations and enforce appropriate corrective measures. Promoting environmental responsibility among developers is essential, including the mandatory rehabilitation of project sites upon completion to restore degraded soil and minimise long-term ecological harm.

### 10.2. Options for legal governance mechanisms

A comprehensive and integrated approach is necessary when considering legal governance mechanisms to address the impact of industrial facilities, infrastructure projects, and the energy transition on soil prevention and restoration in Africa.

#### 10.2.1. Environmental Impact Assessments (EIAs) and Strategic Environmental Assessments (SEAs)

Mechanism:

- Mandatory EIAs for all industrial and infrastructural projects, including renewable energy installations, that may significantly impact the soil with a specific "soil impact assessment" pursuant to Article 14 of the Model Law.
- SEAs for energy transition policies and plans, assessing cumulative impacts on soil resources.

Purpose:

- Identify and mitigate potential soil degradation risks early in the planning process.
- Ensure sustainable development practices.

Implementation:

- Establish clear EIA/SEA guidelines, including soil-specific assessment criteria.
- Ensure public participation and access to information.
- Strengthen the capacity of environmental authorities.

#### 10.2.2. Land use planning and zoning regulations

Mechanism:

- Develop and enforce land use plans that designate industrial, infrastructure, and renewable energy development areas, considering soil sensitivity and ecological vulnerability.
- Implement zoning regulations to control land conversion and prevent soil degradation.

Purpose:

- Minimise soil disturbance and protect fertile agricultural lands.
- Promote sustainable land use practices.

Implementation:

- Integrate soil health considerations into spatial planning.
- Strengthen local government capacity for land use management.
- Ensure community involvement in land use planning.

### 10.2.3. Soil protection and restoration laws

Mechanism:

- Enact specific laws that protect soil resources, regulate soil disturbance, and promote soil conservation practices.
- Establish legal frameworks for soil restoration and remediation of contaminated sites.

Purpose:

- Prevent soil erosion, compaction, and contamination.
- Ensure the restoration of degraded soils.

Implementation:

- Develop soil quality standards and guidelines.
- Establish enforcement mechanisms and penalties for violations.
- Provide incentives for soil restoration and sustainable land management.

### 10.2.4. Waste management regulations

Mechanism:

- Develop and enforce regulations for industrial waste management, including hazardous waste disposal and effluent discharge.
- Promote waste reduction, recycling, and reuse.

Purpose:

- Prevent soil contamination from industrial waste.
- Minimise the environmental footprint of industrial activities.

Implementation:

- Establish waste treatment and disposal standards.

- Strengthen monitoring and enforcement of waste management regulations.
- Promote circular economy principles.

#### 10.2.5. Water resources management laws

Mechanism:

- Implement integrated water resources management laws that regulate water abstraction, protect water quality, and promote water conservation.
- Address soil salinisation and waterlogging issues related to irrigation and drainage.

Purpose:

- Prevent soil degradation caused by unsustainable water use.
- Ensure equitable access to water resources.

Implementation:

- Establish water allocation mechanisms and water quality standards.
- Promote water-efficient irrigation practices.
- Address transboundary water issues.

#### 10.2.6. Contractual agreements and investment treaties

Mechanism:

- Incorporate soil protection clauses into investment contracts and bilateral/multilateral investment treaties (BITs/MITs).
- Establish dispute resolution mechanisms for soil-related issues.

Purpose:

- Set clear environmental obligations for investors.
- Ensure accountability for soil degradation.

Implementation:

- Develop model contract clauses and treaty provisions.
- Strengthen the capacity of dispute resolution bodies.

### 10.2.7. Community participation and empowerment

Mechanism:

- Establish legal mechanisms for community participation in environmental monitoring and enforcing soil protection laws.
- Promote community-based soil management initiatives.

Purpose:

- Enhance local ownership and promote sustainable land management practices.
- Ensure that environmental policies reflect community needs and priorities.

Implementation:

- Provide access to information and capacity building for community organisations.
- Establish mechanisms for public participation in decision-making.

## 10.3. Concrete text for legal provisions

Specific legal provisions can be integrated into national and regional frameworks to effectively address the impact of industrial development, infrastructure, and the energy transition on African soils.

Environmental Impact Assessments (EIAs) and Strategic Environmental Assessments (SEAs)

(1) All industrial facilities and infrastructure projects, including renewable energy installations exceeding [specified size/capacity], shall undergo a mandatory Environmental and Social Impact Assessment (ESIA) before approval. The ESIA shall include a comprehensive soil impact assessment, detailing potential risks of soil degradation and associated mitigation measures.

(2) Article 14 of the Model Law concerning a specific 'soil impact assessment' shall apply.

(3) Strategic Environmental Assessments (SEAs) shall be conducted for national and regional energy transition plans, evaluating the cumulative impacts of renewable energy infrastructure development on soil resources. These SEAs shall inform policy decisions and project planning.

(4) The ESIA must contain a soil remediation and restoration plan in case of soil contamination.

Land use planning and zoning regulations

(1) Municipalities shall develop land use plans that designate areas for industrial, infrastructure, and renewable energy development, considering soil sensitivity and ecological vulnerability. Conversion of prime agricultural land for industrial or infrastructure purposes shall be prohibited unless justified by overriding public interest and accompanied by compensatory measures.

(2) Zoning regulations shall establish buffer zones around industrial facilities and infrastructure projects to minimise soil disturbance and protect surrounding ecosystems. These buffer zones shall be maintained as natural or semi-natural areas.

(3) Renewable energy installations, such as solar and wind farms, shall be sited on degraded or marginal lands whenever feasible to minimise impacts on fertile agricultural soils.

Soil protection and restoration laws

(1) Industrial facilities shall implement soil erosion control measures during construction and operation, including using sediment traps, contour ploughing, and revegetation of disturbed areas. Soil compaction shall be minimised using appropriate construction equipment and techniques.

(2) Contaminated soil resulting from industrial activities shall be remediated to meet soil quality standards established by the national environmental authority. The polluter shall bear the cost of remediation.

(3) The removal and stockpiling of topsoil during construction activities must be done in a way that preserves the biological and chemical properties of the soil.

(4) A national soil health monitoring network shall be established to track soil quality trends and assess the effectiveness of soil protection measures.

Waste management regulations

(1) Industrial facilities shall implement closed-loop systems to minimise waste generation and promote recycling and reuse. Hazardous waste shall be treated and disposed of in accordance with national and international standards.

(2) Effluent discharge from industrial facilities shall comply with water quality standards that protect soil health. Irrigation with treated wastewater shall be subject to soil monitoring and control measures to prevent salinisation and contamination.

(3) Regulations concerning the disposal of solar panels and wind turbine components, at the end of their life cycles, must be established and enforced.

Water resources management laws

(1) Large-scale irrigation projects shall be subject to water use permits and soil salinity monitoring requirements. Water-efficient irrigation technologies shall be promoted to minimise waterlogging and salinisation.
(2) Infrastructure projects, such as roads and railways, shall incorporate stormwater management measures to prevent soil erosion and flooding. These measures shall include using permeable pavements, rain gardens, and constructed wetlands.

Contractual agreements and investment treaties

(1) Investment contracts and bilateral/multilateral investment treaties (BITs/MITs) shall include clauses that explicitly recognise the host state's right to regulate in the public interest, including protecting soil resources. Investors shall be required to comply with national soil protection laws and regulations.
(2) Dispute resolution mechanisms in investment treaties shall consider the environmental impacts of investment projects, including soil degradation. Compensation for soil damage shall be based on the principle of full reparation.

Community participation and empowerment

(1) Local communities shall have the right to participate in environmental monitoring and enforcing soil protection laws. Community-based soil management initiatives shall be supported through capacity building and resource access.
(2) A public environmental complaints mechanism shall be established to report soil degradation incidents related to industrial facilities and infrastructure projects. Whistleblowers shall be protected from retaliation.

## 11. Commentary X: Mining

Mining remains a predominant economic pillar for most African countries, following oil and gas, agriculture, and tourism.[23] It serves as a cornerstone of industrial development, driven by the continent's vast mineral wealth and the rising global demand for strategic resources such as lithium, nickel, graphite, and cobalt, particularly to support energy transitions and accelerated industrialisation. Africa holds approximately 30% of the world's known mineral deposits, including diamonds, cobalt, gold, copper, and uranium, which are extensively mined and contribute significantly to fiscal revenues.[24] While mining intensity varies by mineral and

---

23 Chuhan-Pole et al. (2017).
24 See https://www.unep.org/regions/africa/our-work-africa/, accessed 29 September 2025.

country, 42 of Africa's 55 states are classified as resource-dependent.[25] Among these, eighteen rely primarily on non-fuel minerals, ten on energy or fuel exports, and the remainder on agricultural commodities.

This Commentary highlights three key factors driving the prevalence of mining activities across Africa. First is the availability of strategic mineral resources within specific countries. Second is the degree of economic diversification away from extractive sectors towards alternatives such as tourism and agriculture. Third is the dominant type of mining, which can be either artisanal and small-scale, industrial, large-scale, or a combination of both. These factors—mineral availability, economic diversification, and the mining model—collectively shape the intensity and nature of mining across the continent. For instance, leading gold-producing countries such as South Africa, Burkina Faso, Guinea, and Mali face distinct soil and environmental challenges compared to nations predominantly mining copper and cobalt (e.g., the Democratic Republic of Congo and Zambia) or those centred on diamond extraction (such as Botswana and Namibia).[26]

### 11.1. Description of challenges

Despite generating significant economic and social benefits, both large-scale and artisanal and small-scale mining (ASM) activities pose serious environmental risks to soil across much of Africa. Although many African countries have enacted ecological and mining legislation aimed at mitigating such damage, substantial gaps remain in the practical implementation, compliance, and enforcement of these laws. These deficiencies hinder the ability to balance the gains of the extractive sector with the imperatives of sustainable soil and environmental stewardship.

Both industrial large-scale mining and ASM result in extensive land degradation, albeit through different mechanisms. Industrial mining typically causes severe soil and land disruption through large-scale excavation and the development of deep underground galleries, often rendering land permanently unsuitable for agricultural use. In gold-producing countries, mining activities frequently contaminate soil with toxic substances, including mercury and cyanide, which pose significant health risks to surrounding communities. One of the most critical environmental concerns associated with both mining and mineral processing is the contamination of soils, river systems, and crops through direct emissions and tailings-dam effluents.

Strong political will is essential to ensure the effectiveness of mining regulations that mitigate the environmental impacts of both industrial and artisanal mining. The success of these regulations depends not only on their existence but also on their

25 See https://360mozambique.com/world/africa/top-ten-african-countries-that-heavily-depend-on-mining-exports/, accessed 29 September 2025.

26 Ibid.

consistent implementation, the awareness of all relevant stakeholders, and the strict enforcement of sanctions for non-compliance. However, in many African countries, these efforts are undermined by significant shortcomings, including inadequate environmental standards and weak enforcement mechanisms within existing ecological and mining legislation. Further arising challenges are specified below.

### 11.1.1. Industrial large-scale mining, often undertaken by foreign investors

Industrial and large-scale mining investments in Africa often begin with the acquisition of vast tracts of land, frequently through unfair or illegal means that disregard customary or indigenous land tenure systems. As highlighted in the commentary on land tenure, tenure insecurity, exacerbated by the coexistence of customary and statutory regimes and by the fact that approximately 90% of rural land remains undocumented, poses a significant obstacle to sustainable soil management. This legal ambiguity exposes communities to dispossession, as they lack effective legal recourse when governments allocate their lands to investors.

To safeguard customary land rights and promote soil protection, more inclusive and participatory consultation processes are required to ensure that local communities give free, prior, and informed consent before mining licences are issued. The link between tenure insecurity and soil degradation becomes particularly pronounced in this context. Soil degradation caused by industrial mining spans all phases of the mining lifecycle—preparatory, operational, and closure—resulting in long-term environmental harm. Large foreign conglomerates, which dominate the sector, often fail to implement adequate ecological safeguards. Their operations frequently involve the use of toxic substances such as mercury and cyanide, which degrade soil health, contaminate ecosystems, and harm local livelihoods.

This is compounded by weak regulatory enforcement and investment regimes that favour investors, offering tax incentives and long-term leases, without adequately holding them accountable for environmental impacts. Despite expectations that investors operate within host states' legal frameworks, numerous examples across Africa illustrate how these frameworks fail to address the resulting soil and environmental damage, particularly in the mining sector. Moreover, pollution from industrial mining, particularly from tailings dams and hazardous waste, is often poorly monitored and insufficiently addressed in current legislation, resulting in widespread soil contamination with heavy metals and other toxins.

### 11.1.2. Legal and illegal artisanal and small-scale mining by both foreign investors and local communities

The statistics indicate that 70–80% of African artisanal and small-scale mining operations are illegal, while 20–30% are legal but often improperly overseen, monitored, and evaluated.[27] Failure to consider these dynamics leads to the implementation of inappropriate legislation and industry support schemes. In the case of sub-Saharan Africa, the predominantly 'top-down' approach taken to formalise and support ASM has resulted, inter alia, in the dissemination of inappropriate processing and environmental technologies; the implementation of bureaucratic licensing schemes; and the design of ineffective and/or incompatible regulations.

The dynamics of artisanal and small-scale mining in sub-Saharan Africa vary from country to country but present similar challenges. This type of mining focuses on extracting a wide range of—predominantly—precious minerals and stones, including gold, sapphires, and diamonds. Complex labour hierarchies characterise it, as do unique forms of production and informal systems of assistance, all of which have evolved, for the most part, in an environment devoid of regulation.

A new phenomenon across much of Africa is that artisanal and small-scale mining is being illegally driven by foreign investors who avoid the formalities of large-scale industrial mining. This illegal artisanal and small-scale mining may be carried out using sophisticated machinery, thereby compromising the rural environment and soil more than anticipated.

### 11.1.3. Incidents caused by both industrial large-scale and artisanal and small-scale mining

The core dimensions of good governance with respect to mining include:

- Consideration of the interests of the local communities, primarily concerning access to land;
- mitigating adverse effects on the environment, on soils, and on human health; and
- sharing economic benefits—the interest of the local communities and society in gaining financial benefits from the mining activities.

27 Ondanyo et al. (2024).

## 11.2. Options for legal governance mechanisms

### 11.2.1. Industrial mining, often undertaken by foreign investors: EIA soil standards, permission procedures, CSR, transnational cooperation

Industrial and large-scale mining can harm the environment and natural resources, including soil. Therefore, African countries need to enact mining legislation that minimises these adverse effects and recognises and values the interests of local communities. This necessitates periodic reviews and updates to mining law and policy to ensure alignment with international best practices. Strict environmental standards, including soil standards, must also be implemented. Comprehensive regulations relating to mining waste management, site rehabilitation and remediation, and biodiversity protection must be enacted.

The integration of Corporate Social Responsibility (CSR) should be required of mining companies, with a focus on community engagement, local job creation, and the development of social infrastructure. Institutional capacity building is also necessary to ensure that government agencies can enforce policies effectively and efficiently. Additionally, research and development efforts should be encouraged to foster innovation in environmentally friendly soil management technologies.

Outside direct mining activities, African states need strengthened transparency requirements for foreign contracts and financial flows, particularly in the case of large-scale industrial mining. It is essential to promote local participation and CSR while also ensuring compliance with and enforcement of environmental standards.

With Africa's evolving technological outlook, it is possible to establish anonymous reporting mechanisms for violations and create strong national public online platforms for transparent access to environmental impact reports, mining permits, and data on emissions, mining waste, and soil degradation. Innovative technologies, such as drones and remote monitoring, are also encouraged to improve environmental oversight.

### 11.2.2. Official artisanal and small-scale mining: same, stronger involvement of traditional leaders

The initiatives in this section can be institutionalised through the traditional leadership structures of local communities. Artisanal and small-scale mining is essential for local community participation and socio-economic needs across Africa, contributing to economic growth and employment in many African nations. African governments must encourage responsibility through training, financial support, and incentives for implementing sustainable soil governance. Additionally, institutional capacity-building is necessary to ensure that government regulatory agencies can effectively enforce policies and legislation that address the adverse effects of mining on soils across Africa.

Artisanal and small-scale mining is primarily informal and unorganised, with minimal support or intervention from African governments. A dedicated continental and regional approach based on multi-sectoral and multidisciplinary cooperation would be needed to invest in, improve, and adopt affordable, cleaner, safer, and more efficient alternative mining techniques. Incidents caused by industrial mining must be subject to strict liability, ensuring that the polluter pays for all consequential harm. This will help to address detrimental environmental effects, injury, diseases, and premature deaths.

#### 11.2.3. Illegal mining, mainly in the form of small-scale or artisanal mining

Providing a coordinated assessment of environmental and public health issues associated with artisanal and small-scale mining in Africa is essential. While illegal mining must be severely sanctioned, it is crucial to minimise it by establishing a conducive and simplified legal framework that facilitates artisanal mining.

### 11.3. Concrete text for legal provisions

The proposed legal text may be integrated into existing mining and environmental laws, as each country deems fit. The provisions must be tailored to each country's circumstances. While many suggestions may be proposed for mining, this text primarily focuses on soil conservation in the mining sector.

Legislative text is essential in the following:

Interpretation
"Artisanal mining" refers to traditional and customary mining operations that primarily utilise rudimentary methods and manual tools to extract minerals from the surface and shallow depths.
"Minerals" refer to (…) [definition should include soil]
"Small-scale mining" concerns (…) [definition may limit the area of mining coverage, number of people employed, amount of initial investment made, and amount of ore produced in a year, etc.]
"Large-scale mining" concerns (…) [definition may limit the area of mining coverage, number of people employed, amount of initial investment made, and amount of ore produced in a year, etc.]

International mining standards

(1) Any prospecting or mining operation must be conducted in accordance with good international mining industry practice.

(2) The principles set out in [environmental legislation] shall
   (a) apply to all prospecting and mining operations and any matter or activity relating to such operation; and
   (b) serve as guidelines for the interpretation, administration, and implementation of the environmental requirements of this [mining] law.

Regulation of small-scale and artisanal mining[28]

(1) A person who intends to carry on any artisanal mining, small-scale mining, or large-scale mining shall apply to the [competent authority] for an appropriate mining licence in the prescribed manner and form on payment of a prescribed fee.

(2) Artisanal mining shall only be undertaken by a [citizen] or a [co-operative wholly composed of citizens] or [any person].

(3) Small-scale mining shall only be undertaken by a [wholly citizen-owned company] or [a body corporate having a minimum of (...) percent of its shares held by citizens of [Country X]; or a co-operative society registered in [Country X] having a minimum of (...) percent of its member being citizens of [Country X].

Environmental/Soil Impact Assessments[29]

(1) In accordance with good international mining industry standards, the applicant for a mining licence or any renewal of either shall prepare and submit a comprehensive Environmental Impact Assessment (EIA).

(2) The EIA shall contain a specific "soil impact assessment" pursuant to Article 14 of the Model Law.

(3) Notwithstanding subsection (1), an application for a small scale mining licence shall be accompanied by a report on the anticipated impact of mining operations on the environment and any measures to be taken to assess, prevent, or minimise such impact, including proposals for –
   (a) the prevention or treatment of soil pollution;
   (b) the treatment and disposal of waste; and

28 This section deals with eligibility requirements, requirements for a licence application to an appropriate mining licence, and a specific requirement for development.

29 Soil management and conservation plans should include the segregation, proper placement, and stockpiling of clean soils and overburden material for site remediation. If topsoil is pre-stripped, it must be stored for future rehabilitation to preserve its integrity. Storage areas should be temporarily protected or vegetated to prevent erosion, and any exposed soils or erodible materials should be promptly revegetated or covered. Subsection (3) requires SSMs to submit a simplified environmental impact assessment.

(c) the reclamation and rehabilitation of land and soil disturbed by mining operations.

Environmental considerations

(1) In considering whether to grant a mining licence, the competent authority shall consider the need to –

(a) conserve and protect the soil and features of cultural, architectural, archaeological, historical, or geological interests;

(b) ensure that any mining or mineral processing activity prevents any adverse socio-economic impact or harm to human health, in or on the land over which the right or licence is sought; and

(2) A mining licence holder shall implement appropriate soil conservation measures before, during, and after mining operations.

Soil rehabilitation and remediation processes[30]

(1) The holder of a mining licence shall ensure that their mining area is rehabilitated from time to time and ultimately reclaimed, so far as is practicable, in a manner acceptable to the competent authority.

(2) Notwithstanding subsection (1), during and after operations in any mine, excavation, or waste dump, the licence holder must take necessary measures to maintain and restore topsoil and return the land substantially to its original condition.

(3) If there is any dispute as to the extent of the measures necessary to comply with the requirements of this section, the holder of a mining licence may refer the question to arbitration.

(4) If a mining licence holder fails to meet the obligations under this section, the Minister may restore the area after notifying the holder and granting a reasonable period for action. The restoration cost becomes a debt owed to the government, recoverable in a competent court.

(5) The competent authority may cancel the mining licence where the mining licence holder does not comply with the terms of the mining licence.

30 Generally, holders of small-scale mining licences are the same as holders of large-scale exploitation licences, except that certain environmental, social, labour, and reporting obligations are often lighter for SSM licence holders because their operations are smaller in size and impact. Their licences are shorter than the terms of large-scale exploitation licences, and their projects involve a much smaller investment.

Capacity building[31]

(1) The competent authority shall regularly conduct a training course for [any person] or [artisanal miners] who apply for a licence under this law and do not have relevant qualifications.
(2) A course, in accordance with subsection (1), shall cover topics such as good mining practices and soil resource management in mining.
(3) A holder of a small-scale mining licence or large-scale mining licence shall carry out a scheme of training and employment of local employees in each phase and level of operations, taking into account the safety requirements and the need to maintain acceptable standards of efficiency in the conduct of the operations.
(4) Failure by a holder of a mining right to comply with the provisions of subsection (3) shall be regarded as a material breach. If such a person holds a small-scale or large-scale mining licence, the licence may be suspended or cancelled.

Risk monitoring and management measures for artisanal and small-scale mining[32]

(1) A competent authority may, at a reasonable time, and on the production of the appropriate authorisation
  (a) enter, inspect, and examine a mine in a manner that does not unnecessarily impede or obstruct the working of the mine;
  (b) examine and inquire into
    (i) the state and condition of a mine or part of the mine and of matters and things that pertain to the mine in so far as they relate to the safety or health of persons employed in the mine; and
    (ii) matters relating to these regulations, to minimise environmental damage caused by mining and mining-related operations.
  (c) enforce compliance with these regulations.
(2) A competent authority may, by written notice to a holder of a mining licence or the manager of a mine, order

31 This provision enables the government to develop skills for artisanal miners. Additionally, SSMs and large-scale mining operators are required to provide training to their employees. The government may offer refund-based incentives to companies that provide such training. Effective compliance monitoring requires significant government capacity; where capacity is limited, mining licence holders should publish annual progress reports to facilitate public oversight.

32 Mine inspections ensure operations comply with legal standards. Most mining laws, health and safety regulations, and national laws mandate regular inspections, as reflected in the ILO Safety and Health in Mines Convention, 1995 (No. 176). Consequently, countries often require biannual or annual inspections, as well as one before a new mine opens. Investigative inspections targeting high-risk areas or practices may follow risk assessments or complaints, underscoring the need for anonymous non-compliance reporting by the public and mine workers. Effective inspections rely on inspectors' expertise and clear procedural rules, with non-compliance leading to remediation opportunities or penalties based on the level of risk.

(a) the cessation of operations in, and the withdrawal of any or all persons from the mine or part of the mine where the inspector considers necessary in the interest of safety, health, or the environment; or

(b) the holder or the manager of the mine to remedy the situation immediately or within the time specified by the Inspector.

Corporate Social Responsibility[33]

(1) The holder of a small-scale or large-scale mining licence shall assist in the development of mining communities affected by its operations to promote sustainable development, enhance the general welfare and the quality of life of the inhabitants, and shall recognise and respect the rights, customs, traditions, and religion of local communities.

(2) In pursuance of subsection (1), the holder of a small-scale or large-scale mining licence shall enter into a written community development agreement with the host community.

(3) The community development agreement shall consider the unique circumstances of the licence holder and host community. Issues to be addressed in the agreement may include environmental and socio-economic management methods and procedures, as well as enhancements to local governance.

(4) A community development agreement agreed and signed by the authorised representatives of a small-scale or large-scale mining licence and its host community shall be submitted for approval to the competent authority, who shall, if the agreement meets the relevant requirements, approve such agreement within [X] calendar days of it being submitted.

Reports and access to data

(1) A mining licence holder shall maintain records of all geological information obtained by, or on behalf of, the holder, including data on soil properties.

(2) A mining licence holder shall submit to the competent authority the geological information obtained by, or on behalf of, the holder.

33 A key factor in promoting community development is aligning corporate social responsibility with local goals. The laws should clearly guide the negotiation and drafting of Community Development Agreements (CDAs), which must require consultation with local communities to set project priorities and ensure alignment with local government development plans. Additionally, CDAs should establish formal mechanisms, such as a representative committee comprising the mining company, the local community, and the government, to monitor implementation, produce annual progress reports, and hold regular meetings.

## 12. Commentary XI: Migration

A complex interplay of push factors and pull factors, including national movements, cross-border flows, conflict, and environmental stressors, shapes migration in Africa. These migration patterns have significant implications for land use across the continent. In many cases, migration leads to the abandonment of agricultural land, particularly in rural areas, which contributes to land degradation and shifts in land management practices. According to the Intergovernmental Panel on Climate Change (IPCC), global warming is projected to drive a sharp increase in internal displacement, with estimates ranging from 51 to 100 million internal migrants by 2050.[34] Economic pressures, including the search for employment, declining agricultural profitability, and limited financial resources, are major drivers of rural-urban migration in Africa. These dynamics particularly affect the youth, who often leave rural areas in pursuit of better opportunities, resulting in ageing populations and increasing tracts of uncultivated land. Environmental stressors, such as land degradation, water scarcity, and the growing frequency of extreme weather events, further compel communities to migrate in search of more viable agricultural conditions. Moreover, conflict, political instability, and insecure land tenure discourage long-term investment in land and soil management, frequently leading to the abandonment of farmland and the breakdown of rural livelihoods.

Recognising these complex dynamics, the Migration Policy Framework for Africa and its Plan of Action (2018–2030) provides a comprehensive roadmap for managing migration effectively while maximising its developmental benefits.[35] It promotes the protection of migrants' rights, regional cooperation, and the integration of migration into national development plans. In this Commentary, the term "migration" refers to the movement of people across national or international borders, whether voluntary or involuntary, driven by various factors[36] that may influence sustainable soil management. This Commentary examines the challenges and opportunities associated with African migration in the context of sustainable soil management and explores legal and policy options to enhance migration governance.

### 12.1. Challenges

Managing migration for various reasons poses significant challenges, especially (albeit not uniquely) concerning soil management. When people migrate within a country or

34 See https://www.ipcc.ch/report/ar6/wg2/downloads/report/IPCC_AR6_WGII_Chapter16.pdf.
35 See https://au.int/sites/default/files/documents/35956-doc-au-mpfa-executive-summary-eng.pdf.
36 See https://www.fao.org/migration/en, accessed 29 September 2025.

across borders, it can impact agricultural practices, land use patterns, and soil quality in several ways.

### 12.1.1. Land abandonment

Migration often leads to agricultural land abandonment as farmers leave rural areas in search of "greener pastures," better opportunities in urban centres, or abroad. This can result in neglected farmland, leading to soil degradation and a loss of fertility. Land abandonment due to migration is a growing global challenge with far-reaching environmental, economic, and social consequences. From a soil management perspective, the consequences of land abandonment are immediate and long-term. Without active farming practices, abandoned land becomes vulnerable to erosion, compaction, and nutrient depletion.[37] As soil conservation methods such as crop rotation and organic fertilisation are no longer employed. Over time, this reduces the land's ability to support sustainable agriculture. The lack of soil management also encourages the growth of invasive plant species, which alter soil composition and further degrade its quality. In regions prone to extreme weather events, such as droughts or heavy rainfall, the absence of protective vegetation exacerbates soil erosion. While some abandoned land may experience a "fallow effect," in which natural regeneration of soil properties occurs, this is contingent on the land remaining undisturbed by overgrazing or illegal cultivation. Land abandonment also triggers a feedback loop: as soil quality declines and agricultural activity decreases, rural economies suffer, further driving migration and intensifying the cycle of land degradation.

### 12.1.2. Changes in land use and agricultural practices

Migration can significantly affect agricultural practices and soil management, with both positive and negative consequences. Migrants often introduce new agrarian techniques or abandon traditional practices, which can affect soil health and productivity. In regions where migrants settle, agricultural land may be converted to residential or commercial use, altering soil composition and reducing its capacity to support sustainable agriculture. The forced displacement of people due to violence, political instability, or resource-based conflicts places additional pressure on host regions, resulting in overexploitation of fragile ecosystems and further soil degradation. In some cases, unplanned agricultural expansion by displaced populations leads to unsustainable practices such as slash-and-burn farming, accelerating

37 Maxwell (2025).

deforestation,[38] soil erosion, and biodiversity loss. However, abandoned lands in conflict-affected areas may naturally regenerate due to the fallow effect, allowing them to recover specific chemical, physical, and biological properties. On the other hand, the abandonment of farmlands can lead to a loss of soil fertility, erosion, compaction, and the invasion of non-native plant species. Meanwhile, in areas receiving migrants, agricultural intensification often leads to the overuse of chemical fertilisers, pesticides, and other inputs, degrading soil health over time.

### 12.1.3. Pressure on urban infrastructure and environmental impacts

Rapid migration from rural to urban areas places significant pressure on urban infrastructure while posing serious challenges to soil management and ecological sustainability. As cities expand, fertile agricultural land is often converted into urban areas,[39] leading to soil sealing that prevents water absorption, disrupts drainage systems, and increases the risk of flooding and food insecurity. Unregulated urbanisation also contributes to soil pollution through improper waste disposal and industrial activities, degrading land quality. The loss of vegetation exacerbates soil erosion, making areas more prone to landslides and sedimentation in water bodies. Large-scale migration can have broader environmental consequences, including deforestation, habitat loss, and increased pressure on natural resources, which negatively impact soil quality and the provision of ecosystem services. Food security is also threatened, as reduced local agricultural production drives up prices and increases reliance on food imports. The rapid urban expansion into abandoned farmland exacerbates resource competition, making land restoration efforts more difficult.

## 12.2. Options for legal governance mechanisms

Migration-driven land abandonment presents significant challenges to soil management and environmental sustainability. Without proper intervention, abandoned agricultural lands are vulnerable to erosion, nutrient depletion, and biodiversity loss. To prevent soil degradation and promote sustainable land use, preventive measures that support land restoration, enhance agricultural practices, and mitigate environmental pressures in both rural and urban areas are essential. Effective governance mechanisms, including policy interventions, financial incentives, and

38 Kyere-Boateng & Marek (2021).
39 Omasire (2024).

community engagement, safeguard soil health and ensure long-term environmental resilience amid land-use changes associated with migration.

### 12.2.1. Preventive measures for soil degradation on abandoned land

The following options are possible for preventing soil degradation due to migration:

(1) Implement soil conservation programs, incentivise land restoration, and implement specific policies addressing abandoned agricultural lands.
(2) Encouraging rural-urban linkages can help mitigate the effects of migration on both urban infrastructure and rural agricultural systems.
(3) Engaging multiple stakeholders, including local governments, NGOs, private sector actors, and migrants

To prevent soil degradation from abandoned agricultural land, governments can implement soil conservation programs that incentivise land restoration. Programs could include financial support for landowners to rehabilitate degraded land and reintroduce sustainable farming practices such as crop rotation, organic fertilisation, and agroforestry. In conflict-affected areas, international organisations and governments can collaborate to promote soil restoration and provide technical support for land regeneration. Specific policies addressing abandoned agricultural lands, such as incentivising natural regeneration or supporting the reintroduction of agriculture or agroforestry, could help mitigate the impacts of migration-driven land abandonment. Governments can offer grants or subsidies to private landowners and community groups to invest in land restoration, soil rehabilitation, and biodiversity conservation.

Governance mechanisms could focus on fostering economic opportunities in rural areas, such as through rural development programs that create jobs and reduce the need to migrate. Strengthening connections between urban and rural areas through transportation, trade, and technology can also facilitate the sustainable exchange of resources and ideas that support soil management and agricultural practices.

Create effective governance mechanisms that facilitate the integration of migrants into new areas. This includes encouraging participatory planning for land-use decisions and promoting collaboration among urban planners, environmentalists, and agricultural experts to ensure that urban and rural communities are supported in sustainably managing their land and resources.

### 12.2.2. Improving land use and agricultural practices

Improving land use and agricultural practices is possible through:

(1) Strengthening land tenure systems in areas experiencing migration, especially those with displaced populations.
(2) Implementing policies that grant land rights to migrants and displaced populations.
(3) Promoting sustainable agricultural practices among new migrants and existing rural populations.

In areas experiencing migration, especially those with displaced populations, strengthening land tenure systems can provide security for migrants and existing residents. Secure land tenure encourages investment in land restoration and sustainable agricultural practices. Governments can implement policies that grant land rights to migrants and displaced populations, ensuring that they can access and sustainably manage land for agricultural purposes.

Governance mechanisms can focus on promoting sustainable agricultural practices among both new migrants and existing rural populations. This includes supporting the adoption of agroecology, agroforestry, and organic farming practices. Farmers should receive education and extension services on soil management techniques that enhance soil fertility and prevent erosion. Additionally, displaced populations should be trained on sustainable farming techniques to prevent environmental degradation.

### 12.2.3. Reducing pressure on land in urban areas and environmental impacts

The following options are possible:
(1) Promoting integrated land-use planning at rural and urban levels to balance agricultural, urban, and environmental needs.
(2) Establishing systems for monitoring soil health and land use across rural and urban areas.
(3) Enforcement of land-use regulations and incentives for responsible practices.

Governments can promote integrated land-use planning at rural and urban levels to balance agricultural, urban, and environmental needs. This approach should include zoning regulations that prevent the over-conversion of agricultural land into urban areas, preserve agricultural land, and promote sustainable urban development that minimises soil sealing and environmental degradation. This could involve establishing urban growth boundaries and incentivising landowners to preserve rural land for agricultural purposes. Urban areas experiencing rapid migration should integrate resilience planning into their development strategies. This includes investing in green infrastructure, such as permeable surfaces, green spaces, and urban agriculture, to mitigate soil sealing and improve soil health. Urban resilience planning should also focus on improving drainage systems and reducing flood risks by preserving the natural water cycle and ensuring sustainable waste management practices.

To reduce environmental impacts, governments can establish systems for monitoring soil health and land use across rural and urban areas. Implementing stronger environmental regulations to prevent overexploitation of land and ecosystem degradation in both host and departure regions will help address the environmental impacts of migration. Enforcement of land-use regulations and incentives for responsible practices, such as reforestation and sustainable farming, can mitigate soil degradation and preserve biodiversity.

## 12.3. Concrete text for legal provisions

The following is intended as a point of consideration. It outlines a potential approach to formulating a law that regulates the core elements of migration from a sustainable soil management perspective. This draft would have to be adapted to national needs and the national legislative structure.

General provisions

Objective:
This law establishes governance mechanisms, policies, and programs that prevent soil degradation, promote land restoration, and ensure sustainable land use in areas affected by migration-driven land abandonment. Engaging all relevant stakeholders in land and resource management aims to protect soil health, preserve biodiversity, strengthen rural-urban linkages, and enhance environmental resilience.

Scope:
This law applies to all public, private, and community-managed lands within the national territory affected by migration, land abandonment, or environmental degradation. It covers rural and urban areas, including abandoned farmlands, conflict-affected zones, rapidly urbanising regions, and areas designated for land-use planning, soil restoration, or biodiversity conservation. Its provisions apply to government bodies, local authorities, landowners, farmers, private sector actors, communities, migrants, and displaced populations.

Definitions:
"Soil conservation programs and land restoration" involve government-led or supported efforts to rehabilitate degraded or abandoned agricultural lands, restore soil health, and enhance biodiversity.

"Sustainable farming practices", such as agroecology, crop rotation, and organic farming, promote long-term soil productivity while minimising environmental impacts.

"Natural regeneration" supports ecosystem recovery with minimal intervention.

"Land tenure security" ensures legal protection of land rights for individuals and communities, including migrants and displaced populations.

"Integrated land-use planning and urban resilience planning" aim to balance rural and urban development, prevent environmental degradation, and strengthen resilience through Green Infrastructure and sustainable land management.

"Rural-urban linkages" promote resource exchange and development synergies.

"Biodiversity conservation" ensures ecosystem balance

"Participatory governance" guarantees inclusive decision-making involving all stakeholders, including government, communities, private actors, and vulnerable groups.

Soil conservation and land restoration programs:

(1) The state shall establish and implement Soil Conservation Programs to restore degraded and abandoned agricultural lands and prevent further soil degradation. These programs shall include:
  (a) Financial grants or subsidies to landowners, farmer groups, and community organisations for soil rehabilitation, restoration, and biodiversity conservation projects.
  (b) Promote sustainable farming practices, including crop rotation, organic fertilisation, and agroforestry, to improve soil health and productivity.
  (c) Support natural regeneration policies, allowing abandoned lands to recover naturally or by reintroducing sustainable agriculture or agroforestry.

(2) In conflict-affected areas, the state shall collaborate with international organisations to provide technical assistance and financial resources for soil regeneration and sustainable land management.

Strengthening rural-urban linkages and economic resilience:
The state shall implement rural development programs to create employment opportunities, reduce migration pressures, and support sustainable land management in rural areas.

Measures shall include:

(1) Strengthening transportation, trade, and technological connections between urban and rural areas to support sustainable resource exchange and soil management practices.
(2) Encouraging stakeholder engagement, including local governments, NGOs, private sector actors, and migrant communities in decision-making processes.
(3) Promoting participatory land-use planning, ensuring collaboration between urban planners, environmentalists, and agricultural experts to balance land use and resource management.

Secure land tenure and sustainable agricultural practices:

(1) The state shall guarantee secure land tenure rights for migrants, displaced populations, and local communities to encourage investment in land restoration and sustainable agricultural practices.

Land tenure systems shall:

(2) Provide legal agricultural land access for migrants and displaced populations, promoting self-reliance and environmental sustainability.
(3) Support adopting sustainable agricultural methods through targeted policies and programs, including agroecology, agroforestry, and organic farming.
(4) Ensure access to education and extension services on soil management, fertility enhancement, and erosion control techniques for all farmers, including displaced populations.

Integrated land-use planning and urban resilience:
The state shall promote integrated land-use planning at rural and urban levels to balance agricultural, urban, and environmental needs.

Measures shall include:

(1) Enacting zoning regulations and urban growth boundaries to preserve agricultural lands, limit urban sprawl, and prevent excessive land conversion.
(2) Offering financial incentives to landowners who preserve rural land for agriculture rather than urban development.
(3) Integrating urban resilience planning into migration-affected urban areas, including investments in green infrastructure such as permeable surfaces, green spaces, and urban agriculture, improved drainage systems to mitigate flood risks and preserve the natural water cycle, and sustainable waste management practices to protect soil and water resources.

Monitoring, environmental protection, and biodiversity conservation:

(1) The state shall establish monitoring systems to assess soil health and land-use changes across rural and urban areas.
(2) Environmental regulations shall be strengthened to prevent land overexploitation, ecosystem degradation, and biodiversity loss.
(3) The state shall promote reforestation, ecosystem restoration, and sustainable farming practices through financial incentives and legal obligations to ensure long-term environmental resilience and biodiversity preservation.

Multi-stakeholder involvement and participatory governance:

(1) All relevant stakeholders, including local governments, community groups, NGOs, private sector actors, migrants, and displaced populations, shall be involved in the planning, implementing, and monitoring land-use and soil conservation programs.
(2) Participatory governance mechanisms shall ensure transparency, inclusiveness, and accountability in land and soil resource decision-making processes.

## 13. Commentary XII: Pesticides

The use of pesticides in Africa plays a crucial role in safeguarding crops and enhancing agricultural productivity, thereby contributing significantly to food security and economic stability across the continent. However, the safe and effective management of pesticides remains a challenge due to varying national regulations, economic disparities, and limited access to training, safety equipment, and monitoring systems. Misuse or overuse of pesticides can lead to severe environmental damage, health risks to soil, animals, and humans, and socio-economic consequences for farmers and communities. While pesticides are crucial for boosting crop yields and ensuring food security in Africa, their misuse can pose food safety risks[40] and negatively affect soil microbiota, structure, composition, and fertility. This impact includes disruptions to nutrient availability and absorption for plants.[41]

Recognising these challenges, African countries have taken steps to improve pesticide management, notably through the Policy for the Harmonisation of Pesticide Registration in Africa.[42] Developed in 2012, this policy seeks to establish a unified framework for pesticide registration, strengthen regulatory systems, and promote cooperation among member states. Harmonised registration processes ensure that only

---

40 See https://www.ipcc.ch/site/assets/uploads/sites/4/2022/11/SRCCL_Chapter_5.pdf, accessed 7 April 2026.

41 Navshree et al. (2025).

42 See https://auiapsc.org/2012/04/15/harmonization-of-pesticides-registration-in-africa-2012/, accessed 29 September 2025.

safe and effective pesticides are used, reducing regulatory duplication, facilitating trade, and supporting sustainable agricultural development.

Strengthening legislation, monitoring, and enforcement remains essential for controlling pesticide quality, use, labelling, and distribution, ultimately protecting soil, animal, and human health, as well as ecosystems, and advancing Africa's agricultural sector. This Commentary aims to analyse the challenges of pesticide use in Africa and to explore policy options to improve pesticide management and achieve sustainable soil management.

## 13.1. Challenges

Smallholder farmers in many African countries face significant challenges in accessing quality pesticides, leading to reliance on counterfeit products, ineffective pest control, and environmental and health risks. Weak regulations, poor waste management, pest resistance, limited adoption of sustainable alternatives, and logistical barriers further threaten agricultural productivity and food security.

### 13.1.1. Limited access to quality pesticides

Approved pesticides are often too expensive for most African farmers, forcing them to rely on more affordable but unregulated alternatives. These low-cost options are often counterfeit or of poor quality, providing minimal pest protection while posing significant risks to crops, the environment, and human health.[43] As a result, African farmers remain vulnerable to crop losses despite their efforts to control pests. The high cost of certified pesticides also fuels the smuggling of illegal chemicals, further undermining agricultural productivity and threatening food safety and environmental sustainability. Poor import and distribution mechanisms exacerbate access to pesticides, particularly in landlocked countries. Indeed, high transportation costs, inadequate storage facilities, and weak distribution networks drive up prices of quality pesticides and may lead to shortages, especially during peak agricultural seasons.

### 13.1.2. Lack of regulation and oversight

Weak regulatory institutions in many African countries contribute to the widespread importation and sale of unapproved or banned pesticides. Insufficient enforcement mechanisms enable the illegal trade of pesticides to flourish, exposing farmers and

43 Kassem et al. (2021).

consumers to hazardous chemicals and undermining sustainable agriculture. The unapproved pesticides from illicit markets, which often bypass safety regulations, may harm soil health. Penal law and sanctions are needed to prevent the continuation of illegal markets. At the same time, regional bodies such as the Sahelian Committee of Pesticides and the East African Community oversee pesticide regulation.[44] These institutions often struggle with resource constraints and limited institutional support, hindering their ability to effectively monitor and control the distribution of hazardous chemicals. Additionally, the lack of governance over pesticide waste is a critical issue in many African countries. Farmers, especially in rural areas, often lack the infrastructure, resources, and awareness to dispose of pesticide containers safely. Pesticide misuse and improper waste management lead to severe environmental consequences, including soil degradation, water contamination, biodiversity loss, long-term health risks for farming communities, and an increased potential for pest resistance. In some cases, farmers suffer pesticide-related illnesses due to direct exposure.[45]

### 13.1.3. Lack of ecological alternatives and capacity building

The lack of environmental alternatives to chemical pesticides and the insufficient capacity building for farmers in most African countries reinforce the continued reliance on harmful pesticide practices. While integrated pest management strategies and biopesticides are promoted as sustainable alternatives, their adoption remains limited. This is primarily due to the immediate effectiveness of chemical pesticides, which are widely regarded as the most reliable solution for pest control, delivering quick results despite their significant long-term environmental and health consequences. The lack of ecological alternatives is further exacerbated by insufficient training on the safe use of pesticides[46] and the unavailability of reliable, accessible ecological options. The absence of effective training programs and support systems for farmers exacerbates the risks of pesticide overuse and misuse. For instance, many farmers are unaware of the benefits of integrated pest management or biopesticides and lack the technical support to implement these methods effectively. Additionally, limited access to information, resources, and technology hinders farmers' ability to transition from chemical-based practices to more sustainable alternatives. Furthermore, research institutions often lack the necessary scientific equipment and financial resources to develop cost-effective, efficient alternatives to chemical

44 See https://insah.cilss.int/du-csp-au-coahp/ and https://www.eac.int/documents/category/pesticides, accessed 29 September 2025.
45 Anderson & Isgren (2021).
46 Naré et al. (2015).

pesticides, thereby hindering the development and accessibility of ecological solutions.

## 13.2. Options for legal governance mechanisms

Effective legal governance mechanisms are crucial for enhancing pesticide management in Africa, ensuring the safe use of pesticides while safeguarding human health and the environment. Strengthening national legislation, harmonising regional regulations, enforcing pesticide registration requirements, and establishing waste management laws are key measures to enhance oversight, reduce risks, and promote sustainable agricultural practices across the continent.

### 13.2.1. Improving accessibility to quality pesticides

The following key options can improve accessibility to quality pesticides:

(1) Implementation of legal governance mechanisms plays a vital role in improving access to high-quality pesticides in African countries, ensuring that their production, distribution, and use are safe, sustainable, and comply with international standards.

(2) Developing fair pricing policies to ensure quality pesticides are affordable for smallholder farmers.

(3) Developing a partnership between governments and the private sector to enhance accessibility.

(4) Harmonising pesticide regulations through regional organisations can help ensure consistency and alignment across member states.

Pesticides must undergo registration for approval, including toxicological testing and environmental impact assessments, to ensure safety. This process is crucial for protecting human health and the environment. Governments should establish regulations that set pesticide quality standards, such as maximum residue limits in food, and ensure compliance with international safety standards. For instance, all pesticides must be registered with a national regulatory authority, undergo thorough testing to ensure safety and efficacy, and minimise risks associated with harmful or ineffective products. It is necessary to ensure that farmers, particularly in rural areas, can access quality products while preventing counterfeit pesticides from entering the market.

Legal frameworks should ensure affordable access to quality pesticides, with subsidies or support programs for low-income farmers and measures to prevent price manipulation.

Governments should liaise with private-sector stakeholders and offer incentives to expand access to high-quality pesticides, particularly in underserved regions. It should encourage local pesticide production to help reduce import dependence, promote job creation, and ensure pesticides meet local needs.

Regional collaboration, particularly through bodies such as the African Union and the Regional Economic Communities (RECs), can help align pesticide regulations across countries, ensure consistent standards, and facilitate trade. Legal frameworks should regulate the cross-border movement of pesticides, ensuring the safe and controlled trade of products through customs checks and international partnerships to prevent the spread of substandard pesticides.

### 13.2.2. Improving regulation and oversight

Options for improving the regulation and oversight of pesticides involve:

(1) Developing and implementing dedicated national legislation on pesticides to control hazardous pesticides and regulate waste and packaging.
(2) Developing soil-related environmental standards to avoid the contamination of soils using pesticides.
(3) Establishing comprehensive monitoring systems to track pesticides throughout their lifecycle.
(4) Harmonising pesticide regulations at the regional level to maintain consistent safety standards across borders.

Control of Pesticide Distribution and Sales regulates pesticide distribution by granting licences only to companies that meet strict safety and quality standards. One key measure is the strict control of pesticide distribution to prevent the introduction of counterfeit or non-compliant products. Governments can strengthen this control by imposing quotas or restrictions on the import of hazardous or outdated pesticides. This should be established through specific national legislation on pesticides. Control of Hazardous Pesticides involves banning or strictly limiting the use of highly hazardous pesticides to protect human health and the environment. Regulation of Waste and Packaging involves establishing laws for the proper disposal of pesticide containers and residues to prevent environmental contamination.

Monitoring and Traceability is a robust monitoring system that should track pesticides from production to use, ensuring compliance with safety guidelines. Governments must implement monitoring mechanisms and sanctions to enforce compliance through inspections and audits, with severe penalties for violations, including fines and imprisonment. Regional coordination and harmonisation aims to harmonise pesticide regulations across member countries of regional bodies, promote consistent safety standards, and facilitate trade.

#### 13.2.3. Strengthen ecological alternatives and capacity building

The following options are possible:

(1) Promoting sustainable agricultural practices by offering subsidies and incentives for pesticide alternatives.
(2) Encouraging research into and the development of environmentally friendly pest control methods.
(3) Implementing training and certification programs.

The government's role in promoting sustainable practices is to foster sustainable agriculture by offering subsidies and incentives to adopt alternatives to chemical pesticides, such as biopesticides and integrated pest management (IPM). These mechanisms support a transition toward more environmentally friendly and health-conscious pest control methods. By providing financial support for these alternatives, governments reduce the reliance on harmful chemical pesticides, benefiting public health and the environment.

Training and certification programs are to ensure the safe and responsible use of chemicals. Governments can establish certification programs that require individuals to demonstrate an understanding of best practices, correct dosage application, and the potential health risks associated with pesticide use. These programs can help ensure that only qualified personnel handle pesticides, thus minimising risks to human health and the environment.

Encouraging research and adoption of alternatives involves supporting research into alternative pest control methods that are less harmful to the environment and human health. Policies can be introduced to fund research in biopesticides and other sustainable agricultural techniques. Such measures can foster innovation in pest management, creating safer options for farmers and reducing the long-term environmental impacts of pesticide use.

### 13.3. Concrete text for legal provisions

This proposal is intended as a point of consideration. It outlines a potential approach to formulating a law that regulates the core elements of pesticide governance. This draft would need to be adapted to national needs and the national legislative structure.

General provisions

Objective:
This law establishes governance mechanisms to regulate, distribute, and use pesticides, ensuring safety, sustainability, and compliance with international standards.

Responsible pesticide management protects human health, preserves the environment, and promotes agricultural productivity.

Scope:

This framework governs the entire lifecycle of pesticides, including their production, importation, exportation, sale, and use, ensuring strict oversight from market entry to application. It establishes explicit authorisation and registration processes to verify product safety and efficacy before distribution. Additionally, it mandates robust monitoring and enforcement mechanisms to prevent non-compliance and mitigate risks associated with pesticide use. Proper waste management regulations are enforced to prevent environmental contamination from residues and packaging. Furthermore, the framework promotes training and certification programs to ensure pesticide handlers apply best practices. Lastly, it encourages the adoption of sustainable pest control alternatives to reduce reliance on harmful chemical pesticides and support environmentally friendly agricultural practices.

Definitions:

Key terms in this framework define essential concepts for effective pesticide regulation and management.

A "pesticide" refers to any substance used to prevent, destroy, or control pests, while a biopesticide is derived from natural sources, offering a more sustainable alternative.

"Integrated pest management" (IPM) combines various pest control methods to minimise environmental and health risks.

"Registration" is the approval process that ensures pesticides meet safety and efficacy standards before market entry.

"Counterfeit" pesticides are mislabelled or fail to comply with safety regulations.

"Certification" means officially recognising individuals or entities that adhere to proper pesticide handling practices.

"Residue limits" mean the maximum allowable pesticide residues in food to protect consumer health.

"Hazardous pesticides" pose or cause significant risks to human health or the environment, requiring strict regulation or prohibition.

"Sustainable alternatives" refer to all other options that promote eco-friendly pest control methods, reducing reliance on synthetic chemicals.

The "regulatory authority" is the designated body overseeing pesticide compliance, enforcement, and safety measures.

Quality control and distribution

(1) Pesticides must comply with national and international safety standards, including maximum residue limits in food and environmental safety benchmarks.
(2) The distribution and sale of pesticides shall be restricted to licensed entities that meet regulatory requirements.
(3) Importing hazardous or obsolete pesticides is prohibited unless authorised for specific scientific or environmental remediation purposes.
(4) Measures shall be taken to prevent counterfeit pesticides from entering the market, including regular inspections and strict enforcement of licensing requirements.

Affordability and accessibility

(1) Governments shall implement policies to ensure that high-quality pesticides remain affordable, including subsidies and financial support for smallholder farmers.
(2) To reduce dependence on imports, incentives and regulatory support shall be provided to promote local pesticide production.
(3) Regional cooperation mechanisms shall be established to harmonise pesticide regulations, ensure uniform safety standards, and facilitate trade.

Regulation of hazardous pesticides

(1) Highly hazardous pesticides (HHPs) shall be subject to strict control, with potential bans or phased-out use where safer alternatives exist.
(2) The government shall promote the adoption of integrated pest management (IPM) and biopesticides through policy incentives and research funding.
(3) Public awareness campaigns shall educate farmers and consumers on the risks of hazardous pesticides and the benefits of ecological alternatives.

Waste management and environmental protection

(1) The disposal of pesticide containers and residues shall be regulated to prevent environmental contamination.
(2) Manufacturers and distributors shall be required to implement take-back programs for used pesticide containers.
(3) Pesticide application near water sources, protected areas, and sensitive ecosystems shall be subject to stringent environmental safeguards.

Capacity building and certification

(1) All pesticide applicators must undergo mandatory training and obtain certification before handling or applying pesticides.

(2) Certification programs shall include best practices for pesticide application, risk mitigation, and safety precautions.
(3) Governments shall collaborate with research institutions and private stakeholders to promote education and capacity-building initiatives in sustainable pest management.

Monitoring, compliance, and sanctions
(1) A national monitoring system shall be established to track pesticides from production to end-use, ensuring compliance with regulatory standards.
(2) Regular inspections and audits shall be conducted to verify adherence to pesticide handling and application safety protocols.
(3) Violations of pesticide regulations, including the sale of counterfeit or banned pesticides, shall be subject to strict penalties, including fines, licence revocation, and legal action.

## 14. Commentary XIII: Pastoralism

Livestock and agricultural systems have a profound influence on soil fertility across Africa. The continent hosts fifteen distinct farming systems, with rain-fed cropping and pastoralism being the most prevalent.[47] Trees and shrubs also play essential roles in many of these systems. Pastoralism—derived from the Latin word pastor, meaning herder—is characterised by mobility, rangeland use, and a reliance on livestock, particularly cattle. This extensive form of pastoralism is primarily practised in arid and semi-arid regions with limited access to infrastructure and services. It typically combines livestock rearing with dryland cropping. Pastoralists in Africa number approximately 268 million people, accounting for more than a quarter of the continent's population, and occupy around 43% of Africa's total land area.[48] However, climate change and population growth have led to a decline in per capita access to livestock and land resources. These pressures, if left unchecked, are likely to exacerbate soil degradation, environmental inequality, and vulnerability among pastoralist communities. This Commentary analyses the role of pastoralism in soil governance, identifies its legal and ecological challenges, and proposes legislative options and model provisions to support sustainable pastoral land management.

47 Dixon et al. (2020).
48 FAO (2018: 1).

### 14.1. Contextualising pastoralism

Pastoralism in Africa serves as both a livelihood strategy and a production system for many communities residing in arid and semi-arid regions. These areas are marked by considerable spatial and temporal variability in rainfall, often resulting in unpredictable and uneven distribution of grazing resources. In response, pastoralists strategically employ livestock mobility to optimise access to available forage and water. Mobility—often seasonal—is a defining characteristic of pastoral systems, enabling resilience in the face of environmental uncertainty. However, movement patterns vary depending on local ecological conditions, land tenure systems, and the types of livestock reared. This dynamic adaptation highlights the importance of flexible land-use governance and supportive policies in sustaining pastoralism in a changing climate. Pastoral regions in Africa are found in the following natural zones:

(1) the Mediterranean and Saharan zone in North Africa, spanning from Morocco in the west to Egypt in the east, including Algeria, Tunisia, and Libya;
(2) the sub-Saharan tropical and equatorial zone, extending from the edges of the Sahara Desert in the north to the Kalahari Desert in the south; and
(3) the southern zone, encompassing Namibia, Botswana, Zimbabwe, Mozambique, Swaziland, Lesotho, and South Africa.

### 14.2. Challenges

The identified natural zones exhibit distinct soil characteristics that shape the implications of pastoralism and its associated challenges, varying from one region to another. However, the predominant challenge in pastoralism remains land degradation, primarily driven by social and economic factors such as poverty, population growth, inadequate governance and political representation, and restricted land rights and access.

The laws, legislative frameworks, and strategies across Africa differ significantly. No specific pastoral policies or regulations in southern Africa explicitly address pastoral land tenure issues. In contrast, governments in West and East Africa have enacted several pastoral laws to safeguard pastoral land and facilitate livestock mobility. Despite these efforts, existing pastoral laws across the continent often fail to address soil-related issues associated with pastoralism. Even the African Union's Policy Framework for Pastoralism in Africa: Securing, Protecting, and Improving the Lives, Livelihoods, and Rights of Pastoralist Communities (2010) does not address soil-related issues in pastoralism.

## 14.3. Options for legal governance mechanisms (policies and institutions)

Many global, regional, and national policies affect the pastoral farming system. Critical among these policies are governance and political participation (including security), economic development (agriculture, livestock, and markets), natural resources (including land biodiversity and water), and development cooperation (including aid and humanitarian assistance). Inappropriate policies and developmental interventions favoured crop-based agriculture and sedentary livestock production in the past. This inappropriateness has stemmed from a lack of pastoralists' participation and influence in decision-making. In recent years, policies have shown renewed support for pastoralism. Policy attention is also increasingly focusing on conservation and rangeland ecosystems, facilitating transboundary livestock movement, and promoting inclusiveness in the local policy process. In this vein, the proposed legislative intervention is meant to promote sustainable pastoralism.

### 14.3.1. Option 1: reforming existing soil laws to include management of pastoral lands

This legislative proposal recommends enhancing current soil legislation by incorporating measures to prevent, mitigate, or manage soil erosion on both arable and pastoral lands, tailored to each country's specific conditions. It also advocates reforming existing pastoral land management laws to integrate sustainable soil management practices. Integrating pastoral issues into existing soil legislation, and *vice versa*, enables a comprehensive approach to sustainable soil management.

### 14.3.2. Option 2: introducing pastoral land management law

This option entails enacting separate pastoral land management laws to address the administration of pastoral land (access), establishing mechanisms to achieve sustainable use of soil in pastoral lands, developing grazing management mechanisms, clarifying the responsibilities of pastoralists and the government, and implementing rangeland condition monitoring. Existing regional treaties/protocols, such as the ECOWAS Protocol on Transhumance, 1998, and Nouakchott Declaration on Pastoralism, 2013, and the African Union Policy Framework for Pastoralism in Africa: Securing, Protecting, and Improving the Lives, Livelihoods, and Rights of Pastoralist Communities, 2010, may be considered as building blocks towards achieving sustainable pastoralism.

## 14.4. Proposed legal text and annotations

### Definitions

"Pastoral lands" refer to the use and management of resources that allow animal husbandry. They include areas of natural vegetation such as savannah and forest, as well as agricultural lands where the animals are put to common grazing after the harvest.

### Objectives

The objects of the laws are as follows:

(1) to ensure that all pastoral land is well managed and utilised prudently and
(2) to provide for—
  (a) the effective monitoring of the condition of pastoral land;
  (b) the prevention of degradation of pastoral lands;
  (c) the rehabilitation of the land in cases of damage;
(3) to provide a form of tenure of state land / communal / tribal land for pastoral purposes; and
(4) to provide the community with a system for accessing pastoral lands.

### General duties

A pastoralist shall carry out pastoral activities in accordance with good land management practices; prevent degradation of the land and soil resources; and endeavour, within the limits of financial resources, to improve the condition of the land and soil.

### Conditions for access to pastoral lands

(1) The competent authority shall, upon application [by a community or individual], grant access to pastoral lands.
(2) A permission or authorisation to access pastoral lands shall be subject to the following land management conditions, providing for—
  (a) an obligation to ensure that the number of stocks on the land or a particular part of the land does not exceed the maximum levels specified in the law, except with the prior approval of the competent authority;
  (b) an obligation to maintain existing constructed stock watering points in proper working order; and
  (c) an obligation to close off specified areas on the land, or to close or move specified access points on the land, to rehabilitate degraded land.

Destocking[49]

If the competent authority is of the opinion that pastoral land has, from any cause, been damaged, or is likely to suffer damage or deteriorate, and that to prevent, arrest or minimise damage to or deterioration of the land and soil, or to rehabilitate the land or soil, it is necessary that action under this section be taken, the competent authority may, by notice in writing to the [pastoralist/occupier of the pastoral land], require him/her to do any one or more of the following:

(1) remove a specified number of stocks from the land or a particular part of the land;
(2) keep the amount of stock on the land or a particular part of the land to a specified level, or to keep no stock at all on that land;
(3) carry out specified improvements on the land; and
(4) adopt or desist from specified land management practices, in accordance with the terms of the notice.

## 15. Commentary XIV: Urbanisation

Africa is experiencing unprecedented urban growth, which is rapidly reshaping its landscapes and resource bases. While urbanisation offers potential avenues for economic development and improved living standards, it also presents significant environmental challenges, particularly regarding soil and land degradation. Urbanisation refers to the growing concentration of population in urban areas, which drives land-use changes and often leads to soil degradation from infrastructure development and waste accumulation. This Commentary analyses urbanisation in Africa as a major driver of soil and land degradation and proposes solutions for addressing the numerous challenges.

49 Most pastoral lands are managed communally due to the unpredictability of resources and the need for mobility. Policies that shift toward individualised land use tend to lead to conflict and environmental degradation. In contrast, when governments support communal land tenure, pastoral communities benefit. Therefore, to ensure sustainable land and soil management, it is essential to recognise communal land rights. This Commentary does not propose full legislative text for every component of pastoral land management laws. The suggested provisions can be incorporated into soil and pastoral land management legislation. It is essential to assign specific responsibilities to pastoral land users, particularly the obligation to prevent land and soil degradation. Overstocking is a major challenge on pastoral lands, underscoring the need to maintain livestock numbers within the lands' carrying capacities.

## 15.1. Description of challenges

Globally, future urban area expansion is expected to cause significant food production losses, reduce biodiversity, and increase land-use change emissions, jeopardising human livelihoods and the natural environment. As of 2023, Africa is highly urbanised, with Gabon the most urbanised African country at 90%, followed by Djibouti, Libya, São Tomé and Príncipe, and Algeria, all with over 75%. At the lowest scale of urbanisation in Africa are countries such as Malawi, Rwanda, Niger, and Burundi, which have less than 20% urbanisation. The rest of the African countries, such as South Sudan, have urbanisation rates ranging from 21% to 40%; while most countries, such as Equatorial Guinea, Botswana, South Africa, Morocco, Cameroon, Ghana, Namibia, Zambia, Madagascar, and others, remain within the higher rates of 41% to 74%.[50]

Urbanisation, in its narrower sense, refers to the increasing proportion of a population residing in urban areas. It typically results from rural-to-urban migration, as individuals relocate from the countryside to towns and cities in search of better economic opportunities, services, and living conditions.[51] The broader perspective of urbanisation incorporates "all the social, economic, biophysical and institutional changes that result from and accompany urban growth."[52] With urbanisation comes industrialisation and infrastructural development, which are necessary for economic growth. Although urbanisation is highly correlated with economic development, it does not necessarily cause it.

Urbanisation has diverse effects on the environment. For instance, on the African continent, one of the fastest urbanising regions, food systems are also transforming rapidly. This puts immense pressure on food security in the world's most food-insecure region.

Further, rapid and unplanned urbanisation presents a significant challenge in Africa. Projections indicate that by 2050, over 60% of Africa's population will live in urban areas, up from approximately 40%.[53] These high levels of urbanisation also pressure the government to secure land for new settlements, sometimes at the expense of land designated for ecological preservation, such as forests and other protected areas, which are crucial for soil health and overall environmental regeneration.

Among other challenges, urbanisation in Africa has largely translated into the establishment of slums, increased poverty, and widening inequalities. A definitional appraisal of "urban sprawl" has established that the term covers six categories: pattern, process, nature, location, actors, and factors.[54] While urbanisation may drive economic

50 Statista (2023); OECD (2025a).
51 Smit (2021).
52 Ibid.
53 OECD (2025a).
54 Dadashpoor & Shahhossein (2024).

development, alter the urban form, and influence production technologies, citizen lifestyles, and societal values, it can also negatively impact social equity, public health, and the physical and natural environment, specifically soil, air, and land, thereby increasing pollution and related diseases.

Consequently, rapid urban population growth intensifies human activities and accelerates environmental degradation, such as soil depletion. In Africa, rapid urbanisation is responsible for converting forests and wetlands into residential, industrial, and agricultural zones, stressing ecosystems and increasing soil vulnerability.

Urbanisation and infrastructure development often progress in tandem, placing immense pressure on soil resources. One of the most critical consequences is the loss of fertile soils through soil sealing—the covering of land with impermeable materials such as concrete and asphalt for buildings, roads, and other infrastructure. This process permanently impairs the soil's ecological functions. Furthermore, many African cities have historically been established on prime agricultural land, intensifying the challenge. As urban areas expand, valuable land and fertile soils are lost, reducing the availability of arable land for food cultivation and threatening long-term food security.

Rapid and unplanned urbanisation, accompanied by a growing human population and other associated anthropogenic activities in Africa, is also generating large amounts of waste, leading to problems with waste disposal and management. In most African countries, the most common practices of waste processing and management include landfilling, incineration, unscientific dumping, and vermi-composting. The first three of these methods pose drawbacks to soil sustainability, including soil and groundwater contamination, environmental pollution from biomass burning, and impacts on human health and environmental hygiene. For these reasons, when African governments formulate urbanisation policies, it is essential to strike a balance between economic, social, and ecological considerations by integrating health-oriented and sustainable soil governance measures.

Africa's soils face mounting threats from a waste management crisis driven by rapid urbanisation, inadequate infrastructure, and weak regulatory enforcement. Uncontrolled dumping and widespread contamination are prevalent, particularly in rapidly growing cities that are ill-equipped to manage the increasing volumes of municipal, industrial, and hazardous waste, including e-waste. Limited recycling capacity and the absence of circular economy strategies further exacerbate the situation. Financial constraints and public disengagement hinder progress, while climate change–induced disasters accelerate the spread of pollutants. A coordinated and urgent response is required, one that includes robust regulatory frameworks, targeted infrastructure investments, public education campaigns, and international cooperation, to safeguard Africa's critical soil resources and ensure long-term environmental resilience.

The escalating volume of waste across Africa poses a serious environmental threat, requiring urgent, sustainable management strategies to prevent widespread soil contamination. Rapid urbanisation, industrial expansion, and evolving consumption patterns have led to an unprecedented increase in solid and hazardous waste. Traditional disposal practices, such as open dumping and poorly regulated landfills, expose soils to significant risks. Leachates from these sites, containing heavy metals, pathogens, and other pollutants, infiltrate the soil, compromising fertility, agricultural productivity, water quality, and public health. To address this, implementing integrated waste management systems is essential. These should prioritise waste reduction, recycling, and the safe treatment and disposal of hazardous materials. Additionally, promoting circular economy principles, where waste is reimagined as a resource, can substantially reduce soil contamination while contributing to broader sustainability goals across the continent.

Healthy soils also form the foundation of adequate green infrastructure, offering vital ecosystem services that help buffer the impacts of rising temperatures and extreme weather events. This is especially critical in urban environments, where the urban heat island effect significantly amplifies climate-related health risks. Soils' capacity to sequester atmospheric carbon dioxide and support vegetation helps regulate temperature, while their ability to absorb and store water reduces flood risks and enhances drought resilience. Moreover, structurally intact soils prevent erosion and support slope stability during severe weather events, while their biodiversity underpins ecosystems that are more resilient to environmental stress.

Investing in soil health, therefore, is not merely an environmental priority; it is an essential strategy for building climate-resilient, sustainable urban and rural landscapes that can withstand the escalating challenges of the 21st century.

## 15.2. Options for legal governance mechanisms

Various legal governance mechanisms can be employed to effectively address soil and land degradation driven by urbanisation in African countries. These mechanisms focus on regulating land use, encouraging sustainable practices, and enforcing environmental protection. The key options include:

(1) Upgrading informal settlements by providing integrated infrastructure and services that target marginalised groups, including the poor, youth, women, and the elderly. African governments should act proactively to ensure orderly urban development by defining and implementing clear urban development strategies.
(2) Mobilising urban financing from local and foreign investors and ensuring these resources are efficiently and adequately allocated between central and local governments' urban projects in Africa.

(3) Improving human capital through equal access to education and healthcare services and facilities for all categories of citizens to meet labour market needs across Africa.
(4) Diversification of economic activities in African countries by creating new economic hubs oriented towards high sustainable and value-added production and exportation. These reforms should be more inclusive to ensure that all categories of citizens, regardless of their age, race, gender, ethnicity, or socio-economic conditions, have equal access to adequate housing, basic infrastructure and services, and equal job opportunities.
(5) Urbanisation in Africa is necessary, but must be strategically planned and managed, utilising practical local and international urban and land-use planning tools and adhering to relevant legislation. In this context, several key technical proposals are recommended:
    (a) The establishment of effective national solid waste management policies.
    (b) Creation of viable institutional, legal, and financial frameworks tailored to different levels of governance.
    (c) Update respective country urban laws and policies to consider soil-specific sustainability.
(6) Dedicated care for urban soils and infrastructure in Africa:
    (a) Urban infrastructure – careful management of gardens, parks, and lawns, bioretention systems, and green roofs;
    (b) Urban agriculture; and
    (c) Urban forestry.
(7) Land planning is the first tool for reducing the impacts of urbanisation on soils by preventing higher-quality soils from sealing; implementing compensation measures such as urban greening and de-sealing; and mitigating the loss of ecosystem services provided by soils, reducing the degree of imperviousness. Containment of urban expansion is unlikely, especially in developing countries. Moreover, although promoting dense urban development can reduce built-up areas and many additional externalities (e.g., transport-related carbon emissions), it entails significant trade-offs with critical urban ecosystem services, such as the loss of green spaces, thereby reducing overall urban sustainability. Therefore, considering land use alongside urban ecosystem services and biodiversity, land planning should always be tailored to the specific area or region in Africa.
(8) Soil de-sealing can help compensate for what was sealed during urbanisation and the regeneration and reuse of so-called brownfield sites. Outside Europe, soil de-sealing has been employed mainly in North America, including in several examples of the re-naturalisation of brownfields. However, if this option is pursued in high-income, high-density African countries where available land for further urban development is relatively scarce, the cost of

the practice could be high due to the likely need for decontamination. Additionally, de-sealing is unlikely to compensate for the quantitative loss of land, given the urban growth rate.

(9) To effectively combat soil contamination from escalating waste in Africa, a comprehensive legal framework is essential, encompassing national and local waste management laws, Extended Producer Responsibility schemes, stringent landfill and hazardous waste regulations, circular economy promotion, community involvement, robust enforcement, and international cooperation. This multi-faceted approach prioritises waste reduction, recycling, and safe disposal, ensuring environmental protection and sustainable development through clear standards, monitoring, and collaborative efforts.

(10) Healthy soils are critically important in urban areas for adapting to climate change, particularly increased temperatures, droughts, and heavy rainfall events. Town planning that integrates sufficient green and blue regions and practical management tools can significantly enhance urban resilience.

Town planning for green and blue areas:

(1) Green infrastructure integration:
    (a) Incorporate parks, green roofs, walls, urban forests, and community gardens into urban planning.
    (b) Preserve and restore existing natural areas within cities.
(2) Blue infrastructure integration:
    (a) Create and restore wetlands, ponds, rain gardens, and permeable pavements to manage stormwater and enhance water infiltration.
    (b) Daylight buried streams and rivers to restore natural water flow and ecological functions.
(3) Connectivity:
    (a) Establish green corridors and networks to connect green and blue areas, promoting biodiversity and facilitating wildlife movement.
    (b) These corridors also allow for the movement of people, reducing the heat island effect.

15.3. Explanations of different options

Land use planning and zoning: Implementing regulations to demarcate zones for urban growth, agriculture, and conservation, controlling sprawl, and protecting sensitive areas. This requires strong local governance, public involvement, and robust enforcement.

Environmental Impact Assessments (EIAs): Mandating EIAs for development projects to evaluate and mitigate soil and land impacts, ensuring sustainable practices and accountability. As entailed in the Model Law, the EIA shall entail a specific "soil impact assessment" (Article 14 Model Law). This necessitates clear guidelines, competent assessors, and public access to information.

Soil and land conservation laws: Enacting laws to protect soil, regulate extractive industries, and promote conservation, preventing erosion and maintaining fertility. This demands effective enforcement, public awareness, and incentives for sustainable land management.

Waste management regulations: Developing and enforcing rules for waste disposal to prevent contamination, encourage recycling, and ensure safe handling of hazardous materials. This requires infrastructure investment, public education, and regulatory compliance.

Water resources management: Implementing laws to regulate water use, protect quality, and promote conservation, preventing degradation and ensuring equitable access. This requires inter-sectoral coordination and stakeholder involvement.

Urban agriculture regulations: Promoting sustainable urban farming practices to enhance food security and soil health. This requires technical support, land access, and integration with urban planning.

Enforcement and compliance: Establishing strong mechanisms for monitoring, inspections, and penalties to enforce environmental laws. This requires funding, trained personnel, and transparent legal processes.

Community participation: Encouraging community involvement in planning and enforcement to enhance local ownership and ensure policy relevance. This requires capacity building and access to information.

Regional and international cooperation: Fostering collaboration to address transboundary issues and share best practices. This requires participation in agreements and partnerships with international bodies.

## 15.4. Management tools for climate adaptation in urban areas

Soil health management:

- Promote using compost and organic matter to improve soil structure and water-holding capacity.
- Implement soil remediation techniques to address contamination.
- Regulate the use of heavy machinery in urban green spaces.

Water-sensitive urban design (WSUD):

- Integrate WSUD principles into urban development to manage stormwater and enhance water conservation.

- Utilise permeable pavements, rain gardens, and constructed wetlands to reduce runoff and improve water quality.

Urban forestry management:
- Develop urban forestry plans that select climate-resilient tree species and promote tree canopy cover.
- Implement tree maintenance programs to ensure tree health and longevity.

Early warning systems:
- Establish early warning systems for extreme weather events, such as heat waves, floods, and droughts.
- Develop emergency response plans to mitigate the impacts of these events.

Climate modelling and risk assessment:
- Conduct climate modelling and risk assessments to identify vulnerable areas and prioritise adaptation measures.
- Use data-driven approaches to inform urban planning and decision-making.

Community engagement:
- Engage local communities in the planning and implementation of climate adaptation measures.
- Promote public awareness and education on the importance of healthy soils and green infrastructure.

Policy and regulation:
- Create and enforce policies that protect urban soils.
- Incentivise green building practices.
- Regulate waste disposal to prevent soil contamination.

### 15.5. Concrete text for legal provisions

The following outlines concrete legal provisions that could be incorporated into legislation addressing soil and land degradation driven by urbanisation in Africa. These examples are designed to be specific and actionable.

Land use planning and zoning:
- Urban development zones shall be delineated in municipal development plans, clearly demarcating areas for residential, commercial, industrial, and agricultural use. The conversion of prime agricultural land for non-agricultural

purposes within designated agricultural zones is prohibited without explicit authorisation from the Ministry of Agriculture.
- Local authorities shall establish mandatory greenbelts around urban centres, with a minimum width of [specified meters], to prevent urban sprawl and preserve natural ecosystems. These greenbelts shall be protected from development and maintained as public green spaces.

Environmental Impact Assessments (EIAs):
- All urban development projects exceeding [specified area] or involving [specified activities] shall require a mandatory Environmental Impact Assessment (EIA) conducted by a certified environmental consulting firm. The EIA shall assess the project's potential impacts on soil, land, water resources, and biodiversity.
- EIAs shall include a specific 'soil impact assessment' including a detailed soil management plan, outlining measures to prevent soil erosion, maintain soil fertility, and minimise land disturbance during construction and operation. The soil management plan shall be subject to public review and approval by the environmental regulatory authority.

Soil and land conservation laws:
- Mining and quarrying activities shall be subject to strict rehabilitation requirements, including restoring excavated areas to their original topography and revegetating disturbed lands with native plant species. A rehabilitation bond shall be required to ensure compliance.
- Farmers and landowners shall implement soil conservation practices, such as contour ploughing, terracing, and cover cropping, in areas prone to soil erosion. The Ministry of Agriculture shall provide technical assistance and financial incentives to support these practices.

Waste management regulations:
- Municipalities shall establish integrated waste management systems, including separate collection of recyclable materials, composting organic waste, and safe disposal of hazardous waste. Landfilling of untreated municipal solid waste is prohibited.
- Industrial facilities shall be required to treat wastewater to meet specified discharge standards before releasing it into the environment. Monitoring and reporting wastewater discharge shall be mandatory and subject to regular inspections by environmental authorities.

Water resources management laws:

- Water abstraction permits shall be required for all large-scale water users, including industries, agricultural operations, and urban water supply systems. Water allocation shall prioritise essential human needs and environmental flows.
- Urban stormwater runoff shall be managed through the implementation of green infrastructure, such as rain gardens, permeable pavements, and constructed wetlands, to minimise soil erosion and water pollution.

Urban agriculture regulations:

- Municipalities shall designate areas for urban agriculture, including community gardens, rooftop gardens, and vertical farms. Access to land and resources shall be provided to urban farmers, especially marginalised communities.
- Urban agriculture practices shall comply with sustainable agriculture standards, including organic fertilisers, integrated pest management, and water-efficient irrigation techniques.

Enforcement and compliance mechanisms:

- Environmental regulatory authorities shall conduct regular inspections of development projects, industrial facilities, and agricultural operations to ensure compliance with environmental laws. Penalties for violations shall be proportional to the severity of the offence and shall include fines, remediation orders, and project suspension.
- A public environmental complaints mechanism shall be established to report violations of environmental laws. Whistleblowers shall be protected from retaliation.

Community participation and empowerment:

- Local communities shall be involved in developing and implementing land use plans and environmental management strategies. Public hearings and consultations shall be conducted to gather community input.
- Community-based environmental monitoring programs shall be established to track soil and land degradation and assess the effectiveness of environmental policies.

Regional and international cooperation:

- The government shall participate in regional environmental agreements and initiatives to address transboundary environmental issues, such as desertification and water resource management.

- The government shall seek technical and financial assistance from international organisations to support the implementation of sustainable land management practices and environmental protection measures.

Climate change, urbanisation, and infrastructure

Climate-resilient infrastructure planning:

- All new urban infrastructure projects (roads, bridges, water systems, energy grids) shall undergo a Climate Resilience Assessment, evaluating potential climate change impacts (flooding, heatwaves, sea-level rise) over the project's lifespan and incorporating adaptation measures.
- National and municipal infrastructure development plans shall integrate climate change projections and risk assessments, prioritising investments in resilient infrastructure that can withstand future climate impacts.
- Infrastructure projects located in coastal areas must include a sea level rise impact study and take into account the projections of sea level rise for the next 100 years.

Urban planning and development controls:

- Urban planning regulations shall incorporate climate change adaptation measures, including:
  - Designating flood-prone areas as green spaces or permeable zones.
  - Mandating the use of heat-resistant building materials and designs.
  - Promoting the development of green infrastructure (parks, green roofs, urban forests) to mitigate the urban heat island effect.
- Municipalities shall develop and enforce zoning regulations that restrict development in areas vulnerable to climate hazards (floodplains, coastal zones, areas prone to landslides).

## 16. Commentary XV: Tenure rights

Land refers to parts of the earth that support agriculture, provide habitats, and harbour natural resources. This definition of land encompasses the physical land and all objects thereon, including the soil and subsoil, water bodies and their associated living organisms, as well as the air and atmosphere above. From a socio-cultural perspective, land is a religious and ancestral resource of significant value, serving as sacred sites and burial grounds for generations, thereby forming part of the cultural heritage. As a source of socio-cultural well-being for a people, land constitutes a vital spiritual link and the primary means of communication between them, the dead/ancestors, and their god. As an ancestral gift, land before colonisation was held in trust by members of customary communities to protect and pass on to future generations, which is why it could not be alienated through sales, as this would have depleted the family or community patrimony. Furthermore, from a socio-economic perspective, land provides for basic sustenance. Again, land is utilised from both economic and political perspectives for wealth creation and as a means of power and control. In contemporary times, land constitutes a form of capital that generates wealth or is used to create more wealth due to the economic value it commands.

Land tenure has been defined as "the terms under which individuals, households or social groups hold land and natural resources."[55] Land tenure is a crucial aspect of landholding and a key consideration in any discussion regarding the sustainable management of land and soils. Land governance in Africa has become a central concern in recent decades. One of the concerns is land tenure security, which refers to how secure individuals feel about 'their rights' to land, how such land rights are recognised by law, and safeguarded by competent state authorities. Concerns about land tenure security are triggered by the continuous surge in the market value of land, as it has increasingly become an economic commodity, and a corresponding increase in demand for this versatile resource. Land tenure security concerns are also provoked by urban expansion, as well as by the social and political dimensions and the agro-ecological functions of land as an invaluable asset. The impacts of all these land interests have triggered a call for sustainable land management (SLM), succinctly captured by the concept of 'Land Degradation Neutrality' (LDN), which was adopted as part of the 2030 Agenda for Sustainable Development in 2015. Introduced by the United Nations Convention to Combat Desertification (UNCCD),[56] LDN aims to achieve a state in which the amount and quality of land resources remain stable or increase, preventing the net loss of healthy and productive land.

Land tenure systems and their degree of security have implications for sustainable or unsustainable land management, which must be understood within specific socio-economic and legal contexts.[57] Land tenure systems can guarantee tenure security and work favourably for SLM.[58] Evidence is unequivocal that secure land tenure is an indispensable precondition for sustainable land and soil management. Despite substantial evidence linking land tenure security to SLM, the governance frameworks necessary to guarantee such security remain generally weak across many African countries. At the core of land tenure security is the recognition and protection of land rights, namely, the rights to access, use, and ownership, which constitute a fundamental prerequisite and key determinant of effective land and soil stewardship. However, tenure security in Africa is undermined by a host of structural, legal, and institutional

---

55 IPCC (2019: 749).

56 The United Nations Convention to Combat Desertification (UNCCD) is the driving force behind LDN, serving as the sole legally binding international agreement linking environment and development to sustainable land management.

57 See IPCC (2019: 70).

58 Ibid.

challenges that significantly hinder the sustainable management of land and soil resources. Land tenure governance across Africa is premised on a shared historical legacy of colonialism/foreign administration, inequality, tenure diversity, and fragmentation.[59] The persistence of tenure insecurity, decades after African countries' independence and despite ongoing land tenure reforms, raises questions about the genuineness and effectiveness of these reforms. Without effective land governance systems that guarantee tenure security, it will be challenging to manage land sustainably. Security of tenure is a decisive factor for sustainable land management and, consequently, crucial for soil protection.

This Commentary examines land tenure systems in Africa, identifies structural challenges to tenure security, and proposes legal and institutional mechanisms to strengthen equitable land governance and support sustainable land and soil management.

## 16.1. Description of the challenges of land tenure security that are drawbacks for sustainable land/soil management in Africa

According to the IPCC report,[60] unclear land tenure rights breed tenure insecurity and undermine incentives to manage land and soil sustainably. Land tenure insecurity is a serious constraint to the sustainable management of land and soils in Africa. Despite decades of land tenure reforms across Africa, challenges persist in establishing optimal land tenure arrangements that can ensure the achievement of the expected goals, including providing security for all and, above all, sustainability. Sustainability in this regard refers to the consequential environmental and social benefits of secure land tenure, such as reducing pollution, preventing land and biodiversity degradation, mitigating climate change, enhancing productivity, ensuring food security, and alleviating poverty. The challenges, some of which vary across the different countries and regions of Africa, are many and range from:

### 16.1.1. Duality of land tenure – statutory/formal and customary

There are two primary forms of land tenure systems in Africa: statutory/formal land tenure, which is based on written rules, and customary land tenure, which is based on unwritten rules, norms, and practices. Until the colonial period, the customary land tenure system dominated land management in the various pre-state communities. The duality of land tenure is a significant challenge that does not bode well for SLM. There

59 Bayer (2021: 47).

60 See Nabuurs et al. (2022: 825).

is a disparity between statutory/formal land tenure and customary land tenure systems. Formal/statutory land titles, which are generally considered superior to customary land tenure in most African countries, are associated with higher perceptions of tenure security than customary land tenure.

The most important feature of the customary land tenure system is that an individual's or family's, or group's rights to hold land in a specific community are based on membership in the socio-political community, ethnic group, clan, or family with the land in common trust.[61] Under this system, land has been acquired, possessed, and transferred within community regimes based on norms derived from longstanding practices commonly established by the village, clan, or tribal community.[62] Recognising that customary land tenure systems are not uniform across Africa can be beneficial. They are diverse and vary significantly across countries, states, and regions, reflecting the unique histories, cultures, and socio-political structures of different communities.

Another key feature of customary land tenure in Africa is that land rights are usually earned through 'son of the soil' entitlements.[63] However, it is common for both strangers and 'sons of the soil' to pay for such land rights.[64] Even though such land may still be collectively owned, individuals can claim rights to use a specified piece of land through long-term occupation and possession. In many communities, this right of use is transferable to other family members and those who can pay. Generally, customary tenure systems often prohibit land sales, especially to non-group members, to maintain community control and ownership. Until the neo-liberal reforms, outright sales of such lands were uncommon, although informal sales were common.

Additionally, customary land tenure systems have remained essentially unchanged, having been influenced by colonial and post-independence government interventions, and continue to adapt to social, economic, political, and cultural shifts. Customary tenure in contemporary times ranges from what is known as 'permissive occupancy' of state lands in some countries, such as Zimbabwe, to formalised customary tenure regimes that allow the registration of collective and individual titles in countries such as Burkina Faso, Uganda, Rwanda, and Tanzania.[65] In African countries, customary lands can be under the authority of traditional leaders or the control of large clans or families.

The conflict between statutory land tenure and customary land tenure often culminates in the loss of land rights for the poorest and marginalised. This has implications for unsustainable land-use practices and negative consequences for land and soil degradation, as they may use unsustainable methods to establish rights and

61 Chigbu et al. (2022: 664).
62 Ibid.
63 Chimhowu (2019: 898).
64 Ibid.
65 Wily (2011: 458).

claims to land. There is growing recognition that modern land laws must build on customary land tenure norms and practices. Some African countries have adopted legislation that protects customary land tenure rights.[66]

### 16.1.2. Costly and complex/cumbersome procedures for establishing formal land titles under statutory law

The procedures for acquiring formal land titles under statutory law in many African countries are often costly, complex, and bureaucratically burdensome, disproportionately favouring wealthy, well-connected individuals over marginalised populations and those with limited means. While legal frameworks may formally guarantee every person—natural or legal—the right to own, use, enjoy, and dispose of land, these rights are, in practice, inaccessible to the average citizen.[67] The requirements for securing land titles are frequently beyond the financial and logistical reach of ordinary people. As a result, land ownership tends to concentrate in the hands of the state, large corporations, religious institutions, national elites, and affluent individuals, particularly as land becomes increasingly scarce due to declining fertility and rising economic value.[68] Furthermore, land titling processes are often characterised by inefficiency, opacity, and corruption. In addition to being slow and expensive, the procedures may be marred by unfair dealings, such as double land sales and administrative or judicial decisions that cancel land titles, often to the advantage of influential actors. Consequently, even those who manage to secure land titles may still face insecurity. This pervasive uncertainty discourages long-term investments in land. It fosters unsustainable land-use practices, as occupiers may avoid conservation efforts or exploit soil resources unsustainably out of fear of eviction or dispossession. Ultimately, such systemic challenges undermine both equitable access to land and adequate soil protection across the continent.

### 16.1.3. "Land-grabbing" and dispossession of local communities

Another significant challenge to land tenure security in Africa is land grabbing—the large-scale acquisition or leasing of land, often involving the dispossession of local communities and future generations from community and family lands. State authorities frequently facilitate these large-scale land acquisitions (LSLAs) in

---

66 Cotula (2007).

67 In legal terms, a natural person or (physical person) is a human being. In contrast, a moral person (or legal person) is an entity, such as a corporation or organisation, granted legal rights and responsibilities.

68 Cameroon's Country Report by Tamasang in Ruppel et al. (2025: 29, 32, 75).

collusion with powerful actors, including foreign investors, natural resource and agribusiness companies, and domestic elites. Land grabbing is particularly prevalent in Africa, where vast tracts of land are being secured for commercial agriculture, mining, and infrastructure development. LSLAs are a threat to tenure security and SLM, but the nature and scale of the threat are not well understood.[69] Based on cross-checked data for completed lease agreements in Ethiopia, Ghana, and Tanzania, LSLAs cover 1.9%, 1.9%, and 1.1% of each country's total arable land.[70] The literature presents differing views on whether these acquisitions involve marginal lands or already utilised lands, potentially displacing existing users.[71]

Although one of the cited justifications for LSLAs is that they can boost food production on a larger scale, they also contribute to land tenure insecurity, enabling unsustainable land-use practices by land grabbers and resulting in negative consequences such as land and soil degradation.

### 16.1.4. Traditional leaders

A twin challenge accompanying LSLAs and the dispossession of local communities is the corruption and co-optation of traditional leaders by state authorities. This often occurs through promises of political favour, material benefits, or enhanced status. In many instances, traditional authorities are pressured or incentivised to endorse land deals that undermine the rights and livelihoods of their communities. This issue is particularly acute in peri-urban areas, where land is highly sought after for urban expansion and commercial development.

Collusion between traditional authorities and formal land administration services has been widely condemned, including during national debates held as part of the Convention on Land in Guinea.[72] Such practices not only compromise community trust and traditional governance structures but also exacerbate tenure insecurity and fuel land conflicts. They highlight the urgent need for stronger legal safeguards, transparent land governance, and mechanisms for genuine community consultation and consent in land transactions.

69 IPCC (2019: 70).
70 Ibid.: 750.
71 Ibid.
72 Gret (2024).

### 16.1.5. Wanting inclusive land governance across Africa, giving rise to corruption and land disputes

Inclusive land governance, defined as the meaningful participation of all stakeholders with an interest in land, is generally lacking in many African countries.[73] Yet such participation is vital to upholding the rule of law and ensuring the long-term sustainability of land and soil management. In practice, applicants for land titles often fail to engage with or consult individuals and communities with legitimate interests in the land. In the absence of inclusive consultation, some applicants resort to corrupt practices, such as bribing local stakeholders or government officials involved in the land titling process. These actions undermine transparency and accountability, frequently giving rise to land disputes that destabilise tenure arrangements and obstruct efforts toward sustainable land use and soil protection.

### 16.1.6. Gender discrimination regarding access to land, use, and ownership across Africa

Land tenure security is a key enabler of women's empowerment and a critical factor in achieving sustainable land and soil management, particularly for women, who make up a large proportion of smallholder farmers in Africa. While many African countries have made progress in adopting legislation that promotes gender equality in land access, use, and ownership, women's rights to land remain constrained in practice. Discriminatory customary norms, combined with weak enforcement of legal provisions, continue to limit women's ability to inherit, acquire, or retain land. In many communities, customary systems often exclude women from land inheritance, which remains a primary means of acquiring land. As a result, women are frequently confined to smaller, fragmented plots, which reduces their capacity to invest in and implement sustainable land and soil management practices.

### 16.1.7. Inadequate recognition of customary land tenure rights and the eminence of the state as the primary steward of all lands across Africa

Local communities and indigenous peoples in Africa often lack formal recognition of their land tenure rights. The IPCC's Fifth Assessment Report identifies the non-recognition of customary tenure, loss of possession rights, and insecure tenure as key socio-economic risks of implementing climate change mitigation strategies in the

73 Bayer (2021: 47).

Agriculture, Forestry, and Other Land Use (AFOLU) sector.[74] These risks apply equally to efforts aimed at promoting sustainable land management (SLM). Where customary land systems are unrecognised, undermined, or unenforced by the state, tenure insecurity is likely to result. Across Africa, states frequently assert sovereign stewardship over land, designating vast areas as national or state lands. This legal framing enables governments to reallocate customary lands, often without adequate consultation or compensation, for large-scale agricultural or mining investments. Such practices marginalise vulnerable communities, undermining their trust in state institutions and increasing the likelihood of conflict, land degradation, and unsustainable land use as acts of resistance to dispossession.[75]

### 16.1.8. Diversity of land tenure systems in Africa

African countries exhibit a range of land tenure systems, including customary tenure, formal or statutory tenure, and hybrid systems, with varying degrees of individual, communal, and state control. Pre-colonial practices, colonial legacies, and post-independence policies often influence these systems. Regarding the factors that affect land tenure diversity, pre-colonial tenure systems were established by pre-state communities. Regarding colonial legacies, colonial governments typically introduced formal land tenure systems that replaced or superseded customary practices. Regarding post-independence policies, governments have implemented various land policies, some aimed at promoting private land ownership, while others focused on protecting customary land rights. In modern times, population growth, urbanisation, investments, and economic development have put pressure on land resources, leading to changes in land tenure systems. All of these, in one way or another, contribute to conflicts and tenure insecurity. A discussion of land tenure security in the context of sustainable land and soil management in Africa must consider the implications of informal/customary and modified customary land tenure systems.[76] A significant percentage of Africa's total land area is managed under some form of these customary or communal tenure systems, and only a small fraction is formally recognised by the governments of a few countries. Customary land rights span various categories of land but are difficult to assess accurately due to a lack of legal recognition, inadequate reporting, and limited access to reporting systems.[77] It is reported that in 2005, only 1% of the land in Africa was legally registered.[78]

---

74 Smith et al. (2014: 853).
75 Mazwi & Mudimu (2021: 225).
76 IPCC (2019: 749).
77 Ibid.
78 Ibid.

#### 16.1.8.1. Customary land tenure systems

Customary land tenure systems are based on traditional norms, rules, and practices that have evolved within specific communities. The characteristics are as follows:

- Land is often seen as a communal resource, with access and use rights determined by kinship, lineage, and community membership.
- Rights are often tied to specific social roles and responsibilities within the community.
- Land is typically not considered a commodity to be bought and sold, but rather as a source of livelihood and social identity.

Thus, in communal land tenure systems, land is held collectively by a community, and community needs and decisions determine access. Individuals may have the right to use land for specific purposes, such as farming or grazing, but not necessarily the right to own it. In some communities, only male children can inherit land, while in other communities, land is inherited by both males and females. In patrilineal systems, land ownership and inheritance are handed down through the male line.

#### 16.1.8.2. Formal or statutory land tenure systems

On the other hand, formal or statutory land tenure systems are based on laws and regulations established by national governments, which recognise and protect land ownership and use rights. Formal or statutory land tenure systems exhibit the following characteristics:

- Land can be owned privately, communally, or by the state.
- Land ownership and use rights are registered and documented.
- Land can be bought, sold, and used as collateral for loans.

Regarding private land ownership, natural persons, individuals, and corporations have the right to own and manage land.

Regarding state land ownership, governments own and control land and may lease or allocate it to individuals or organisations. In some countries, such as Cameroon, a distinction is made between state and private land. It includes lands belonging to public bodies and state-controlled national lands, which the state can classify or incorporate for environmental or developmental purposes. It can also be allocated to corporations through investment leases. Thus, individuals or organisations can lease land from the government or other landowners for a specific period.

#### 16.1.8.3. Hybrid and informal systems

Many African countries have formal and informal land tenure systems, with customary tenure systems often coexisting with formal or statutory systems. In some countries, customary tenure systems are not formally recognised and frequently operate outside formal legal frameworks, with land rights determined by customary norms and practices. Such informal systems can be vulnerable to conflict and insecurity, as they are not always legally recognised or protected. Clashes and disputes can arise between customary and formal land tenure systems.

### 16.2. Issuance of more than one title over the same piece of land

In many cases, multiple land titles are issued over the same parcel of land, resulting in disputes and tenure insecurity. This problem is often rooted in poor land administration, including inadequate record-keeping, weak institutional capacity, and corruption within land governance systems. Such uncertainty is deeply frustrating for landholders and may discourage long-term investment in sustainable land use. Instead, it can incentivise exploitative or short-term land management practices, ultimately harming soil health and undermining SLM. The cumulative effect of these challenges underscores the urgent need for comprehensive land tenure reform across Africa. Robust, transparent, and accountable tenure systems are crucial for securing land rights, mitigating conflict, and promoting responsible stewardship of soil resources.

### 16.3. Options or mechanisms that can safeguard land tenure security in Africa

Understanding the interactions between land tenure security and SLM in Africa must be grounded in the relationship between land tenure systems and soil security. Tenure security is a decisive factor for SLM and soil protection.[79] Strengthening land tenure security can facilitate the adoption of soil conservation measures, thereby contributing to SLM.[80] Land tenure security can be safeguarded or achieved through various legal and non-legal mechanisms if land tenure rights are clearly defined and well-established.

79 IPCC (2019: 749).
80 Ibid.: 287.

### 16.3.1. Main focus: Legal mechanisms that safeguard land tenure security to be considered in accordance with each country's specificity in Africa

To strengthen SLM, African countries should adopt legal mechanisms that protect tenure security and stability. These mechanisms may include the provision of formal land titles, long-term leases, and the formal or legal recognition of customary land tenure systems, preferably enshrined in national constitutions. Importantly, such measures should reflect the diverse tenure systems that exist across the continent. However, while these approaches hold promise, existing research indicates only medium confidence that land titling and the recognition and respect of indigenous and communal tenure systems consistently result in improved SLM outcomes. The effectiveness of these legal interventions often depends on broader governance factors, including implementation capacity, institutional integrity, and the degree of community participation in land governance processes.[81]

### 16.3.2. Legal option one: Formal title or freehold land tenure

Formal title or freehold land tenure is a traditionally Western concept of individual property rights that envisages absolute land rights, implying the right to own, control, manage, use, and dispose of land. While such land rights are held in perpetuity, the state may expropriate the land when it is targeted for public purposes (for example, road construction, urban expansion, etc.). Formal title is the most secure form of land tenure in Africa.[82] During this tenure, landowners often invest in sustainable land and soil management practices.

### 16.3.3. Legal option two: Long-term lease under leasehold land tenure

A lease is a contract by which one party, known as the lessor, conveys land, property, services, etc., to another, known as the lessee, for a specified time. Under a leasehold, land tenure rights are based on the notion of renting for a specified period. Such leases can be long or short. A long-term lease, typically involving a 99-year lease, is considered a highly secure form of land tenure. Under this mechanism, land belonging to one entity, either the state or an individual (the lessor), is, by contractual arrangement, leased to another entity or person (the lessee). The lease agreement is then registered against the title of that land to create effective and enforceable land rights. Leasehold land tenure has been primarily associated with large-scale farming

81 Ibid.: 70.
82 Kasimbazi (2017: 9).

and elite land ownership regimes.[83] In some jurisdictions, such as Uganda, non-citizens are only eligible for leases.[84] Under short-term leases, land usually suffers greater degradation, as tenant farmers may be unwilling to undertake sustainable land management or soil protection measures because they do not have the land long enough to realise the benefits of their investments. On the contrary, long-term leases support sustainable land and soil management, as leaseholders feel more secure and tend to improve the land, just as title owners do.

#### 16.3.4. Legal option three: Formal recognition of customary land tenure, especially in constitutions

Under customary land tenure, land is administered according to the customs of local and indigenous communities, rather than under statutory tenure or a formal title system. Under customary land tenure, land ownership is vested in a tribe, group, family, or community and allocated by customary authorities or traditional leaders. Customary land rights are often flexible and overlapping, allowing individuals and groups to use local lands and their appurtenant resources. Access to land is typically restricted by kinship or ethnicity, excluding outsiders and restricting land sales. Individuals or families within a community may be allocated land for their individual or family use. Still, if they leave the land unused, it may return to the community. This is the most common type of tenure in Africa. For example, approximately 70% of Kenya's land tenure is customary.[85]

Customary land tenure systems in Africa are increasingly vulnerable to the misuse of state power, particularly under the pretext of eminent domain, which has often facilitated state-led encroachment onto customary lands. In practice, this has disproportionately affected people experiencing poverty, who are typically unable to afford formal land registration, resulting in a lack of secure tenure. Scholars and policy assessments have observed that customary tenure arrangements often provide only weak legal protection, especially in contexts where state law does not formally recognise or enforce such rights.[86] However, where tenure security is ensured for customary landholders and communities, it tends to promote the retention of traditional knowledge and practices, many of which support SLM and soil protection. Strengthening the legal recognition of customary tenure can thus serve not only to safeguard livelihoods but also to reinforce ecologically sound land stewardship.

---

83 Ibid.

84 Ibid.

85 Ibid.

86 Lang (2017: 116).

### 16.4. Additional focus: Non-legal mechanisms to be mentioned or considered as supplementary tools for safeguarding land tenure security by countries/regions in Africa

Some incentive mechanisms (non-legal tools that can safeguard land tenure security) that can encourage farmers to invest in degraded lands and own them to avoid continuous pressure on already scarce fertile lands include:

- providing them with manure free of charge; and
- granting interest-free loans.

### 16.5. Annotations: explanation of the different options for safeguarding land tenure security in Africa (pros and cons for each option/system)

The significant socio-political and legal changes for SLM require a wide range of land governance mechanisms.

#### 16.5.1. Explanation of formal title as an option for safeguarding land tenure security in Africa

Formal land title under statutory law is widely recommended as one of the most robust mechanisms for safeguarding land tenure security in Africa. Once established, such a title is typically deemed absolute, definite, and difficult to challenge. Even in cases where it is contested, formal institutions often possess the legal and administrative strength to adjudicate and enforce rights effectively. Accordingly, a formal title offers landowners and users the highest degree of tenure security, which can incentivise the adoption of SLM practices.

However, despite these advantages, the statutory land titling system can also generate significant exclusion. Access to a formal title is often contingent on an individual's ability to navigate complex, costly, and bureaucratic procedures—conditions that tend to favour elites and marginalise people with low incomes. As a result, this model of land tenure recognition can entrench inequality and undermine broad-based access to land. In contrast, customary land tenure systems are typically grounded in communal norms and collective responsibility, prioritising inclusion and social welfare over exclusivity. These systems enable community members to access and use land in ways that support familial livelihoods and social cohesion. Therefore, while formal titling provides legal certainty, it may simultaneously undermine the inclusive principles embedded in customary land governance, with implications for equity and sustainability.

### 16.5.2. Explanation of long-term lease

Long-term leases, typically extending up to 99 years, are widely regarded as a highly secure form of land tenure. Lessees under such arrangements often enjoy a level of tenure security comparable to that of formal titleholders. This sense of stability incentivises long-term planning, investment, and land stewardship, thereby promoting SLM. In contrast, short-term lease arrangements tend to offer little security or incentive for tenants to invest in land improvement or conservation. Short-term tenants may avoid implementing SLM practices, as the limited duration of their lease does not allow sufficient time to realise the benefits of such investments. Thus, lands under short-term leases are often more vulnerable to degradation and unsustainable exploitation. In this regard, long-term leases not only support tenure security but also enable environmentally sound land-use practices by allowing lessees adequate time to recoup costs and enjoy the benefits of their stewardship.

Long-term lease as an option for safeguarding land tenure security in Africa offers several opportunities for sustainable land/soil management, including:

- Encouraging investment in land and soil improvement as it provides land users, such as farmers, the security and stability to invest in their land, leading to improved soil health and overall productivity.
- Offering stability and predictability and promoting sustainable practices, enabling investors to plan and invest in long-term projects, and to adopt sustainable land management practices, reduce fertiliser use, as they can see the long-term benefits of the sustainable land management practices, especially regarding soil protection.
- Enabling diversified land management systems by supporting agroforestry is essential for improving soil health and reducing erosion and pollution.
- In some cases, long-term leases are inheritable, further increasing the security of tenure and encouraging long-term investment, crucial for soil sustainability.

### 16.5.3. Explanation of formal or legal recognition of customary land tenure

One of the key shortcomings of customary land tenure systems, highlighting the need for formal or legal recognition, is their vulnerability to abuse of power. These abuses often occur under the guise of state ownership or through interference by foreign investors and traditional leaders who exceed or misuse their authority. This has facilitated widespread encroachment on customary lands, often with little to no compensation for the affected communities. Despite such vulnerabilities, customary tenure remains a foundational element of land law in virtually all African countries.[87]

87 McAuslan (2006).

Another significant limitation is that customary tenure does not provide the same level of security as private land titles. Its lack of formal recognition and its operation outside statutory frameworks often leave communities exposed to tenure insecurity and legal marginalisation. To address this, customary land rights should be legally recognised, ideally through constitutional provisions that guarantee rights of ownership, access, and use, rather than merely confining customary claims to occupation and use of "national land" owned and controlled by the state.[88] The importance of securing customary tenure is further underscored by empirical evidence from the Intergovernmental Panel on Climate Change (IPCC), which finds a strong correlation between secure communal tenure and lower deforestation rates. Forest preservation, in turn, helps prevent soil erosion and maintain soil fertility, thereby enhancing conditions for SLM.[89] Legal recognition of indigenous and customary land rights through targeted reforms is, therefore, not only a matter of equity and justice but also a cost-effective and contextually appropriate strategy for improving soil protection and land governance across Africa.[90]

Another critical shortcoming of the customary land tenure system that necessitates formal recognition is the security risk posed by competing claims from multiple rights holders, especially in areas subject to diverse uses such as agriculture, grazing, and fishing. These challenges are particularly acute in regions facing socio-political and climatic instability, such as the Sahel, where climate-induced stressors contribute to conflict between farmers, pastoralists, and fisherfolk, all competing for limited fertile land and water resources.

Customary institutions, though culturally embedded and historically resilient, often lack the regulatory capacity to manage such complex and overlapping claims effectively. The absence of formal mechanisms to recognise and adjudicate these rights exacerbates insecurity, especially where rights are informal and undocumented.

To address this, a customary land registration system, administered at the local level, has been proposed. Such a system would allow community members to register their lands under customary tenure, offering an accessible and cost-effective alternative to formal titling in rural areas. However, communities often express deep scepticism toward local administrations, fearing corruption, lack of transparency, and elite capture. From the perspective of grassroots communities, entrusting local governments with land management responsibilities can alienate them from decision-making processes and expose them to power imbalances, particularly when local officials allocate land to politically connected elites without proper consultation.

To overcome these challenges, any customary registration scheme must be grounded in participatory governance and incorporate robust safeguards. This could be achieved by establishing land commissions composed of trusted community

---

88 Wily (2011: 24).
89 IPCC (2019: 749).
90 Ibid.

figures, such as elders, kinship heads, and clan leaders, to authenticate and supervise land claims. National legislation could provide that, while formal titles may be issued in rural areas, customary land rights documented through certificates of customary ownership should be equally recognised and provide adequate tenure security. This approach allows both systems to coexist and complement one another, reflecting the socio-legal pluralism present in most African contexts.

The constitutional recognition of customary tenure is crucial. While many African states have acknowledged the legal and/or legitimate status of various land tenure systems, tenure security remains narrowly tied to statutory titles, such as individual land titles and leases. This reality excludes many who customarily hold land but lack the resources to navigate costly and complex formal titling processes. Legal reform that establishes a dual tenure system comprising statutory and customary tenure offers a path forward for enhancing tenure security and promoting SLM.

A further justification for such reform is the potential for greater local and indigenous buy-in, where legal recognition of customary systems fosters legitimacy, trust, and stewardship over land. The alignment of formal legal systems with community norms can help translate tenure security into sustainable land-use practices, with positive spillover effects for soil conservation, biodiversity, and climate resilience.

While a dual system is normatively sound and socially responsive, its practical implementation is contingent upon political will. Where feasible, it would involve land titling under statutory law in urban, peri-urban, and certain rural areas, as well as customary land registration in rural areas, through less burdensome and more inclusive procedures. Such an approach would ensure that legal pluralism is not merely tolerated but institutionalised, forming the bedrock of a more equitable and sustainable land governance regime in Africa.

### 16.5.4. Other options/mechanisms in response to the challenges of land tenure security

Other ways of carrying out land tenure reform to appropriately safeguard tenure security across Africa, to enhance sustainable management of land and soils on the continent are:

- Formulation of comprehensive national land management legislation/acts, or policies.
- Establishment of national land tenure agencies that supervise all transactions relating to acquiring formal land titles, leases, and registration of customary lands in respective countries.
- Guarantee fairness and certainty in granting land titles with secured access, ownership, and use rights. Tenure security is essential for adopting sustainable

land management practices. This is especially true in an era characterised by payment for ecosystem services, in which landowners are encouraged to restore and rehabilitate degraded land, cultivate and store carbon, and receive payment for that carbon through the Crediting Mechanism.

- Implement land tenure reforms that ensure the participation or involvement of those interested in land that is the subject of any transaction to overcome the lack of inclusive land governance across Africa.
- Implement land tenure regimes that recognise and uphold the co-existence of both statutory and customary tenure systems. Secure land tenure, especially for communally managed lands, helps reduce large-scale and arbitrary land appropriations.[91]
- Simplify the complex/cumbersome procedures for establishing formal land titles and institute less complex/cumbersome and less costly methods for registering customary lands.
- Institute strict measures to guard against land-grabbing and corruption of traditional leaders and ensure adequate compensation to those whose lands are expropriated for public interest. If the public-interest goal is not attained, such land should revert to its owners. To overcome LSLAs, governments can implement policies that impose restrictions on the size of land sales/leases; reinforce pressure on agribusiness companies to agree to Voluntary Guidelines on the Responsible Governance of Tenure of Land, Fisheries and Forests in the Context of National Food Security, or similar principles; strengthen existing land law and land registration systems; in partnership with NGOs, make use of community monitoring systems and enhance protests against LSLAs.[92]
- Secure land rights, including for customarily held lands, can incentivise users to adopt long-term SLM practices that benefit soil protection.
- Encouraging traditional rulers to abolish customs and practices that discriminate against women, especially those that prohibit women from inheriting land. Empowering women can bolster SLM, a goal achieved through policy instruments that account for gender differences.[93] The overwhelming presence of women in many land-based activities, including agriculture, provides opportunities to mainstream gender policies, overcome gender barriers, enhance gender equality, and increase SLM.[94]
- Enhance and digitalise record-keeping to stamp out corruption and issuing more than one land title over the same parcel of land.
- Above all, the IPCC recommends more research on the optimal tenure mix, including low-cost land certification, redistribution reforms, market-assisted

---

91 IPCC (2019: 287).
92 Ibid.: 750.
93 Ibid.: 70.
94 Ibid.

reforms, gender-responsive reforms, and collective forms of land tenure such as communal and cooperative land tenure.[95]

### 16.6. Proposed text for legal provisions for safeguarding land tenure security in Africa

(1) The law guarantees every citizen the right to own, use, control, and dispose of land. However, the enjoyment of these rights is conditioned on proof of a land title/certificate or a certificate of customary ownership in the case of customary land, duly established in accordance with laid down rules and procedures.
(2) Natural persons and corporate bodies of foreign nationality or corporations wishing to invest in a country may conclude lease agreements to have access to land. Such a lease may be granted over urban or rural lands. Deeds drawn up for this purpose shall bear the prior approval of the minister in charge of lands, under penalty of being null and void.
(3) Owners of both long-term and short-term leases shall invest in land improvement, foster long-term land planning, and promote efficient resource use.
(4) The Constitution or this law hereby recognises the co-existence of both statutory land tenure systems, consisting of the issuance of private land titles, and customary land tenure systems, consisting of the issuance of a certificate of customary ownership.
(5) Occupants of lands in rural and peri-urban areas who cannot afford to register such lands under formal land titling systems may apply for such lands to be registered and a certificate of customary ownership issued under the customary land tenure system.
(6) This law establishes a national land tenure agency that is in charge of supervising all transactions relating to the acquisition of formal land titles, leases, and registration of customary lands in the country.

## 17. Commentary XVI: Traditional leaders

This Commentary advocates for sustainable soil governance that recognises the vital role of traditional leadership in Africa as custodians of local customs and the land. It further promotes inclusive governance by encouraging the integration of traditional knowledge systems with modern scientific approaches.

95 Ibid.: 287.

Soil is a fundamental natural resource, composed of minerals, organic matter, gases, liquids, and a vast array of organisms that together sustain life on Earth. Its formation is a gradual process that occurs over thousands of years through the weathering of rocks and the decomposition of organic materials. Soil plays an indispensable role in supporting terrestrial ecosystems by providing physical stability and essential nutrients for plant growth, serving as a habitat for countless organisms crucial to biodiversity and ecological balance, and acting as a natural carbon sink that contributes to climate change mitigation.

Despite its critical importance, soil is increasingly under threat due to population pressures, rapid industrialisation, and climate change. These forces drive soil degradation through erosion, nutrient loss, and contamination, which in turn accelerate desertification and diminish the land's capacity to sustain life. In response, there is an urgent need for all relevant stakeholders to engage actively in the sustainable management of soil resources. Among these, traditional leaders hold a unique position. As stewards of customary land and repositories of indigenous knowledge, they are indispensable actors in efforts to protect and restore Africa's soils.

## 17.1. Soil governance

Soil governance encompasses the policies, institutions, and processes that direct the management, conservation, and sustainable use of soil resources. It plays a critical role in ensuring food security, preserving biodiversity[96], mitigating climate change, and sustaining vital ecosystem services.

Soil governance has the following components: policy framework, institutional structures, regulatory mechanisms, stakeholder engagement, capacity building, research, and monitoring.

Well-governed soil exhibits several characteristics that contribute to its health, productivity, and sustainability, thus supporting sustainable agriculture and food security.

### 17.1.1. Key stakeholders in soil governance in Africa

Soil governance in Africa involves a diverse range of stakeholders who play critical roles in managing and sustainably using soil resources. These include national and regional governments, which are responsible for developing and enforcing policies and regulations; farmers and agricultural communities, who are the primary stewards of the land; and research institutions that provide essential data and technical support.

96 See Hinz & Ruppel (2008); Hinz et al. (2012).

Non-governmental organisations and environmental groups contribute to soil health through advocacy, awareness-raising, and community initiatives. At the same time, the private sector, including agribusiness and mining companies, has a significant impact on soil health through their operations. International organisations and development partners support policy development, funding, and regional collaboration. Indigenous communities and traditional leaders offer invaluable local knowledge, and policymakers and urban planners influence long-term land-use patterns. Despite the broad range of actors involved, soil governance in Africa faces significant challenges, including widespread land degradation and erosion, fragmented land tenure systems, high population pressure, weak policy frameworks, socio-economic inequalities, and competing land uses such as mining and urban development. These challenges require inclusive, well-coordinated, and context-specific strategies that integrate traditional knowledge with modern science to ensure effective and sustainable soil management across the continent.

### 17.1.2. Traditional leaders in Africa

Traditional leaders in Africa are individuals who wield authority within their communities based on long-standing cultural, historical, and social norms rather than formal political systems. They are widely respected for their roles in governance, conflict resolution, and the preservation of cultural heritage. Over time, the structure and functions of traditional leadership have evolved significantly, influenced by historical events such as colonialism, apartheid, and independence movements, as well as by processes of Westernisation, modernisation, and constitutional reforms. Today, traditional leadership operates within increasingly pluralistic state structures, where it must coexist and sometimes intersect with formal legal and political institutions.

A simplified pattern of the structure of traditional leaders includes:

- Chiefs, Kings, or Queens: The conventional leadership apex structure and symbol of unity, and the primary decision maker for the community.
- Council of Elders or Advisors: Council of Elders/Advisors, consisting of respected members of the community, who can even advise the community.
- Lineage heads: They often play a crucial role in managing the affairs of their respective family lines. Age grades and societies play a significant role in governance, as they are organised according to age or initiation and contribute to decision-making, conflict resolution, and the enforcement of community norms.
- Traditional courts: Where applicable, they (still) deal with matters of land disputes, marital issues, and minor offences, and they are presided over by chiefs, elders, or other designated individuals.

- Religious leaders: They provide spiritual guidance, preside over ceremonies, and serve as advisors to the communities. Depending on the system, they may also be integrated into the traditional leadership structure. Effective traditional leadership relies on deeply rooted cultural knowledge and heritage, wisdom and experience, integrity and honesty, empathy and compassion, conflict resolution skills, advocacy and community mobilisation skills, among other attributes. In fact, it fosters societal harmony with the respective communities.
- Traditional leaders: They can play a pivotal role in soil governance through their deep-rooted influence in local communities and customary systems. Their contributions span a range of activities, including land administration and management, the resolution of land-related conflicts, and the protection of communal natural resources. They often serve as custodians of customary land rights and play integral roles in local governance structures. Traditional leaders also contribute to the development and implementation of national land policies by articulating community interests, and they are frequently involved in environmental conservation efforts. Additionally, they help regulate agricultural practices, promote culturally rooted land use traditions, and support broader community development initiatives. Their active participation is essential for achieving inclusive, culturally appropriate, and sustainable soil governance across Africa.

### 17.1.3. Land tenure and traditional soil governance

#### 17.1.3.1. Land tenure

Land tenure refers to the rights and arrangements regarding the use, control, and transfer of land. Secure land tenure is essential for effective soil management as it influences the farmers' willingness to invest in long-term soil health.

Land tenure in Africa is diverse and complex, varying significantly across the continent due to historical, cultural, and socioeconomic factors. The common land tenure systems include customary, freehold, leasehold, and public land tenure.

The simplified African regional land tenure systems comprise the following:

(1) East Africa: (Kenya, Uganda, Tanzania) - A Mixture of customary, freehold, and leasehold systems, and land tenure systems reforms are focused on formalising customary rights and improving governance.

(2) Southern Africa: (South Africa, Zimbabwe, Namibia) - Pluralistic approaches in land ownership due to colonialism, apartheid, land redistribution, and tenure reforms.

(3) West Africa: (Ghana, Nigeria, Côte d'Ivoire) - Predominant customary systems, with increasing pressure on land due to population growth and commercial agriculture.
(4) North Africa: (Egypt, Morocco, Algeria) - A mixture of state-owned, private, and communal lands, with varying degrees of formalisation and registration.

Community land in Africa has several distinct characteristics that vary across different regions and communities. This includes collective ownership, customary tenure systems, community rights to use, cultural significance, sources of essential community resources, and vulnerability to external pressures, and can be both a source of community conflicts and a basis for community livelihoods. It is integral to the social, economic, and cultural fabric of many African societies and embodies the interplay between traditional practices and modern legal frameworks.

17.1.3.2. Traditional and modern soil governance practices

Traditional and modern soil governance practices have evolved in response to shifting societal structures, agricultural systems, and environmental challenges. The central challenge today is to effectively integrate traditional knowledge with modern scientific approaches to establish sustainable and culturally relevant soil governance systems. Traditional practices include customary land tenure systems, shifting cultivation, crop rotation, fallowing to naturally restore soil fertility, indigenous knowledge systems, and communal labour arrangements. In contrast, modern soil governance emphasises national soil management strategies, such as integrated soil fertility management, climate-smart agriculture, and public–private partnerships. Harmonising these approaches offers a pathway toward resilient and inclusive soil governance frameworks in Africa.

17.1.3.3. Soil law implementation in community land

Soil law implementation refers to the legal frameworks and practices that govern land use management and the preservation of soil resources within a community's territory. It includes aspects of land rights, sustainable practices, regulatory frameworks, community engagement, conflict resolution, and awareness creation.

## 17.2. Soil law implementation by traditional leaders on community land

Traditional leaders enforce laws within their communities using a variety of mechanisms rooted in customary law, cultural norms and practices, and societal structures.

The enforcement of laws can differ depending on the community, while specific customs *inter alia* include:

- Community consensus: Traditional leaders often operate through community consensus, consulting with clans, families, or influential members to reach a collective agreement on matters. Their authority stems from the respect they command, and decisions are expected to be respected and honoured by community members.
- Customary trials and mediation: In cases of disputes or breaches of customary law, traditional leaders may conduct trials or mediation based on customary law. They gather evidence, listen to testimony, and make determinations that are binding within the community. In many jurisdictions in Africa, however, the criminal law enforcement has moved to state jurisdiction.
- Social pressure: Traditional leaders leverage social relationships and norms to enforce laws. Community members are discouraged from breaking rules, as this may result in social ostracism or loss of respect within the community.
- Restorative justice: Many traditional systems emphasise restorative justice, focusing on repairing societal harm by restoring relationships rather than merely punishing offenders. Leaders may facilitate discussions between the offending and aggrieved parties to reach mutually agreeable resolutions.
- Incentives and rewards: Traditional leaders sometimes use incentives to encourage compliance with laws and regulations. This can include public recognition, community support, or rewards for individuals who adhere to customary practices.
- Cultural sanctions: Non-compliance may result in cultural sanctions, such as fines, public shaming, or rituals intended to restore societal harmony. These sanctions reinforce the community's norms and motivate adherence to traditional laws and values.
- Accountability through elders and councils: Traditional leaders are often supported by elder councils or committees that assist in lawmaking and enforcement. They help to monitor adherence to customs and provide guidance on appropriate actions and sanctions.
- Education and awareness: Traditional leaders may conduct educational efforts to inform community members about laws and the importance of adhering to them for the community's well-being. The effectiveness of law enforcement by traditional leaders relies heavily on the support structures vested in them by

the state, their moral authority, the respect they command within the community, and the collective adherence to shared customs and beliefs.

## 17.3. Challenges facing the implementation of soil law in community lands

Implementing soil law on community land, particularly when involving traditional leaders, can present a range of challenges. These include, among others:

- Authority and jurisdiction conflicts: Traditional leaders may have their own systems of governance and dispute resolution, which could conflict with formal legal frameworks. This duality can create confusion over authority and jurisdiction, potentially leading to conflict. Soil management often involves multiple stakeholders, including local communities, government agencies, and the private sector. Different interests and objectives can lead to a lack of cohesive strategies, making it challenging to implement new soil laws.
- Inadequate legal awareness: Traditional leaders and community members may not be fully aware of soil laws nor receive adequate support or recognition from government authorities, which can lead to noncompliance or misunderstanding of legal requirements. This limits their authority and effectiveness in enforcing soil laws. Additionally, existing laws and regulations may not effectively address current soil threats, such as erosion, contamination, and degradation, nor do they encourage sustainable land-use practices.
- Cases of mismanagement: Even when soil laws are in place, enforcement can be weak due to a lack of political will or inadequate monitoring systems. Mismanagement and abuse of authority can create a culture of impunity, in which individuals and organisations are not held accountable for violating the law.
- Resource limitations: Implementing soil laws requires resources, such as funding for capacity building and awareness creation programs, materials for sustainable practices, alternative livelihoods for those affected by regulations, or technology for soil management. Traditional leaders in rural areas require access to these resources to bridge gaps among traditional practices, legal requirements, monitoring, and enforcement.
- Lack of awareness and knowledge: Traditional leaders are equipped with the necessary wisdom that, in addition, can acquire knowledge or training about modern agricultural practices and soil laws. This knowledge complementarity can foster effective implementation and enforcement, leading to best practices that prioritise sustainable soil management. They can be instrumental in making their communities more resilient by overcoming resistance to, for

instance, new regulations or practices introduced by soil laws that replace unsustainable traditional practices.

- Conflict resolution: Traditional soil governance structures may vary significantly between different communities based on the influence and power of traditional leaders, which can strengthen the rights of all in their community. The application of and adherence to soil law can differ significantly between communities depending on the influence and power of traditional leaders. Traditional conflict-resolution mechanisms aligned with legal processes can improve soil management.
- Climate change impacts: Traditional leaders have known about climate change before modern science detected it. Yet an improved scientific understanding of sustainable soil practices and environmental conservation among traditional leaders and community members can positively impact compliance with and the implementation of soil laws. Changing weather patterns and extreme weather events can exacerbate soil degradation, putting additional pressure on governance systems to respond effectively. Increased droughts, floods, and erosion, as well as biodiversity loss, can strain traditional coping mechanisms and require new approaches. Traditional leaders often have the power to adapt to these changing conditions while working within the constraints of existing laws.
- Land use conflicts: Customary land tenure systems can clash with statutory land laws. This can lead to confusion and disputes over land ownership and usage rights, hindering the effective implementation of soil conservation measures. Competition among agricultural, urban, and industrial land uses can also lead to conflicts that undermine sustainable soil governance. Rapid population growth is increasing pressure on land resources, leading to unsustainable farming practices and deforestation. This may call on traditional leaders to strike a balance between the needs of their communities and the need to protect soil resources. While engaging the community is crucial, traditional leaders can foster trust and collaboration on the importance of soil laws.
- Vulnerability of local communities: When it comes to giving effect to enforceable sustainable soil practices, traditional governance systems can promote and protect the rights and needs of local communities, particularly marginalised groups, women, youth, and people with disabilities. External actors, such as commercial farmers, mining companies, or government agencies, sometimes exert pressure on traditional leaders to prioritise economic development over soil conservation. Political affiliations and pressures can erode the authority of traditional leaders, leading to unsustainable land-use practices.
- Technological adaptation: The rapid development of new technologies for monitoring and managing soil health can be integrated into traditional

governance systems, leading to improved soil practices. Furthermore, a lack of comprehensive, accessible data on soil health, use, and management practices can hinder effective decision-making. Addressing these challenges requires a collaborative approach that considers both ecological and socio-economic factors in soil governance. In such processes involving traditional leaders, the government, communities, and other key stakeholders are essential to success.

## 17.4. Options for the role of traditional leaders in implementing soil law

Incorporating traditional leadership into the implementation of soil law can create a more inclusive and culturally relevant approach to managing soil resources, ultimately supporting the achievement of sustainable development goals in African communities. Traditional leaders play a crucial role in implementing soil law across various regions in Africa, leveraging their influence and local knowledge. Their roles in soil governance include:

### 17.4.1. Conflict resolution in implementing soil law

Conflict resolution in soil governance addresses disputes over land use, ownership rights, and resource management through culturally embedded practices and customary laws. Involving traditional leaders for conflict resolution ensures local buy-in as they have the necessary authority and respect within their communities to mediate conflicts, including those related to land and soil usage, which can minimise disputes and contribute to a more peaceful coexistence in the application of culturally appropriate methods and narratives that both resonate with community values, facilitate understanding and contribute to a resolution of soil conflicts (e.g. land tenure conflicts, resource allocation, encroachment, "land grabbing", environmental degradation and conflicting government policies). Thus, the effective conflict-resolution mechanism relies on the active involvement of traditional leaders in soil governance, as they are trusted for their authority, legitimacy, integrity, knowledge, and wisdom. It is essential to acknowledge the role of traditional leaders in conflict mediation and collaborative governance, and to include provisions for establishing multi-stakeholder committees that incorporate diverse voices. These committees should integrate traditional authorities into broader governance structures to promote sustainable practices and embed indigenous knowledge systems and early warning mechanisms for conflict into soil governance. By implementing these strategies, traditional leaders can help foster more sustainable, inclusive, and equitable land use across Africa.

### 17.4.2. Advocacy and awareness

Advocacy refers to the efforts to influence decision-makers and raise public awareness about the importance of soil governance. Traditional leaders can play a crucial role in mobilising the local population to recognise the importance of soil health, protect and sustainably utilise soil resources, and engage with local and national governments to promote national policies that protect soil resources and support sustainable agricultural practices.

### 17.4.3. Mismanagement

Mismanagement in soil governance frequently occurs during the implementation of soil laws, resulting from inadequate enforcement, poor planning, and a lack of expertise and training. Such deficiencies can lead to ineffective regulation, resulting in environmental degradation, economic losses, social inequality, and a decline in public trust. To mitigate these effects, it is essential to adopt robust strategies, including strengthening oversight mechanisms, enhancing transparency, building institutional and technical capacity, promoting public participation, creating incentives for compliance, enforcing penalties for violations, and fostering collaborative governance across all levels.

## 17.5. Legal mechanisms to strengthen the enforcement of soil law by traditional leaders

Some of the approaches can include the following non-conclusive set of measures:

- Corresponding customary and statutory land laws: Legal frameworks that recognise and respect customary land tenure systems, while promoting sustainable land management practices.
- Raising awareness and building capacity: Providing training and education to traditional leaders and community members on soil laws, sustainable land management practices, and the overall benefits of soil conservation.
- Strengthening enforcement mechanisms: Enhancing monitoring systems, increasing transparency, and holding individuals who violate soil laws liable.
- Empowering women: Ensuring that women have equal rights and opportunities in land ownership and decision-making processes.
- Addressing climate change: Implementing climate-smart agriculture practices and investing in adaptation measures to reduce the impacts of climate change on soil resources.

- Promoting sustainable livelihoods: Providing alternative livelihood options for those affected by soil conservation measures, such as eco-tourism, agroforestry, or small-scale enterprises.

# Legislating into the future: soil law, AI, and digitalisation

*Ruda Murray & Oliver C. Ruppel*

"It is customary to offer a grain of comfort, in the form of a statement that some peculiarly human characteristic could never be imitated by a machine. I cannot offer any such comfort, for I believe that no such bounds can be set." —Alan Turing, 1951

## 1. Introduction

Artificial intelligence (AI) has been called "the new electricity."[1] In less than a decade, technologies once confined to science fiction (e.g., robots, algorithms, and adaptive digital companions) have become part of everyday life. In 2023 alone, the United States (US) Food and Drug Administration approved 223 AI-powered medical devices, compared to only six in 2015.[2] Autonomous vehicles are no longer experimental: Waymo now delivers more than 150,000 self-driving rides weekly in the US, while Baidu's Apollo Go robotaxis operate across multiple Chinese cities.[3] In 2024, nearly 80% of businesses worldwide reported using AI tools.[4] In December 2024, an AI system known as "The Fourth Judge" was employed to score a world championship boxing match in Riyadh, Saudi Arabia.[5] In 2025, Albania made history by appointing Diella, the world's first AI-powered virtual minister, to oversee public procurement.[6] In August 2025, Malaysia launched the world's first AI-powered bank (Ryt Bank), led by YTL Group and Sea Limited.[7] What seemed futuristic has become an integral part of how societies function, communicate, and govern.

The scale of investment underscores this shift. Between 2013 and 2024, the US attracted nearly USD 500 billion in private AI funding,[8] followed by China (USD 119 billion), the United Kingdom (UK) (USD 28 billion), and Canada and Israel (around USD 15 billion each).[9] In 2024, US institutions produced 40 major AI models, while

1 See https://www.gsb.stanford.edu/insights/andrew-ng-why-ai-new-electricity, accessed 29 September 2025.

2 Stanford University (2025: 3).

3 Ibid.

4 Ibid.

5 See www.forbes.com/sites/brianmazique/2024/12/21/oleksandr-usyk-vs-tyson-fury-2-results-winner-scorecards-reaction, accessed 27 October 2025.

6 See https://www.politico.eu/article/albania-apppoints-worlds-first-virtual-minister-edi-rama-diella/, accessed 27 October 2025.

7 See https://www.artificialintelligence-news.com/news/malaysia-launches-ryt-bank-its-first-ai-powered-bank/, accessed 30 October 2025.

8 See https://www.visualcapitalist.com/visualizing-global-ai-investment-by-country/#google_vignette, accessed 29 September 2025.

9 Ibid.

China created 15 and Europe produced just 3.[10] Global trade in goods that enable AI reached approximately USD 2.3 trillion in 2023.[11] These figures reflect not only economic ambition but also a geopolitical race to shape the digital rules of the future. This race increasingly forces countries into binary choices between US and Chinese technologies, raising profound questions of sovereignty, autonomy, and security.

AI is also entering the realm of governance, including environmental governance. It offers opportunities to improve transparency, anticipate ecological risks, and strengthen enforcement. Yet it also raises pressing questions: Who controls the data on which AI depends? How are algorithmic decisions made, and who is accountable when they cause harm? Can digital governance frameworks genuinely promote soil protection and environmental justice, or do they risk entrenching existing inequalities under the guise of innovation?

Environmental governance often struggles with fragmented national laws and policies—especially in understudied sectors where coherence is crucial but poorly theorised. Legal materials are scattered across languages, jurisdictions, and political contexts, making systematic cross-country comparison difficult. Recent advances in behavioural and cognitive-scale AI provide a glimpse of what governance assistance might look like. For instance, "Centaur," a model fine-tuned on the large-scale Psych-101 dataset (covering millions of human decisions across hundreds of experiments), can predict and simulate human behaviour in any scenario expressible in natural language.[12] Its ability to generalise across unseen tasks and align with human neural patterns suggests how similar systems could eventually help policymakers model institutional performance, anticipate stakeholder responses, and test regulatory outcomes before implementation. Such cognitive-level modelling, when applied ethically, could transform governance from a reactive to an anticipatory approach.

AI can thus help close existing governance gaps by parsing multilingual legal corpora, mapping duties and institutions, and flagging inconsistencies or omissions—providing an evaluative lens on governance frameworks within a chosen environmental domain and a baseline for evidence-based reform.

This chapter explores the convergence of soil governance, AI, and digitalisation. Soils underpin food security, biodiversity, and climate regulation, yet they remain largely invisible in legal frameworks. At the same time, digital technologies are transforming how societies collect, manage, and regulate soil data. From AI-powered soil monitoring to blockchain-enabled land tenure, these tools hold potential to reshape environmental law. They can support predictive regulation, strengthen compliance, and make governance more adaptive. But they also carry risks of data colonialism, algorithmic opacity, and digital exclusion, particularly for smallholder farmers and indigenous communities.

---

10 Stanford University (2025: 3).

11 WTO (2025: 21).

12 Binz et al. (2024).

Against this backdrop, this chapter asks: How should soil law be redesigned to integrate AI and digitalisation to advance sustainable soil management (SSM)—by safeguarding data sovereignty, transparency, accountability, and equity—rather than reproducing digital colonisation and environmental harm? To answer this, the chapter proceeds in four steps. First, it traces the origins of AI and big data and their evolving applications, clarifying the "moving target" for regulators. Second, it examines SSM's governance mechanisms and shows how digital tools can both strengthen and undermine them (including energy/water footprints, bias, and exclusion). Third, it analyses legal and policy approaches at national, regional, and international levels and assesses their relevance to soils. Finally, it interrogates digital colonisation, focusing on soil data sovereignty in Africa (including a South African case study), and briefly surveys broader AI developments shaping this terrain. It proposes pathways—such as data commons, method transparency and guardrails, standardised soil-health indices, and rights to audit and contestation—for inclusive, transparent, and ecocentric legal frameworks.

Ultimately, this chapter argues that soil law must evolve in tandem with digitalisation. Only by integrating soil health, digital rights, and the ethical use of AI into future legislation can societies ensure that soils, often overlooked as expendable resources, are recognised as central to planetary sustainability in the digital age.

## 2. Understanding AI: origins, forms, and evolving applications

AI only truly entered public debate in November 2022, when ChatGPT abruptly pushed the concept into everyday consciousness. Yet the idea of creating machines capable of independent action is far older.[13] Greek philosophers speculated about artificial life more than two millennia ago,[14] while Archytas of Tarentum reportedly built a mechanical dove around 400 BCE.[15] Leonardo da Vinci designed a humanoid automaton in 1495.[16] The fascination with self-operating machines is thus deeply rooted in human imagination.

AI's formal history as a scientific field began in 1956 with the Dartmouth Summer Research Project on Artificial Intelligence. John McCarthy and colleagues proposed that every aspect of learning and intelligence could, in principle, be described precisely enough for a machine to simulate it.[17] Since then, AI has evolved into an umbrella concept encompassing a spectrum of systems capable of performing tasks traditionally

13 Singh (2020).
14 Bedini (1964).
15 Chondros (2017).
16 Moran (2006).
17 See https://home.dartmouth.edu/about/artificial-intelligence-ai-coined-dartmouth, accessed 29 September 2025.

associated with human intelligence, including learning, reasoning, problem-solving, language use, and decision-making.

## 2.1. Forms of AI

Britannica defines AI as "the ability of a digital computer or computer-controlled robot to perform tasks commonly associated with intelligent beings."[18] The United Nations Educational, Scientific, and Cultural Organisation (UNESCO) explains that, "[b]uilt from data, hardware and connectivity, AI allows machines to mimic human intelligence such as perception, problem-solving, linguistic interaction or creativity."[19] According to the European Commission:

> Artificial intelligence (AI) refers to systems designed by humans that, given a complex goal, act in the physical or digital world by perceiving their environment, interpreting the collected structured or unstructured data, reasoning on the knowledge derived from this data and deciding the best action(s) to take (according to pre-defined parameters) to achieve the given goal. AI systems can also be designed to learn to adapt their behaviour by analysing how the environment is affected by their previous actions. As a scientific discipline, AI includes several approaches and techniques, such as machine learning (of which deep learning and reinforcement learning are specific examples), machine reasoning (which includes planning, scheduling, knowledge representation and reasoning, search, and optimization), and robotics (which includes control, perception, sensors and actuators, as well as the integration of all other techniques into cyber-physical systems).[20]

At its core, AI is not a single technology but a continuum that ranges from narrow or "weak" AI (Artificial Narrow Intelligence, ANI)—systems designed for specific tasks, such as voice assistants, facial recognition, and recommendation engines, which are fast and efficient but lack a general understanding[21]—to the still-theoretical realm of Artificial General Intelligence (AGI), which would replicate human-like adaptability across many domains.[22] Within this spectrum sits generative AI, capable of creating original text, images, audio, or code by learning from large datasets (e.g., ChatGPT, DALL·E, Codex).[23] Much of modern AI is driven by Machine Learning (ML), a subset in which models learn from data and improve performance without explicit programming, encompassing branches such as deep learning, natural language processing, computer vision, and reinforcement learning.[24] Underpinning all of this is Big Data—the high-volume, high-velocity, and high-variety information streams that fuel training

---

18 See https://www.britannica.com/technology/artificial-intelligence, accessed 29 September 2025.

19 See https://www.unesco.org/en/artificial-intelligence, accessed 29 September 2025.

20 European Commission (2018: 7).

21 For example, Google's DeepMind, Facebook's facial recognition technology, Apple's 'Siri', Amazon's Alexa, and Tesla's and Uber's self-driving vehicles. McLean et al. (2023); Flowers (2019).

22 McLean et al. (2023).

23 Jackson et al. (2024); Zhang et al. (2025).

24 Ibrahim & Abdulazeez (2021); Bowman (2024); Chinnaiyan et al. (2024); Gaur et al. (2023).

and inference—whose analysis enables insights and decisions that would otherwise be impractical or impossible.[25]

A widely cited operational criterion for identifying AI is the Turing test, which asks whether a person, engaged in natural-language exchange with a purported AI system, cannot reliably distinguish it from a human.[26] A positive result is taken as *prima facie* evidence of intelligence. In addition to such evidentiary markers, autonomy constitutes a central attribute of AI. Autonomous systems can generate outputs that are not fully predetermined by programmers, even when they originate from human-specified objectives and constraints.[27] This capacity for non-preprogrammed responses is both intellectually and practically valuable, enabling AI systems to generate novel and unexpected solutions that humans might overlook due to habitual patterns or cognitive biases.

## 2.2. Applications across sectors

AI now permeates nearly every domain of human activity: in health, it assists with diagnosing diseases, personalising treatments, and supporting the regulatory review and approval of medical devices; in finance, it powers fraud detection and algorithmic trading; in agriculture, it enables crop monitoring, precision irrigation, and predictive yield modelling; in environmental stewardship, it models climate change, tracks deforestation, detects pollution, and monitors compliance; and in law and governance, it supports legal research, case prediction, and automated decision-making in areas such as parole or welfare.[28]

The potential and risks of AI are visible across diverse sectors. Google's Air View+ provides real-time air quality data in India, combining AI, sensors, and satellite imagery.[29] In the Amazon, AI detects illegal logging, while in South Africa, smart collars track rhinos and alert rangers to distress signals, bolstering anti-poaching efforts.[30]

---

25 Wang et al. (2021).

26 Martinez (2019: 1024).

27 Ibid.: 1026.

28 Selvakumar et al. (2025); Mishra & Mishra (2023); Gatla (2024); Johnson et al. (2021); Patil (2024); Mwangi & Njoroge (2024); Tironi & Lisboa (2023).

29 See https://www.sandtech.com/insight/ai-for-environmental-monitoring/, accessed 29 September 2025; Rautela & Goyal (2024); See https://economictimes.indiatimes.com/tech/technology/google-maps-launches-air-view-in-india-real-time-hyperlocal-air-quality-info/articleshow/115489441.cms?from=mdr, accessed 29 September 2025.

30 See https://www.sandtech.com/insight/ai-for-environmental-monitoring/; https://news.microsoft.com/source/latam/features/ai/project-guacamaya-rainforest-deforestation/?lang=en; https://news.mongabay.com/2021/08/new-artificial-intelligence-tool-helps-forecast-amazon-deforestation/, accessed 29 September 2025; Teixeira et al. (2023).

The justice system offers even more striking illustrations.[31] In Australia, the Judicial Information Research System (JIRS) assists judges in criminal sentencing by analysing vast datasets of past decisions through neural networks.[32] China has taken further steps, establishing "smart courts" in Beijing, Suzhou, and Hangzhou.[33] Litigants can file cases and attend hearings entirely online, with the average case resolved in 40 days and hearings lasting 37 minutes. Nearly all rulings (98%) are accepted without appeal, underscoring both efficiency and compliance.[34] These courts also employ Xiao Fa, an AI-powered assistant that translates complex legal rules into plain language.[35] While it was originally accessible only in courthouses, it is now integrated with Aegis, a WeChat-based platform that handles 30,000 daily queries with 85% accuracy.[36] Together, they reduce barriers to justice by making legal information widely accessible. Similar initiatives are emerging elsewhere. In Europe, the Claudette system, developed at the European University Institute, assists plaintiffs, defendants, and lawyers by assessing litigation risks and estimating the likelihood of success in court.[37]

It must be acknowledged that AI systems differ significantly in design and capability, and they are not always employed in ways consistent with their original or intended objectives. For example, in 2023, a US judge imposed sanctions on two New York lawyers after they submitted a legal brief containing fictitious case citations—all generated by the AI chatbot ChatGPT.[38] In the case of *Mata v Avianca, Inc.* (a routine personal injury case), the plaintiff's attorney, limited by a restricted legal research subscription, utilised ChatGPT to assist in drafting a response to a motion to dismiss.[39] Relying on the chatbot, the attorney submitted an affirmation citing multiple cases, including *Varghese v China Southern Airlines Co., Ltd.*, which appeared to support tolling the statute of limitations under the Montreal Convention due to Avianca's bankruptcy. However, that case, along with several others cited, was entirely fabricated by ChatGPT, complete with invented quotes and legal citations. This highlights the risks of overreliance on generative AI in legal practice, particularly when outputs are not correctly verified, and underscores the need for human oversight and accountability in the use of AI tools. Notably, the judge did not criticise the use of ChatGPT or generative AI itself: "[t]echnological advances are commonplace and there is nothing inherently improper about using a reliable artificial intelligence tool for assistance."[40]

31 See https://www.thomsonreuters.com/en-us/posts/ai-in-courts/humanizing-justice/, accessed 29 September 2025; Bell et al. (2022).

32 Tahura & Selvadurai (2022).

33 See https://www.lexisnexis.ca/en-ca/ihc/2020-02/robot-justice-chinas-use-of-internet-courts.page, accessed 29 September 2025.

34 Ibid.

35 Chen & Li (2020: 8–9).

36 Ibid.

37 Zhou (2024).

38 Lyon (2023).

39 2023 WL 4138427 (S.D.N.Y. June 22, 2023).

40 Lyon (2023: 11).

Instead, the real issue was the failure to verify its output, and its reliance as the primary research tool was described as an example of "poor and sloppy research." A similar incident occurred in 2023, in an appellate decision by the Texas Court of Appeals.[41] There is also *Park v Kim* (US),[42] where an attorney relied on fake, AI-generated legal citations in a filing; *Kruse v Karlan* (US),[43] where a litigant filed a brief with multiple fake, AI-generated legal citations; and *Kohls v Ellison* (US),[44] where lawyers used expert testimony, reports, and affidavits with fake citations and false information generated by AI in court.

In South Africa, the courts have not been as open-minded to the use of AI. In *Parker v Forsyth NO*, where the plaintiff's attorneys relied on ChatGPT for legal research, without verifying its accuracy, the court stated:

> In this age of instant gratification, this incident serves as a timely reminder to, at least, the lawyers involved in this matter that when it comes to legal research, the efficiency of modern technology still needs to be infused with a dose of good old-fashioned independent reading. Courts expect lawyers to bring a legally-independent and questioning mind to bear on, especially, novel legal matters, and certainly not to merely repeat in parrot-fashion, the unverified research of a chatbot (...) The embarrassment associated with this incident is probably sufficient punishment for the Plaintiff's attorneys.[45]

Further, in *Mavundla v MEC: Department of Co-Operative Government and Traditional Affairs KwaZulu-Natal*,[46] a traditional leadership dispute in KwaZulu-Natal, the court encountered a troubling issue with AI-generated legal content. Mavundla's legal representatives submitted a supplementary notice of appeal containing numerous case citations. However, upon review, the court discovered that several of these cited authorities could not be found in any recognised legal database. By design, ChatGPT is not intended to be a legal research tool. When tested on the Uniform Bar Exam (US), OpenAI's GPT-4 language model (released in 2023) outperformed 90% of human test takers.[47] However, it is essential to note that the free version of ChatGPT does not run on GPT-4 and, by comparison, performed significantly worse, scoring better than only 10% of human test-takers.[48] While an AI model running on GPT-4 can perform well when paired with a dedicated legal database, ChatGPT itself lacks access to platforms such as LexisNexis and Westlaw, which are essential for conducting reliable and up-to-date legal research.[49] As a language-based chatbot, ChatGPT can generate legal-

---

41 Ibid.: 8.

42 91 F.4th 610, 614–16 (2d Cir. 2023).

43 692 S.W.3d 43, 53 (Mo. Ct. App. 2024).

44 24-cv-3754 (LMP/DLM) (D. Minn. Jan 10, 2025).

45 (1585/20) [2023] ZAGPRD 1 (29 June 2023) paras 90-91; See https://www.derebus.org.za/what-have-the-courts-said-about-the-ethical-use-of-artificial-intelligence-in-legal-practice/, accessed 27 October 2025.

46 2025 (3) SA 534 (KZP) (8 January 2025); Petse & Phindelo (2025).

47 See https://law.stanford.edu/2023/04/19/gpt-4-passes-the-bar-exam-what-that-means-for-artificial-intelligence-tools-in-the-legal-industry/, accessed 27 October 2025.

48 Ibid.

49 See https://www.spellbook.legal/learn/chatgpt-for-lawyers, accessed 27 October 2025.

sounding arguments and even cite cases; however, these may be invented or outdated, as it relies solely on its pre-existing training data and is not connected to live legal databases.

These developments illustrate both the transformative potential and the persistent fragility of AI integration across sectors. Whether in environmental monitoring, judicial efficiency, or legal practice, the value of AI depends on responsible design, ethical deployment, and human oversight. The growing number of cases involving fabricated citations or unverified outputs serves as a cautionary reminder that technological sophistication cannot substitute for professional diligence. As AI becomes more deeply embedded in decision-making systems, the challenge is not simply to adopt it but to cultivate the institutional, ethical, and legal frameworks that ensure it advances—rather than undermines—the integrity of human judgment.

### 2.3. The moving target

The boundary between digitalisation and AI is fluid. As once-novel technologies become commonplace, definitions shift, making AI a "moving target" for regulators. Crucially, AI is never neutral: its outputs reflect the data and values on which it is trained. ML begins with large datasets, from which computers extract patterns and generate their own algorithms.[50] Unlike traditional programming, the model then applies these learned patterns to new data. But because humans curate training data, AI systems often reproduce the biases in that data. For example, self-driving car systems struggled to detect people of colour because the training images underrepresented them.[51] In disaster-risk management, algorithms that privilege affluent districts while overlooking marginalised ones do not deliver fairness; they entrench vulnerability and widen existing inequalities.[52]

AI's potential to reduce bias has been tested in the criminal justice system. A Tulane University study examined 50,000 Virginia convictions in which judges used AI to assess the risk of reoffending.[53] While AI recommendations reduced gender disparities in sentencing, racial gaps persisted; judges were less likely to follow AI advice when the defendant was a person of colour. This highlights AI's dual role: it can promote consistency, yet human prejudice can still distort outcomes. Furthermore, transparency remains a concern. Many judicial AI systems rely on opaque "black box" reasoning, raising questions about accountability and fairness.[54] A 'black box' refers to a

50 Thornton (2023).

51 See https://www.vox.com/future-perfect/2019/3/5/18251924/self-driving-car-racial-bias-study-autonomous-vehicle-dark-skin, accessed 29 September 2025.

52 Zhan & Liao (2024).

53 See https://news.tulane.edu/pr/ai-sentencing-cut-jail-time-low-risk-offenders-study-finds-racial-bias-persisted, accessed 29 September 2025.

54 von Eschenbach (2021).

tool that produces a score without revealing its inputs or logic, sometimes even shielded by trade-secret claims. In court settings, that opacity makes it hard for defendants to challenge errors, for judges to give reasons that can be appealed, and for oversight bodies to detect disparate impact. In other words, even if AI can improve consistency, a lack of explainability and auditability risks entrenching or hiding bias.

US case law illustrates the risks. In *State v Loomis,* a COMPAS risk score contributed to the determination of a six-year sentence, although the defendant was not given insight into the algorithm.[55] The Wisconsin Supreme Court upheld the ruling, treating COMPAS as a legitimate tool despite its opacity.[56] By contrast, in *Kansas v Walls*, the court ordered disclosure of the complete diagnostic assessment used in sentencing, recognising the need for transparency.[57] More recently, *In Re Matter of Weber* exposed the dangers of relying on generative AI: an expert who used Microsoft Copilot was unable to explain how it produced its financial calculations, thereby undermining the credibility of his testimony.[58]

Even at the supranational level, structural biases are evident. Studies of AI applied to European Court of Human Rights (ECtHR) decisions have shown that models trained on judges' summaries often reinforce reasoning aligned with the outcomes, rather than substantively engaging with the law.[59] This raises doubts about whether such systems analyse legal precedent or mimic linguistic cues.

The pitfalls of overstated claims are evident in the case of DoNotPay, a startup that branded itself as "the world's first robot lawyer."[60] The US Federal Trade Commission found that it had not tested its AI to the standard of a human attorney and lacked professionals to verify its outputs.[61]

Together, these examples demonstrate that while AI can streamline processes and reduce certain inequities, it can also amplify hidden biases, undermine transparency, and pose risks when deployed without oversight. The same concerns arise in the governance of agricultural and soil data. Just as courts risk relying on opaque "black box" systems, farmers may be asked to trust AI-driven soil or crop recommendations without insight into how outputs are generated, what data they rely on, or whose interests

55 *State v Loomis* (2016) WI 68, 371 Wis. 2d 235, 881 N.W.2d 749; Freeman (2016); Gualdi & Cordella (2021). COMPAS (Correctional Offender Management Profiling for Alternative Sanctions) is a proprietary risk-assessment tool developed by Northpointe (now Equivant) that some US courts use at bail, sentencing, and parole to estimate a person's risk of reoffending (general and violent). It draws on questionnaire answers and administrative data (e.g., age, prior arrests/convictions, employment, substance-use history) and outputs risk categories/deciles.

56 *Loomis v Wisconsin*, 881 N.W.2d 749 (Wis. 2016), cert. denied, 137 S.Ct. 2290 (2017).

57 *State of Kansas v John Keith Walls*, pp. 116, 027, The Court of Appeals of the State of Kansas (2017).

58 See https://law.justia.com/cases/new-york/other-courts/2024/2024-ny-slip-op-24258.html; https://www.freereferral.com/blog/disqualification-of-expert-witness-for-artificial-intellegence-use, accessed 29 September 2025.

59 Ibid.

60 See https://gizmodo.com/donotpay-has-to-pay-up-over-worlds-first-robot-lawyer-2000503265, accessed 29 September 2025.

61 *In re DoNotPay, Inc.*, No. C-4812 (F.T.C. Jan. 14, 2025).

they ultimately serve.[62] In both domains, reliability depends not only on technical design but also on institutional safeguards, accountability, and fair distribution of benefits. Crucially, the quality and diversity of training data are critical: entire climate zones—tropical, arid, mild-continental, and polar tundra—are markedly underrepresented in AI research for agricultural soil health, despite spanning vast areas of Central and South America, Africa, Central and South Asia, and Australia.[63] Suppose AI systems are trained on narrow, imported, or incomplete datasets. In that case, they risk misclassifying soil health, overlooking local realities, and promoting one-size-fits-all recommendations ill-suited to African (and other) contexts.[64] To ensure global applicability, future work should prioritise high-quality, standardised datasets from these under-sampled regions, as well as the rigorous use of bias detection and mitigation methods in datasets and models.

In the worst case, unchecked bias becomes a system driver rather than a bug: a handful of powerful agri-tech platforms, trained on skewed data and optimised for a narrow notion of "efficiency," could standardise practice across regions, marginalising indigenous and local agronomies honed over centuries.[65] In such a stunted trajectory, long-term soil vitality is traded for short-term output: biased systems privilege input-heavy farming, driving widespread application of synthetic fertilisers and pesticides that degrade soil structure, deplete organic matter, and damage the microbial webs that underpin healthy soils—locking farmers into an input treadmill to maintain yields on exhausted land.[66] The biodiversity fallout would be severe: monocultures and intensive pesticide use depress pollinators, natural enemies, and other wildlife, weakening ecological regulation, triggering more frequent pest outbreaks and disease, and eroding the resilience of food systems.[67]

Ensuring diverse, locally relevant soil data feeds into AI systems is therefore essential, not only to improve accuracy but also to uphold equity and resilience in agricultural decision-making. That aim also requires transparency, contestability, and oversight, so that recommendations are explainable, open to challenge, and aligned with the interests of farmers and communities, rather than solely with corporate logics.

62 Gardezi et al. (2023).
63 Schweng et al. (2026: 12).
64 See https://prism.sustainability-directory.com/scenario/algorithmic-bias-in-soil-health-management-systems/, accessed 29 September 2025.
65 Ibid.
66 Ibid.
67 Ibid.

## 2.4. Sustainable soil management and governance

SSM addresses the multiple pressures contributing to soil degradation and seeks to ensure the long-term health and resilience of soils.[68] Because soils underpin food security, biodiversity, climate regulation, and human livelihoods, their governance is inherently crosscutting. Pressures arise from agriculture, urbanisation, infrastructure, mining, and industrial activity, while climate change intensifies risks through droughts, flooding, and water scarcity. Poverty and insecure land tenure further drive unsustainable practices, weakening resilience.[69]

SSM relies on four main mechanisms:[70] First, SSM starts with reliable data.[71] That means taking field-level measurements of soil conditions, analysing and interpreting the results, and then sharing the information in usable formats with policymakers, regulators, farmers, and the public. Good data enables evidence-based decisions and creates a common factual baseline for action. Second, land-use planning and zoning can shield fertile soils from permanent sealing by urban growth, infrastructure, or industrial projects.[72] Effective planning relies on comprehensive, up-to-date information, and AI can assist by processing large datasets and transforming raw measurements into actionable insights. Digital soil maps that layer soil status, weather patterns, current land uses, and the legal status of ownership and tenure are powerful tools for guiding sustainable planning choices.[73] Third, binding, enforceable soil quality standards set thresholds for acceptable interference and empower authorities to restrict harmful activities when those limits are exceeded.[74] Because soil degradation has many dimensions—erosion, compaction, loss of organic matter, salinisation—developing robust standards is complex and resource-intensive. New digital technologies can support this work by improving monitoring accuracy, analysing large datasets, and grounding the standards in sound evidence. Lastly, long-term soil protection depends on broad recognition of soil's value. Although awareness is improving, soils continue to receive insufficient attention in policy debates. Targeted outreach to politicians, the private sector, civil society, and young people can foster a shared commitment to stewardship.[75] Digital tools can accelerate this by delivering audience-specific materials—adapted to local languages, levels of technical knowledge, and preferred visual styles—that clearly convey the importance and vulnerability of soil.

---

68 Ginzky & Ruppel (2025a: 252).

69 Ginzky (2023: 535).

70 Ginzky (2022).

71 Ginzky & Ruppel (2022: 44–45).

72 Ginzky & Ruppel (2025b: 32); Ginzky & Ruppel (2025a: 252).

73 Statement of a Soil scientist during a workshop on 8 April 2025 in Stellenbosch, South Africa, "Digitalisation, AI, Sustainability and Soil Protection: Multiple Perspectives"; Ginzky & Ruppel (2025a: 253).

74 Ginzky (2021); Ginzky (2022).

75 Ginzky & Ruppel (2025b: 33).

For decades, soils have been treated as expendable, often overshadowed by air and water in environmental law. Yet soils are non-renewable on human timescales: they take centuries to form but can be degraded within years. Recognising soils as a vital, fragile resource demands governance approaches that are both comprehensive and enforceable.

Digital technologies offer significant opportunities to strengthen soil governance. While field data remains the foundation, digital tools can accelerate analysis, enhance accuracy, and make soil information more accessible to a diverse range of users. The applications of AI in soil science are diverse and impactful, falling into several key branches. The first branch focuses on monitoring and predicting soil health, utilising AI to develop predictive models based on soil properties, microbiome data, sensors, and satellite imagery.[76] This analytical power extends to the very foundation of soil fertility. A second branch focuses on analysing the soil microbiome, where AI tools build predictive models of microbial interactions and their impact on nutrient cycles.[77] Furthermore, AI provides critical insights into soil composition, with specific techniques predicting soil organic carbon levels to forecast global carbon dynamics and identify soils at higher risk of $CO_2$ release, thereby informing sequestration and sustainable carbon management strategies.[78]

These advanced technologies enable the real-time monitoring and management of inputs, such as fertilisers, pesticides, and irrigation systems. AI plays a crucial role in detecting soil contamination, estimating heavy metal concentrations from soil spectra, and determining nutrient levels in real time.[79] AI tools for soil moisture and water management integrate monitoring and prediction to analyse climatic parameters and provide farmers with irrigation recommendations, thereby reducing water stress and fostering more sustainable, resilient farming practices.[80] Remote sensing, when combined with AI, offers powerful applications for soil management, including detecting land-use changes and estimating soil quality from images.[81] Techniques that interpret soil colour and vegetation from drone or satellite imagery can estimate organic matter and moisture.[82]

Equally important is the dissemination of this complex information. AI can be harnessed to produce audience-tailored outputs, such as translating information into local or indigenous languages, adapting content to varying levels of technical complexity, and using visualisation tools to make data more accessible and meaningful to diverse stakeholders.[83]

76 Rosca & Stancu (2025: 17–18).
77 Ibid.
78 Ibid.
79 Ibid.
80 Nalwimba (2024); Mienye et al. (2024).
81 World Economic Forum (2024).
82 Rosca & Stancu (2025: 17–18).
83 World Economic Forum (2024); Nalwimba (2024).

## 2.5. Digitalisation, power asymmetries, and sustainability risks

While digital technologies offer great potential for soil governance, they also carry environmental, social, and economic risks. If left unmanaged, these risks could undermine the very sustainability goals that digitalisation aims to support.

First, regarding environmental risks, digitalisation relies on substantial amounts of energy and water.[84] Recent analyses suggest that producing a single image using a state-of-the-art generative model consumes roughly as much electricity as charging a typical smartphone once.[85] By 2027, AI's overall power demand could rival that of countries such as the Netherlands or Argentina.[86] Data centres require cooling systems, often in regions already experiencing water scarcity.[87] Recent estimates suggest that a single conversational session with a leading chatbot (roughly 20–50 prompts and replies) can indirectly consume about the equivalent of a 500 ml bottle of water through evaporative cooling, depending on location, cooling technology, and grid mix.[88] Scaled across millions of sessions, this translates into a substantial aggregate water footprint. In 2022, Google reported that its data centres withdrew roughly 25 billion litres of water and consumed nearly 20 billion litres for on-site cooling—about 77% of which was potable.[89] Typically, around 80% of water withdrawn by data centres is "consumed" (lost) through evaporation.[90] If energy is derived from fossil fuels, emissions rise and may outweigh the environmental benefits of precision agriculture or reduced fertiliser use.

Second, regarding the social risks, two challenges stand out, both of which are explored further below: The first is data privacy and misuse; soil data, when linked to farmers or geolocation, can reveal sensitive information.[91] Without clear rules on ownership, accountability, and liability, private actors may exploit data at the expense of smallholders.[92] The risks are not merely theoretical, as demonstrated by the significant cyberattack against DeepSeek, a Chinese AI startup, in early 2025, which resulted in the leak of data from over a million users.[93] This incident underscores concerns raised by security researchers about the neglect of basic cybersecurity measures on some digital platforms, highlighting a clear and present danger that extends to the agricultural

84 Harvey (2025); see https://www.theguardian.com/technology/2025/apr/10/energy-demands-from-ai-datacentres-to-quadruple-by-2030-says-report, accessed 29 September 2025.

85 Hacker (2023).

86 Ibid.

87 Barratt et al. (2025); https://www.theguardian.com/environment/2025/apr/09/big-tech-datacentres-water, accessed 29 September 2025.

88 Hacker (2023: 5).

89 Ibid.: 7.

90 Ibid.

91 Ginzky & Ruppel (2025a: 254).

92 OECD (2024a and b).

93 See https://www.darkreading.com/cyberattacks-data-breaches/deepseek-breach-opens-floodgates-dark-web, accessed 29 September 2025.

sector, where protecting proprietary farm and location data is paramount. The second is the digital divide: One-third of the world's population remains offline.[94] Digital technologies depend on a reliable power supply. Yet load-shedding and power cuts remain a daily reality in many developing countries.[95] Rural areas are particularly affected, limiting the use of digital tools precisely where they are most needed for soil and agricultural management.[96] Investments in AI and digital infrastructure are concentrated in the Global North, leaving many countries in the Global South behind.[97] An Oxford Insights assessment of 181 countries reveals that many regions in the Global South, particularly sub-Saharan Africa, parts of Central and South Asia, and certain areas of Latin America, rank lowest in preparedness to implement AI in public services.[98] The report emphasises that effective AI development relies on a supportive operating environment, including a robust technology sector, reliable data infrastructure, and a clear strategic direction focused on governance and ethical standards. Without basic infrastructure, even the most advanced digital applications cannot function effectively, leaving rural farmers and communities excluded from the benefits of innovation.[99]

Third, regarding economic risks, inclusive access is vulnerable to restrictions due to high costs and technical barriers, which could exacerbate disparities in agriculture. Investment in digitalisation and AI is disproportionately concentrated in the Global North.[100] For instance, training sophisticated AI models can cost several million dollars.[101] Canada unveiled a USD 2.4 billion package to strengthen its AI infrastructure, while China introduced a USD 47.5 billion fund to accelerate semiconductor production. France has committed USD 113 billion to advancing AI capabilities, while India has pledged USD 1.25 billion. Saudi Arabia's ambitious Project Transcendence, valued at USD 100 billion, aims to position the country as a leader in AI.[102] Most African and other developing countries cannot match these levels, leaving them dependent on technologies, platforms, and expertise imported from abroad. In Nigeria, for instance, despite its relative technical advancement, around 90% of software is imported, with local efforts confined largely to producing add-ons or extensions for mainstream products.[103] A handful of global technology companies dominate the digital sector. Their

---

94 See https://www.destatis.de/DE/Themen/Laender-Regionen/Internationales/Thema/wissenschaft-technologie-digitales/_inhalt.html, accessed 29 September 2025; Ginzky & Ruppel (2025a: 254-255).

95 AU (2024b: 14); Okolo et al. (2023: 38).

96 Okolo et al. (2023: 41).

97 Ruthmann-Bloem (2023).

98 See https://oxfordinsights.com/ai-readiness/ai-readiness-index/, accessed 29 September 2025.

99 Arakpogun et al. (2021). See also https://news.un.org/en/story/2023/07/1138827, accessed 29 September 2025.

100 For example: African Union Development Agency (2021:45); von Carlowitz, Züfle & Schmid (2025).

101 For further information see https://www.weforum.org/stories/2023/01/davos23-ai-divide-global-north-global-south/, accessed 29 September 2025.

102 Stanford University (2025: 4).

103 Birhane (2020: 396).

control over platforms, algorithms, and services risks creating monopolies and undermining fair competition. Robust national and international competition rules are needed to prevent dependency on a few powerful actors.[104] Furthermore, many countries in the Global South face shortages of skilled personnel to design, adapt, and govern digital technologies. Many African AI experts work abroad, contributing to a talent drain that weakens local capacity and expertise. Farmers and end-users may also lack the literacy and training necessary to benefit from digital services.[105] These services include mobile phones and the internet, as well as newer tools such as big-data analytics, blockchain, drones, satellite imagery, AI/machine learning, and remote sensing—used both on farms (e.g., drones for spraying) and as support services (e.g., blockchain traceability or mobile weather alerts).[106]

There is a clear need to address market power concentrations through effective regulatory frameworks. Given that many leading technology companies operate in highly globalised markets, international regulation is crucial to ensure accountability and equitable access.[107] Achieving agreement on shared international standards, however, is likely to become increasingly challenging in the current geopolitical climate. At the same time, the accumulation of market power within domestic economies also calls for strong national oversight to curb monopolistic practices and safeguard fair competition.[108] These risks and challenges vary depending on the specific digital tools and applications involved. For instance, it will be necessary to examine whether the deployment of AI in fertiliser use is so energy-intensive that it negates the environmental benefits of reduced fertiliser application, and whether access to such technologies risks exacerbating existing economic inequalities among farmers.[109]

Taken together, these environmental, social, and economic risks highlight that digitalisation is not a neutral process. Its outcomes depend on context, regulation, and capacity. Without proactive governance, digital tools intended to strengthen soil management may unintentionally deepen existing inequalities and environmental pressures. The challenge, therefore, is not whether to embrace digitalisation, but how to design rules and institutions that ensure its benefits reach farmers and ecosystems alike.

These risks point to a broader structural challenge: digitalisation, environmental degradation, and socio-economic inequality cannot be governed in isolation. As the German Advisory Council on Global Change (WBGU) emphasises, future-oriented policymaking requires an integrated understanding of security—one that places the protection of natural life-support systems at its core.[110] Climate change, biodiversity

104 OECD (2024a: 33).
105 Okolo et al. (2023: 40).
106 Abdulai et al. (2023).
107 Ginzky & Ruppel (2025a: 255).
108 Ibid.
109 Ibid.
110 WBGU (2026: 1).

loss, pollution, land degradation, and desertification are no longer peripheral environmental concerns but are among the most significant long-term risks to societal stability, economic systems, and democratic resilience. From this perspective, soil governance must be understood as a foundational element of integrated security policy. The WBGU highlights that sustainable agricultural systems, soil conservation, and climate-resilient land management are essential not only for environmental protection but for ensuring food security, social cohesion, and geopolitical stability.[111] At the same time, the rapid expansion of AI and digital infrastructures introduces new vulnerabilities, including dependencies on external technologies, risks to information integrity, and widening global inequalities in digital capacity. A future-oriented legal response must therefore move beyond fragmented regulatory approaches and instead embed soil governance, digital governance, and socio-ecological resilience within a multidimensional security architecture. This includes integrating environmental risks into early-warning systems, strengthening international cooperation, reducing technological dependencies, and ensuring that digital innovation aligns with long-term sustainability goals.[112] Without such integration, efforts to regulate AI and digitalisation risk reinforcing, rather than mitigating, the structural vulnerabilities they seek to address.

### 2.6. Governing AI: law, power, and accountability

AI has been described as "summoning the demon."[113] While hyperbolic, the remark reflects widespread concern that without proper regulation, AI may produce harms that are irreversible or uncontrollable. Clear governance frameworks are, therefore, essential to maximise benefits while minimising risks. The evidence shows a landscape already skewed toward large-scale, industrial farming. The "bias" in datasets and models is not a technical hiccup—it mirrors entrenched social inequities and power imbalances. Left unchecked, it will grow worse, driving ecological decline, widening injustice, and further concentrating control in corporate hands.[114]

Yet the persistence of these risks cannot be explained solely by regulatory delays or oversight failures; it reflects deeper structural constraints within the global political economy of artificial intelligence. A growing body of scholarship suggests that the current impasse in international AI governance persists because major powers prioritise strategic and economic advantage over cooperation, private actors retain disproportionate control over data and technological infrastructure, and international

111 Ibid.: 5.

112 Ibid.: 4.

113 See https://www.cnet.com/science/elon-musk-we-are-summoning-the-demon-with-artificial-intelligence/, accessed 29 September 2025.

114 See https://prism.sustainability-directory.com/scenario/algorithmic-bias-in-soil-health-management-systems/, accessed 29 September 2025.

institutions lack both enforcement capacity and technical expertise. In such a context, global coordination remains limited, fragmented, and largely non-binding. Meaningful governance progress may therefore only become politically feasible when the costs of regulatory inaction become too significant to ignore. Historical experience demonstrates that durable governance regimes are rarely the product of foresight alone, but are instead catalysed by crisis, moments in which systemic failure collapses political resistance and creates narrow windows for institutional innovation. This suggests that the challenge for AI governance is not only to develop normative frameworks in advance, but to ensure that legal, technical, and institutional mechanisms are sufficiently developed to be rapidly operationalised when such windows emerge.[115]

Globally, legislative attention to AI is increasing rapidly. Between 2016 and 2024, the AI Index tracked bills and statutes mentioning "artificial intelligence" across 114 countries; of these, 39 countries adopted at least one AI-related law, resulting in a cumulative total of 204 AI-related enactments.[116] Over 70 countries have now developed and implemented national strategies or policies focused on AI, with the majority of these initiatives concentrated in high-income and upper-middle-income countries.[117] This compares with just 16% of lower-middle-income economies and only 8% of low-income economies.[118] References to AI in legislative proceedings rose by over 20% between 2023 and 2024 alone.[119] In the Global South, where public awareness of algorithmic bias, privacy, and accountability remains limited, strong governance is crucial. By 2025, 36 of Africa's 55 countries had adopted data protection laws, of which 31 guard against automated decision-making.[120] Only 26 had functioning data protection authorities, of which only fifteen established an expert body on AI.[121] However, no African country had yet enacted dedicated AI legislation, and only eight had adopted AI policy frameworks or strategies (twelve).[122] This patchwork highlights the unevenness of AI readiness across the continent, creating a

115 Wilkinson et al. (2026).

116 Stanford University (2025: 337).

117 WTO (2025: 69–70).

118 Ibid.

119 Stanford University (2025).

120 Makulilo (2024: 43); See https://www.trust.org/toolkit/part-2-emerging-ai-governance-in-africa/domestic-ai-governance/, accessed 29 September 2025.

121 To stay up to date, see https://iapp.org/resources/article/global-ai-legislation-tracker/, https://www.trust.org/toolkit/part-2-emerging-ai-governance-in-africa/domestic-ai-governance/, accessed 29 September 2025; Andere & Kathure (2024).

122 See https://www.whitecase.com/insight-our-thinking/ai-watch-global-regulatory-tracker-african-union, https://www.lawyershub.org/news/post/artificial-intelligence-and-parliaments-in-africa, https://www.dentons.com/en/insights/articles/2024/june/13/ai-regulation-and-policy-in-africa, https://www.trust.org/toolkit/part-2-emerging-ai-governance-in-africa/domestic-ai-governance/, accessed 29 September 2025; Davis et al. (2022).

vacuum that allows external actors to dominate Africa's digital landscape with minimal accountability.[123]

The challenges associated with digitalisation in the context of soil governance are not merely technical but reveal a deeper structural problem within contemporary legal systems. The rapid pace of technological development, particularly in fields such as AI, the Internet of Things, and data-driven agriculture, has outstripped the capacity of existing regulatory frameworks to respond effectively.[124] As a result, regulatory systems are frequently reactive, fragmented, and ill-equipped to anticipate or manage emerging risks. This temporal mismatch creates a persistent governance gap, where technologies are widely deployed before their implications are fully understood, leaving both ecosystems and communities vulnerable. This challenge is compounded by significant information asymmetries between regulators, industry actors, and affected communities. Policymakers often lack access to the technical knowledge, data, and predictive capacity necessary to make informed decisions, while private actors—particularly large technology firms—retain disproportionate control over both technological development and the data that underpins it.[125] In the context of soil governance, this asymmetry is especially pronounced, as soil data is increasingly captured, processed, and commercialised through digital platforms that are often external to the jurisdictions in which the data originates. This dynamic risks reinforcing existing inequalities and contributing to new forms of digital dependency and extraction.

At the same time, the transboundary nature of digital technologies further complicates governance efforts. Data flows, algorithmic systems, and digital infrastructures operate across national borders, challenging traditional concepts of jurisdiction, accountability, and regulatory authority.[126] Actions undertaken in one jurisdiction may have far-reaching environmental, economic, and social consequences in another, while fragmented regulatory approaches create inconsistencies, gaps, and opportunities for regulatory arbitrage. In such a context, purely national or sectoral approaches to regulation are insufficient. These dynamics are exacerbated by institutional fragmentation. Digital technologies frequently fall within overlapping or unclear regulatory mandates, resulting in a diffusion of responsibility across multiple agencies.[127] In some cases, this leads to duplication and inefficiency; in others, critical risks fall through the cracks altogether. Soil governance, already characterised by fragmented legal and institutional frameworks, is particularly vulnerable to these dynamics. The integration of digital technologies into soil management, therefore, risks entrenching, rather than resolving, existing governance deficiencies.

123 Salami (2024).
124 OECD (2025b: 87).
125 Ibid.: 90.
126 Ibid.: 91–92.
127 Ibid.: 97 & 111–112.

Traditional regulatory approaches are poorly suited to these conditions. Law has historically operated through relatively static, "set-and-forget" models, whereby rules are designed, enacted, and only periodically reviewed.[128] However, such approaches are incompatible with the dynamic and rapidly evolving nature of digital technologies. By the time regulatory interventions are implemented, the technologies in question may already have evolved, rendering existing rules obsolete or ineffective. This highlights the need for a fundamental shift in regulatory design and governance philosophy. In response, there is growing recognition of the need for more adaptive, anticipatory, and integrated forms of governance. Anticipatory governance approaches—incorporating tools such as horizon scanning, strategic foresight, and early-stage stakeholder engagement—offer a means of identifying emerging risks and opportunities before they become entrenched.[129] Such approaches emphasise iterative policy cycles, continuous learning, and the integration of diverse forms of knowledge, including scientific, technical, and local expertise.

For soil governance, this shift is particularly significant. It requires moving beyond fragmented, sector-specific regulation towards a more holistic framework that integrates environmental protection, digital governance, and socio-economic considerations. This includes recognising soil not only as a resource to be managed but also as a critical component of broader socio-ecological systems that underpin food security, climate resilience, and human well-being. It also necessitates addressing questions of data ownership, technological sovereignty, and equitable access to digital tools and infrastructures. Governing soil in the digital age demands more than incremental reform. It requires a reconfiguration of legal and institutional frameworks to address the interconnected challenges of technological innovation, environmental degradation, and global inequality. Without such a shift, efforts to harness digital technologies for sustainable soil management risk reproducing the very power imbalances and governance failures they seek to overcome.

### 2.6.1. The 2024 OECD Study

The Organisation for Economic Co-operation and Development (OECD) conducted a comprehensive study between 2023 and 2024 on the risks, benefits, and policy implications of AI.[130] Its Expert Group on AI Futures, comprising around 70 specialists from various regions and disciplines, published its findings in December 2024.[131]

The report identified ten priority policy actions, including:[132]

128 Ibid.: 91.
129 Ibid.: 92–93.
130 OECD (2024a).
131 See https://oecd.ai/en/site/ai-futures, accessed 29 September 2025.
132 Ginzky & Ruppel (2025a: 256–259).

Establishing more explicit liability rules for AI-related harms. Because new digital technologies, including AI, carry inherent risks of harm, transparent and enforceable liability regimes are indispensable. Such frameworks must reflect the distinctive features of AI systems—especially their complexity, autonomy, and opacity—and clarify how accountability is allocated. This involves defining the legal standards of causation and establishing rules for assigning the burden of proof in cases of harm. Without this clarification, it will be challenging to guarantee justice for affected parties, safeguard rights, and promote responsible innovation.

Defining "red lines" to prohibit AI uses that violate fundamental rights. Clear red lines may be necessary where AI applications infringe on fundamental rights, such as human rights or privacy. In such cases, outright prohibitions should apply. Beyond individual rights, the prospect of severe adverse impacts on broader public goods, such as democratic integrity or climate stability, can also justify adopting strict regulatory measures, including bans on specific applications.

Requiring disclosure of key information about AI systems. Disclosure of the information underlying AI applications is essential, particularly to enable consumers to make informed choices and to counterbalance the power asymmetry between AI developers, users, and those affected by the technology. As the number and influence of AI applications continue to grow, ensuring such transparency becomes ever more critical.

Implementing risk management procedures across the AI lifecycle. Certain types and categories of new digital technologies may pose significant risks to the public good during both their development and deployment. To address these concerns, robust risk assessment and management mechanisms must be designed and agreed upon. Such assessments should be conducted before market entry and then continuously monitored and revised throughout the technology's deployment.

Preventing excessive concentration of market power. The concentration of market power poses a significant challenge to ensuring equitable access to new digital technologies and maintaining transparency regarding the conditions under which they are developed and deployed. Such concentration risks slowing technological progress, hindering economic growth, and creating structural imbalances between developers and users on the one hand, and consumers on the other. To mitigate these risks, appropriate international regulation, particularly competition rules, is essential to safeguard fair access, stimulate innovation, and prevent the adverse effects of excessive market concentration.

Investing in AI safety, transparency, and interpretability research. The safety of AI systems is paramount and must be understood in multiple dimensions. First, AI must be aligned with human values and respect human rights. Second, high-risk AI applications require rigorous assessment and management, supported by appropriate safeguards. Third, systems must demonstrate robustness, i.e., safety, reliability, and resilience to deviations from their intended purpose. Together, these principles underpin the trustworthy and responsible deployment of AI. In parallel, technological development must prioritise explainability, interpretability, and transparency to reduce bias and other systemic deficiencies.

Expanding education and retraining to address labour disruptions. Capacity building is essential to ensure the availability of skilled human resources for the development and deployment of AI and other digital technologies. This requires investment in both higher education and continuous on-the-job training. Importantly, capacity-building initiatives must also consider the specific perspectives, priorities, and needs of the Global South, where resource constraints and developmental challenges demand tailored approaches.

Ensuring broad stakeholder participation to strengthen trust and democracy. Stakeholder involvement in all decision-making processes is vital. Such participation is not only instrumental in refining, developing, and improving AI applications but also serves as a trust-building exercise. By ensuring inclusiveness and transparency, stakeholder engagement can strengthen confidence in both democratic processes and the rule of law, thereby reinforcing the legitimacy of AI governance.

Mitigating wider forms of power concentration (technological, economic, political). This dimension closely relates to mitigating competitive dynamics but places greater emphasis on broader forms of power concentration. It highlights how excessive concentrations of power—whether economic, technological, or political—can pose significant risks to public goods and therefore require careful regulatory oversight.

Taking targeted actions to secure specific societal benefits of AI. This dimension underscores the need for governance frameworks that actively secure the realisation of anticipated benefits, rather than merely facilitating them indirectly or passively. Currently, most governance approaches tend to enable potential benefits only incidentally, without ensuring that these are fully realised or fairly distributed. To close this gap, more direct, outcome-oriented measures are required—frameworks that not only support innovation but also guarantee that its benefits are effectively delivered and equitably shared.

While comprehensive, the report underemphasised three dimensions critical for the Global South: persistent deficits in power supply, infrastructure, and digital literacy; risks of deepening the global digital divide; and environmental trade-offs, such as the energy and water footprint of AI. Therefore, while the OECD framework offers a valuable foundation, its Global North bias limits its applicability in contexts where soils, agriculture, and basic infrastructure remain existential concerns.

### 2.6.2. Legislation at the national level

At the national level, regulating digital technologies in the context of soil governance reveals both the breadth of relevant laws and the gaps between them. Soil management is inherently cross-sectoral: effective regulation depends not on a single statute but on a patchwork of provisions across multiple domains. Most countries lack dedicated soil laws. Instead, general environmental statutes and sector-specific provisions shape soil governance. Relevant areas include agricultural law (fertilisers, pesticides, land use); urban and regional planning; industrial and mining regulation; water management; and nature conservation. This fragmentation is often criticised, but it is unavoidable given the soils' cross-cutting role. It does, however, complicate the integration of digital tools into soil governance.

The African Union's (AU) Continental Artificial Intelligence Strategy identifies a wide range of existing laws as relevant for AI and digital governance, including:[133] intellectual property law; electronic communications and transactions law; whistle-blowing and disclosure law; access to information law; personal data protection law; cybersecurity law; consumer protection law; antitrust and competition law; and laws promoting inclusion and empowerment of marginalised groups. Together, these frameworks form the legal foundation for regulating digital innovation, protecting rights, and ensuring that new technologies support equitable outcomes.

Despite this, digitalisation is rarely addressed in soil-related legal frameworks. The *International Yearbook of Soil Law and Policy* has not explicitly covered the interface between digital technologies and soil governance in any of its six volumes, nor have the recent *Soil Security* special issues.[134] Likewise, the AU's AI Strategy omits explicit references to environmental protection or climate law.

This separation reflects a broader trend: debates on digitalisation are often siloed from debates on environmental sustainability, even though they are increasingly interdependent. Bridging this gap is critical if soil governance is to keep pace with technological change.

#### 2.6.2.1. Examples at the regional and national level

Technological change advances at a pace that often outstrips the law. Legal frameworks, typically designed to manage stable and measurable risks, struggle to keep pace with innovations that rapidly transition from "cutting-edge" to commonplace. This constant cycle of adjustment forces regulators to address not only technical risks but also deeper ethical and societal questions of fairness, dignity, and non-discrimination. Yet these values are interpreted differently across societies, making harmonisation difficult and producing fragmented regulatory approaches.[135]

---

133 AU (2024b: 32).

134 See https://www.umweltbundesamt.de/en/topics/international-yearbook-of-soil-law-policy, accessed 29 September 2025. For the two special issues: https://www.sciencedirect.com/special-issue/10VQ9HFPD6Z; and https://www.sciencedirect.com/special-issue/1006G3251R7.

135 WTO (2024).

Countries in the Global North, with stronger infrastructure, investment, and expertise, are better positioned to shape the trajectory of AI. At the same time, many in the Global South remain constrained by persistent deficits. By 2015, over 100 AI-related policies had already been implemented across all high-income economies.[136] Upper-middle-income economies reached this milestone in 2018, while lower-middle-income and low-income economies have yet to achieve this level of policy development.[137] Without deliberate safeguards, the digital revolution could entrench dependency rather than promote inclusion. At the same time, AI offers opportunities for leapfrogging traditional barriers to development. With appropriate governance, digital tools can support sustainable agriculture, strengthen climate adaptation, and promote more inclusive soil management. For many developing economies, the central challenge is not whether to engage with AI, but how to do so without replicating past patterns of reliance on external models.

The AU has increasingly shifted its institutional focus to AI governance. This trajectory began with the 2019 Sharm el-Sheikh Declaration, adopted by AU Ministers responsible for Communication and Information Technologies under the Specialised Technical Committee on that subject.[138] The Declaration reaffirmed earlier AU digital initiatives, including the Policy and Regulatory Initiative for Digital Africa (PRIDA), as well as existing cybersecurity and data protection frameworks, setting out an ambitious vision for an inclusive digital society and economy. It called on Member States to accelerate the implementation of the Digital Transformation Strategy for Africa (2020–2030), ratify the Malabo Convention, promote digitalisation across sectors such as postal services and financial systems, and establish national Internet Governance Forums. Institutionally, the Declaration mandated the AU Commission to mobilise resources to implement the digital strategy and established a working group on AI to develop a unified continental position. It also proposed an Africa-wide framework for capacity building and the establishment of an AI think tank aligned with Agenda 2063 and the UN Sustainable Development Goals (SDGs). Building on these foundations, the Continental Artificial Intelligence Strategy for Africa, adopted by the AU Executive Council in 2024, seeks to guide national AI strategies, governance frameworks, and capacity-building efforts.[139] Complementary efforts by the African Commission on Human and Peoples' Rights, notably Resolution 473 (2021), underscore the need to ensure that AI, robotics, and emerging technologies are developed and deployed in ways consistent with African values and human rights.[140] The Malabo Convention on Cybersecurity and Personal Data Protection, adopted in 2014 and entering into force

136 WTO (2025: 70).

137 Ibid.

138 ALT Advisory (2022: 6).

139 See https://fpf.org/blog/global/the-african-unions-continental-ai-strategy-data-protection-and-governance-laws-set-to-play-a-key-role-in-ai-regulation/, accessed 27 October 2025.

140 See https://presscouncil.org.za/2025/05/14/african-commission-study-charts-path-for-ethical-ai-in-africa/, accessed 27 October 2025.

in 2023, remains the AU's key binding instrument, setting comprehensive standards for e-commerce, data protection, and cybersecurity. Yet only sixteen states have ratified it so far, underscoring ongoing implementation challenges.

National efforts signal early steps toward regional convergence. South Africa released its National Policy Framework on AI in 2025, setting ethical guardrails for responsible use, mandating transparency in algorithmic decisions, and prioritising public safety—seeking to spur innovation while protecting rights.[141] Nigeria's National AI Strategy (2023) aims to drive growth in agriculture, finance, and health, while pairing that ambition with clear ethical and regulatory safeguards.[142] Kenya launched its National AI Strategy 2025–2030, focused on ethical, inclusive, innovation-led adoption.[143] Rwanda's National AI Policy (2023) emphasises fairness and transparency, sets guidance for public-sector use (including smart-city applications), and invests in regulator training.[144] Egypt's National AI Strategy (2025–2030) strikes a balance between economic objectives and oversight, requiring ethical thresholds for AI in public services and the development of monitoring frameworks across various sectors, including transportation.[145] Mauritius's National AI Strategy (2018) targets economy-wide gains in productivity and quality of life, pairing priority use cases with plans to build an innovation ecosystem and a fit-for-purpose regulatory framework.[146]

The Continental AI Strategy identifies agriculture as a key sector for AI innovation, promoting centres of excellence, knowledge sharing, and awareness-raising about AI's potential and risks. While these initiatives focus broadly on agriculture, their relevance extends to soil protection and management, as soil governance forms the ecological foundation of agricultural systems. Similarly, the Soil Initiative for Africa (SIA) integrates digital technologies across its priority areas, particularly in data-driven soil monitoring and integrated planning.[147] However, the SIA remains silent mainly on regulatory guidance for digital tools—highlighting the broader challenge of fragmented, uncoordinated national frameworks and the need for continental coherence in governing AI for sustainable soil management.

141 See https://www.techpolicy.press/scaffolding-for-the-south-africa-national-ai-policy-framework/, accessed 27 October 2025.

142 See https://africa.businessinsider.com/local/markets/from-data-to-ai-inside-nigerias-leading-blueprint-for-africas-digital-sovereignty/e6r7cxj, accessed 27 October 2025.

143 See https://www.covafrica.com/2025/04/kenyas-ai-strategy-2025-2030-signals-for-global-companies-operating-in-africa/, accessed 27 October 2025.

144 See https://theconversation.com/ai-policies-in-africa-lessons-from-ghana-and-rwanda-253642, accessed 27 October 2025.

145 See https://techafricanews.com/2025/09/04/egypt-aims-for-ai-leadership-in-the-middle-east-and-africa-with-new-national-strategy/, accessed 27 October 2025.

146 See https://www.legal500.com/developments/thought-leadership/ai-regulation-and-policy-in-africa/, accessed 27 October 2025.

147 See https://sia.faraafrica.org/, accessed 27 October 2025.

Against this backdrop, several major regulatory models dominate global debates on AI. Each provides valuable lessons for integrating AI into soil governance, though they carry essential limitations:

#### 2.6.2.2. EU Artificial Intelligence Act (EU AI Act)

Adopted in June 2024 after years of negotiation, the EU AI Act is the first comprehensive legislative framework for AI.[148] According to Article 113, the regulation will formally take effect on 2 August 2026, although compliance with Chapters I and II will be required as of 2 February 2025. As of 2 August 2025, the AI Act's Chapter V obligations for General-Purpose AI apply to any model first placed on the EU market on or after that date. Models already on the market before 2 August 2025 have a two-year grace period—until 2 August 2027—to comply (Article 111(3)). A "general-purpose AI model" under the AI Act is a model trained with extensive datasets and compute that can generate language (text/audio), images, or video and shows broad functional generality—i.e., it can perform many distinct tasks and be integrated into a wide range of downstream systems. Models used only for research, development, or prototyping before market placement are excluded. Examples include GPT-4, Google Gemini, and Llama 3.1; social media chatbots are built on these models. On 18 July 2025, the European Commission published draft guidelines clarifying how the AI Act's provisions apply to these models.[149]

As a regulation, the Act applies directly in all Member States. In its 2020 White Paper, the European Commission highlighted risks such as privacy intrusions, constraints on freedom of expression, affronts to human dignity, and discriminatory outcomes (e.g., in hiring) as key AI harms—classifying them as non-material threats to fundamental rights, distinct from material risks to safety and health.[150] Accordingly, the Act's architecture is explicitly risk-based, classifying AI systems according to the level of risk they pose to health, security, or fundamental rights. This orientation has led many observers to describe the EU's regulatory model as explicitly human-centric, reflecting its emphasis on safeguarding public goods and fundamental values.[151]

148 Regulation (EU) 2024/1689 of the European Parliament and of the Council of 13 June 2024 laying down harmonised rules on artificial intelligence and amending Regulations (EC) No 300/2008, (EU) No 167/2013, (EU) No 168/2013, (EU) 2018/858, (EU) 2018/1139 and (EU) 2019/2144 and Directives 2014/90/EU, (EU) 2016/797 and (EU) 2020/1828 (Artificial Intelligence Act). Available at: https://eur-lex.europa.eu/legal-content/EN/TXT/PDF/?uri=OJ:L_202401689; Ginzky & Ruppel (2025a: 261–263).

149 See https://digital-strategy.ec.europa.eu/en/library/guidelines-scope-obligations-providers-general-purpose-ai-models-under-ai-act, accessed 29 September 2025.

150 See https://commission.europa.eu/system/files/2020-02/commission-white-paper-artificial-intelligence-feb2020_en.pdf, accessed 29 September 2025.

151 Pirozolli (2024).

Under the EU's AI Act, systems deemed to pose "unacceptable" risk are outright prohibited.[152] These include manipulative AI targeting vulnerable groups (e.g., voice-activated toys that incite dangerous behaviour in children); social scoring systems; biometric categorisation and identification in public spaces. "High-risk" systems may operate only if they meet strict safeguards:[153] a lifecycle risk-management process (Article 9); training and testing on data suitable for the intended use (Article 10); comprehensive technical documentation (Article 11); automatic logging of key events (Article 12); clear information for deployers about risks and proper use (Article 13); and effective human oversight during operation (Article 14). These include AI used in critical infrastructure, education, employment, law enforcement, border control, and legal interpretation. Before being marketed or put into service, they must pass a conformity assessment (Article 16). In addition, general-purpose AI models are split into those that create systemic risks and those that do not (Article 52a), with different obligations applying to each category. Limited and minimal-risk systems (such as generative AI models like ChatGPT) fall into this category and are subject to transparency and copyright rules. To support innovation, the Act also mandates the creation of AI regulatory sandboxes, enabling the controlled testing of new systems. A regulatory sandbox is a soft-law tool commonly used for emerging technologies such as AI: it lets startups and other innovators trial their products in real-world conditions within a controlled, regulator-supervised setting.[154]

The European Commission has also released a General-Purpose AI Code of Practice, drafted by independent experts, and endorsed it as a suitable voluntary instrument for providers to show alignment with the AI Act.[155] The Code centres on transparency, copyright compliance, and model safety and security. Providers are invited to sign it, and by doing so, formally commit to following its principles.

For soil governance, the EU AI Act will apply where soil-related AI systems are placed on the EU market. However, criticism has emerged: environmental impacts are not explicitly included in the risk framework, and stakeholder participation (e.g., farmers, civil society) is not required in the risk classification process.[156] The AI Act leaves significant sustainability risks largely untouched. It contains no binding provisions on the energy and water use of data centres, the associated greenhouse-gas emissions, or the mounting problem of e-waste—issues flagged by the European Parliament's research service—beyond pointing to voluntary codes of conduct.[157] There are virtually

152 See https://www.europarl.europa.eu/topics/en/article/20230601STO93804/eu-ai-act-first-regulation-on-artificial-intelligence#ai-regulation-in-europe-the-first-comprehensive-framework-4, accessed 29 September 2025.

153 Ibid.

154 See https://www.trust.org/toolkit/part-2-emerging-ai-governance-in-africa/the-continental-response/, accessed 29 September 2025.

155 See https://ec.europa.eu/commission/presscorner/detail/en/ip_25_1787, accessed 29 September 2025.

156 Müller (2022: A6).

157 Wörsdörfer (2023).

no explicit references to climate change, ecological sustainability, environmental protection, or "green AI."[158] As Floridi notes, the framework remains predominantly anthropocentric, centring on human rights impacts while sidelining environmental harms.[159] These omissions reduce transparency and inclusiveness, undermining the Act's potential to support sustainability.

Notably, some emerging economies in the Global South, including Mexico, are edging toward the EU's template.[160]

#### 2.6.2.3. China's regulatory concept

China can be considered a frontrunner in AI regulation.[161] Since 2022, it has introduced a series of targeted measures: the Algorithm Recommendation Regulation (2022), which sets rules for fairness and transparency in recommendation systems; the Deep Synthesis Regulation (2023), which governs "deepfake" and synthetic media technologies; Generative AI Regulation (2023), which requires security assessments before deployment of generative AI; and the Ethical Review Measures (draft, 2023), which obliges universities, research bodies, and companies engaged in sensitive technologies to establish ethics committees.[162]

Unlike the EU, China does not classify AI systems by risk levels or prohibit particular applications. Instead, regulation is designed to ensure that AI serves state priorities, with an emphasis on ethics, security, and social stability. As a result, China's regulatory framework has often been characterised as "state-centric," in contrast to the EU's explicitly human-centric approach.[163]

Notably, China does not yet have a single comprehensive AI statute. Plans for an overarching AI law were removed from the 2025 legislative agenda, signalling a preference for a phased regulatory strategy rather than immediate codification.[164] Instead of adopting a unified framework, China currently relies on a combination of targeted regulations, sector-specific rules, technical standards, and regulatory pilots to govern AI development and deployment. This incremental approach allows regulators to test governance mechanisms, refine safety and transparency requirements, and respond to emerging risks while maintaining regulatory flexibility and limiting compliance burdens for industry. However, the absence of a unified statute also leaves companies navigating a fragmented governance landscape, with overlapping obligations across

158 Ibid.

159 Floridi (2021).

160 Ibid.

161 For full discussion, see Filipova (2024); Karpiuk-Wawryszuk & Kasprowicz (2025).

162 Quoted from Xu et al. (2023: 9-10); Ginzky & Ruppel (2025a: 263-264).

163 Randazzoa & Hill (2025: 4).

164 See https://eastasiaforum.org/2025/12/25/china-resets-the-path-to-comprehensive-ai-governance/, accessed 15 March 2026.

different regulatory instruments. Therefore, coordination among transparency rules, safety testing requirements, and data governance frameworks remains a key challenge within China's evolving AI governance model.

As in the EU, environmental considerations remain largely absent from China's AI governance framework.[165] This omission limits the relevance of the Chinese model for SSM, particularly in contexts where ecological protection and land-resource governance are central policy objectives.

### 2.6.2.4. Singapore's model framework

Although less publicised than the EU and China's approaches, Singapore provides essential guidance, having introduced its Model Artificial Intelligence Governance Framework in 2019 and updated it in 2020. The framework is built on two overarching principles: AI decisions should be explainable, transparent, and fair, and AI systems should be human-centric, safeguarding people's interests, safety, and well-being.[166]

These principles are elaborated through four areas of guidance. First, organisations are encouraged to establish or adapt internal governance structures to incorporate values, responsibilities, and risk management in algorithmic decision-making. Second, the framework helps determine the appropriate level of human involvement in AI decision-making, using tools such as a "probability–severity of harm" matrix to assess risk appetite. Third, it addresses operations management, outlining factors for developing, selecting, and maintaining AI models, with a particular focus on data management. Finally, it provides strategies for communicating with stakeholders and management on the use of AI solutions.

As a central technology hub in Asia, Singapore's approach has a regional influence, illustrating how voluntary frameworks can promote the responsible adoption of AI. Unlike regulatory mandates, the model relies on industry uptake, allowing for rapid refinement through practical experience.[167] Its rules- and risk-based approach balances innovation with protection, recognising that sustainable AI development requires advancing competitiveness while safeguarding rights and trust.

The framework's emphasis on human-centricity goes beyond ethics, treating it as a business imperative. AI systems are expected to enhance human capabilities, respect autonomy, and preserve oversight in consequential decisions. This ensures that technology strengthens, rather than substitutes, human judgement—building the trust essential for widespread adoption.

---

165 See https://www.chathamhouse.org/2022/03/challenges-ai, accessed 29 September 2025; Birkstedt et al. (2023).

166 See https://www.pdpc.gov.sg/-/media/files/pdpc/pdf-files/resource-for-organisation/ai/sgmodelaigovframework2.pdf, accessed 29 September 2025.

167 Lousqui (2025).

Singapore's Model AI Governance Framework for Generative AI ("GenAI Framework"), issued on 30 May 2024 by the Infocomm Media Development Authority and the AI Verify Foundation, offers a detailed soft-law instrument that couples high-level principles with operational guidance across nine interlocking dimensions.[168] It assigns accountability *ex ante* across the technology stack and provides *ex post* redress mechanisms (including indemnities and insurance); sets out data-governance expectations focused on quality, lawfulness (privacy and copyright), and the use of privacy-enhancing technologies; requires trustworthy development and deployment through lifecycle safety practices, context-specific risk assessment, and standardised, plain-language disclosures; establishes proportionate incident management encompassing proactive vulnerability reporting and thresholds for mandatory notification; envisages third-party testing and assurance supported by standard benchmarks and, in time, accreditation; embeds security-by-design complemented by GenAI-specific controls (such as input-risk filters and digital forensics); promotes content provenance via watermarking, cryptographic proofs, and uniform labelling; prioritises safety and alignment research and development (e.g., reinforcement learning from AI feedback, post-training evaluations, and mechanistic interpretability) alongside public research institutes; and advances "AI for public good" through equitable access, improved public service delivery, workforce upskilling, and attention to environmental footprints. Framed for voluntary adoption by regulators and firms alike, the GenAI Framework is readily transposable to data-intensive domains such as soil information systems, where its emphasis on data quality, provenance, independent assurance, and clear user disclosures would materially strengthen the trustworthiness and local grounding of AI.

Regarding sustainability, the Framework acknowledges that generative AI entails significant energy and water consumption, with implications for climate objectives. It calls for coordinated action across the ecosystem to develop and deploy energy-efficient compute, track and measure the lifecycle carbon footprint of training and inference, and host AI workloads in data centres that apply best-in-class efficiency practices and utilise low-carbon energy sources or pathways. It assigns a primary role to AI developers and equipment manufacturers in conducting research and development on green computing techniques and in adopting energy-efficient hardware.

In January 2026, the Infocomm Media Development Authority introduced the Model AI Governance Framework for Agentic AI, the first comprehensive governance guide specifically addressing risks associated with agentic AI systems—AI systems capable of autonomously planning and executing multi-step tasks to achieve user-defined goals.[169] Like Singapore's earlier AI frameworks, the model remains voluntary but aims to help organisations manage regulatory exposure and legal accountability under existing laws. The framework identifies new risks arising from the increased

---

168 Allen et al. (2025); Avery Foundation (2024).

169 See https://www.eversheds-sutherland.com/en/global/insights/singapore-understanding-singapores-new-model-framework-for-agentic-ai-governance, accessed 15 March 2026.

autonomy of agentic systems, including erroneous or unauthorised actions, biased decision-making, data breaches, and disruptions to interconnected digital systems. To address these concerns, the guidance proposes governance measures across four key dimensions: assessing and bounding risks before deployment; ensuring clear human accountability and meaningful oversight; implementing technical safeguards such as testing, monitoring, and fail-safe mechanisms; and strengthening transparency and user responsibility through disclosure and training. The framework forms part of Singapore's broader "AI for Public Good" strategy and reflects the country's incremental, multi-layered approach to AI governance. Rather than imposing binding legislation, Singapore relies on voluntary governance frameworks, regulatory guidance, and industry standards to encourage responsible AI deployment while maintaining flexibility for innovation.

#### 2.6.2.5. The USA's AI Action Plan

The US has so far favoured a market-led, sectoral patchwork: no comprehensive federal statute, a reliance on voluntary guidance and agency rules, and an increasingly uneven mosaic of state laws.[170] One of the most prominent soft-law initiatives is the Blueprint for an AI Bill of Rights, released in October 2022 by the White House Office of Science and Technology Policy.[171] The blueprint sets out five guiding principles intended to shape the responsible design, deployment, and governance of AI systems. These include the development of safe and effective systems, the protection of data privacy, notice and explanation when AI is used, safeguards against algorithmic discrimination, and the availability of human alternatives and oversight in high-stakes decisions. Although the Blueprint is non-binding, it has influenced federal procurement practices, agency risk assessments, and broader discussions on trustworthy AI governance. It reflects the US's broader regulatory philosophy, which relies on voluntary standards, sector-specific regulation, and public-private collaboration rather than comprehensive federal legislation.

On 23 July 2025, the Trump administration released a 28-page strategy, "Winning the Race: America's AI Action Plan", prepared pursuant to Executive Order 14179, which tasked presidential advisers to craft a roadmap to sustain and strengthen US leadership in AI in support of human flourishing, economic competitiveness, and national security.[172] The Action Plan itself is non-binding—it imposes no mandatory steps on agencies or the private sector—but outlines a comprehensive set of

170 See https://www.softwareimprovementgroup.com/us-ai-legislation-overview/, accessed 29 September 2025; Lousqui (2025).

171 See https://bidenwhitehouse.archives.gov/ostp/ai-bill-of-rights/, accessed 15 March 2026.

172 See https://www.whitehouse.gov/wp-content/uploads/2025/07/Americas-AI-Action-Plan.pdf, accessed 29 September 2025.

recommended policy actions for federal departments across various domains. In parallel, President Trump issued three executive orders to operationalise the Plan's priorities: restricting federal procurement of "biased" AI models, streamlining permits for data centres and other AI infrastructure, and promoting an export strategy for US AI systems. Unlike the Plan, these orders create binding obligations for federal agencies. Taken together, the Action Plan and the accompanying orders constitute the administration's most precise and comprehensive AI policy guidance to date.

However, read as a whole, the Action Plan prioritises rapid deployment of AI infrastructure over environmental safeguards.[173] It recommends accelerated permitting by streamlining or reducing regulations under environmental laws and directs agencies to identify federal lands for large-scale data centre and generation projects. These measures de-prioritise soil stewardship—increasing the risk of soil sealing, erosion, and contamination—and are not consistent with a sustainability-oriented approach.

#### 2.6.2.6. The UK's emerging AI framework

The UK has initially pursued a light-touch, sectoral approach to AI governance, relying primarily on existing regulatory frameworks rather than adopting a comprehensive AI statute.[174] In recent years, however, the UK has begun to move toward more structured regulation through a series of proposed and sector-specific laws.[175]

Several draft bills illustrate this shift. The Artificial Intelligence (Regulation and Workers' Rights) Bill (2023) focused on AI use in the workplace, proposing requirements for transparency, employee consultation, and safeguards against algorithmic discrimination, but it has not progressed through Parliament.[176] A broader Artificial Intelligence (Regulation) Bill introduced in 2024 proposes establishing a central AI Authority to coordinate regulators, promote regulatory sandboxes, and oversee accountability measures, such as appointing organisational AI officers and ensuring transparency regarding AI systems and training data.[177]

Additional legislative initiatives include the Public Authority Algorithmic and Automated Decision-Making Systems Bill (2024), which would require public authorities to conduct algorithmic impact assessments and publish transparency records before deploying automated decision systems.[178] In contrast to these horizontal proposals, the Automated Vehicles Act represents the UK's first enacted AI-specific

173 See https://diginomica.com/us-ai-action-plan-part-one-beware-its-local-and-environmental-consequences-warns-amc, accessed 29 September 2025.

174 Ritchie et al. (2025).

175 For a discussion, see Hilliard et al. (2026).

176 See https://www.tuc.org.uk/research-analysis/reports/artificial-intelligence-regulation-and-employment-rights-bill, accessed 20 March 2026.

177 See https://bills.parliament.uk/publications/59353/documents/6128, accessed 20 March 2026.

178 See https://bills.parliament.uk/bills/3760, accessed 20 March 2026.

legislation, focusing on the safety, licensing, liability, and oversight of autonomous vehicles.[179]

Despite these emerging initiatives, the UK's AI governance landscape remains fragmented. Existing laws—particularly data protection legislation—continue to serve as the primary enforcement mechanisms for AI-related harms, with regulatory actions largely led by the Information Commissioner's Office.[180]

### 2.6.2.7. South Korea's AI Basic Act

South Korea has adopted a comprehensive yet innovation-oriented approach to AI governance through the Framework Act on Artificial Intelligence Development and Establishment of a Foundation for Trustworthiness (AI Basic Act), which was enacted in December 2024 and entered into force on 22 January 2026.[181] Overseen by the Ministry of Science and Information and Communication Technology, the law establishes a national framework to promote AI development while ensuring safety, transparency, and public trust.

The Act adopts a risk-based governance model that applies to organisations whose AI activities affect South Korea, including foreign companies providing AI services to domestic users. Particular obligations apply to "high-impact AI" systems—those affecting sectors such as healthcare, transportation, energy, public administration, and biometric technologies.[182] Providers of such systems must implement risk management measures, disclose AI use, and may undergo voluntary inspections or certification mechanisms designed to strengthen trust. Generative AI services must also label AI-generated content and notify users when outputs are produced by AI systems.

Compared with the EU's regulatory framework, South Korea's approach is less restrictive and more innovation-focused.[183] Rather than imposing strict pre-market conformity assessments or prohibiting specific AI practices, the Act relies more heavily on post-market oversight, voluntary certification, and soft-law governance principles, while leaving low-risk AI largely unregulated. The law also incorporates industrial policy objectives, including regulatory sandboxes, research support, and infrastructure development to promote AI competitiveness.

Enforcement under the new framework is expected to remain relatively limited, with penalties capped at modest levels and a transitional grace period for

179 See https://www.legislation.gov.uk/ukpga/2024/10/contents, accessed 20 March 2026.

180 Unver & Odusola-Stevenson (2025).

181 For a discussion, see Hilliard et al. (2026).

182 See https://fpf.org/blog/south-koreas-new-ai-framework-act-a-balancing-act-between-innovation-and-regulation/, accessed 20 March 2026.

183 See https://www.theguardian.com/world/2026/jan/29/south-korea-world-first-ai-regulation-laws, accessed 20 March 2026.

compliance.[184] In practice, most AI-related enforcement actions have so far occurred under data protection law, overseen by the Personal Information Protection Commission.[185]

### 2.6.2.8. Brazil's emerging AI regulatory framework

Brazil has been among the first jurisdictions to explore comprehensive AI legislation. Since 2019, several bills have been introduced to establish principles and governance structures for artificial intelligence. Early proposals, including Bill No. 5051/2019 and Bill No. 21/2020, emphasised human dignity, privacy, transparency, and human oversight, seeking to ensure that AI systems enhance rather than replace human decision-making while safeguarding fundamental rights.[186] A subsequent proposal, Bill No. 872/2021, further highlighted principles such as autonomy, democratic oversight, bias prevention, and continuous risk management.[187]

The most advanced initiative is Bill No. 2338/2023, adopted in December 2024, which introduces a risk-based regulatory framework broadly comparable to the EU AI Act.[188] The law identifies a range of high-risk AI applications, including systems used in critical infrastructure, healthcare, employment decisions, credit assessment, biometric identification, law enforcement, migration management, and public administration. Providers of such systems must conduct impact assessments, implement risk management and data governance measures, ensure transparency, and comply with data protection legislation. The framework also prohibits certain high-risk practices, such as manipulative systems exploiting vulnerable groups or social scoring by public authorities.

The legislation includes enforcement mechanisms such as fines of up to 2% of annual revenue or R$50 million, as well as potential suspension of AI systems. However, enforcement activity in Brazil remains limited and has largely arisen under data protection law rather than AI-specific regulation.[189] Oversight by the Autoridade

184 See https://www.littler.com/news-analysis/asap/understanding-south-koreas-new-ai-law-key-considerations-multinational-employers, accessed 20 March 2026.

185 See https://iapp.org/news/a/south-korea-s-pipc-flexes-its-muscles-what-to-know-about-ai-model-deletion-cross-border-transfers-and-more, accessed 20 March 2026.

186 See https://www.holisticai.com/blog/brazil-ai-legislation-proposals, accessed 20 March 2026.

187 For a discussion, see Hilliard et al. (2026).

188 See https://www.holisticai.com/blog/brazil-ai-legislation-proposals, accessed 20 March 2026.

189 See https://cms.law/en/int/expert-guides/ai-regulation-scanner/brazil#:~:text=Brazil%20does%20not%20yet%20have,%2C%20security%20measures%2C%20and%20accountability, accessed 8 April 2026.

Nacional de Proteção de Dados (ANPD) has included actions against companies such as Meta for unlawful processing of personal data used to train AI systems.[190]

### 2.6.2.9. Russia's experimental approach to AI governance

Russia initially adopted a light-touch approach to AI governance, relying on national strategies and government initiatives rather than comprehensive legislation. Early policy measures included the Federal Programme on the Digital Economy of the Russian Federation and the National Strategy for the Development of Artificial Intelligence (2019), which set out long-term objectives to advance AI capabilities through 2030.[191] The strategy emphasises cooperation between government, industry, and scientific institutions while promoting principles such as security, human autonomy, risk-based regulation, and the prohibition of delegating morally responsible decisions to AI systems. Amendments introduced in 2024 further refined governance principles and expanded access to datasets—such as medical, anonymised personal, and industrial data—to support AI development.

In terms of legislation, Russia has primarily focused on regulatory sandboxes rather than broad horizontal regulation.[192] The 2020 Moscow experimental legal regime (Law 123-FZ) established a framework that allows companies to test AI technologies outside existing regulations for up to 5 years.[193] This initiative was expanded nationwide through the Experimental Legal Regimes in Digital Innovation Law (258-FZ) of 2021, enabling controlled experimentation with AI technologies in sectors such as healthcare, transportation, finance, and agriculture.[194] Amendments adopted in 2024 introduced additional safeguards, including mandatory civil liability insurance for participants testing AI systems within these experimental regimes.

Enforcement activity related to AI remains limited in Russia. Most regulatory activity focuses on experimentation and technology development rather than punitive oversight. However, recent policy proposals suggest a shift towards more assertive state control, with Russia considering sweeping powers to ban or restrict foreign AI tools that do not comply with domestic regulatory requirements, including data localisation and alignment with so-called "traditional values".[195]

---

190 See https://fpf.org/blog/processing-of-personal-data-for-ai-training-in-brazil-takeaways-from-anpds-preliminary-decisions-in-the-meta-case/#:~:text=The%20ANPD%20issued%20a%20preventive,suspension%20of%20that%20processing%20activity, accessed 20 March 2026.

191 For a discussion, see Hilliard et al. (2026).

192 See https://law.asia/russia-ai-regulations-legal-framework-ethics/, accessed 20 March 2026.

193 See https://regulations.ai/regulations/RAI-RU-MO-FN1A2XX-2020, accessed 20 March 2026.

194 Mamina & Kobzeva (2021).

195 See https://www.reuters.com/business/russia-give-itself-sweeping-powers-ban-or-restrict-foreign-ai-tools-2026-03-20/, accessed 20 March 2026.

### 2.6.3. The international level

International debates on AI governance have accelerated in recent years, but binding global rules remain elusive.[196] Instead, the landscape is marked by non-binding principles, regional strategies, and fragmented bilateral initiatives.[197] For soil governance, this fragmentation creates uncertainty, as soil-related AI tools may be subject to inconsistent standards depending on where they are deployed. Notably, the OECD has proposed creating an international intergovernmental body, comparable in structure and mandate to the Intergovernmental Panel on Climate Change (IPCC), tasked with monitoring global AI developments, producing regular assessments, and making its analyses publicly accessible to policymakers and civil society alike. Such a body could provide the much-needed epistemic authority and shared evidence base to counteract fragmentation and build trust in global governance processes.[198]

The Council of Europe Framework Convention on AI (2024) is the most advanced initiative to date, developed under the auspices of the Council of Europe—a regional organisation distinct from, but overlapping with, the EU. The Convention represents the first attempt to establish binding international standards on AI governance, focusing on human rights, democracy, and the rule of law. However, it has not yet secured the necessary number of ratifications to enter into force. It was formally opened for ratification in September 2024.[199] To date, signatories include the EU, the UK, Canada, Georgia, Japan, and the US. In terms of its stated purpose, Article 1 of the Convention affirms that the design, development, and deployment of AI systems across their entire lifecycle must be "fully consistent with human rights, democracy, and the rule of law."[200]

On 10–11 February 2025, the second AI Summit was co-hosted by France and India, bringing together representatives from over 100 countries, as well as civil society, the private sector, and research institutions. The meeting concluded with the adoption of the *Statement on Inclusive and Sustainable Artificial Intelligence for People and Planet.* Signed by approximately sixty states, including China, the statement underscored the "importance of reinforcing the diversity of the AI ecosystem". It affirmed the need to continue multisectoral dialogue, with clear priorities and next steps. It also stressed that effectively harnessing AI's benefits will depend fundamentally on "trust and safety." Notably, Russia, the UK, and the US did not sign the statement.[201]

196 Ginzky & Ruppel (2025a: 264).
197 WTO (2024).
198 Ibid.
199 See https://www.elysee.fr/en/sommet-pour-l-action-sur-l-ia, accessed 29 September 2025.
200 Council of Europe Treaty Series - No. 225, Council of Europe Framework Convention on Artificial Intelligence and Human Rights, Democracy and the Rule of Law (2024), available at https://rm.coe.int/1680afae3c, accessed 7 April 2026.
201 See https://www.elysee.fr/en/emmanuel-macron/2025/02/11/statement-on-inclusive-and-sustainable-artificial-intelligence-for-people-and-the-planet, accessed 29 September 2025.

Despite divergent approaches, a standard set of values is gaining traction. These principles were first advanced in academic circles[202] and subsequently developed under the auspices of international organisations such as the World Trade Organisation (WTO),[203] the OECD,[204] and the United Nations.[205] A notable example is the set of principles adopted by UNESCO in November 2021, which articulate core values to guide the development and deployment of AI. These include:[206] proportionality and "do no harm"; fairness and non-discrimination; transparency and explainability; human oversight and accountability; privacy and data protection; sustainability and climate responsibility; multi-stakeholder governance.[207]

One complementary proposal is Public Constitutional AI: instead of leaving "AI constitutions" to engineers or vendors, a jurisdiction would run a participatory process (including citizens' assemblies, public comment, civil-society input, and expert input) to draft a binding set of principles for high-risk and frontier systems.[208] Providers must train, fine-tune, and audit models against this public constitution, publish "constitutional audit" reports and failure cases, and offer contestability rights (including explanations, appeals, and remedies) to affected individuals. Regular reviews (e.g., every two to three years) update the rules as risks evolve. This shifts legitimacy from private policy to public law—tackling opacity and ensuring that AI used in soil governance and SSM aligns with locally endorsed rights and values.

On 18 August 2025, the UN General Assembly created two new mechanisms: the Global Dialogue on AI Governance and the Independent International Scientific Panel on AI. The Global Dialogue will convene annually (two days) to bring governments and stakeholders together to address the development of safe, secure, and trustworthy AI; promote interoperability and compatibility among national and regional governance approaches; ensure robust human oversight consistent with international law; and advance open-source software, open data and open AI models.[209] The Panel—a 40-member, multidisciplinary, geographically diverse body—will advise the UN on AI's opportunities, risks, and impacts, produce a flagship annual study, and serve as the expert engine that feeds analysis and options into the Global Dialogue. Although non-binding, these forums can set influential soft-law benchmarks—on transparency, auditability, and data governance—that will shape procurement terms, donor

202 Okolo et al. (2023) with further references.
203 Ruppel (2022b); WTO (2024).
204 OECD (2024a).
205 See https://unsceb.org/principles-ethical-use-artificial-intelligence-united-nations-system, accessed 29 September 2025.
206 See UNESCO (2021: 10). UNESCO clearly stated that the scope of application only refers to the mandates and tasks of UNESCO.
207 Ibid.: 20–25.
208 Abiri (2024).
209 UNGA A/79/L.118, 'Terms of reference and modalities for the establishment and functioning of the Independent International Scientific Panel on Artificial Intelligence and the Global Dialogue on Artificial Intelligence Governance' (18 August 2025).

conditionalities and domestic rulemaking. They offer African states and other Global South actors a venue to press for standards on locally representative training data for agricultural AI, protections for soil and farm data sovereignty, requirements for explainability ('black-box' mitigation), and attention to sustainability costs (energy and water use of AI infrastructures). Properly leveraged, the Dialogue and Panel could help align AI deployment in SSM with principles of equity, accountability and environmental stewardship.

From the AU Continental Artificial Intelligence Strategy (2024),[210] the UNESCO Recommendation on the Ethics of Artificial Intelligence,[211] and the Windhoek Statement on Artificial Intelligence in Southern Africa,[212] the following overlapping and mutually reinforcing principles emerge:

- Principle of Foundational Data Governance. AI systems are built on data, making their governance a central concern. This goes beyond mere collection to encompass questions of quality, ethics, and relevance. To be effective, data must be high-quality, inclusive, and locally grounded, so that AI solutions can avoid bias and remain applicable in African contexts. Equally important is the ethical and secure sharing of data, guided by robust frameworks that protect against misuse. At the same time, there is growing momentum toward openness—establishing trustworthy "gold standard" datasets, shared repositories, and a broader digital commons that can foster innovation while safeguarding legal and ethical standards.
- Principle of Rights-Based Protection and Agency. This principle centres on the individual, ensuring that the development of AI does not come at the expense of fundamental human rights. Legislative frameworks must embed privacy by design, requiring impact assessments, transparency, and independent oversight so that individuals remain in control of their personal data. Equally vital are safeguards to prevent harm, particularly in high-risk applications such as facial recognition and in handling sensitive biometric, genetic, or health data. Ultimately, protecting data subject rights, including the ability to access, correct, or delete personal information, remains a non-negotiable cornerstone of responsible AI governance.
- Principle of Contextual and Africa-Centric Innovation. AI must be designed for and by Africa, reflecting the continent's unique realities, challenges, and opportunities. Innovation should be channelled toward solving pressing regional issues such as health, agriculture, and climate change, rather than importing models that lack local relevance. This also requires valuing and integrating indigenous knowledge systems, ensuring that technologies resonate

210 AU (2024b).
211 See https://www.unesco.org/en/articles/recommendation-ethics-artificial-intelligence, accessed 29 September 2025.
212 See https://unesdoc.unesco.org/ark:/48223/pf0000383197, accessed 29 September 2025.

with cultural and ecological contexts. Equally important is the pursuit of technological sovereignty: building local capacity so that Africa becomes not only a consumer but also a producer and shaper of AI, thereby safeguarding its digital future.

- Principle of Inclusive and Equitable Development. This principle seeks to ensure that the benefits of AI are distributed fairly and that no one is left behind. Bridging the digital divide requires active investment in foundational infrastructure such as electricity, connectivity, and data centres, particularly in rural and disadvantaged areas. Equally important is advancing gender equality and inclusion through gender-responsive policies, promoting women in STEM fields, and safeguarding against algorithmic biases that risk marginalising vulnerable groups. Finally, capacity-building efforts must prioritise youth, women, and other marginalised communities, enabling their full participation in the AI ecosystem and ensuring that digital transformation fosters equity rather than exclusion.
- Principle of Capacity and Ecosystem Building. Sustainable AI development requires holistic investment in human capital, infrastructure, and supportive environments. Education and literacy are foundational, ranging from broad public awareness campaigns to advanced academic programmes and dedicated centres of excellence. At the same time, infrastructure investment, particularly in computing capacity, green data centres, and high-performance computing, must be treated as essential rather than optional. Equally critical is support for innovation, through incubators, hubs, and creative funding mechanisms that can nurture start-ups and stimulate digital entrepreneurship across the continent.
- Principle of Proactive and Adaptive Governance. The fast pace of AI demands governance that is both anticipatory and flexible. Policymaking must look ahead to identify potential risks and opportunities, rather than merely reacting to harms that have already occurred. Legal and regulatory frameworks should also be regularly reviewed and revised to ensure they remain responsive to rapid technological change. Ultimately, effective governance requires genuine multi-stakeholder collaboration among governments, the private sector, civil society, and academia to balance innovation, accountability, and the public interest.
- Principle of Regional Collaboration and Global Partnership. No single country can manage the challenges of AI governance in isolation. This principle emphasises the importance of unity and active engagement on the global stage. Cross-border harmonisation is vital, with interoperable standards and regional policy alignment enabling collaboration and scale. At the same time, global engagement must ensure that African voices and expertise are meaningfully represented in international AI governance forums, shaping norms rather than

passively receiving imposed solutions. Shared resources, such as collaborative platforms, secure data sharing, and the exchange of best practices, are equally essential for building trust and strengthening collective capacity across borders.

Taken together, these principles move away from a purely technocratic view of AI. They advocate for a model where AI is a tool for sustainable development rather than just profits or surveillance; rooted in ethical values and human rights from its inception; built on a foundation of sovereignty and self-determination, ensuring Africa controls its own digital destiny; and inclusive by design, aiming to reduce existing inequalities rather than exacerbate them.

This framework presents a vision of AI that is not merely adopted from elsewhere but is consciously and deliberately built to serve the specific needs and values of the African continent and similar regions.

## 3. Africa, digital colonisation, and the struggle for soil data sovereignty

### 3.1. Dependency, surveillance, and exclusion

"The future is already here – it's just not evenly distributed."[213] This aphorism captures Africa's position in the global digital economy: on the cusp of technological transformation, yet at risk of repeating historical patterns of extraction and dependency. AI and digitalisation hold immense potential for soil protection and SSM. Still, without adequate governance, they may entrench inequalities and strip communities of their most fundamental resource. Nowhere is this tension more visible than in the treatment of soil data.

A cautionary parallel is Senegal's "Akon City": an American-owned USD 6 billion venture marketed in 2018 as a tech-utopian hub that would deliver jobs, hospitals, and "smart" infrastructure. However, it required large tracts of land near Mbodiène, with residents either relocated or pressured to relinquish their land amid disputes over compensation.[214] Years later, little of the promised city materialised, and in 2025, authorities pivoted away from the plan. The arc is familiar in AI rollouts: grand narratives of transformation justify displacement and private control, while local communities absorb the risks and costs.

Data derives value from use, not mere volume.[215] Its worth often rises combinatorially when linked with other datasets—becoming greater than the sum of its parts.[216]

213 See https://www.goodreads.com/quotes/681-the-future-is-already-here-it-s-just-not-evenly, accessed 29 September 2025.

214 See https://www.bbc.com/news/articles/c8xvrv21drjo, accessed 29 September 2025.

215 OECD/WTO (2025: 12).

216 Ibid.

Data also carries both inherent and option (potential) value: information unused today may be strategically valuable tomorrow. Because data is non-rivalrous and can be copied and shared at near-zero marginal cost, multiple actors can reuse it simultaneously for diverse purposes, multiplying its overall utility.[217] Soil data occupies a complex and ambiguous position in law and governance. By itself, it is often considered "non-personal." Yet once linked to geolocation coordinates, ownership records, or farm identifiers, it becomes sensitive, even personal information. This legal ambiguity is not merely theoretical. Decades of data governance experience demonstrate that datasets deemed "anonymised" or "non-personal" can often be re-identified with minimal auxiliary information. Classic examples from health and consumer data illustrate how cross-referencing supposedly de-identified datasets with publicly available records can accurately identify individuals.[218] These cases underscore a structural weakness in data protection regimes that rely on formal anonymisation while ignoring linkage risk and data aggregation dynamics.

Farmers across Africa often unknowingly surrender their data rights, which are frequently hidden in the fine print of contracts with agribusinesses or technology firms.[219] These contracts usually assign ownership of valuable datasets to multinational corporations, giving them disproportionate control over agricultural markets, credit systems, and even input supply chains.[220] The problem of data colonialism would intensify under such arrangements: when a handful of platforms control farm and soil data, producers lose any real say over how it is used or who captures the gains. The result is a kind of digital feudalism—value created by land and farmers' labour is siphoned off and concentrated in the hands of platform owners.[221] Instead of democratising information and empowering growers, AI is being harnessed to enforce enclosure, lock-in, and corporate extraction.

In practice, soil data is treated as a commodity, traded and monetised far from the fields where it originates. The African data centre market is projected to exceed USD 5 billion by 2026, but most facilities remain under foreign ownership.[222] The result is a widening gap in digital sovereignty that mirrors—and risks deepening—the North–South divide. The asymmetry in bargaining power leaves farmers with little capacity to negotiate terms or benefit from the economic value of their data. This imbalance raises fundamental questions of justice, sovereignty, and control over Africa's digital future. Scholars increasingly describe this situation as digital colonisation: the decentralised extraction and control of citizens' data, often without their explicit consent,

217 Ibid.
218 Cajueiro & Celestino (2026: 81).
219 Wiseman et al. (2019).
220 Lawyers Hub (2024).
221 See https://prism.sustainability-directory.com/scenario/algorithmic-bias-in-soil-health-management-systems/, accessed 29 September 2025.
222 See https://onixdatacentres.com/2024/05/07/data-centre-innovations-africa-adca-report/, accessed 29 September 2025.

through networks owned and operated by foreign technology companies.[223] It is not limited to Western firms. Chinese companies, too, have become central actors, introducing new forms of dependency.

In 2021, China's AI market was valued at roughly USD 23.196 billion, with projections of about USD 61.855 billion by 2025.[224] Between 2000 and 2014, China undertook digital projects in 44 African countries, with approximately half of these projects concentrated in Nigeria, Ethiopia, and Zimbabwe.[225] Over the past two decades, Huawei is estimated to have built around 50% of Africa's 3G networks and 70% of its 4G networks, deepening Chinese firms' embedment in the continent's information infrastructure.[226] Currently, more than 266 China-backed technology initiatives operate in Africa, many of which involve AI-related deployments, such as 5G infrastructure, data centres, smart-city platforms, and surveillance systems.[227] Hikvision opened a Johannesburg office and, via a local partner, deployed roughly 15,000 surveillance cameras across the city in 2019.[228] In 2021 alone, China reportedly earmarked USD 8.43 billion for Africa-focused digital and AI initiatives spanning high-performance computing, big data, the Internet of Things, AI, blockchain, quantum computing, cross-border e-commerce, smart cities, telemedicine, and internet finance.[229]

Therefore, the risk of dependency is not hypothetical. In 2016, for example, Facebook announced plans to build population-density maps for much of Africa using computer vision, population data, and high-resolution satellite imagery. Framed as "creating knowledge about Africa's population distribution," "connecting the unconnected," and "enabling humanitarian aid," the project effectively positioned a private platform as the authority over what counts as legitimate demographic knowledge.[230] In 2018, the Chinese AI start-up CloudWalk Technology signed an agreement with Zimbabwe to provide facial recognition systems. In exchange, Zimbabwe's citizens became a testing ground for algorithmic training datasets. Marketed as "win–win cooperation," the deal exemplified how access to African data can advance foreign technology while leaving African governments dependent on imported tools.[231] Since 2020, Google has invested over USD 200 million in AI-driven social initiatives worldwide, focusing on addressing challenges such as wildfires, hunger, and public health emergencies.[232] In July 2025, it opened an AI Community Centre in Ghana to foster local innovation and

223 Png (2022); Salami (2024).
224 Tinarwo & Babu (2023: 3).
225 Ibid.: 6.
226 Ibid.
227 Ibid.
228 Gravett (2022: 6).
229 Tinarwo & Babu (2023: 7).
230 Birhane (2020).
231 Travers (2024).
232 See https://restofworld.org/2025/africa-ai-for-good-big-tech/, accessed 29 September 2025.

pledged an additional USD 37 million to "AI for Good" projects across Africa.[233] Other major technology companies, including Microsoft, Meta, Amazon, and Apple, are pursuing similar ventures. McKinsey & Company estimates that the widespread adoption of generative AI in Africa could generate up to USD 100 billion in annual economic value across sectors.[234] Google currently operates two AI laboratories on the continent, located in Accra, Ghana, and Nairobi, Kenya. From these hubs, at least three models have been released addressing climate change, public health, and urban planning. Its global hydrological model, for instance, utilises satellite data to forecast floods up to seven days in advance, covering approximately 460 million people across 41 African countries.[235] In March 2025, Google launched MetNet in Nairobi—an AI-powered precipitation-forecasting tool available through Google Search—that helps farmers make crucial decisions, such as timing fertiliser applications to avoid rainfall losses.[236] Chinese Agricultural Technology Development Centres have become flagship aid projects, with 23 now operating across Africa, initially financed by China's Ministry of Commerce.[237] In Zambia, the Sunagri Investments–run centre showcases "smart farming" tools such as drones.[238] China has also donated five plant-protection drones to Zambia to help raise agricultural productivity.[239]

Yet while these initiatives are presented as serving the public good, they also consolidate corporate influence over vulnerable communities. Microsoft's Project Ellora, for example, has faced scrutiny in India for using rural labourers to collect speech data, despite their limited access to smartphones or the internet and the unlikelihood that they would benefit from the resulting technology.[240] Similarly, in Argentina, the company drew backlash for gathering personal data from young girls in Salta province under the pretext of predicting teenage pregnancies years in advance.[241] In Africa, too, the billions poured into cloud data centres, undersea cables, and startup ecosystems

---

233 See https://www.connectingafrica.com/ai/google-commits-37m-to-advancing-ai-in-africa, accessed 29 September 2025.

234 See https://www.mckinsey.com/capabilities/quantumblack/our-insights/leading-not-lagging-africas-gen-ai-opportunity, accessed 29 September 2025.

235 See https://blog.google/intl/en-africa/company-news/outreach-and-initiatives/5-ways-were-bringing-ai-innovations-to-people-across-africa/#:~:text=Forecasting%20floods%20up%20to%207%20days%20in%20advance&text=Google%20Research's%20global%20hydrological%20AI,460M%20people%20across%20the%20continent, accessed 29 September 2025.

236 See https://medium.com/@FromLagosto/googles-ai-forecasts-rain-for-africa-a-game-changer-in-weather-prediction-567b5c8f02eb, accessed 29 September 2025.

237 See https://www.iied.org/chinese-engagement-african-agriculture-not-what-it-seems, accessed 30 October 2025.

238 See https://chinaglobalsouth.com/analysis/case-study-chinese-agricultural-firm-uses-drones-to-fight-pests-in-zambia/, accessed 30 October 2025.

239 See http://www.china.org.cn/world/Off_the_Wire/2025-03/19/content_117775557.htm, accessed 30 October 2025.

240 See https://restofworld.org/2025/africa-ai-for-good-big-tech/, accessed 29 September 2025.

241 See https://notmy.ai/news/case-study-plataforma-tecnologica-de-intervencion-social-argentina-and-brazil/, accessed 29 September 2025.

should not be mistaken for altruism. Training local developers or expanding internet access through ventures such as Starlink may increase connectivity, but it also binds users to corporate platforms where alternatives are scarce. It is the digital equivalent of building a highway into a remote town and then charging a toll for every car: the infrastructure is valuable, but the toll—continuous dependence on proprietary systems—is the real business model.[242]

At the agricultural level, smallholder farmers, who form the backbone of African food systems, often cannot access digital tools that require costly hardware, broadband internet, or advanced literacy.[243] Even when technology arrives, it is frequently introduced through "doing good in Africa" programmes in which a major tech company sponsors apps, sensors, or platforms for local communities. For example, in recent years, pesticide and fertiliser companies have rolled out a surge of mobile "decision-support" apps for farmers—purporting to advise on what to plant, how much to spray, and when to harvest.[244] The offer looks generous and is gratefully accepted. Still, the hidden price is data extraction: the company harvests farm- and community-level data at scale, which then feeds its proprietary products and markets—the real money lies in the data, not the donation. These tools are also commonly bundled with input packages supplied by the same corporations that own the data and algorithms, creating lock-in to closed ecosystems that tilt the playing field against local innovators and turn farmers into data providers without informed consent, benefit-sharing, or data-sovereignty protections. Meanwhile, governments struggle to regulate technologies and cross-border data flows that evolve far faster than legislative processes.

In data-rich regions and on capital-intensive farms, technology providers can harvest large volumes of high-frequency information, including regular soil assays, plot-level field trials, yield monitors on new tractors, drone imagery, and in-field sensor streams.[245] They train algorithms on these datasets and market highly granular prescriptions for fertiliser rates, pesticide applications, and harvest timing. The predominance of monocropping on such operations further simplifies modelling and narrows uncertainty, making optimisation comparatively straightforward. Smallholders face the inverse conditions. Decades of structural adjustment have hollowed out public extension across much of the Global South, leaving little coordinated collection of field data. Most small farms cannot afford the machinery and sensors that feed commercial platforms. The result is sparse, noisy, and uneven datasets, from which providers can draw only low-quality inferences. Models trained primarily on data from large, monocropped systems then generalise poorly to diverse, intercropped, or rain-fed smallholder contexts—producing advice that is at best irrelevant and at worst harmful, while

242 See https://medium.com/woza-business/africa-rising-or-africa-exploited-big-techs-world-domination-plan-0c41dc1024ed, accessed 29 September 2025.

243 Abdulai et al. (2023).

244 See https://grain.org/en/article/6595-digital-control-how-big-tech-moves-into-food-and-farming-and-what-it-means, accessed 29 September 2025.

245 See https://www.myfarmweb.com/.

deepening existing inequalities in access to agronomic knowledge and digital services.[246]

For Africa, digital sovereignty is inextricably linked to soil sovereignty. Soils underpin food security, livelihoods, and resilience to climate change, yet they are under mounting pressure from erosion, nutrient depletion, desertification, and competing land uses. AI is often presented as a way for Africa to leapfrog developmental constraints by providing tools such as digital soil maps, predictive modelling, and precision agriculture systems. These could indeed optimise fertiliser use, conserve water, and provide early warnings of soil degradation.[247] There are promising soil- and agriculture-focused initiatives, such as Nuru, which was developed in collaboration with Tanzanian farmers. This initiative utilises a mobile app that functions offline to detect cassava plant diseases, safeguarding a staple crop for over 500 million people.[248] Then there is AI Farmer (formerly Hi Saai) in South Africa, which provides digital extension services that bridge access gaps for smallholder farmers.[249] Around 100 AI start-ups have been established, attracting over USD 140 million in seed funding, primarily concentrated in Nigeria's fintech sector.[250] South Africa leads in AI start-ups, followed by Nigeria and Kenya. Africa's first AI factory—a collaboration between Cassava Technologies and Nvidia—is being built in South Africa, with further facilities planned across Kenya, Nigeria, Morocco, and Egypt.[251] Still, the advancement and rollout of AI technologies remain highly uneven globally, with a pronounced divide between developed and developing countries.[252]

These examples demonstrate the potential of locally adapted AI, particularly when designed for accessibility and offline use. Yet they remain exceptions in an ecosystem dominated by multinational corporations. The contrast is instructive: while local initiatives show what is possible, the prevailing reality is that most farmers continue to face deep-seated concerns about trust, ownership, and control of their data. Farmers consistently express mistrust of digital service providers, citing issues such as:[253] lack of clarity around ownership and use of data collected through farm machinery and smart farming tools; risk of farms being re-identified by combining de-identified datasets with satellite imagery and government soil maps; fears that soil data on carbon content, fertiliser use, or biodiversity could lead to taxation, regulation, or negative consumer perceptions. Attitudes often differ when data is shared with government

246 See https://grain.org/en/article/6595-digital-control-how-big-tech-moves-into-food-and-farming-and-what-it-means, accessed 29 September 2025.
247 Castro et al. (2024); Kumar et al. (2024); Awais et al. (2023).
248 Arakpogun et al. (2021).
249 See https://saai.org/en/saai-launches-artificial-intelligence-platform-for-family-farmers/, accessed 29 September 2025.
250 Arakpogun et al. (2021).
251 See https://iafrica.com/africas-first-ai-factory-underway-as-cassava-and-nvidia-deploy-3000-gpus-in-south-africa/, accessed 29 September 2025.
252 Arakpogun et al. (2021).
253 Chichaibelu et al. (2023).

agencies, academic researchers, or private companies, reflecting different levels of trust and perceived risk.[254]

Consent cannot be meaningful if farmers do not understand the potential uses of their data or lack the ability to enforce their rights. Agricultural data has increasingly become a valuable asset and tradable commodity.[255] The way in which benefits and risks are distributed during this technological transition is primarily shaped by who controls the data and determines its uses.

Beyond individual datasets, there is significant power in data aggregation at scale. At present, this concentration of value primarily resides with powerful corporate actors—not only in the agricultural input and farm machinery industries, but also within the broader sphere of "Big Tech.".[256] Digital technologies will only benefit farmers if they have both access to the data and the capacity to influence its governance, that is, to decide how the data may be used, by whom, and for what purposes. Certain types of agricultural data, such as income or household information, are highly sensitive and require stringent safeguards. Others, such as weather records, are generally not viewed as problematic when shared publicly.[257]

Ensuring that data ownership contributes to data justice requires more than formal rights on paper. It must be coupled with capacity-building for farmers and workers to understand their entitlements, as well as structural enforcement mechanisms.[258] Otherwise, the prevailing system continues to place the burden of privacy protection on the individual "data subject"—the farmer or worker—who often lacks the time, expertise, or resources to navigate and exercise these rights.[259]

### 3.2. The South African example

South Africa offers a microcosm of the challenges surrounding agricultural and soil data governance in Africa. There is no single regulator for soil data; instead, governance is shaped indirectly by multiple laws and regulations. At the highest level, the Constitution of 1996 establishes rights that frame the use of data: the privacy rights (Section 14), dignity (Section 10), equality (Section 9), freedom and security (Section 12), access to information (Section 32), and freedom of expression, including scientific research (Section 16). The Constitutional Court has emphasised that privacy safeguards a "sphere of private intimacy and autonomy without interference," though this sphere is limited.[260] These values, combined with the Constitution's supremacy

254 Ruder & Wittman (2025).
255 Uyar et al. (2024).
256 Ruder & Wittman (2025).
257 Ibid.
258 Barton et al. (2025).
259 Ruder & Wittman (2025).
260 *Botha v Smuts* [2024] ZACC 22 (9 October 2024) at para 84.

(Section 2) and commitment to the rule of law, provide the foundation for regulating personal and environmental data, including soil data.

At the regional level, the Southern African Development Community (SADC) Model Law on Data Protection provides a valuable point of comparison.[261] Under the Model Law, soil data classification depends on whether it is linked to identifiable individuals or communities. Purely environmental information, such as soil chemistry, moisture levels, or erosion risk, typically does not qualify as personal data. However, when soil data is tied to farmers, households, or communal tenure systems through GPS coordinates or land records, it falls within the scope of personal data. It must be processed lawfully and fairly, with the consent of those affected. The Model Law also permits collection without consent where it serves the public interest, scientific research, or environmental protection, provided that safeguards are in place. In principle, this enables large-scale soil monitoring for climate change adaptation or food security, provided it is overseen by a competent authority to ensure transparency and accountability. Importantly, anonymisation and aggregation are framed as key tools for balancing governance needs with the rights and expectations of farmers and communities.

South Africa's domestic regime, however, reveals the gaps between regional aspirations and national implementation. Environmental statutes, such as the National Environmental Management Act 107 of 1998 (NEMA), regulate access to and the protection of ecological information. Yet soil data remains uncoordinated and scattered across government departments, universities, agribusinesses, and international organisations, with accessibility varying from open access (government/research) to restricted proprietary use (private firms). The Protection of Personal Information Act (POPIA) 4 of 2013, which has been in force since July 2021, is South Africa's primary data protection law. While POPIA protects the processing of personal information of natural and juristic persons, it does not expressly regulate non-personal data such as soil metrics.[262] Nevertheless, soil data linked to identifiable farmers or landowners may indirectly fall under its scope.

The Electronic Communications and Transactions Act 25 of 2002 (ECTA) is South Africa's primary statute governing electronic communications and e-commerce, designed to prevent abuses in the digital environment. Section 20 specifically addresses "automated transactions," i.e., contracts concluded where one or both parties use an automated system. It confirms that a binding agreement—and corresponding contractual rights—arises upon the conclusion of such a transaction, and that the parties are bound even if they did not personally review the system's actions. Section 20 also provides that a material error in an automated transaction can render the

261 See https://www.itu.int/en/ITU-D/Projects/ITU-EC-ACP/HIPSSA/Documents/FINAL%20DOCUMENTS/FINAL%20DOCS%20ENGLISH/sadc_model_law_data_protection.pdf, accessed 29 September 2025.

262 Coetzee (2024).

agreement void, subject to specified conditions. Accordingly, contracts formed using AI as an electronic agent fall within Section 20's scope and protections.

POPIA lays down eight conditions for lawful processing: accountability, processing limitation, purpose specification, further processing limitation, information quality, openness, security safeguards, and data subject participation. Farmers must provide consent, be notified of the collection, and retain the right to access or correct their information. The Act also regulates automated decision-making (Section 71), prohibiting legally consequential decisions based solely on automated processing unless contractual or legal safeguards are in place to ensure fairness and transparency.

Under Section 72, a responsible party may transfer personal information to a foreign country only where a lawful transfer basis exists. This is satisfied if the foreign recipient is subject to a law, binding corporate rules, or a contract that affords an adequate level of protection—i.e., provisions substantially similar to POPIA's conditions for lawful processing and to Section 72's onward-transfer restrictions. Alternatively, a transfer may proceed with the data subject's consent; where it is necessary for performance of a contract with the data subject (or pre-contract measures at their request); where it is necessary for the conclusion or performance of a contract in the data subject's interests between the responsible party and a third party; or, in limited cases, where the transfer is for the data subject's benefit and it is not reasonably practicable to obtain consent, but the data subject would likely have consented.

Yet vague wording leaves key questions unresolved: Is human confirmation after an automated decision sufficient?[263] What transparency obligations apply? Compounding this, POPIA does not obligate decision-makers to notify data subjects when automated decisions are made, making enforcement of rights difficult.[264]

AI systems often transform the data they ingest—reconstructing it into latent features, combining it with other sources, and continuously updating models—thereby limiting organisations' oversight of how the information they collected is modified and reused. The opacity of these processes makes it hard for individuals to understand how their data is being used, undermining meaningful notice and informed consent.[265]

This weakness reflects broader structural concerns. POPIA deliberately avoids regulating ownership.[266] A defensible view is that a newly created piece of digital information comes into being ownerless (*res nullius*). Its original acquisition occurs by appropriation/occupation: the first person who both intends to own it and exercises effective control over it becomes its owner, meaning universities, agribusinesses, or technology firms can establish control and claim ownership.[267] Ownership rights then

263 Davis & Trott (2024).

264 See https://www.derebus.org.za/has-popia-adequately-prepared-people-to-exercise-their-right-not-to-be-subject-to-automated-decision-making/, accessed 29 September 2025.

265 Davis & Trott (2024); Mbonye / Moodley / Nyika (2024).

266 Thaldar (2025); See https://theconversation.com/who-owns-digital-data-about-you-south-african-legal-scholar-weighs-up-property-and-privacy-rights-249741, accessed 29 September 2025.

267 Ibid.

enable data to be licensed or monetised as an economic asset, often without reciprocal benefit to the farmers or communities who generated the underlying information. Put differently, on a property view, a new instance of personal information can be owned, but not necessarily by the data subject. The party best placed to acquire ownership is the one on whose device the information is first recorded (i.e., tech company), since that party exercises control from the outset and needs only the intention to own to acquire title.[268]

This is particularly concerning in light of recent research that found existing mechanisms in data protection law (e.g., the right of access to information, as provided for in Section 5(g) of POPIA) ineffective for determining how a data subject's personal information is used in automated processing.[269] The research found that some of the largest companies are unable to provide meaningful responses to data subjects' requests to understand whether and how their personal information is used in automated processing and whether this is in line with the provisions of POPIA.

South Africa has begun to grapple with these gaps through broader digital and AI policy initiatives. Key developments include:

- AI Governance: Establishment of the Fourth Industrial Revolution (4IR) Commission (2019),[270] AI Institute of South Africa (2022),[271] and the draft National AI Plan (2024).[272]
- Research Oversight: The Academy of Science of South Africa (ASSAf) Code of Conduct for Research, initially developed for approval by the Information Regulator, has since been reconstituted as a voluntary POPIA Compliance Framework following regulatory feedback.[273] While not formally adopted as a binding code, it remains an important governance instrument that complements POPIA in guiding research activities in South Africa, including the sharing of data with international collaborators.[274]
- National AI Policy Framework (2024): Nine strategic pillars, including ethical AI, transparency, fairness, privacy, and bias mitigation.[275]

---

268 Ibid.

269 Davis et al. (2022).

270 See https://www.gov.za/news/media-statements/president-cyril-ramaphosa-appoints-commission-fourth-industrial-revolution-09, accessed 27 October 2025.

271 See https://aii-sa.co.za/, https://www.cair.org.za/, accessed 27 October 2025.

272 See https://www.michalsons.com/focus-areas/artificial-intelligence-law/national-ai-policy-guidance-and-overview, https://www.ppmattorneys.co.za/south-africas-draft-national-ai-plan/, https://www.werksmans.com/legal-updates-and-opinions/the-ai-national-policy-south-africas-initial-step-to-establish-an-ai-policy-and-regulatory-framework/, accessed 27 October 2025.

273 Gooden & Thaldar (2024).

274 Academy of Science of South Africa (2025:4).

275 See https://www.dcdt.gov.za/sa-national-ai-policy-framework/file/338-sa-national-ai-policy-framework.html, accessed 27 October 2025.

- National Data and Cloud Policy (2024): Promotes data sovereignty, cloud security, and digital transformation.[276]
- On 3 December 2024, during its G20 presidency, South Africa launched a Task Force on AI, Data Governance, and Innovation for Sustainable Development.[277]
- The Department of Communications and Digital Technologies has submitted the Draft National AI Policy to Cabinet for approval and gazetting in South Africa, with publication anticipated in March 2026.[278] Following approval and official gazetting, the Draft AI Policy will be released for public consultation. The government has adopted a sector-specific, multi-regulator approach rather than establishing a single dedicated AI authority, thereby embedding AI governance within existing regulatory frameworks.[279] The policy is structured around six core pillars aimed at promoting the responsible development and ethical deployment of AI: capacity and talent development; AI for inclusive growth and job creation; responsible governance; ethical and inclusive AI; cultural preservation and international integration; and human-centred deployment.

The above was merely a brief explanation of the problem, using South Africa as an example, but AI regulation in Africa is severely lacking.

Scholars have noted that the rise of digital technologies has placed significant pressure on international human rights law, as existing legal frameworks were not designed to address data-driven surveillance, profiling, and automated decision-making.[280] Rather than negotiating new binding treaties, regulators and courts have largely responded by stretching existing norms of international human rights law through dynamic interpretation, applying established rights—such as privacy, dignity, autonomy, and equality—to new technological contexts.[281] This strategy has produced a fragmented and uneven protective landscape. On the one hand, many digital risks have been addressed through legal regimes that sit outside international human rights law, including data protection, consumer protection, and administrative law.[282] While these frameworks offer important procedural safeguards, they are typically individualised, sector-specific, and weakly enforced, and they struggle to address structural power asymmetries or collective harms. On the other hand, courts have sought to integrate

276 See https://www.michalsons.com/blog/south-african-national-policy-on-data-and-the-cloud/74319, accessed 27 October 2025.

277 See https://g20.org/g20-south-africa/g20-presidency/, accessed 27 October 2025.

278 See https://www.fasken.com/en/knowledge/2026/03/ai-regulation-progress-in-south-africa-a-further-step-in-the-right-direction-2, accessed 20 March 2026.

279 See https://www.bakermckenzie.com/en/insight/publications/2026/02/south-african-ai-policy-moves-towards-approval, accessed 20 March 2026.

280 International Commission of Jurists (2022:24); Bakiner (2023); Rodrigues (2020).

281 Shany (2025: 458).

282 Ibid.

certain "digital rights" into existing human rights treaties through purposive interpretation, on the premise that formal treaty reform is politically unlikely.[283] The literature identifies a paradox at the heart of this approach. The more unlikely new international human rights treaties appear, the more interpretative flexibility is relied upon to fill normative gaps.[284] Yet this reliance simultaneously reduces incentives to develop clearer, binding instruments to address systemic digital harms. As a result, interpretative expansion often masks—rather than resolves—the absence of comprehensive legal protection.

This dynamic is directly relevant to the governance of soil data in Africa. In most African countries, the only relevant law addressing automated decision-making is data protection legislation, which has significant gaps regarding AI, including algorithmic bias, accountability, transparency, and the broader societal effects of automation.[285] Significant legal ambiguity also surrounds issues such as deepfakes, AI-generated art, and the ownership rights of works created by AI. To strengthen soil protection through digitalisation and AI, South Africa and African states more broadly must move beyond fragmented personal data regimes. This requires a National Soil Data Policy to define ownership and access rights; AI-specific environmental regulations to ensure accountability in soil monitoring; open and inclusive data-sharing frameworks that balance private and public interests; and investments in digital literacy to empower farmers as co-creators of value in the soil data economy.[286]

## 4. Latest dynamics and developments

The rapid evolution of AI, digital trade, and data governance is reshaping global economic, legal, and environmental systems. The 2024–2025 cycle has seen unprecedented convergence between trade law, intellectual property (IP), digital sovereignty, and sustainability policy, indicating a shift from fragmented innovation approaches toward coordinated digital governance. Within this landscape, Africa is increasingly positioned as both a laboratory for experimentation and a catalyst for new models of global cooperation.

The conversation around AI often oscillates between utopian optimism and dystopian anxiety. Yet the central challenge is neither technological progress nor automation itself, but the unequal distribution of its benefits. As millions of jobs face disruption, the key question is not whether AI will transform labour markets, but who will capture the gains it generates. Without broad access to capital, infrastructure, and income security, AI risks deepening existing inequalities rather than expanding global

283 Ibid.: 463–468; For a discussion, see Pajuste (2025).
284 Ibid.: 461.
285 Davis & Trott (2024).
286 See https://www.fluxmans.com/article/ai-regulation-south-africa, accessed 29 September 2025.

opportunity. In this sense, AI is not a neutral force: it amplifies pre-existing asymmetries in wealth, capacity, and institutional strength. This dynamic is already visible across the Global South. Middle-income economies such as Brazil, China, India, and Indonesia are increasingly able to integrate AI into existing industrial systems.[287] By contrast, many African economies—where informal employment dominates—remain structurally unprepared for large-scale AI adoption.[288] At the lower end of the income spectrum, countries risk losing their comparative advantage in labour-intensive service sectors without gaining footholds in AI-driven industries, as automation accelerates a pattern of "jobless growth." At its core, AI is reshaping the global distribution of income by shifting returns from labour to capital. Countries with strong technological ecosystems can accumulate domestic AI capital, while others remain dependent on foreign platforms and infrastructure. This creates a new axis of inequality within the Global South itself, dividing AI adopters from AI-dependent economies.[289]

AI governance is transitioning from voluntary ethical principles to binding law. Risk-based, transparency-driven frameworks are becoming the global norm, with extraterritorial effects that influence domestic policymaking. Alongside these developments, multi-stakeholder initiatives at global and regional levels aim to align technological innovation with human rights, safety, accountability, and societal benefit. The International Bar Association's Strategic Plan exemplifies this trend, proposing measures to integrate AI responsibly into the legal profession by supporting smaller firms through training and financial incentives, developing governance standards on privacy and data security, and revising ethical guidelines to ensure AI-generated work complies with professional standards.[290] Similarly, new international instruments, such as the OECD's Expert Group on AI Futures, the EU's AI Act, the UN's Global Digital Compact (GDC), and the AU's AI Strategy, seek to bridge the digital, data, and innovation divides. The GDC, annexed to the Pact for the Future, provides a blueprint for global cooperation by promoting inclusive connectivity, digital literacy, human rights–based governance, and ethical oversight of emerging technologies, ensuring that technological progress supports sustainable and equitable development.[291]

Evolving notions of digital sovereignty complement these frameworks. Control over data, infrastructure, and code has become a central geopolitical objective.[292] In practice, however, the pursuit of digital sovereignty may also enable more intrusive forms of state control. Recent evidence highlights the rapid expansion of AI-enabled mass surveillance systems across parts of Africa, often implemented through foreign

287 See https://www.giga-hamburg.de/en/publications/giga-focus/automation-and-inequality-social-safety-nets-in-the-age-of-ai, accessed 20 March 2026.

288 Ibid.

289 Ibid.

290 IBA (2024: 10).

291 See UN (2023a and b).

292 Fritzsche & Spoiala (2022: 21).

technology partnerships.[293] Reports indicate that several African governments have invested heavily in AI-powered facial recognition, biometric tracking, and smart surveillance infrastructure, frequently justified in terms of urban modernisation and security.[294] Yet in many cases, these systems operate in contexts of limited regulatory oversight, raising serious concerns about proportionality, legality, and the protection of fundamental rights. These developments illustrate that digital sovereignty is not inherently emancipatory: without robust legal safeguards, it may instead reinforce new forms of technological dependency and state-led control.

While Europe advances human-centric governance through initiatives such as the Digital Markets Act, the AI Act, and the Global Gateway, China extends its influence through the Digital Silk Road.[295] Africa finds itself navigating between these competing models while asserting its technological autonomy through regional initiatives such as the AU–EU Digital for Development Hub, which promotes data sovereignty, shared standards, and multi-stakeholder dialogue.[296] The EU's experience in building a Digital Single Market provides valuable lessons for Africa's own efforts to develop a continental digital market under the African Continental Free Trade Area Agreement (AfCFTA).[297] Still, success will depend on capacity building, localisation of standards, and sustained investment in digital skills.

Recent initiatives further illustrate Africa's growing emphasis on building sovereign digital capacity through strategic partnerships. In February 2026, the African Union Commission concluded a landmark Memorandum of Understanding with Google to advance AI and digital transformation across the continent.[298] Moving beyond mere technology adoption, the partnership focuses on strengthening long-term resilience through investments in digital and cloud infrastructure, skills development, research and innovation ecosystems, and responsible AI governance frameworks. Crucially, it reflects a shift from digital access towards digital agency, emphasising locally relevant innovation, multilingual AI systems, and the development of domestic technical capacity. Such initiatives signal an emerging model of cooperative digital sovereignty in which Africa seeks to shape, rather than simply adopt, global technological systems.

At the same time, international trade institutions are becoming critical arenas for AI-trade governance. Through instruments such as the Technical Barriers to Trade (TBT) Agreement, the Trade-Related Aspects of Intellectual Property Rights (TRIPS)

---

293 See https://www.theguardian.com/global-development/2026/mar/12/invasive-ai-led-mass-surveillance-in-africa-violating-freedoms-warn-experts, accessed 20 March 2026.

294 Ibid.

295 Daniels et al. (2022: 5–7).

296 Fritzsche & Spoiala (2022: 24-25); see https://www.weforum.org/stories/2025/01/europe-digital-sovereignty/, accessed 27 October 2025.

297 Daniels et al. (2022: 6).

298 See https://au.int/en/pressreleases/20260217/auc-google-sign-partnership-advance-africas-sovereign-ai-digital-capacity, accessed 20 March 2026.

Agreement, and the General Agreement on Trade in Services (GATS), the WTO facilitates transparency, harmonisation, and mutual recognition of AI-related goods and services.[299] The WTO's World Trade Report 2025 estimates that, given supportive policies, AI could increase the value of international trade in goods and services by almost 40% by 2040, driven by productivity gains and lower trading costs.[300] However, to ensure those gains are broadly shared, the report emphasises the need to close the digital divide, invest in skills, and maintain an open and predictable trading system. The TBT Agreement encourages members to participate in developing international standards and to use them as the foundation for domestic regulation, thereby reducing unnecessary divergence and compliance costs.[301] Mutual Recognition Agreements (MRAs) further enable countries to recognise each other's certifications, facilitating the cross-border flow of digital products. However, developing economies often lack the capacity to fully engage in these technical forums. Within Africa, it is estimated that digital upgrades could benefit 600,000 formally registered firms and 40 million microbusinesses.[302] A case in point is WFP's 'Maano—Virtual Farmers Market' pilot in Zambia: an app that links smallholders with traders, provides real-time price signals, and closes transactions securely.[303] The AfCFTA Digital Trade Protocol could transform this landscape, provided it reflects regional realities and strengthens institutional capacity to manage innovation responsibly.[304] Embedding practical, farmer-facing use cases—such as e-payments, e-signatures, data protection, platform interoperability, and SME onboarding—would help translate connectivity into inclusive market access.

Algorithms—the foundational components that enable AI to learn, predict, and make autonomous decisions—play an increasingly central role in the commerce sector. They enhance efficiency in financial trading and online pricing, yet they also raise complex issues under competition law.[305] While increased price transparency can promote competition, algorithmic pricing can lead to coordinated behaviour, price discrimination, or the exploitation of market power.[306] Competition law, traditionally concerned with consumer welfare in terms of price, choice, quality, and innovation, must now adapt to the algorithmic economy. Detecting algorithmic collusion, dominance abuse, and resale price maintenance has become an enforcement challenge, underscoring the need for robust oversight and accountability mechanisms to ensure that technological advancement aligns with fair-market principles.

Beyond competition law, digitalisation and AI are also reshaping traditional understandings of intellectual property and inventorship, including in the agricultural sector.

299 WTO (2024); da Fonseca Azevedo (2024: 8).
300 WTO (2025: 6).
301 WTO (2024: 68); WTO (2021: 20–21).
302 Signé (2024: 150).
303 See https://innovation.wfp.org/project/virtual-farmers-market, accessed 30 October 2025.
304 Lemma et al. (2024).
305 Barfield (2018: 2).
306 Bostoen (2025: 178).

Digital, data-driven agriculture is poised to play a pivotal role in increasing global food output by approximately 60% to feed an estimated 9.3 billion people by 2050.[307] With millions of on-farm sensors now deployed, an average farm currently generates about 500,000 data points per day, a figure projected to climb to around 4 million daily by 2036.[308] Agricultural farm data (and, by extension, soil data) is less likely to be protected under current copyright systems.[309] While raw data itself is not patentable, its analysis may lead to patentable inventions. Derivative works—such as analytical reports or digital models generated from farm data—could qualify for copyright protection.[310] This highlights the importance of clear agreements governing farmers' data disclosure, ensuring that ownership or benefit-sharing arrangements are established for any inventions or intellectual property derived from shared data. To foster trust between farmers and ag-tech providers while laws catch up, several voluntary, farmer-centric data agreements have emerged. These include the US Privacy and Security Principles for Farm Data, the Australian Farm Data Code, France's Charte sur l'utilisation des données agricoles, Switzerland's Charter on the Digitalisation of Agriculture and Food, and the EU's Code of Conduct.[311] These instruments generally recognise farmers' ownership or control over their data and establish baseline rules for privacy, security, access, and fair use.

More broadly, as AI systems increasingly contribute to creative and inventive processes, questions arise over authorship, ownership, and patent eligibility.[312] Most jurisdictions maintain that only natural or juristic persons can be inventors, yet South Africa's acceptance of the DABUS patent in 2021 signals a potential paradigm shift.[313] These trends also open debates about whether AI should be granted some form of legal personhood.[314] Under TRIPS, transparency and disclosure requirements for AI-generated innovations are becoming vital for balancing innovation incentives with accessibility.[315] These developments illustrate how AI is transforming the moral and legal foundations of creativity, demanding a re-examination of existing IP frameworks to ensure that protection mechanisms remain relevant in the digital age.

Meanwhile, digitalisation is redefining sustainability imperatives. AI can model energy efficiency, forecast environmental risks, and optimise resource management, but it also contributes to carbon emissions, electronic waste, and widening

307 Yu et al. (2025: 1).
308 Ibid.
309 Uddin (2024: 5).
310 Ibid.: 11.
311 Ibid.: 2.
312 WIPO (2019: 19).
313 See https://www.nortonrosefulbright.com/en-za/knowledge/publications/2a3c551a/ai-inventorship-on-the-horizon-part-1, accessed 27 October 2025.
314 See Forrest (2024); Baeyaert (2025).
315 WTO (2024: 44, 46 & 75–76).

inequalities.[316] The emerging field of digital sustainability law links AI regulation to environmental commitments under the WTO and the Paris Agreement, positioning sustainability and inclusivity as benchmarks for legitimate digital transformation.[317] Africa's Continental AI Strategy reinforces this view, framing digitalisation not merely as an economic opportunity but as a pathway toward ecological resilience and intergenerational justice.

Across these diverse developments, a more profound structural transformation is becoming visible: the gradual convergence of AI regulation, digital trade, intellectual property, and environmental governance into a single, interoperability-driven system. Several interlocking dynamics define this emerging digital order—the assertion of data and technological sovereignty as a foundation of self-determination; the integration of sustainability and equity as prerequisites for legitimacy; and the growing reliance on evidence-based, transparent policymaking to guide innovation responsibly. Together, they mark a shift from fragmented technological experimentation to coordinated digital stewardship. For Africa, this transformation represents both a challenge and an opportunity. Through the Continental AI Strategy, the Digital Transformation Strategy (2020–2030), and the AfCFTA Digital Trade Protocol, the AU is laying the groundwork for a distinctly African model of digital governance—people-centred, rights-based, and ecologically grounded. Success will depend on closing the AI and data divides through infrastructure investment, institutional capacity-building, and equitable access. Recent AU–G20 cooperation might facilitate this: At the G20 on AI for Africa Conference (September–October 2025), UNESCO launched the AI Initiative for Africa to scale ethical, people-centred AI—committing to train 15,000 civil servants, 5,000 judges and prosecutors on using AI, and, via the SPAARK-AI Alliance of public-administration schools (now spanning 45 African states), to cascade this capacity continent-wide.[318] Working with the AU on its continental AI strategy, UNESCO also unveiled a Technology Policy Assistance Facility with case studies, training resources, and expert directories to help governments craft AI roadmaps aligned with international standards.

Ultimately, these intertwined trends point toward a maturing global digital order that seeks to balance innovation with accountability, autonomy with interdependence, and growth with sustainability.

---

316 See https://www.unep.org/topics/digital-transformations/sustainable-digitalization, accessed 27 October 2025.

317 Aslam et al. (2025).

318 See https://www.unesco.org/en/articles/ai-africa-unesco-unveils-new-solutions-its-development-g20, accessed 6 November 2025.

## 5. Conclusion: governing AI and digitalisation for sustainable soils

The UN Trade and Development's *Technology and Innovation Report 2025* depicts a bifurcated AI landscape. A small cohort—approximately 100 firms, primarily based in the US and China—accounts for roughly 40% of private research and development. At the same time, 118 countries, mainly in the Global South, are underrepresented in rule-making arenas.[319] The market is expected to inflate to an estimated USD 4.8 trillion by 2033, with valuations tripling in 2023 and nearly tripling again in 2024.[320] Compute and infrastructure are likewise concentrated: the US holds about one third of TOP500 supercomputers and over half of total computational performance; China is second with 80 machines but under a tenth of US compute; most hyperscale data centres remain US-based, with only a few developing economies (notably Brazil, China, India, and the Russian Federation) hosting comparable assets.[321] Training costs for frontier models have increased by approximately 2.4 times per year since 2016 and are now dominated by hardware, pushing development into the hands of large tech companies.[322] In 2023, the US accounted for ~70% of global private AI investment (USD 67 billion), followed by China (USD 7.8 billion) and India (USD 1.4 billion), which ranked tenth.[323] Between 2000 and 2023, the US and China accounted for approximately one-third of AI publications and around 60% of AI patents.[324] Most GenAI breakthroughs—and top-tier talent (≈approximately 50% from China, 18% from the US, and 12% from Europe)—are clustered in these regions.[325]

That concentration is not a neutral backdrop. It determines who writes the code, curates the datasets, and defines the "best practices" now being adopted in agriculture, environmental governance, and law. As AI moves into SSM, these upstream asymmetries risk being reproduced downstream—in how soils are mapped, monitored, and monetised, and in who captures the value of the data. For SSM, these tools hold enormous promise, from improving monitoring and planning to strengthening accountability. Yet their deployment also raises profound risks: high energy and water consumption, widening socioeconomic divides, market concentration, opaque data practices, and the erosion of trust, as farmers and communities lack real agency over their information.

Realising the benefits of digitalisation requires more than technological optimism. Reliable, site-specific field data remains indispensable, and without it, even the most sophisticated systems cannot deliver meaningful insights. Equally important is governance: who controls data, how it is shared, and under what conditions. Without clear

319 UNCTAD (2025: 8–9).
320 Ibid.: 6.
321 Ibid.: 21.
322 Ibid.: 22.
323 Ibid.
324 Ibid.: 23.
325 Ibid.

rights, farmers risk becoming data subjects rather than empowered participants in digital transitions.

At the international level, broad principles for AI are beginning to take shape; yet a global consensus on key concepts remains elusive. The absence of specific standards for risk assessment and public goods, such as democracy, human rights, and climate stability, leaves critical gaps. Proposals, such as an intergovernmental panel on AI modelled on the IPCC, illustrate how a collective framework for monitoring, evaluation, and knowledge sharing could develop.

Nationally, effective legislation will require interdisciplinary approaches that integrate soil science, digital innovation, and legal design. Discussions on soil management and digitalisation can no longer proceed in parallel; they must converge. Existing models, such as the EU AI Act, provide valuable guidance; however, frameworks must remain flexible and adaptable to the rapid pace of technological change.

While AI has advanced soil research, three gaps persist: (1) over-reliance on narrow predictors instead of spatial/temporal and decision-making approaches; (2) scarce data from neglected regions; and (3) non-comparable soil-health indices.[326] Legally, these map onto duties to: require transparency of methods and guardrails for any soil-relevant AI used in permitting, subsidies, planning, or enforcement; build a data-protection-compliant Soil Data Commons that prioritises underserved regions; and adopt national, versioned, openly specified soil-health indices for cross-site, multi-year reporting.

AI also forces uncomfortable legal questions. In contexts where environmental protection laws exist only on paper—undermined by corruption, capture, or weak enforcement—AI systems trained on ecological thresholds and legal criteria could, in theory, enforce rules more consistently than compromised human institutions.[327] Yet handing enforcement to opaque "black-box" models creates new risks: when code is inscrutable, errors cannot be contested, bias is hard to detect, and discretion can be laundered through algorithmic outputs. That combination—apparent objectivity coupled with opacity—both threatens entrenched discretionary power and offers it a new veil, making governments reluctant to delegate and communities unable to scrutinise. The lesson is clear: legal systems fail less from a lack of tools than from a lack of political will. AI may expose these failures, but it cannot resolve them without strong oversight, algorithmic transparency (including explainability, audit trails, and the right to challenge automated decisions), and democratic legitimacy.

Unlike earlier technologies, modern AI—especially deep-learning systems—cannot be straightforwardly inspected, specified, or audited against regulations; their behaviour arises unpredictably from training rather than deliberate design.[328] Still, the proven oversight models from high-risk sectors, such as aviation and nuclear energy,

326 Birkstedt et al. (2023).
327 Kumar (2025).
328 Judge et al. (2025).

should not be abandoned. Policymakers must instead manage the risks posed by today's opaque models while supporting the development of AI architectures that can be rigorously proven safe. Drawing from AI safety research and prior regulatory experience, effective governance will likely depend on consolidated authority, licensing regimes, mandatory disclosure of training data and model parameters, formal verification of system behaviour, and the capacity for rapid intervention.[329]

We should not frame AI regulation as a battle of extremes. Instead, it should represent a careful effort to strike a balance between individual and societal safety and the need to foster innovation. Navigating these trade-offs requires clarity and a nuanced understanding of several critical issues. Defining AI remains inherently difficult; vague definitions introduce legal uncertainty and weaken regulatory effectiveness.[330] Because AI applications differ across sectors, technologies, and data types, a uniform regulatory approach may prove both ineffective and counterproductive.[331] Yet there is broad agreement that AI systems must uphold privacy, fairness, transparency, accountability, and the preservation of individual freedoms.[332] Regulation should safeguard these principles precisely and proportionately.

Given AI's sectoral diversity, effective governance requires inclusive processes that bring together governments, scientists, legal experts, and civil society. Certification mechanisms can clarify liability and incentivise adherence to safety standards, while regulatory sandboxes provide controlled environments to test innovations before deployment.[333] Policymakers must also ensure regulators have sufficient technical expertise, invite public participation, and craft frameworks that remain adaptive to technological change.[334] Over-regulation risks stagnation; under-regulation risks harm. The solution lies in flexible, evidence-based regulation that protects rights while promoting responsible progress.

Crucially, this requires a shift in how regulation itself is conceived. Rather than relying on static "set-and-forget" legal frameworks, governments must adopt more responsive, adaptive approaches that evolve with technological change. This includes embedding anticipatory governance tools—such as horizon scanning, strategic foresight, and early-stage stakeholder engagement—within regulatory processes, alongside iterative policy cycles that allow for continuous learning, feedback, and adjustment.[335] Such approaches can help close persistent information gaps and better align legal frameworks with rapidly changing technological realities. At the same time, digital technologies themselves offer new tools for improving regulatory design and implementation. Advanced data analytics, regulatory experimentation, and digital

329 Ibid.
330 Cajueiro & Celestino (2026: 90).
331 Ibid.
332 Ibid.
333 Ibid.
334 Ibid.
335 OECD (2025a: 87).

monitoring systems can support more evidence-based decision-making, enhance enforcement capacity, and reduce administrative burdens in increasingly complex governance environments.[336] However, realising these benefits depends on strengthening institutional capacity and coordination. Without investment in skills, expertise, and cross-sectoral collaboration, there is a risk that digital innovations will fall between regulatory silos, exacerbating fragmentation rather than resolving it.[337] Future-ready governance, therefore, depends not only on better rules but on stronger institutions. Building cohesive, well-resourced, and technically capable regulatory systems—at both national and international levels—is essential to ensure that digitalisation supports, rather than undermines, sustainable soil management and broader socio-ecological objectives.[338]

The way forward lies in hybrid governance systems, which combine AI's speed, consistency, and pattern recognition with human judgment, ethical safeguards, and robust accountability. To harness AI's potential for soils while mitigating its risks, a layered governance model is essential: binding regulation, moral guidance, and strong local agency, particularly in the Global South. That, in turn, demands data: African governments should update national soil maps and build publicly accessible, interoperable soil-data platforms; partner with universities, research institutes, and extension services to generate and validate high-quality local datasets; and require that agricultural AI be trained, tested, and benchmarked on locally representative data rather than foreign proxies. For Africa, this means developing context-sensitive, socially grounded soil governance frameworks—rooted in local knowledge, open standards, and clear rights to access and benefit from data—rather than importing external models wholesale.

Ultimately, the question is not simply how to govern AI, but to what end. If digitalisation is to advance soil law, its foundations must be justice, sustainability, and human dignity, not efficiency or profit alone. These values must be embedded into the very architecture of AI systems that generate, interpret, and disseminate soil data. In this emerging legal order, the challenge is not to resist digital change, but to ensure that technological innovation strengthens the protection of soils—our most fragile and indispensable resource. Only then can AI and digitalisation become true allies in building a more just, democratic, and sustainable future.

336 Ibid.
337 Ibid.
338 Ibid.

# Soil governance and digital transformation in the African Union: a comparative legal analysis from a European Union perspective

*Ines Dehaene*

## 1. Introduction

The significance of digitalisation and environmental stewardship has gained increasing recognition, particularly considering the pressing imperative to safeguard the planet and its natural resources. Within this context of environmental protection and sustainable development, particular emphasis must be placed on soil, the foundation of terrestrial ecosystems and human existence.

Healthy soil is indispensable to food security, sustainable livelihoods, and long-term economic development, particularly in Africa, where a substantial proportion of the population relies on agriculture.[1] Soil also functions as a pillar of global supply chains and climate resilience, serving as a carbon sink, mitigating floods, droughts, and erosion, and sustaining biodiversity and essential ecosystem services.[2] Africa accounts for approximately 60%[3] of the world's remaining agricultural land, and 95% of all food production is contingent upon the maintenance of healthy soils.[4]

African soils are presently in a deplorable condition. Between 75 and 80% of the continent's arable land has already been degraded, resulting in an annual loss of approximately 30–60 kilograms of nutrients per hectare.[5] The drivers of soil degradation are multifaceted and largely anthropogenic, with unsustainable land-use practices, climate change, and excessive fertiliser use playing central roles. Additional contributing factors include overgrazing, mining activities, erosion, deforestation, industrial pollution, inadequately regulated foreign investment, rapid urbanisation, entrenched poverty, insecure land tenure, and global crises, such as the COVID-19 pandemic.[6]

Digitalisation and soil health are closely interlinked, as digital technologies can serve as effective tools for safeguarding soil health. In agriculture, digital tools increase productivity, improve efficiency, and promote sustainability, thereby supporting sound soil management.[7] Digital technologies facilitate systematic data collection and dissemination, enabling a shift from reactive responses to preventive and evidence-

1 AU (2024a: 7–8).
2 Ibid.: 10.
3 World Economic Forum (2024: 6).
4 Ibid.: 4.
5 AUDA-NEPAD (2023: 1–2).
6 Ginzky & Ruppel (2025b: 23–25).
7 Nalwinban (2024: 6).

based strategies.[8] Concrete initiatives, such as the Soil4Africa Project, illustrate the practical application of these technologies for soil health.[9]

At the same time, the adoption of digital technologies in Africa faces substantial barriers. Smallholder farmers face limited digital literacy, inadequate infrastructure, high costs, gender disparities, and language constraints, while digitalisation also entails risks, including cybercrime, labour displacement, and broader socio-economic challenges.[10] For digital tools to function effectively in soil protection, management, and monitoring, a coherent and comprehensive policy or legislative framework is indispensable.

Yet policies and regulations relating to soil and digitalisation, and their intersection, remain far from comprehensive. There is no binding continental regulatory framework addressing soil protection, digitalisation, or artificial intelligence, and initiatives such as the Soil Initiative for Africa remain non-binding.[11] Consequently, no comprehensive regime governs the use of digital tools for soil management and protection, revealing a significant lacuna in African legislation. Nevertheless, recent developments within the AU indicate emerging momentum with the Model Law on Soil Management in Africa signalling a potential shift towards a more coordinated regulatory approach.[12]

This chapter, partially based on several conference presentations and the author's master's thesis in law conducted at Stellenbosch University, examines the following central research question: "To what extent can the AU, inspired by the example of the EU and adapted to the institutional, cultural, and economic context of Africa, develop, implement, and enforce a regulatory instrument that regulates the use of digital tools for effective soil management, monitoring, and protection?"

To address this question, this chapter offers recommendations for the effective and comprehensive regulation of digital technologies as tools for soil management, protection, and monitoring within the AU, drawing on the EU example.

8 AU (2020: 33–35).

9 See https://www.soils4africa-h2020.eu/the-project, accessed 4 July 2025.

10 Nalwinban (2024: 23–27); see https://stemmenvanafrika.nl/talen-van-afrika/, accessed 4 July 2025.

11 AUDA-NEPAD (2023: 19).

12 See https://www.africanparliamentarynews.com/2025/11/pan-african-parliament-adopts-landmark_7.html, accessed 28 March 2026.

## 2. Soil, digitalisation, and the African context: legal framework and characteristics

### 2.1. The African Union's policy and legal instruments on soil and digitalisation

#### 2.1.1. Soil governance and soil health

The prevailing regulatory and policy framework of the AU contains no explicit reference to soil; nonetheless, certain provisions may be regarded as indirectly pertinent. The Constitutive Act, notably Article 13(1)(c), which enumerates areas intrinsically connected to soil use and management, is indirectly relevant.[13] Beyond the Constitutive Act, the AU's policy ambitions are articulated in Agenda 2063, its long-term strategic framework. Although the Agenda does not establish a dedicated soil policy, it does acknowledge issues closely connected to soil governance, such as erosion and fertility.[14]

In contrast to indirect references to soil in the AU's core instruments, regional conventions and treaties provide explicit legal provisions on soil protection. The most notable in this regard is the Revised African Convention on the Conservation of Nature and Natural Resources, which remains the sole continental instrument to prescribe specific measures relating to soil.[15]

In addition to binding regulations, conventions, and treaties, the governance of soil in Africa is shaped by a range of soft-law instruments, including the Draft African Union Strategy on Climate Change, the Climate Change and Resilient Development Strategy and Action Plan for Africa, and the Nairobi Declaration on Climate Change.[16]

While these climate-oriented instruments address soil only indirectly, a second set of frameworks has emerged with a more explicit focus on agriculture and soil governance. These initiatives, though likewise non-binding, are designed specifically to tackle soil degradation and to promote sustainable soil management across the continent. Central to this is the New Partnership for Africa's Development (NEPAD), established to guide member states in pursuing their development objectives. Within this framework, the Comprehensive Africa Agriculture Development Programme (CAADP) was formulated as a policy instrument to promote sustainable agriculture, enhance food security, and stimulate economic growth. As one of the central pillars of Agenda 2063, CAADP has also provided the institutional basis for the African Union Commission's 2020 call to create a Soil Initiative for Africa (SIA). The SIA seeks to address soil degradation through innovative fertiliser use, the application of proven technologies, and the development of enabling policies and institutions to sustain long-term soil management. It is structured around two principal components: the Draft

13 Art 13(1)(c) Constitutive Act of the African Union 2000.
14 See https://www.nepad.org/agenda2063, accessed 25 September 2025.
15 Kassner & Ruppel (2025: 760-770).
16 Ibid.: 770–774.

Framework Document of the Soil Initiative for Africa and the African Fertiliser and Soil Health Action Plan (AFSH Action Plan). The SIA is conceived as a long-term initiative, with an evaluation planned after the first ten years to inform the next decennial plan.[17]

In addition to AU initiatives, the African Soil Partnership, established under the Food and Agriculture Organisation's Global Soil Partnership, supports African states in protecting and sustainably managing their soil resources through coordinated regional action. While non-binding, it underscores the importance of international cooperation and capacity-building in African soil governance, complementing efforts under NEPAD, CAADP, and the SIA.[18] Against this background of largely indirect and non-binding instruments, the Model Law on Soil Management represents a notable step towards greater normative coherence.

On the diplomatic front, at the twentieth session of the African Ministerial Conference on the Environment (AMCEN), held in July 2025, African environment ministers adopted Decision AMCEN/20/Dec.1, which aims to Strengthen Soil Governance and Land Restoration in Africa. The Decision called for the development of guidelines for a continental soil governance framework.[19] During the Sixth Ordinary Session of its Sixth Legislature on 6 November 2025, the Pan-African Parliament (PAP) adopted the continent's first Model Law on Soil Management.[20] With this, Africa has taken a historic step forward for sustainable development, food security, and environmental protection. Officially titled "Model Law on Soil Management in Africa", it provides countries with a model legal framework to safeguard their soils and strengthen resilience to climate change. It encompasses all dimensions of soil governance, including sustainable agriculture and food security, climate mitigation and adaptation, soil use regulation and planning, data management, digitalisation and innovation, public participation, indigenous knowledge, and gender equity. Additionally, it addresses rehabilitation, enforcement, and dispute settlement mechanisms. The Model Law includes a full section on Soil Data, Digitalisation, Monitoring, and Innovation.[21] Following the PAP's adoption of the Model Law, the resolution is normally forwarded to the AU Assembly of Heads of State and Government for final approval. Once approved, the Model Law can be sent to and disseminated among national parliaments and the public. The Model Law for Soil Management in Africa includes a toolbox for domestication and implementation designed to contribute to more coordinated soil governance across the African continent. The Model Law can contribute to a more effective integrated soil protection agenda, which, in turn, favours land degradation

17 AU (2024a: 1).

18 See https://www.fao.org/global-soil-partnership/regional-partnerships/africa/en/, accessed 6 July 2025.

19 Ruppel & Murray (2025).

20 See https://pap.au.int/en/news/press-releases/2025-11-06/african-parliamentarians-adopt-continents-first-model-law, accessed 28 March 2026.

21 Ibid.

neutrality (LDN), enhances land and soil restoration and soil health, in the interest of climate change resilience, and supports more biodiversity protection, re-naturalisation, and food security. Moreover, the Model Law can serve as a blueprint piece of legislation—together with an implementation toolbox—that can also digitally enable domestic legislators to create, monitor, and implement tailored soil legislation to support more coordinated soil management, protection, monitoring, and enforcement.

### 2.1.2. AI and other digital tools

While the preceding section has outlined the legal and policy dimensions of soil governance and soil health, it is equally necessary to consider the emerging role of digital technologies and the corresponding policy and legal instruments.

The Government AI Readiness Index indicates that Sub-Saharan Africa faces significant structural obstacles to AI adoption, including a lack of reliable official data, weak and fragmented governance structures, and ongoing political instability. Although private actors and citizens are not formally precluded from deploying AI tools, the absence of institutional support and accessible data constrains their effective use. Progress is required not only in building the necessary technological infrastructure but also in establishing coherent regulatory frameworks that ensure legitimacy, accountability, and legal certainty in the use of AI.[22]

Notwithstanding the absence of a comprehensive regulatory framework safeguarding the continent from the risks associated with AI and other digital technologies, the governance of AI has begun to attract growing institutional attention within the AU. The 2019 Sharm el-Sheikh Declaration reaffirmed earlier AU decisions and strategies, including the Policy and Regulatory Initiative for Digital Africa (PRIDA), and articulated the ambition of creating an integrated and inclusive digital society. It further mandated the promotion of the Digital Transformation Strategy for Africa (2020–2030), the ratification of the Malabo Convention, and the establishment of an AI working group.[23] In 2024, the AU Executive Council adopted the Continental Artificial Intelligence Strategy for Africa, aimed at advancing national AI strategies, governance frameworks, capacity-building initiatives, and resource mobilisation.[24]

Complementing these efforts, the African Commission on Human and Peoples' Rights adopted Resolution No. 473 in 2021, calling for a regulatory framework ensuring that AI deployment remains aligned with the needs and aspirations of African

---

22 Fuentes et al. (2021: 5 & 44–46).

23 African Union (Specialised Technical Committee on Communication and Information Technologies) 2019 Sharm El Sheikh Declaration AU/STS-CICT-3/MIN/Decl. 3-7.

24 AU (2024b: 1); see https://www.whitecase.com/insight-our-thinking/ai-watch-global-regulatory-tracker-african-union, accessed 7 July 2025.

populations.[25] At the continental level, the most significant binding instrument remains the African Union Convention on Cyber Security and Personal Data Protection (the Malabo Convention), which entered into force in 2023 and establishes a legal framework governing electronic commerce, data protection, cybercrime, and cybersecurity, although only fifteen states have ratified it.[26] In parallel, several member states have developed national AI strategies and institutional mechanisms, reflecting a fragmented but emerging pattern of regulatory convergence. The development of AI governance on the continent thus remains in an incipient stage.[27]

#### 2.1.3. The intersection between soil and digitalisation

Having considered the AU's policy and legal instruments on soil governance and on AI and other digital tools, it is necessary to examine the extent to which these domains converge. The central question is whether continental regulation and policy initiatives explicitly address the intersection of soil governance and digitalisation, namely the digitisation of soil management, protection, and monitoring.

The Continental Artificial Intelligence Strategy for Africa identifies agriculture as one of its key priority sectors, aligning its focus areas with Agenda 2063 and the Sustainable Development Goals (SDGs). The Strategy acknowledges that digital technologies are already being applied on a limited scale in agriculture and advances recommendations to promote the wider adoption of AI, support member states in integrating AI into the agricultural sector, establish centres of excellence, and raise awareness of both the potential benefits and risks of AI use. While these recommendations relate primarily to agriculture more broadly rather than to soil, they are directly relevant to soil protection, management, and monitoring.[28]

The Soil Initiative for Africa likewise identifies digital technologies as instruments to advance soil protection and management. Priority Area 1 provides that digital technologies may be utilised and that access to such tools should be ensured. Priority Area 2 highlights the importance of leveraging digitally enabled products and services, and Priority Area 3 underscores the need to establish effective soil information systems to support data-driven decision-making and monitoring. By contrast, Priority Area 4 does not explicitly address the regulation of digital technologies.[29] Taken together, the aforementioned instruments acknowledge the potential of digitalisation for soil management, protection, and monitoring, yet they fall short of providing a coherent regulatory

25 ALT Advisory (2022: 6).
26 Ibid.: 6–7.
27 Fuentes et al. (2021: 44–46).
28 AU (2024b: 38).
29 AU (2024b: 7–12).

framework to address the specific legal challenges posed by the digitisation of soil governance.

### 2.2. Critical analysis of the legal and policy framework

A central concern is the considerable gaps in African legislation regarding soil, digitalisation, and their intersection. At present, there exists neither a comprehensive nor a binding regulatory framework specifically dedicated to soil protection, management, and monitoring, nor a framework capable of governing the use of digital technologies in soil governance and mitigating the risks associated with their deployment.[30] Although significant gaps remain, a recent normative development, the adoption of a continental Model Law on Soil Management by the Pan-African Parliament, demonstrates an emerging shift towards more structured soil governance.

Implementation deficiencies further undermine effectiveness. AU member states are under no obligation to submit implementation reports under the African Convention on the Conservation of Nature and Natural Resources, and, in the absence of a dedicated supervisory body and amid chronic financial constraints, this weakens compliance.[31] Similar shortcomings characterise AI governance, where national initiatives remain isolated and poorly coordinated, leading to overlaps and gaps in regulatory frameworks. Although a Continental AI Strategy has been adopted, its objectives still need to be translated into enforceable measures, leaving the AU with the dual challenge of harmonising national initiatives while respecting member states' sovereignty.[32]

The rapid pace of technological progress in artificial intelligence requires regulatory and policy frameworks that are sufficiently flexible to adapt without constant reform, yet acute infrastructure deficits in Africa hinder the establishment of coherent and unified AI governance. At the same time, the growing influence of international corporations raises concerns of "AI colonialism", whereby African states risk becoming passive consumers of externally developed technologies rather than active participants in shaping and deploying them, thereby affecting regulatory autonomy and long-term digital sovereignty.[33] Data regulation presents additional challenges, as prevailing frameworks emphasise individual privacy and neglect the collective dimension of data, allowing private corporations to exploit unprotected collective data to the detriment of farmers. Farmers, as primary stakeholders, are often excluded from policymaking processes and lack the financial and technical resources required to utilise digital technologies.[34] Finally, while the continent has produced numerous soft-law instruments, their

30 Kassner & Ruppel (2025: 761–762).
31 Ibid.
32 ALT Advisory (2022: 13).
33 Njoroge (2024).
34 Canfield & Ntamabirweki (2024).

non-binding nature results in weaker compliance. Although binding frameworks are called for to ensure consistency and enforcement, such instruments often prove more cautious and less ambitious in their regulatory scope.[35]

### 2.3. Contextual factors affecting policy creation, implementation, and enforcement

The shortcomings in AU frameworks on soil governance and digitalisation are intertwined with broader political, institutional, and economic conditions that shape policy creation, implementation, and enforcement. The AU, composed of 55 member states and possessing both intergovernmental and limited supranational characteristics, adopts decisions through a consensus-based process involving the Assembly, the Executive Council, the Specialised Technical Committees (STCs), the AU Commission, and other bodies. Legislative initiatives originate from the Commission, member states, or STCs, are reviewed by the Permanent Representatives' Committee, and ultimately require approval by the Executive Council or Assembly, with decision-making generally proceeding by consensus.[36]

Reliance on consensus slows responses to crises and results in diluted policies based on the lowest common denominator. Although member states are formally equal, more powerful states exert informal influence through economic, diplomatic, or military leverage, and the process lacks transparency due to undisclosed negotiations. Divergences in culture and policy priorities further complicate consensus, while the Pan-African Parliament's lack of genuine legislative authority so far undermines the Union's democratic legitimacy.[37] While this seems to be gradually changing, the soil protection status on the African continent remains weak: there is a severe lack of dedicated soil protection laws, soil protection responsibilities are highly fragmented, weak governance leads to inconsistent policy implementation, and difficulties in tracking progress in soil protection persist. Many existing soil-related laws are outdated, failing to incorporate modern conservation techniques or reflect the latest scientific knowledge. As a result, they are ineffective at addressing contemporary challenges such as climate change, soil erosion, food insecurity, and the demands of growing industrial agriculture. Public knowledge about soil health is generally low. There are limited education and training programs for farmers, and extension services are scarce. This leaves many communities unaware of proper soil management practices, exacerbating soil degradation. Soil data is often not collected or is inaccessible, hindering farmers and communities from assessing soil health or advocating for its protection. Uncertainty over land ownership, especially in communal systems, discourages long-term investment in soil care.

35 Kassner & Ruppel (2025: 778).
36 Amani Africa (2022: 2 & 10–21).
37 Ncube (2020).

Conflicts between traditional and statutory laws further complicate soil protection efforts, with many communities unaware of their land rights and therefore easily violating national land tenure laws. In many African countries, there is inadequate regulation of foreign investments in land use. This results in unsustainable land practices and soil degradation, as foreign investors typically prioritise short-term profits over long-term soil health. Rural and marginalised communities face significant barriers to accessing legal action to protect soil, allowing soil degradation to continue unchecked and leaving these communities vulnerable to unsustainable land-use practices. Therefore, the new Model Law on Soil Management provides a toolbox of options and approaches to support national parliaments in developing domestic solutions tailored to national challenges and purposes.

Although the AU adopts regulations, directives, recommendations, declarations, and resolutions, ambiguously drafted decisions at times hinder their effective execution. Insufficient financial resources further undermine implementation. Reliance on external donors, underutilised resources, bureaucratic inefficiencies, and weak follow-up and accountability mechanisms compound these challenges, while fragmentation among member states and limited coordination prevent the consistent application of the instruments adopted.[38]

Enforcement mechanisms exist under Articles 23 and 4(h) of the Constitutive Act, allowing sanctions and intervention in cases of serious violations, with the Assembly and Peace and Security Council (PSC) playing central roles and the African Court on Human and Peoples' Rights issuing binding judgments.[39] In practice, however, sanctions have shown a limited deterrent effect due to weak coordination with the Regional Economic Communities (RECs) and the Regional Mechanisms,[40] normative inconsistency,[41] insufficient political will, and inadequate technical and financial resources.

## 3. The European Union framework

### 3.1. The European Union's policy and legal instruments on soil and digitalisation

#### 3.1.1. Soil governance and soil health

Since the Single European Act of 1987, the EU has held competence to regulate soil protection. Although for decades no legal instrument had been dedicated exclusively

38 See https://issafrica.org/iss-today/why-arent-more-african-union-decisions-on-security-implemented, accessed 9 July 2025.

39 Amani Africa (2022: 11–13 & 19).

40 See https://au.int/en/recs, accessed 9 July 2025; https://au.int/en/directorates/about-conflict-management, accessed 9 July 2025.

41 Arts 3, 5(1) & 22 of the Protocol on Relations between the African Union (AU) and the Regional Economic Communities (RECs) (25 January 2008) signed on 27 January 2008.

to soil, the issue has increasingly attracted attention across a wide range of EU strategies, most notably the European Green Deal. The Green Deal is a comprehensive development strategy that indirectly addresses soil-related concerns through its broader commitments to climate action and biodiversity preservation. To complement the commitments of the Green Deal, the EU Soil Strategy for 2030 was adopted in November 2021. The Soil Strategy sets medium-term targets for 2030 and long-term objectives for 2050.[42] It calls for the development of a dedicated legislative proposal on soil health and for intensified research, data collection, and monitoring.[43]

To give effect to these commitments, the EU adopted the EU Soil Monitoring and Resilience Directive (Soil Monitoring Law), which entered into force on 16 December 2025 and is the first comprehensive, dedicated legislative instrument for soil-related challenges. The EU member states have until 16 December 2028 to transpose the Directive's provisions into their national legal systems. The first reporting deadline concerning the implementation of the Directive and the assessment of soil health is set for 16 December 2031.[44]

The law's primary objective is to address the principal threats to European soils, namely erosion, loss of soil organic matter, salinisation, contamination, compaction and sealing, and the loss of soil biodiversity. In addition, the legislation addresses all dimensions of soil degradation and applies to all soil types, including forest, urban, and agricultural soils. The Directive establishes the legal framework necessary to achieve healthy soils across the European Union by 2050.

To attain these objectives, the Directive establishes several key measures. It requires member states to systematically monitor and assess soil health, supports farmers and other land managers in enhancing soil resilience, and introduces specific provisions to address contaminated sites within the EU. Moreover, it promotes the generation and dissemination of knowledge on soil conditions, thereby reinforcing the EU's climate and biodiversity objectives and its broader commitments to competitiveness and food security.[45]

The adoption of this legislative instrument must be understood within the broader framework of the EU's environmental competencies. Under Article 192(1) of the Treaty on the Functioning of the European Union (TFEU), the EU is empowered to act in the field of environmental policy, with the European Commission holding the right of legislative initiative. The justification lies in the transboundary nature of soil degradation, whose consequences extend beyond national borders and cannot be effectively contained by individual member states. Moreover, reliance solely on national action risks generating distortions in competition, since the stringency of environmental

42 Heuse (2022: 3-4).

43 See https://environment.ec.europa.eu/topics/soil-health/soil-strategy-2030_en, accessed 9 July 2025.

44 See https://www.consilium.europa.eu/nl/press/press-releases/2024/06/17/soil-monitoring-law-eu-on-the-pathway-to-healthy-soils-by-2050/, accessed 9 July 2025.

45 See https://environment.ec.europa.eu/topics/soil-health/soil-monitoring-law_en#timeline, accessed 3 March 2026.

regulation would vary considerably across member states. The Directive, therefore, seeks to close legal gaps and to strengthen the internal market by harmonising environmental standards across the Union.

In this light, the Commission has opted for a directive rather than a regulation. By selecting a directive, the Commission allowed member states discretion in its implementation, ensuring adaptation to national contexts while aligning with Union-wide objectives.[46]

### 3.1.2. AI and other digital tools

While the previous section examined the European Union's soil-related strategies and the adopted EU Soil Monitoring and Resilience Directive, the analysis would be incomplete without the parallel developments in digital regulation.

Several legislative instruments provide direct support for technological innovation and digital infrastructure, including the Digital Europe Programme Regulation, Horizon Europe, the Pilot Regime for Distributed Ledger Technology, and the European Chips Act, while additional instruments address digital connectivity, data governance, intellectual property, cybersecurity, consumer protection, and the digital transformation of the financial sector. In sum, the Union is progressively shaping the digital transition through a broad legislative programme that addresses innovation, infrastructure, data governance, cybersecurity, competition, and consumer protection to construct a secure, fair, and future-proof digital environment.[47]

Attention is devoted to the EU AI Act, which constitutes the cornerstone of the Union's regulatory approach to artificial intelligence. The EU AI Act (Regulation (EU) 2024/1684), adopted in July 2024, establishes the conditions under which artificial intelligence systems may access the European Single Market. Its dual objective is, on the one hand, to mitigate risks associated with the deployment of AI, and, on the other, to foster innovation within the Union. The Act reflects the Union's broader endeavour to strike an appropriate balance between trust, the protection of fundamental rights, and the operation of market forces.[48]

The EU AI Act adopts a risk-based regulatory approach. It distinguishes between four levels of risk: unacceptable risk, high risk, limited or transparency risk, and minimal or no risk. Systems categorised as presenting an unacceptable risk are strictly prohibited. High-risk systems may be placed on the market only if they comply with stringent regulatory obligations. Limited-risk systems are subject to transparency requirements, obliging providers, namely the developers or entities placing AI systems on the Union market, to disclose the use of AI where necessary to preserve trust. Such

46 European Commission (2023: 9–11).

47 Meuck et al. (2025: 21–50).

48 Ibid.: 53–55.

providers must also ensure that AI-generated content is identifiable and, in certain circumstances, clearly and visibly labelled. By contrast, AI systems assessed as entailing minimal or no risk remain outside the scope of specific regulatory obligations.[49]

Each member state is required to designate a supervisory authority responsible for ensuring compliance with the rules applicable to high-risk AI systems and for withdrawing non-compliant products from the market. At the Union level, supervisory competences are distributed among several institutions. A newly established AI Office serves as the central authority for supervising powerful general-purpose AI models. Within the Commission, the Directorate-General for Communications Networks, Content, and Technology (DG CNECT) assumes responsibility for innovation policy, information and communications technology, and emerging technologies. In addition, the European Artificial Intelligence Board convenes national supervisory authorities from all member states to coordinate implementation.[50] General-purpose AI (GPAI) models are subject to a distinct regime. They must comply with specific transparency obligations and, where they pose systemic risk, implement comprehensive risk management measures.[51]

### 3.1.3. The intersection between soil and digitalisation

The Soil Strategy for 2030 expressly acknowledges digitalisation as an instrument for protecting and monitoring soils. In its Communication to the European Parliament, the Council, the European Economic and Social Committee and the Committee of the Regions, the Commission observed that "we need to know more about soil". The Commission identifies three dimensions of this objective: the digital agenda, soil data and monitoring, and soil research and innovation.[52]

Within the 'soil and digital agenda', the Union emphasises the use of digital technologies to strengthen soil governance. A central element is the Copernicus Programme.[53] The Soil Strategy calls for greater reliance on the Joint Research Centre to develop the European Soil Observatory (EUSO) and on the European Environment Agency to establish the Land Information System for Europe (LISE).[54]

Alongside the digital agenda, the Soil Strategy highlights the need for reliable data and systematic monitoring, building on the Land Use/Cover Area Frame Survey (LUCAS). The Strategy proposes creating a stronger legal basis for the LUCAS soil

49 See https://digital-strategy.ec.europa.eu/en/policies/regulatory-framework-ai, accessed 11 July 2025.

50 Meuck et al. (2025: 56).

51 Ibid.: 58–60 & 64–65.

52 European Commission *Communication from the Commission to the European Parliament, the Council, the European Economic and Social Committee and the Committee of the Regions: EU Soil Strategy* COM (2021) 699 Final 20-23.

53 See https://www.copernicus.eu/en, accessed 3 August 2025.

54 European Commission Communication (2021: 20).

module.[55] In addition to monitoring, the Soil Strategy places strong emphasis on research and innovation. It calls for the establishment of large-scale, carefully designed programmes to generate further knowledge on sustainable soil management. The Strategy also highlights the close link between innovation and digitalisation. Because innovative approaches often rely on costly digital methods and data-driven research, their effectiveness depends on sustained investment. Of particular importance is the explicit call to promote the development and deployment of digital and remote sensors, mobile applications, and portable measuring instruments for assessing soil quality.[56]

The EU Soil Monitoring and Resilience Directive's articles do not themselves regulate or mandate the use of digital tools for soil protection, management, or monitoring. While the Directive anticipates the use of remote sensing products and refers to establishing a digital portal with publicly accessible georeferenced data, these elements serve primarily as supportive instruments for data collection and transparency rather than as legally binding obligations to deploy specific digital technologies.[57] The Directive is designed to reinforce and operate alongside the land use, land-use change, and forestry (LULUCF) framework. It therefore strengthens harmonised monitoring and reporting structures but contains no provision that imposes a general obligation on member states to deploy, standardise, or regulate digital tools or artificial intelligence systems in soil governance.[58] In fact, the Directive created an EU-wide soil health monitoring framework that mandates comparable soil data, contaminated-site remediation planning, and measures on land take and emerging contaminants, thereby offering a regulatory benchmark for other regions.[59]

The EU AI Act establishes a risk-based regulatory framework governing the placing on the market, the use, and the supervision of AI systems within the Union. Article 6, read together with Annex III, identifies sectors that are automatically designated as high risk unless it can be demonstrated that they do not pose a significant threat to health, safety, or fundamental rights. Agriculture and soil are not expressly included in Annex III. Nevertheless, digital systems used in soil management may fall within Annex III (2) when they form part of, or directly affect, the functioning of critical infrastructure sectors, such as water management, food supply systems, or environmental monitoring networks. In such cases, their classification would depend not on the agricultural nature of the system itself, but on its functional integration into infrastructure designated as critical under the Act.[60]

55 See https://joint-research-centre.ec.europa.eu/eu-soil-observatory-euso_en, accessed 3 August 2025; European Commission (2021: 21–22).

56 European Commission Communication (2021: 22).

57 See https://www.cuatrecasas.com/resources/new-eu-directive-on-soil-monitoring-and-resilience-694519fda4ab1032692762.pdf, accessed 3 March 2026.

58 European Commission (2023: 7–9).

59 Ruppel & Murray (2025: 13).

60 Annex III (2) Regulation (EU) 2024/1689 of the European Parliament and of the Council of 13 June 2024 Laying Down Harmonised Rules on Artificial Intelligence and Amending Regulations (2024).

### 3.2. Critical analysis of the legal and policy framework

The EU has established an ambitious framework for soil and AI. The Soil Strategy for 2030 outlines clear policy goals, the EU Soil Monitoring and Resilience Directive is the first-ever Soil Monitoring Law, and the AI Act introduces a comprehensive, risk-based system for AI governance. However, several shortcomings have been identified.

The EU Soil Monitoring and Resilience Directive does not establish legally binding targets.[61] It focuses on monitoring, assessment, reporting, and the principles of sustainable soil management.[62] Member states are required to establish systems to systematically monitor and assess soil health in accordance with common descriptors and EU methodologies. Furthermore, member states must periodically report to the European Commission and the European Environment Agency (EEA) on soil health, land take, and contaminated sites to ensure comparability.[63] The Directive also mandates the identification, registration, and risk assessment of contaminated sites, with the relevant information being made publicly accessible. In addition, it provides for the development of EU-level data platforms, *inter alia*, building upon the EU Soil Observatory, with technical support from the Commission.[64] Concerning soil monitoring and digitalisation, the Directive also devotes explicit attention to these aspects. The use of remote sensing products is anticipated, along with the establishment of a digital portal that provides public access to georeferenced data. However, the Directive does not provide specific provisions governing the use of artificial intelligence, nor does it mandate the use of digital soil-monitoring tools.[65]

Under the EU AI Act, providers of AI systems may determine internally whether their systems qualify as high-risk. Prior approval by a supervisory authority is not foreseen. While AI systems must be registered in a publicly accessible database, the underlying risk assessments are not disclosed. Only competent authorities may request such information, which, in turn, raises concerns about transparency and effective supervision. A further point of discussion concerns the elaboration of technical standards. Responsibility in this regard lies with European standardisation organisations, whose membership includes industrial actors. Critics have argued that these bodies are not sufficiently democratically legitimised, as civil society organisations have limited representation and no voting rights.[66] At the same time, the EU AI Act introduces

61 See https://eeb.org/a-weak-deal-for-europes-soils, accessed 12 July 2025.

62 Directive (EU) 2025/2360 of the European Parliament and of the Council of 12 November 2025 on Soil Monitoring and Resilience (Soil Monitoring Law) OJ L, 2025/2360, 26.11.2025.

63 See https://www.consilium.europa.eu/en/press/press-releases/2025/09/29/council-adopts-new-rules-for-healthier-and-more-resilient-european-soils/, accessed 3 March 2026.

64 See https://mission-soil-platform.ec.europa.eu/news-events/latest-news/soil-monitoring-law-published-eu-official-journal, accessed 3 March 2026.

65 See https://www.cuatrecasas.com/resources/new-eu-directive-on-soil-monitoring-and-resilience-694519fda4ab1032692762.pdf, accessed 3 March 2026.

66 Wachters (2024: 671–718).

important safeguards and benefits for agriculture and soil governance. By regulating the use of AI technologies, the Act has the potential to contribute to more sustainable agricultural practices and to improved soil health across the Union.[67]

### 3.3. Contextual factors affecting policy creation, implementation, and enforcement

The EU adopts a range of legal instruments, including regulations, directives, decisions, recommendations, and opinions. Once an agreement is reached, the legislative act is formally adopted and must be implemented by the member states.[68] One such factor influencing decision-making is the theory of intergovernmentalism, which views international cooperation as a partnership of sovereign states that pool sovereignty only when it serves their interests and highlights how member-state preferences are rooted in domestic political and economic pressures.[69] A further determinant of decision-making is the Union's cultural diversity, as the EU is characterised by the coexistence of distinct national cultures and an institutional framework that promotes dialogue, mutual respect, and equality among member states.[70]

When implementing EU law, it is essential to recognise the characteristics of each type of legal instrument. The primary responsibility for the correct and timely implementation of Union law lies with the member states. The European Commission is charged with ensuring compliance across the Union.[71] To carry out its supervisory role, the Commission uses guidelines, implementation plans, networks of national experts, conformity checks, legal assessments, inspections, and reporting obligations. In performing these tasks, the Commission follows a strategy of "Smart Enforcement", prioritising the prevention of infringements, assisting member states in implementation, and detecting serious or recurring breaches.

The complexity of a legislative instrument significantly affects its implementation. Institutional and administrative capacity, limited resources, and political considerations within member states may hinder compliance. The discretion afforded to member states can create scope for divergent application, leading to differentiated implementation across the Union.[72] The enforcement process is structured in several stages. At the outset, the European Commission gathers information concerning potential instances of non-compliance. Where indications of non-compliance arise, the Commission may initiate a pre-litigation phase, followed by a formal infringement procedure

67 See https://babl.ai/navigating-the-new-frontier-how-the-eu-ai-act-will-impact-the-agriculture-industry/, accessed 12 July 2025.

68 Germond (2016).

69 Hooghe & Marks (2019: 1115–1116).

70 Munos (2017: 150-151 & 154–158).

71 Art 288 of the Treaty on the Functioning of the European Union signed on 11-12-2007 and came into force on 1-12-2009 (OJ C 326/47).

72 Zhelyazkova et al. (2023: 454–456).

under Article 258 of the TFEU. If the member state does not comply, the Commission may refer the case to the Court of Justice of the European Union. When the Court finds a breach, the judgment is binding. Under Article 260 of the TFEU, the Court may impose financial penalties until the member state complies.

In practice, however, the effectiveness of this system is constrained by structural and political factors. The Commission exercises discretion in prioritising cases according to political feasibility, institutional capacity, and the sensitivity of the policy area concerned, and initiates formal proceedings less frequently against larger and more influential member states, as informal or diplomatic solutions are often preferred to formal legal action. Moreover, the infringement procedure is often slow and vulnerable to delaying tactics, places only minimal pressure on member states in its early phases, and keeps communications between the Commission and the member states confidential, thereby restricting public scrutiny and undermining trust in the Union's institutions.[73]

## 4. A legal comparison between the AU and the EU

Based on the previous sections, this part undertakes a structured comparative analysis of the AU and the EU to identify shared approaches, divergences, and potential lessons for regulating the utilisation of digital tools in soil protection and management.

### 4.1. Comparative analysis of legal and policy frameworks for soil and digital governance

#### 4.1.1. Soil governance and soil health

The AU currently lacks binding legislation specifically dedicated to soil protection, monitoring, and management. However, an important recent development warrants attention: the Model Law on Soil Management in Africa marks the AU's first structured, continental attempt to consolidate soil governance within a comprehensive legal framework. Beyond this recent development, soil governance at the continental level remains characterised by indirect references rather than explicit regulation. The Constitutive Act and Agenda 2063 contain only indirect references to soil-related issues, and, apart from the Model Law, no explicit binding regulatory framework has been adopted at the AU level. The only binding instrument so far that indirectly addresses soil health, the African Convention on the Conservation of Nature and Natural Resources, is significantly constrained by weak implementation and monitoring

73 Toshkov (2016).

mechanisms, partly due to limited financial resources. In addition, several non-binding policy instruments, including the Soil Initiative for Africa and the African Fertiliser and Soil Health Action Plan, reflect recognition of soil health, while other policy documents address soil-related matters indirectly. Nevertheless, the absence of a comprehensive, binding legal framework has led to a fragmented, largely aspirational approach.

By contrast, the EU has adopted a more structured legal and policy framework. The EU Soil Strategy for 2030 establishes clear objectives for achieving healthy soils by 2030 and 2050, which are translated into binding legislation through the recently adopted EU Soil Monitoring and Resilience Directive. The Directive is the first relatively comprehensive legislative instrument dedicated specifically to soil-related challenges within the Union. It introduces harmonised monitoring and assessment requirements, obliges member states to establish systematic soil health monitoring systems based on common descriptors and methodologies, and requires periodic reporting to the European Commission and the European Environment Agency to ensure comparability. It further provides for the identification, registration, and risk assessment of contaminated sites, the public accessibility of relevant information, and the development of EU-level data platforms building upon the EU Soil Observatory, thereby strengthening transparency and knowledge generation across the Union.

Although discretion afforded to member states may limit its effectiveness, the EU framework demonstrates a stronger move toward legal consolidation. While the EU has adopted the first comprehensive Soil Monitoring and Resilience Directive, its framework remains primarily monitoring-focused and does not yet integrate all dimensions of soil protection into a single regulatory regime.[74]

#### 4.1.2. AI and other digital transformation tools

The regulatory approaches of the AU and the EU concerning AI differ in their underlying philosophy, legal force, and institutional design. The EU adopts a binding, risk-based regulatory model through the EU AI Act, establishing a centralised governance framework at the Union level. By contrast, the AU's Continental AI Strategy is structured around five pillars and advocates flexible and adaptive regulatory models tailored to member states' specific contexts, rather than prescribing detailed legal obligations.

Institutionally, the divergence is equally pronounced. The AU's approach is characterised by coordination rather than enforcement: the African Union Commission serves as a high-level coordinating body, facilitating cooperation and promoting collaboration among member states and regional actors. This advisory and participatory

74 Kassner & Ruppel (2025: 786–790).

design reflects a bottom-up model that respects the sovereignty and varying capacities of member states. The EU, by contrast, has established a centralised, enforcement-oriented governance structure through the European Artificial Intelligence Board, which ensures consistent interpretation and application of the AI Act and coordinates national enforcement efforts, thereby securing uniformity and legal certainty across the Union.

Despite these structural differences, both organisations recognise the strategic importance of AI and digitalisation and seek to promote responsible governance. However, whereas the EU relies on binding legal obligations and supranational enforcement mechanisms, the AU operates through soft-law instruments and national-level implementation within a continental strategic framework, resulting in differing levels of regulatory uniformity and enforceability.[75]

### 4.1.3. Intersection between digitalisation and soil

The AU so far lacks legal instruments regulating the digitisation of soil protection, monitoring, and management. The new Model Law on Soil Management in Africa, however, represents a normative step towards addressing this gap.[76] In addition, policy instruments such as the Soil Initiative for Africa and the Continental AI Strategy acknowledge the relevance of digital technologies for agriculture and soil health, although they do not provide detailed regulatory guidance on soil-specific digital applications.

By contrast, the EU has explicitly linked digitalisation to soil protection and monitoring. While the EU Soil Monitoring and Resilience Directive recognises, in its recitals, the need to establish a digital soil health data portal at Union level, it does not impose a direct, binding obligation on member states to create or operate such a portal. Nevertheless, the binding requirements for harmonised monitoring, georeferenced data collection, reporting, and public registers indirectly necessitate the development of digital data systems at the national and Union levels.[77] However, the EU AI Act does not specifically address soil management, although relevant systems fall within its risk-based framework.

A further divergence lies in digital infrastructure. The EU operates through interconnected systems, such as LUCAS and Copernicus, embedded within a coherent legal and policy framework.[78] In the AU, digitalisation efforts remain predominantly

---

75 Policy Network on Artificial Intelligence (AI) (2024: 10); Njoroge (2024: 2-4).

76 See https://www.su.ac.za/en/news/pan-african-parliament-adopts-continents-first-model-law-sustainable-soil-management, accessed 28 March 2026.

77 Cf. https://eur-lex.europa.eu/legal-content/EN/TXT/HTML/?uri=OJ:L_202502360, accessed 28 March 2026.

78 European Commission (2021c: 20–22).

project-based and are not anchored within a broader legal framework, and the absence of harmonised technical standards limits coordination at the continental level.[79]

The two regions also diverge in financial and infrastructural support. The EU provides dedicated funding for digital infrastructure in the soil sector, whereas limited financial resources and infrastructural constraints hinder implementation within the AU.[80] In sum, while both the EU and the AU recognise the importance of digital tools in soil governance, the EU's approach is more advanced and more legally and institutionally embedded.

### 4.2. Comparative analysis of norm hierarchy and legal force

The extent of the authority and legal influence exercised by the EU and the AU is shaped by the depth of regional integration achieved within each organisation. In the EU, integration has evolved into a sophisticated political and legal union. By contrast, the AU's integration trajectory has been more complex and uneven, shaped by political diversity and differing levels of state capacity.[81]

EU and AU law distinguish among several legal instruments that reflect different degrees of legal force and methods of implementation. In the EU, regulations are fully binding, directly applicable, and supreme over national law. Directives bind member states as to the result but require national transposition, while decisions bind their addressees, and soft law instruments have limited legal force.

Similarly, the AU distinguishes between regulations, directives, and non-binding instruments. However, although AU regulations are described as "binding and directly applicable", this does not confer genuine direct effect or supremacy. The AU lacks a supranational legal mechanism to ensure the automatic application or primacy of its law over domestic law.[82] The distinction in legal instruments reflects the broader institutional structures underpinning both organisations. The EU embodies a highly developed supranational legal order characterised by the direct effect and supremacy of Union law, allowing binding legal acts to take effect within member states without requiring national implementation. By contrast, the AU operates as a hybrid structure combining intergovernmental cooperation with only limited supranational features. Legislative competences at the continental level remain narrowly defined, member states retain primary authority, and the absence of legal supremacy means that national interests often prevail over continental commitments.[83]

---

79 See https://www.soils4africa-h2020.eu/the-project, accessed 4 July 2025.

80 See https://ec.europa.eu/info/funding-tenders/opportunities/portal/screen/programmes/horizon, accessed 5 July 2025.

81 Adamu & Peter (2016).

82 Amani Africa (2022: 15–16); Mahlangu (2025: 3–5).

83 Adamu & Peter (2016: 52–55); Mahlangu (2025: 5–6).

### 4.3. Comparative analysis of institutional structures and legislative processes

While both the AU and the EU share certain structural features, including parliamentary, executive, and judicial bodies, significant differences remain in the degree of institutionalisation, the distribution of powers, and the procedures by which legal norms are adopted and applied. The EU is characterised by a highly institutionalised and supranational governance structure. The European Commission exercises the exclusive right of legislative initiative and oversees the implementation of EU law, while the European Parliament and the Council act as co-legislators under the ordinary legislative procedure. The Court of Justice of the EU ensures the uniform interpretation and application of EU law through binding judgments with direct effect.

By contrast, the AU operates predominantly on an intergovernmental basis. Ultimate decision-making authority rests with the Assembly, while the Pan-African Parliament has so far largely played an advisory role, lacking legislative competence, except for model law competence. The AU Commission does not enjoy supranational executive powers comparable to those of the European Commission, including the power of legislative initiative. The African Court's jurisdiction depends on the acceptance of individual member states, thereby limiting its authority and hindering the uniform application of its judgments.[84]

These institutional differences are reflected in the legislative processes. In the EU, the legislative process is highly structured and legally integrated.[85] The AU's legislative process is less developed than the EU's and relies heavily on intergovernmental consensus.[86] This consensus-based model contrasts sharply with the EU's decision-making dynamics. The AU's reliance on consensus slows the legislative process and gives informal power relations between member states significant influence over outcomes. By contrast, the EU employs more formalised voting mechanisms. In the Council, decisions are taken by qualified majority, while in the Parliament they are adopted by an absolute majority. This framework results in a faster and more structured legislative process that is less shaped by internal political balances.[87]

Policy network theory further highlights the institutional differences between the two organisations. The theory examines how various actors, such as government bodies, non-governmental organisations, multinational companies, and international institutions, interact in the policymaking process. In the EU, these networks are formalised and embedded in clear procedures. This structure increases transparency and enables non-state actors to participate meaningfully. In the AU, by contrast, such networks are

84 Baba & Mngomezulu (2021).
85 Greenwood & Roederer-Rynning (2018: 123–124).
86 Amani Africa (2022: 10–18).
87 Mahlangu (2025: 4–5).

less formal and less structured, reflecting the organisation's predominantly intergovernmental mode of governance.[88]

### 4.4. Comparative analysis of enforcement and implementation mechanisms

The AU demonstrates a comparatively limited capacity to implement its decisions. This is largely attributable to the predominantly non-binding nature of many of its legal and policy instruments. Even where binding instruments exist, their implementation is undermined by inadequate financial resources, weak institutional coordination, and limited administrative capacity. The AU continues to face significant financial, technical, and institutional constraints that hinder the effective implementation of continental instruments.[89]

By contrast, the EU operates within a highly developed implementation framework, characterised by clear legal obligations, detailed reporting requirements, and strict deadlines. These mechanisms ensure the consistent and effective application of Union law across member states. [90] Compliance cultures also differ. In the EU, comparatively high levels of compliance are sustained by institutional oversight, aligned domestic legal systems, economic incentives linked to the internal market, and peer pressure among member states.[91] In contrast, compliance within the AU is shaped more strongly by domestic political contexts and structural constraints.[92]

So far, the AU also lacks enforcement mechanisms comparable to those of the EU. Although continental institutions exist, their functional capacities remain limited, and the absence of an effective supranational adjudicatory mechanism restricts uniform application.[93] Overall, whereas the EU operates within a legally binding and institutionally robust system, the AU relies largely on non-binding instruments and faces significant structural challenges in ensuring consistent compliance.

Unlike the governments of European states, the governments of African states, when the AU was founded, pursued the goal of preserving their national sovereignty and did not transfer far-reaching powers to the AU. In the strict sense, the AU is not a supranational organisation like the EU, which has its own legislative, executive, and judicial powers within the framework of the powers conferred on it (principle of limited individual authorisation). The AU Assembly, as the highest decision-making body, has the power to define common policies, monitor their implementation, and impose sanctions on member states that fail to comply. Even the Pan-African Parliament, the

88 Ibid.: 3.
89 AUDA-NEPAD (2022: 3).
90 Mahlangu (2025: 6).
91 Ibid.: 5–6.
92 AU (2019: 57–77).
93 Mahlangu (2025: 6–7); Clarke et al. (2019: 1–2).

AU's (intended) legislative body, lacks legislative powers. In this capacity, it can only propose so-called model laws in areas assigned or approved by the AU Assembly. The adoption of these model laws by the AU Assembly does not directly create binding law applicable in the member states.

### 4.5. Comparative analysis of economic resources

The effectiveness of legal frameworks depends not only on institutional design but also on economic resources. Financial means are essential to translate legal commitments into concrete action, particularly in resource-intensive areas such as digitalisation and soil management.

The AU relies primarily on contributions from member states and external donor assistance. However, this funding model creates structural vulnerabilities. Persistent gaps between approved and actual expenditure reveal underlying structural weaknesses. Donor funding is often delayed or withheld, and its overall volume remains unpredictable from year to year. Member state contributions are frequently delayed, partial, or absent. This uneven contribution pattern creates uncertainty about the AU's financial base. As a result, the AU's capacity to achieve fiscal self-sufficiency remains severely constrained.[94]

These structural and financial constraints have direct implications for the AU's capacity to invest in and sustain key policy areas. One example is the digitalisation of agriculture, which requires substantial and stable funding.[95] Because the AU's own financial base remains limited and donor funding is often unpredictable, implementation will rely primarily on external partnerships and coordinated financing mechanisms.[96]

By contrast, the EU operates with a comparatively stable and autonomous financial framework. The EU budget is financed primarily through "own resources",[97] and EU programmes supporting digitalisation in agriculture and soil management, such as Horizon Europe,[98] are financed mainly from the EU budget rather than external donors. Overall, the EU's financial autonomy provides a more stable and predictable basis for regulatory action. In contrast, the AU's reliance on external donors and inconsistent contributions from member states limits its capacity to mobilise resources for effective implementation.

94 Pharatlhatlhe & Vanheukelom (2019: 1–8).
95 AU (2023a: 4–6).
96 Ibid.: 35–42.
97 Deutsche Bank (2020: 45–46 & 50–53).
98 See https://ec.europa.eu/info/funding-tenders/opportunities/portal/screen/programmes/horizon, accessed 5 July 2025.

## 4.6. Comparative analysis of sociocultural influences on policymaking

Sociocultural factors also shape policymaking in both organisations, particularly in areas such as digitalisation and soil governance. The African continent is characterised by significant cultural and linguistic diversity, which represents both an asset and a structural challenge. On the one hand, it constitutes a source of rich cultural heritage, knowledge systems, and local innovation that can inform inclusive policymaking. On the other hand, such heterogeneity complicates the development and implementation of coherent continental policies. Divergent languages, traditions, and governance practices often hinder effective coordination, resulting in policy fragmentation, uneven cooperation, and capacity disparities among member states.[99]

By contrast, the EU operates within a more structured multilingual framework. It has institutionalised multilingualism under the principle of "unity in diversity." All legal and policy documents are systematically translated into these languages to guarantee accessibility and uphold cultural and linguistic rights. While translation slows decision-making, the EU can manage this process because it deals with a limited number of languages and has a well-developed administrative apparatus to support multilingual translation.[100] By contrast, the AU faces far greater linguistic diversity and lacks comparable institutional capacity, making systematic translation much more difficult.[101]

Stakeholder participation constitutes another important dimension. Both organisations formally commit to involving civil society and affected groups in policymaking.[102] A further dimension relates to digital literacy, which plays a crucial role in shaping policy effectiveness. In the AU, low levels of digital literacy among small-scale farmers constitute a major obstacle to the uptake of digital technologies. Europe faces similar challenges: 44% of the EU population lacks basic digital skills.[103] However, in the African context, disparities in infrastructure, expertise, and capital risk exacerbate existing inequalities. Without targeted and inclusive policies, the digitalisation of agriculture may deepen socio-economic divides and exclude vulnerable groups, particularly smallholder farmers.[104]

99 Osemuyi (2024: 22–23).
100 Kuzelewska (2014: 151–152).
101 Ibid.: 161.
102 AU (2023a: 3 & 5); AU (2024b: 1-4 & 16); European Commission (2023: 14 & 43).
103 EIP-AGRI (2020: 3–4).
104 Kudama et al. (2021: 292–300).

# 5. Recommendations for the African Union

## 5.1. Legislative and policy development

### 5.1.1. Develop a binding continental legal framework

The AU, so far, relies on soft-law instruments, such as the Soil Initiative for Africa, which lack enforceability and legal certainty. Unlike the EU, whose supranational legal system enables binding measures with direct effect, the AU's predominantly intergovernmental structure limits its capacity to generate norms that prevail over national law. As a result, continental frameworks function mainly as political coordination tools rather than binding legal instruments. Establishing a binding continental legal framework would strengthen legal coherence, improve compliance, and provide a stable regulatory environment needed to integrate digital tools effectively into soil governance, objectives that soft law cannot achieve.

Insofar it is promising that the new Model Law on Soil Management in Africa offers a comprehensive framework to enable African nations to adapt and domesticate in their national contexts. Key provisions of the Model Law introduce forward-looking concepts, such as:

- Soil Impact Assessments – separating soil assessment from general environmental evaluations, ensuring soil health is independently measured in large-scale projects.
- Public Participation in Soil Governance – requiring that communities be involved in land use decisions before major agricultural or industrial activities commence.
- Zoning and Soil Use Planning – guiding countries on how to allocate land based on soil health and crop suitability.
- Digitalisation and Data Systems – establishing soil information systems to support scientific, data-driven decision-making.[105]

### 5.1.2. Integrate and align existing policy instruments

As proposed in the aforementioned Model Law, regulatory instruments, digitisation, agriculture and soil management instruments should be aligned with the law to ensure coherence and mutual reinforcement. In the EU, the Soil Strategy, the Soil Monitoring Law, and the AI Act are closely interlinked and embedded in broader frameworks, preventing regulatory fragmentation. So far, AU initiatives have operated in parallel

105 See https://spikedmedia.co.zw/pap-adoption-of-model-law-on-sustainable-soil-management-step-toward-food-security-and-climate-resilience/, accessed 1 March 2026.

without legal or institutional integration, limiting their effectiveness and creating gaps in governance. Yet legal integration is essential to enhance regulatory coherence and support the coordinated use of digital tools in soil governance. The Model Law on Soil Management in Africa could be a game-changer within the AU in this regard.

#### 5.1.3. Establish clear regulatory objectives and technical standards

Clear regulatory objectives and harmonised technical standards are essential for providing legal certainty, ensuring consistent implementation, and preventing regulatory fragmentation. As illustrated by the EU AI Act, harmonised technical standards developed by European standardisation organisations play a central role in ensuring legal certainty and interoperability between different digital systems.[106] In the EU, the Soil Strategy and Soil Monitoring Law set clear goals, while the AI Act provides detailed rules for digital technologies. Although the AU has adopted various strategic objectives, these remain fragmented and lack harmonised legal standards. Establishing continent-wide objectives and binding technical standards would strengthen coordination and support the effective integration of digital tools into soil governance.

### 5.2. Institutional design and coordination

#### 5.2.1. Strengthen AU-level legislative and oversight functions

In the EU, institutions such as the European Commission, the European Parliament, and the Court of Justice provide legislative initiative, democratic legitimacy, and judicial enforcement. The Court ensures the uniform application of EU law through binding decisions, while the Parliament exercises legislative powers on behalf of EU citizens. By contrast, the Pan-African Parliament lacks binding legislative authority, and the African Court of Justice is not yet functioning effectively as a supranational adjudicatory body. Strengthening AU-level legislative and oversight functions could provide the institutional foundation needed to achieve regulatory objectives and enhance compliance, coherence, and legitimacy at the continental level.

---

106 Art 40 Regulation (EU) 2024/1689 of the European Parliament and of the Council of 13 June 2024 Laying Down Harmonised Rules on Artificial Intelligence and Amending Regulations.

### 5.2.2. Enhance coordination between member states and Regional Economic Communities

Stronger coordination between member states and RECs is essential for strengthening continental governance. The RECs play a central role in translating AU norms into regional action. As legally recognised building blocks of the Union, they are required under the 2007 Protocol on Relations to harmonise their policies and treaties with those of the AU. Where coordination is weak, divergent legal standards and fragmented frameworks emerge, undermining legal consistency and effective implementation. Coordination among member states within the AU framework is equally important, as the Union's intergovernmental structure places primary responsibility for implementation on the states themselves. In the absence of supranational enforcement mechanisms, collective coordination is essential to ensure the uniform application of AU decisions. Where such coordination is weak, divergent national responses emerge, leading to fragmented implementation and undermining the Union's capacity to act coherently. In this regard, the Model Law on Soil Management represents a significant development within the AU.

### 5.2.3. Develop a centralised soil data platform

A centralised soil data platform is essential to ensure coordinated data collection, accessibility, and transparency at the continental level. In the EU, programmes such as Copernicus are embedded in a clear legal and institutional framework, enabling consistent monitoring and obligating member states to share data. The AU lacks a comparable system. Initiatives such as Soil4Africa attempt to fill this gap but lack a binding legal basis, and data remain fragmented and stored locally.[107] A continental legal instrument requiring data collection and sharing could strengthen coordination and support evidence-based soil governance.

## 5.3. Implementation, compliance, and enforcement

### 5.3.1. Define clear implementation procedures and timelines

Clear implementation procedures and timelines are crucial to translate legal commitments into concrete action. In the EU, instruments such as the Soil Strategy and the Soil Monitoring Law set clear objectives, structured timelines, and reporting obligations, allowing the European Commission to monitor progress and ensure consistent

---

107 See https://www.soils4africa-h2020.eu/the-project, accessed 4 July 2025.

application across member states. By contrast, AU frameworks outline broad policy objectives but lack binding procedures, timelines, or reporting mechanisms, which may lead to fragmented and delayed implementation and limit the effective integration of digital tools into soil governance.

### 5.3.2. Establish monitoring and enforcement mechanisms

Robust monitoring and enforcement mechanisms are essential to ensure compliance with continental obligations. In the EU, supranational bodies such as the European Commission and the Court of Justice monitor implementation and issue binding decisions to secure the uniform application of Union law. The African Court of Justice and Human Rights is envisaged as a continental adjudicatory body, but it is not yet fully operational. Existing enforcement mechanisms are predominantly of political and diplomatic nature. In the field of soil and digitalisation, weak enforcement could exacerbate fragmented data governance and hinder the effective use of digital tools. This institutional gap may weaken compliance and contribute to uneven implementation of continental soil and digitalisation initiatives across member states.

## 5.4. Develop stable and transparent funding mechanisms

Stable and transparent funding mechanisms are crucial to ensure the sustainability and effectiveness of a continental legal framework on soil and digital governance. These policy areas require long-term investments in digital infrastructure, coordinated data collection, and capacity building, which cannot be achieved through ad hoc, unpredictable funding.

Currently, AU initiatives in these fields depend heavily on fragmented and donor-driven financing, which limits long-term planning, undermines implementation, and weakens accountability mechanisms. A clear legal framework should, therefore, define how financial resources are secured, allocated, and monitored. This includes assessing internal funding options, identifying potential external donors and the conditions attached to their support, and creating incentives to attract private sector investment. Importantly, the AU should seek to strengthen its own financial base, drawing inspiration from the EU's use of internally generated resources to fund large-scale programmes. Reducing reliance on external donors could limit exposure to shifting priorities and conditionalities, while providing the financial certainty needed to build digital infrastructure, support coordinated data collection, and ensure effective implementation across member states.

## 5.5. Promote digital inclusion through culturally responsive and technologically adaptive frameworks

Future regulatory frameworks should take existing digital inequalities into account, particularly those between large and small farmers and between men and women. Significant disparities exist between large-scale and smallholder farmers; generally, male farmers have greater access to digital tools, while smallholder and female farmers face financial and educational barriers. Targeted training and subsidy schemes for smallholder farmers could help make digital tools more accessible.

Economic differences between AU member states may also be addressed, for example, through differentiated financial and technical support. Furthermore, regulatory frameworks could benefit from greater flexibility and cultural responsiveness. Setting overarching objectives at the AU level, while allowing member states to adapt implementation to local cultural contexts, may enhance both legitimacy and effectiveness. To address rapid technological developments, a risk-based approach, similar to that applied in the EU's AI framework, could be explored to maintain legal adaptability without frequent legislative changes.

# 6. Conclusion

> The speed of change is growing exponentially, and the new digital means, AI, are deemed to increase our power over nature. Humanity will need to develop an appropriate governance structure for these new technological capabilities, using the Sustainable Development Goals (SDGs) as a useful reference point. Encouraging research and development in sustainable digital technologies and developing appropriate new legal frameworks in parallel seem vital for leveraging the opportunities presented by the digital era. Such an approach is also necessary for using new digital means to improve sustainable soil management continuously.[108]

In this light, the article examined means of digital transformation and the extent to which the AU, inspired by the EU's example and adapted to Africa's institutional, cultural, and economic context, can develop, implement, and enforce a regulatory instrument governing the use of digital tools for more effective soil management and protection.

The analysis demonstrates that the AU currently lacks a comprehensive, binding legal framework to regulate the integration of digital tools into soil governance at the continental level. The newly adopted Model Law on Soil Management is expected to consolidate and streamline existing instruments, including the Soil Initiative for Africa and the Continental AI Strategy, to better recognise the importance of digitalisation. It will also contribute to improved implementation and enforcement mechanisms once domesticated in the AU member states. While structural constraints, including financial dependence on external donors, limited administrative capacity, and the absence

108 Ginzky & Ruppel (2025a: 249–269, 267f).

of supranational legal supremacy, restrict the uniform application of continental norms, the effectiveness of the Model Law will depend on sustained political commitment, institutional strengthening, and stable financing mechanisms at both continental and national levels.

By contrast, the EU operates within a binding and institutionally embedded legal order. Instruments such as the EU Soil Strategy for 2030, the Soil Monitoring and Resilience Directive, and the EU AI Act illustrate how soil governance and digitalisation can be integrated within a structured legal and institutional framework supported by monitoring, reporting, and enforcement mechanisms.

However, the comparative analysis also shows that the European model cannot simply be replicated. Differences in institutional design, levels of integration, financial resources, and socio-economic conditions require context-specific adaptation. The EU experience, therefore, functions as a source of inspiration rather than a template.

As such, the Model Law on Soil Management in Africa comes at a timely moment, offering principles, definitions, institutional designs, and implementation pathways that are adaptable to diverse legal systems of the African continent. Synergies are particularly promising with the EU Soil Monitoring and Resilience Directive, where knowledge exchange on monitoring, data governance, and science-policy interfaces could accelerate progress on both continents through shared research, interoperable datasets, and coordinated capacity-building.[109] For decades, the international plane treated soil as an afterthought, referenced tangentially but rarely the subject of direct obligations. The task before international law, policy, and governance is no longer to justify soil's inclusion but to ultimately build the forum and establish the framework that the planet requires.[110]

While the legal comparability between the two Unions remains asymmetric, the EU Soil Monitoring and Resilience Directive and the Model Law on Soil Management in Africa are evolving soil frameworks that can accelerate progress towards improved digital transformation, soil protection, and monitoring on both continents. While at the international level there may still be a long way to go, at the regional and continental levels, within the AU and the EU, the most recent legislative developments described in this article are promising steps toward improved soil governance.[111]

109 See https://spikedmedia.co.zw/pap-adoption-of-model-law-on-sustainable-soil-management-step-toward-food-security-and-climate-resilience/, accessed 1 March 2026.

110 Ruppel & Murray (2025: 15).

111 These legislative efforts are also in line with the joint declaration that emerged from AU–EU Parliamentary Pre-Summit Meeting, held in Midrand, South Africa on 14-15 November 2025. Therein the Pan-African Parliament (PAP) and the European Parliament (EP) have issued a Joint Declaration under the theme "Renewing Africa-Europe Parliamentary Cooperation in a Changing Global Context". It therein reflected on the 25th anniversary of the formal AU–EU Partnership, which provides a timely opportunity to take stock of progress, identify gaps, and shape a future-oriented partnership anchored in the UN 2030 Agenda for Sustainable Development and AU Agenda 2063. Moreover, the declaration reflects the ambition to renew the "commitment to multilateralism, international cooperation and parliamentary diplomacy founded on the principles of the UN Charter, the

Sustainable Development Goals and the Africa's Agenda 2063 as a means to resolve the complex political, security and socio-economic challenges facing our continents and to promote human rights, democracy, good governance, the rule of law, peace and security." It further expresses the joint commitment "to promote the strengthening of global health, sustainable international agri-food systems, climate resilience." The declaration even calls "for the institutionalization of the parliamentary dimension to make it an integral component of the AU-EU institutional framework", cf. https://pap.au.int/en/documents/2025-11-24/joint-declaration-following-au-eu-parliamentary-pre-summit-meeting, accessed 13 March 2026.

# The decolonisation of Africa's soils: a legal challenge of historical significance

*Oliver C. Ruppel & Ruda Murray*

"African soils cannot be separated from African history because they are, in themselves, historical bodies and they have interacted with human history since its beginning."[1]

## 1. Introduction: soil, justice, and decolonisation

Africa is home to a vast diversity of soils that sustain cultures, economies, and ecosystems.[2] For millennia, communities across the continent cultivated indigenous knowledge systems to maintain soil fertility, conserve water, and protect biodiversity. These practices, embedded in cultural traditions, ensured the long-term resilience of landscapes and the survival of societies. Africa is thus not only rich in natural resources but also in cultural heritage and wisdom that have guided sustainable land management across generations.

This wisdom is reflected in cosmologies, such as the Ethiopian Tewahido Church's belief that human beings are composed of seven elements—three of the soul (thought, communication, and eternal life) and four of the body (wind, fire, water, and soil).[3] In this understanding, soil is not inert matter, but an integral part of human existence itself. Similarly, *Ubuntu* and related African philosophies affirm that life is shared between humans, the non-human world, and the spirit realm: "the land of the people is the people themselves, and the people are the human face of the land."[4] Such worldviews position soil as a living bond between humanity, nature, and ancestry.

The soil's resistance was also central to traditions of anticolonial struggle. Maroon communities—settlements formed by formerly enslaved Africans—drew upon the earth itself as an ally in their defiance of slavery and plantation life. As Wynter notes, they swore oaths of solidarity to one another and against the world of the plantation by "kissing the earth."[5] These practices reveal how soil has long been more than a resource; it has functioned as a ground of resistance, identity, and freedom—a forgotten artefact of the continent's ancestral struggles.

Yet the story of Africa's soils cannot be told without confronting the legacies of colonialism. During the colonial era, fertile lands were expropriated, customary tenure

1 Showers (2006: 118).
2 Ruppel & Ginzky (2024).
3 Woldeyesa & Belachew (2021: 70).
4 Ibid.: 67.
5 Davidson & da Silva (2024: 4).

systems disrupted, and resource use redirected to serve distant markets.[6] The extraction of value was not limited to minerals and crops; it extended to the very fertility of soils, mined for productivity without replenishment. This disruption of ecological and cultural systems has left enduring scars, shaping present-day patterns of land degradation, food insecurity, and environmental vulnerability.

Decolonisation, in its broadest sense, refers to the dismantling of colonial power structures and the enduring legacies they leave behind.[7] This includes the decolonisation of knowledge, which challenges the privileging of Eurocentric perspectives in academia and development discourse. It also extends to the decolonisation of economies by confronting perverse subsidies and financial, trade, and investment structures that perpetuate neo-colonial dependence and exploitation. In this sense, the pursuit of sustainable development may be inherently linked to decolonisation.[8] Many scholars argue that the historical exploitation of resources and the imposition of externally designed development models by colonial powers have left deep and lasting scars on post-colonial societies.[9] These legacies include environmental degradation, social inequality, and economic dependence. Decolonisation in the context of sustainable development, therefore, calls for a shift in power relations. This may require recognition of indigenous and local knowledge systems, which have long offered valuable insights into sustainable resource management and community well-being.[10] It also requires participatory and inclusive decision-making processes so that local voices genuinely shape sustainable development strategies.[11]

Decolonising the environment, therefore, requires decentring Eurocentrism—first by acknowledging the violence of slavery and colonialism, and second by centring indigenous ways of knowing and acting in relation to land and living systems.[12] The distinction between "Western" and "non-Western" views is not essentialist; it reflects how colonial and neo-colonial power structures made European ideas about land reasonable and enforceable, while dismissing African epistemologies as "primitive".[13] At the 1884–1885 Berlin Conference, European powers carved up the continent from afar; people, animals, soils, and vegetation were treated as resources to be catalogued, extracted, and consumed. This cartographic project—the colonial map as *tabula rasa*—imposed a space-based view of Africa as a bundle of natural assets awaiting conversion into capital, detached from grounded life worlds and responsibilities.[14] Its

6 Amanor (2008: 59).
7 Cordonier Segger & Olawuyi (2025: 652).
8 Ibid.: 653.
9 Ibid.: 654.
10 Ibid.: 655–656.
11 Ibid.: 658.
12 Woldeyesa & Belachew (2021: 64).
13 Ibid.: 66.
14 Ibid.

afterlives are visible in fragmented landscapes, insecure tenure, monocultures, chemical dependence, and eroding topsoils. Decolonising soil governance means reversing these logics: restoring land and decision-making authority to communities; recognising customary tenure and guardianship; requiring free, prior, and informed consent; embedding indigenous indicators of soil health alongside scientific metrics; and re-aligning policy instruments, finance, and enforcement with the protection of living soils rather than their depletion.

Precolonial Mali's agroecologies, for example, sustained major urban centres through ring cultivation that built rich anthropogenic soils, grain stores that buffered drought, flood-recession rice in the Inner Niger Delta, and Dina-style coordination of farmers, herders, and fishers.[15] Colonial engineering reversed these logics: the Office du Niger dam and canals introduced forced relocations, salinisation, and disrupted delta flood pulses, undermining rice, fisheries, and pastures.[16] When plantation cotton faltered, policy shifted to rainfed export cotton, undercutting local weaving with cheap imports.[17] Post-independence, a vertically integrated cotton filière deepened input dependence, acidified soils, increased pesticide and herbicide exposure, and reallocated women's labour away from nutrient-dense "sauce crops."[18] The result is the "Sikasso paradox": high commodity output alongside child malnutrition[19]—an emblem of how external models can erode soil health, diets, and agency.

Against this backdrop, the African Union's (AU) 2025 theme, "Justice for Africans and People of African Descent Through Reparations," offers a powerful lens for rethinking soil governance through a justice-based perspective.[20] The AU has emphasised that reparations must address the legacies of slavery, colonialism, apartheid, and genocide. These same legacies are inscribed in the soils of Africa, where depletion and dispossession have gone hand in hand with political and economic subjugation. The campaign for reparatory justice, including the AU's call for a "true new map of Africa," therefore resonates directly with the project of reclaiming soils for African people, cultures, and futures.[21]

At the same time, global climate change is placing unprecedented stress on African soils and ecosystems.[22] Droughts, floods, shifting rainfall patterns, and extreme weather events threaten to undermine food security and strain fragile governance systems. Africa, which has contributed least to global greenhouse gas emissions, is

15 Moseley (2024: 50).
16 Ibid.: 51–54.
17 Ibid.
18 Ibid.: 58–59.
19 Ibid.: 60.
20 African Dialogue Series (2025).
21 See https://edition.cnn.com/2025/08/15/africa/africa-real-size-world-map-campaign-intl, accessed 22 September 2025.
22 Rhodes (2014: 105).

among the least prepared for the severity of these challenges. Soil governance is, therefore, not an abstract concern but a matter of survival, livelihood, and dignity.

In this regard, recent social justice discourse has emphasised that apparent stability often conceals deep structural inequality, and that justice requires more than the formal recognition of rights—it requires the creation of equitable conditions in which those rights can be realised.[23] As Baroness Valerie Amos has cautioned, "stability without equity is fragile."[24] This insight is particularly salient in the African context, where contemporary patterns of soil degradation, land dispossession, and environmental vulnerability remain inseparable from historical injustice and unequal starting points.

African wisdom has long affirmed the deep connection between humanity and the land: "Upon this handful of soil our survival depends."[25] Soils are not lifeless matter but vibrant living systems—cosmoses in miniature—sustaining all biological life. Nearly all the food we consume—over 95%—depends on soils for its production.[26] Yet these foundations are under mounting pressure. Agriculture, mining, infrastructure expansion, and urbanisation drive soil degradation at alarming rates, while poverty and insecure tenure encourage unsustainable practices. The question remains whether *Homo sapiens*—the "wise human"—can live up to its name, or whether we will continue down the path of soil depletion, ecological collapse, and social injustice.

The decolonisation of Africa's soils is, thus, not simply a technical or scientific project. It is a moral and political imperative: to reconnect soil governance with principles of justice, equity, and dignity, and to ensure that Africa's soils serve the needs of its people rather than external interests. The Durban Declaration and Programme of Action (2001) affirmed that slavery, colonialism, and apartheid were crimes against humanity whose legacies demand redress.[27] Building on this foundation, the Accra Declaration on Reparations and Racial Healing (2022) calls for a comprehensive framework of justice to address these enduring harms.[28] Africa's soils, depleted and dispossessed through centuries of extractive rule, embody these legacies. Reclaiming them is not merely an environmental task—it is a reparatory act.

In line with the AU's reparations agenda, this chapter argues that reclaiming Africa's soils must unite science with society and anchor resource management in natural justice. Only then can Africa move from vulnerability to leadership—as a custodian of soils, biodiversity, and ecological futures, not just for itself but for the planet. To that end, this chapter begins by examining international and African frameworks that shape soil governance, highlighting both their promise and

23 See https://www.su.ac.za/en/news/stability-without-equity-fragile-baroness-valerie-amos-warns-7th-social-justice-lecture, accessed 19 March 2026.

24 Ibid.

25 Montgomery (2018).

26 FAO (2023).

27 UN Department of Public Information (2002).

28 See https://reparationscomm.org/docs/the-accra-declaration-on-reparations-and-racial-healing/, accessed 22 September 2025.

limitations. It then turns to colonial legacies and climate justice, tracing how historical exploitation continues to structure present vulnerabilities and claims for reparations. The discussion expands to include the restitution of cultural artefacts, climate neutrality, and just transitions, situating soil within broader struggles for justice and sustainability. From there, the focus shifts to decolonising African soil law and governance, identifying strengths, weaknesses, and systemic gaps. The chapter concludes with recommendations and pathways forward that outline how soils can be reclaimed as foundations for food security, climate resilience, cultural identity, and planetary stewardship.

## 2. International frameworks and the African experience

Global and regional frameworks have become increasingly influential in shaping the governance, conservation, and restoration of soils in Africa. Many of these instruments are non-binding. Yet they carry considerable symbolic and political weight, offering both normative guidance and leverage for national and continental initiatives.
The Revised World Soil Charter (2015) remains a landmark reference point. It highlights soils as the foundation of food security, ecosystem health, and climate regulation, urging states to adopt principles of protection, restoration, and sustainable management. Similarly, the Voluntary Guidelines to Support the Progressive Realisation of the Right to Food (2004), developed with active participation from civil society, provide states with recommendations on access to natural resources, legislation, markets, and education as essential components of food security.

At the broader United Nations (UN) level, the 2030 Agenda for Sustainable Development explicitly integrates soil protection in Goal 15, which focuses on terrestrial ecosystems, forests, desertification, and biodiversity.[29] Within this, Target 15.3 calls for achieving a land degradation-neutral world by 2030. Other relevant goals include Goal 12 on sustainable consumption and production, Goal 13 on climate action, and Goal 17 on partnerships. The UN Convention reinforces the global agenda to Combat Desertification (UNCCD), as clarified by successive COP decisions, particularly COP12, which recognise that soil management is central to ecosystem services and food security.[30]

Notably, while the 2030 Agenda has significantly elevated soil-related concerns within global policy discourse, it is not, in itself, a decolonising instrument.[31] Indeed, critical scholarship argues that the SDGs' underlying architecture tends to work

29 See https://sdgs.un.org/goals, accessed 22 September 2025.

30 See https://www.unccd.int/land-and-life/land-degradation-neutrality/overview, accessed 22 September 2025; UNCCD-SPI Technical Series No. 01, Scientific Conceptual Framework for Land Degradation Neutrality. A Report of the Science-Policy Interface (2017).

31 Telleria (2022).

against decolonisation, remaining tethered to a notion of progress—and an unexamined commitment to economic growth—that helped to generate the very crisis the Agenda seeks to address; its inclusive language can operate as a 'rhetorical shield' that obscures economically driven aspirations.[32] Some scholars suggest that certain SDG targets and indicators implicitly prioritise individualist and consumption-driven development pathways, often measured through gross domestic product (GDP) growth, which may not align with the histories, values, and material realities of post-colonial societies.[33]

As a non-binding framework grounded in universal targets and indicators, the SDGs essentially abstract soil degradation from the historical and structural contexts in which it occurs. Colonial land dispossession, extractive agrarian economies, and the unequal distribution of environmental burdens are not explicitly addressed. Moreover, critics point to the underrepresentation of indigenous and local knowledge systems within the SDG framework.[34] Across Africa, long-standing practices such as crop rotation, intercropping, fallowing, and customary systems of land and water governance have sustained soil health, biodiversity, and community resilience for generations. Yet these knowledge systems are seldom treated as coequal sources of authority. Instead, the emphasis on standardised indicators and global metrics risks marginalising context-specific approaches and discouraging alternative development pathways that prioritise social equity, ecological sustainability, and cultural continuity over narrow economic growth.[35]

As critical scholarship on SDG 15 has shown, the Agenda is notably thin on questions of limits and tends to privilege indicator-driven conservation and management over distributive justice and shared decision-making.[36] In this sense, the Agenda risks flattening historical asymmetries and recasting deeply political questions of land and soil governance as technical challenges of management, capacity, and monitoring.[37] At the same time, the 2030 Agenda creates important normative openings.[38] By recognising land degradation neutrality, ecosystem integrity, climate–soil linkages, and participatory governance, it provides discursive and institutional footholds through which soil can be reframed as a shared ecological commons rather than a mere factor of production. However, as decolonial critiques caution, such openings remain fragile when rights, equity, and interdependencies are not explicitly embedded in the design and implementation of goals, and when participation is implied rather than legally or institutionally secured.[39] Whether these openings translate into

32 Keet & Rafaely (2025: 470–474).
33 Cordonier Segger & Olawuyi (2025: 657–658).
34 Ibid.: 662.
35 Ibid.
36 For a discussion, see Krauss (2021).
37 Hall (2019).
38 Porter & Cook (2023).
39 Triki (2022).

decolonising outcomes depends on how the Agenda is interpreted and operationalised, particularly whether indigenous knowledge systems are treated as co-equal sources of authority, whether soil data and indicators remain locally governed, and whether implementation is linked to tenure reform, distributive justice, and community stewardship.

Beyond the UNCCD, the Food and Agriculture Organization of the UN (FAO) has spearheaded soil-specific initiatives. The Global Soil Partnership (GSP), established in 2011, mobilises governments, academia, civil society, and the private sector to advance sustainable soil management.[40] Its outputs include the Voluntary Guidelines for Sustainable Soil Management (VGSSM), providing structured guidance for policymakers and practitioners, as well as the International Code of Conduct for the Sustainable Use and Management of Fertilisers (2019), which addresses nutrient imbalances and soil pollution while promoting regulation, labelling, education, and responsible use throughout the fertiliser chain.

At the continental level, the AU's Agenda 2063—"the Africa We Want"—outlines a long-term vision for inclusive growth and sustainable development, including secure land tenure, agroforestry, and conservation agriculture. However, soils are not always explicitly mentioned.[41] The 2003 Maputo Declaration on Agriculture and Food Security (Assembly/AU/Decl. 7(II)) committed Heads of State to allocating at least 10% of their national budgets to agriculture and rural development and to implementing the Comprehensive Africa Agriculture Development Programme (CAADP). Under CAADP, Pillar I on "sustainable land and water management" promotes integrated soil fertility management to conserve and enhance soil health. The Malabo Declaration on Accelerated Agricultural Growth and Transformation for Shared Prosperity and Improved Livelihoods (Assembly/AU/Decl. 1(XXIII), June 2014) set time-bound targets—including ending hunger by 2025—thereby placing soil health and conservation at the heart of productivity and resilience.

The African Soil Partnership (AfSP), launched in 2015, represents a coordinated effort to unlock Africa's soil potential, enhancing agricultural productivity and improving food security.[42] Its Regional Implementation Plan (2016) prioritises food security, land restoration, and climate resilience, acknowledging that by 2030, population growth will place unprecedented pressure on soils and rural livelihoods.

Several AU declarations and frameworks further integrate soil into broader agricultural and climate strategies.[43] The Framework and Guidelines on Land Policy

40 See https://www.fao.org/global-soil-partnership/en/, accessed 22 September 2025.

41 See also the Comprehensive African Agricultural Development Programme (CAADP), which is an Agenda 2063 continental initiative designed to promote agricultural development and food security across Africa. It was established by the AU in 2003 as part of the New Partnership for Africa's Development (NEPAD) and is endorsed by African heads of state and government.

42 See https://www.fao.org/global-soil-partnership/regional-partnerships/africa/en/, accessed 22 September 2025.

43 Kassner & Ruppel (2025).

in Africa (2010), developed in collaboration with the UN Economic Commission for Africa (UNECA) and the African Development Bank (AfDB), provide an analytical foundation for secure tenure and sustainable land use. Earlier, the Sirte Declaration (2004) underscored the interdependence of water and agriculture, calling for integrated responses to soil and water degradation. More recently, the AU Climate Change and Resilient Development Strategy and Action Plan (2022–2032) emphasises building resilience through governance reform and adaptation, highlighting soil biodiversity and soil organic carbon as essential to productivity, erosion control, and carbon mitigation.

The AU has also begun to institutionalise soil health as a continental priority. The Soil Initiative for Africa (SIA), launched in 2020, envisions long-term improvements through coordinated policies, programmes, and institutional frameworks.[44] This momentum was reinforced at the Africa Fertiliser and Soil Health Summit (2024) in Nairobi.[45] Under the theme "Listen to the Land", heads of state adopted the Nairobi Declaration, committing to boosting fertiliser production, strengthening smallholder livelihoods, and combating soil degradation. Its ten-year Action Plan now provides a concrete roadmap for governments and stakeholders across Africa.

Taken together, these global and African frameworks increasingly position soil governance at the nexus of food security, climate resilience, and sustainable development. Yet as the country studies in the previous volume of this book demonstrated, the challenge lies less in the absence of policies than in their implementation.[46] International commitments often remain rhetorical, with limited impact on soils and the communities that depend on them.

The UNCCD, often referred to as "Africa's Convention", is perhaps the most directly relevant international instrument for soils. Yet its record is mixed. It has been dubbed the "Cinderella Convention"—"the one that did not make it to the ball"—because of limited attention and funding compared to other environmental treaties, despite its centrality to land management.[47] National Action Plans are often disconnected from mainstream policies, while institutional fragmentation hinders their implementation.[48] Although participation is formally emphasised, local communities—the true custodians of soils—are still too often marginalised.[49] Similar shortcomings mark the UN's sister conventions on climate change and biodiversity, where weak coordination, unreliable funding, and largely declaratory outcomes remain the norm.[50] Global processes, thus, absorb scarce political and financial resources

44 See https://faraafrica.org/soil-initiative-for-africa/, accessed 22 September 2025.
45 See https://au.int/en/AFSH-2024, accessed 22 September 2025.
46 Ruppel et al. (2025).
47 Laurens (2023: 41).
48 UNCCD (2019: 54).
49 Ibid.: 47-52.
50 Akhtar-Schuster et al. (2024).

while concrete action on the ground lags, leaving millions exposed to the daily realities of soil and land degradation.

The consequences are stark. Only around 8% of Africa's land area is covered by soils relatively free from natural constraints to agriculture.[51] Much of the land under cultivation lies in areas unsuitable for farming, while other seemingly suitable areas remain underutilised. Degradation has accelerated as inappropriate practices, often driven by short-term economic pressures, ignore ecological limits. These pressures are compounded by rural poverty, which limits farmers' ability to adopt sustainable practices. The outcome is sobering: an estimated 65% of arable land, 30% of grazing land, and 20% of forests are already degraded across Africa.[52] This widespread decline undermines not only agricultural productivity but also ecological resilience, threatening food security and livelihoods for millions.

This dense web of global and regional frameworks has successfully elevated soil health onto the international policy agenda. Yet as the stark statistics on degradation confirm, charters, declarations, and voluntary guidelines have proven insufficient to reverse the tide, highlighting a broader failure to match political rhetoric with tangible resources and political will. Thus, the future of soil governance in Africa depends on its ability to move beyond the conference room and into the field. This means directly aligning global funding and continental strategies with national and local priorities, empowering communities as central actors in restoration, and ensuring that newer initiatives are measured not by their adoption but by their ability to bridge this very gap.

## 3. Rethinking the challenge: colonial legacies, climate justice, and restitution

In recent years, soil has become a significant concern in social theory, with scholars examining how its materiality interacts with social institutions and cultural imaginings.[53] Far from being an ahistorical substrate, soil is continuously reshaped by human activity and nonhuman forces alike, from the work of earthworms to the application of fertilisers.[54]

For much of the nineteenth and twentieth centuries, "Africa" was narrated through European experience, bureaucratic circulation, and expert reporting. Colonial services rotated officers across territories; as impressions hardened into consensus, London was briefed in the form of generalities.[55] Expert reports often privileged opinion over data,

51 Tetteh (2019: 3).
52 Ibid.
53 Krzywoszynska & Marchesi (2020); Tironi et al. (2021).
54 Meulemans (2020); Clark & Foster (2012).
55 Showers (2006: 121).

laying the groundwork for what Roe later called "crisis narratives."[56] Soil sat at the centre of these stories—laterisation, desertification, fertility decline—frequently blamed on African land users.[57] Late-century debates about "nutrient mining" in the Sahel replicated the pattern: coarse erosion estimates, semi-quantitative nutrient data with wide error margins, and then regional upscaling presented as scientific fact.[58]

A more extended history ties these narratives to systems of exploitation. In *Capitalism and Slavery*, Williams demonstrated that intensive monocrop cultivation in the Caribbean, particularly of tobacco and sugar, led to the rapid depletion of fertile soils. He described this dynamic as the "law of slave production": slavery relied on a cheap, subordinated labour force, discouraging innovations such as crop rotation or scientific farming, while accelerating land depletion.[59] Slavery's most significant defect, Williams observed, was that it "quickly exhausts the soil."[60] No region escaped this logic, as plantation agriculture systematically degraded vast tracts of fertile land.

Rodney extended this analysis in *How Europe Underdeveloped Africa*, emphasising that underdevelopment was not merely economic but also ecological and social.[61] Before colonialism, Africans had cultivated sophisticated ecological knowledge, understanding soils, climates, plants, and their interrelations.[62] This supported diversified agriculture that maintained fertility and ecological balance. Colonialism, however, imposed monocultures—such as rubber in Liberia, cocoa in Ghana, cotton in Uganda, coffee in Angola, and sisal in Tanzania—that steadily impoverished the land.[63] Rodney noted that these crops were "very demanding on the soil," and their widespread cultivation directly contributed to desertification in regions such as Senegal, Niger, and Chad.[64]

Together, Williams and Rodney identify three features of colonial soil degradation. First, the primary divide was not between town and country, as in Europe, but between metropole and colony: Caribbean and African soils were sacrificed for European prosperity, only to be abandoned later.[65] Second, soil exhaustion in the colonies did not provoke a crisis for the colonisers.[66] While Africans faced hunger and malnutrition, European markets remained supplied and profits secure.[67] Third, whereas soil shortages in Europe spurred scientific innovation, such as the development of fertilisers, colonial authorities suppressed comparable improvements in Africa,

56 Roe (1991); Roe (1995).
57 Showers (2006: 122).
58 Ibid.
59 Williams (1944: 145).
60 Ibid.: 7.
61 Davidson & da Silva (2024: 8–9).
62 Rodney (1981: 40).
63 Davidson & da Silva (2024: 9).
64 Rodney (1981: 219).
65 Davidson & da Silva (2024: 10).
66 Williams (1944: 7).
67 Rodney (1981: 236).

devoting negligible resources to agricultural research.[68] The result was a dual process: Africa's economic underdevelopment and the environmental degradation of its soils, each reinforcing the other.[69] Colonial soil regimes exemplify how racial capitalism depleted not only human life but also the very ground beneath it.

These dynamics were particularly stark in South Africa. Before colonisation, African communities practised small-scale mixed farming on communally owned land, producing crops and livestock for subsistence and trade. Before apartheid-era restrictions, the productivity gap between black and white farmers was minimal.[70] Subsequent laws, however, reserved 87% of arable land for white commercial agriculture, confining the African majority to just 13%.[71] Overcrowding made African farming increasingly unsustainable and severed communities from their traditional modes of soil stewardship.

The structural effects of this dispossession persist at the continental scale. According to an African Development Bank survey, 64% of Africa's total land area is currently owned by the state and other institutions, while 36% is privately owned.[72] Much of this state land is leased to farmers through concessions, a system that directly descends from colonial frameworks of expropriation and state control. This ownership pattern illustrates how colonial logics of land alienation and bureaucratic allocation continue to shape access to land, reinforcing tenure insecurities and inequities.

Today, Africa's soil governance challenges remain as much legal and institutional as ecological. Many states still operate under outdated frameworks that fail to integrate indigenous systems of stewardship or reflect contemporary realities.[73] This "colonisation of the law" has resulted in fragmented responsibilities, conflicting tenure regimes, and a weak recognition of soil health in environmental legislation. Meanwhile, foreign investment laws often privilege extractive industries—such as mining, oil, and industrial agriculture—over conservation, perpetuating the exploitative patterns of the colonial era.

These dynamics are increasingly mirrored in contemporary global development frameworks. Related critiques highlight how the SDGs, despite their universal ambitions, may inadvertently reproduce forms of neo-colonial economic dependence. Their emphasis on foreign investment, trade liberalisation, and market-based reform can reinforce reliance on external capital and global markets, often enabling foreign actors to extract value from land, labour, and natural resources while local communities experience limited benefits.[74] In some contexts, this has been associated with ecological degradation, social displacement, gender-based violence, and the

68 Clark & Foster (2012); Rodney (1981: 221).
69 Davidson & da Silva (2024: 9).
70 Davis (2022: 195).
71 Ibid.
72 See https://african.land/blog/article/africas-land-ownership-who-owns-most-of-the-land-b91.
73 Ruppel et al. (2025).
74 Cordonier Segger & Olawuyi (2025: 661).

erosion of cultural heritage, while profits are repatriated abroad. At the same time, neoliberal policy approaches linked to development reform may deepen internal inequalities, as privatisation and liberalisation reduce access to essential resources and expose small-scale farmers and local producers to unfair competition from subsidised imports.[75] Informal economies and subsistence systems—central to livelihoods across much of Africa—are frequently undervalued within such frameworks.

The manner in which the SDGs are implemented further reinforces these concerns. Implementation is often characterised as top-down, driven by international institutions and national governments rather than grounded in genuine local ownership. This risks reproducing colonial dynamics in which development is done to communities rather than with them.[76] In addition, the SDGs' reliance on technocratic and measurement-based models of progress privileges quantitative indicators, despite significant challenges in data collection across many post-colonial contexts. More fundamentally, this emphasis may obscure qualitative dimensions of development, including cultural well-being, dignity, social cohesion, and lived experience, while failing to capture the value of indigenous knowledge and community-based practices.[77]

Land grabbing has emerged as a modern extension of these historical injustices. The FAO defines land grabbing as "the control (whether through ownership, lease, concession, contracts, quotas, or general power) of larger than locally typical amounts of land by any persons or entities (public or private, foreign or domestic) via any means ('legal' or 'illegal') for purposes of speculation, extraction, resource control or commodification at the expense of agroecology, land stewardship, food sovereignty and human rights."[78] Public spending on agriculture in developing countries is limited, especially in Africa, and bank lending to the sector is likewise modest.[79] To close this financing gap, many governments have sought to attract foreign direct investment into agriculture, aiming to facilitate technology transfer, create jobs, improve infrastructure, increase domestic output, and enhance product quality.[80] Yet these gains have not consistently materialised. Across Africa, this practice often mirrors the extractive logics of colonial dispossession, as vast tracts of fertile land are transferred to transnational corporations or elites under the guise of investment or development.[81] Such acquisitions frequently marginalise smallholder farmers, erode customary tenure systems, and disrupt local agroecological practices, thereby deepening rural poverty and accelerating soil degradation. According to the Land Matrix (2020), there are 1,805 concluded deals commonly labelled as "land grabbing," covering more than 50

75 Ibid.
76 Ibid.: 662.
77 Ibid.
78 See https://agrovoc.fao.org/browse/agrovoc/en/page/c_cc39a497?clang=et, accessed 26 October 2025.
79 Tulone et al. (2022: 1).
80 Ibid.
81 Ashukem & Ngang (2022).

million hectares worldwide; 32.8% of these are located in Africa.[82] Mozambique, Ethiopia, and Ghana are the most affected, together accounting for over a third of African deals—205 out of 592—spanning just under 4 million hectares, including about 2 million hectares in Mozambique alone.[83]

The colonial past was marked by violent subjugation, expropriation, and ecological devastation. Some injustices are visible in looted cultural artefacts still housed in European museums; others, such as soil exhaustion or the overuse of the global carbon budget by industrialised states, are less tangible but equally destructive. The connection between colonialism and present-day climate vulnerability is increasingly recognised. Climate indices reveal that the most climate-vulnerable countries are overwhelmingly former colonies.[84] Likewise, the Intergovernmental Panel on Climate Change's (IPCC) Sixth Assessment Report emphasises that "historical and ongoing patterns of inequity such as colonialism" have exacerbated exposure and diminished adaptive capacity.[85] In this sense, both climate change and colonialism distribute risks and vulnerabilities along unjust historical lines.

To respond effectively, it is necessary to move beyond narrow framings such as "desertification" and recognise the broader spectrum of soil degradation: erosion, nutrient depletion, compaction, salinisation, and the loss of organic matter. Most of these processes are anthropogenic, and even natural dynamics are now intensified by human-induced climate change. Addressing them requires a synergistic, adaptive approach that recognises soils as interconnected with water, biodiversity, culture, and livelihoods.

At the same time, soil has always carried meanings that exceed its role as a resource. Herder observed that just as plants thrive in their native soil but wither when transplanted, so too do people draw identity, belonging, and vitality from the ground in which they are rooted.[86] Soil, in this sense, is constitutive of cultural life, shaping and reshaping both human and nonhuman worlds.[87] Cabral developed this insight in explicitly anticolonial terms. For him, soil embodied both the planet's deep geological time and the immediate struggles of politics and production.[88] While colonialism devastated it through cash-crop extraction, Cabral insisted that soil must be treated as a "perennial good," enriched by each generation for the prosperity of the next.[89] More than a passive backdrop, soil was a ground of renewal: as he famously declared, the

82 Tulone et al. (2022: 2).
83 Ibid.
84 Osorio / Manuel / Irwin (2025).
85 IPCC (2022: 12).
86 Herder (2004).
87 Césaire (2012: 33).
88 Cabral (1988: 92); Davidson & da Silva (2024: 12–15).
89 Cabral (1988: 155).

struggle for liberation itself had "created a new man and a new woman on the soil of the African fatherland."[90]

### 3.1. Reparations in the context of climate justice

The UN has long recognised the principle of "common but differentiated responsibilities" in both mitigation and adaptation. Yet many Global North countries, particularly the US, have consistently resisted language that suggests "liability" for climate-related loss and damage.[91] Until COP27 in Sharm el-Sheikh, where parties finally agreed to establish a funding facility for "Loss and Damage," often framed as climate reparations, explicit references to reparations were largely absent from the United Nations Framework Convention on Climate Change (UNFCC) negotiations. Instead, discussions were couched in the technocratic language of "support" or "solidarity," carefully avoiding the politically charged notion of compensation for historical responsibility.[92]

Although climate change affects all countries, its consequences are not experienced in proportion to their impact.[93] The COVID-19 pandemic and the Russian invasion of Ukraine deepened Global South vulnerabilities, compounding debt crises even as extreme climate events became more frequent and destructive.[94] These converging pressures have made reparations claims increasingly urgent, not only as historical redress but also as an essential response to current global inequalities. A growing synergy has, therefore, emerged between the reparations agenda and resistance to what has been described as "climate apartheid": a world where the wealthy insulate themselves from ecological harms while the poor suffer their full force.[95] Despite being responsible for the bulk of historical and ongoing carbon emissions, the Global North has externalised the most severe impacts onto the Global South.[96] Sultana terms this "climate coloniality": the entanglement of Eurocentric hegemony, neocolonialism, racial capitalism, and military domination in producing climate impacts that disproportionately harm racialised and marginalised populations.[97]

A notable feature of global reparations demands, despite their diversity, is their consistent direction towards the same set of countries. Whether the issue concerns slavery and the Atlantic slave trade, colonialism, racial discrimination, genocide, or climate injustice, reparations are overwhelmingly sought from the centres of global

90 Cabral (1973: 25).
91 Fitz-Henry & Klein (2024: 2).
92 Ibid.
93 Malherbe & Oladejo (2025).
94 Fischer & Storm (2023).
95 Long (2024).
96 Hickel (2020).
97 Sultana (2022: 4).

wealth and power. These include Western Europe, the US, Canada, Australia, and New Zealand—countries whose prosperity has historically been built on systems of exploitation and colonisation. Japan is generally included only in relation to broader claims addressed to the "Global North" or "rich countries," such as debt cancellation or climate reparations, rather than specifically in connection with slavery or colonialism.[98] As Acemoglu, Johnson, and Robinson demonstrate, colonial institutions play a central role in these asymmetries. While the North's development pathways fostered strong political and economic institutions, the South inherited extractive systems that entrenched dependency, led to export-oriented economies, and deepened inequalities. These legacies persist, amplifying climate vulnerability and limiting adaptive capacity.[99] A recent study finds that, irrespective of the form or timing of colonisation, it is a significant predictor of a country's climate vulnerability.[100]

One striking feature of reparations debates is their selectivity. Not every historical injustice gives rise to reparations claims today. We do not, for instance, see German calls for compensation for the Allied bombings of Dresden, nor American claims for Pearl Harbour, nor restitution demands for the British burning of the White House in 1814.[101] These events are acknowledged as historical wrongs but are not perceived to structure present inequalities. Reparations gain traction only where past harms continue to shape current distributions of rights, resources, and opportunities. Reparations in such contexts are not backwards-looking charity, but forward-looking repair measures that unwind durable causal chains (such as unjust enrichment and continuing violations) and align the remedy with the current locus of advantage and disadvantage.

Today, such claims have gained prominence to the point that world leaders can no longer dismiss them. Just before COP28 in 2023, John Kerry, then US Climate Envoy, declared that the US would not "under any circumstances" pay climate reparations.[102] In Europe, governments have made modest acknowledgements of slavery and colonial violence, but carefully avoid the term "reparations" and the legal obligations it implies.[103] Consider Germany's engagement with Namibia over colonial atrocities against the Ovaherero and Nama, widely recognised as the first genocide of the twentieth century.[104] Since its independence in 1990, Berlin has established a 'special relationship' based on moral and historical—rather than legal—responsibilities, providing some of the highest per-capita development assistance in its African partnerships.[105] In 2021, Germany formally acknowledged the genocide and

98 Sylla et al. (2024: 586).
99 Acemoglu et al. (2001).
100 Osorio et al. (2025).
101 Wenar (2006: 402).
102 See www.bbc.com/news/world-us-canada-66197366, accessed 22 September 2025.
103 Sylla et al. (2024).
104 Graf (2025: 4).
105 Ibid.

announced a EUR 1.1 billion, 30-year "reconciliation and development programme," explicitly avoiding the terms "reparations" or "compensation."[106] These initiatives have been criticised as tokenistic and entangled with strategic interests, such as Germany's ambitions in Namibia's green hydrogen sector.[107]

Notably, the main public international law obstacle to classifying the atrocities committed against the Herero and Nama by Germany as "genocide" lies in the principle of intertemporal law—the rule that legal acts must be assessed according to the law in force at the time they occurred.[108] When the events took place between 1904 and 1908, no treaty or customary international norm prohibiting genocide yet existed. The 1948 Convention on the Prevention and Punishment of the Crime of Genocide codified the term only after Raphael Lemkin coined it in 1944.[109] Thus, while the crimes clearly satisfy the material elements of genocide under contemporary standards, they cannot be retroactively prosecuted or give rise to state responsibility, as international law generally prohibits *ex post facto* application of criminal norms.[110] Moreover, neither the *ius in bello* applicable at the time nor the 1885 Berlin Congo Act, which merely required colonial powers to protect indigenous populations, created a legally enforceable duty that would have established liability for Germany.[111] Consequently, the atrocities fall outside the binding scope of the 1948 Convention, despite their political recognition as genocide.

Rather than accepting liability, leaders in the Global North have positioned aid as the primary means of achieving climate justice.[112] Yet this framing risks depoliticising reparations by recasting them as charity rather than obligation, while perpetuating neocolonial dependency.[113] Aid, far from being neutral, often functions as conditional finance, entrenching donor leverage.[114] The suspension of US aid to South Africa in early 2025—framed as opposition to land reform but widely seen as political coercion—illustrates how vital programmes can be weaponised, turning dependency into a diplomatic tool.[115]

Aid also deepens debt. Assistance often arrives in the form of loans, requiring repayment through volatile primary commodity exports, which siphon wealth back to the Global North and narrow policy space in the South.[116] Development is then

106 See https://www.bbc.com/news/articles/cy0jkynyln2o, accessed 22 September 2025.
107 De Vita & Goschler (2025); Gabor & Sylla (2023).
108 Ruppel & Schweighofer (2024).
109 Melber (2024: 5).
110 Ruppel & Schweighofer (2024).
111 Ibid.
112 Malherbe & Oladejo (2025).
113 Holmes (2012); Morvaridi (2012).
114 Malherbe & Oladejo (2025); Amin (2009).
115 See https://www.theguardian.com/us-news/2025/mar/06/aid-trump-south-africa; and also https://issafrica.org/iss-today/trump-s-funding-cuts-will-hurt-south-africa-and-the-region, accessed 22 September 2025.
116 Malherbe & Oladejo (2025); Tandon (2011).

narrowly defined in economistic terms—GDP growth, exports, liberalisation—while more equitable, community-based models are sidelined.[117] In this sense, climate aid represents continuity rather than rupture: most climate finance remains tied to Official Development Assistance mechanisms, despite agreements that it should be additional.[118]

This framing also sustains paternalistic narratives. Donor states and NGOs often depict Africa as "the last Eden," a place requiring external guardianship, while obscuring the North's dependence on Southern resources and ecosystems.[119] As Sultana observes, climate aid discourse positions donor countries as "saviours" or sole proprietors of climate solutions.[120] This framing enables them to determine what constitutes a solution, who is deemed worthy of assistance, and under what conditions, while simultaneously obscuring the Global North's historical and ongoing complicity in the climate crisis.[121] As Amin observed, the fundamental asymmetry lies in the opposite direction: the North is dependent on the South for raw materials, labour, and ecological space.[122] Such narratives conceal the structural reality that the Global North itself depends on the extraction of resources from, and the dumping of waste into, the Global South. Recognising this opens the possibility of South–South solidarity—building coalitions that resist climate coloniality and hold governments in the Global South accountable for their commitments to grassroots struggles.[123]

Still, Amin cautions against abrupt withdrawal from aid structures, which would carry severe short-term consequences for dependent states.[124] The challenge, then, is to develop reparative alternatives that avoid reproducing dependency. Reparations, unlike aid, are not acts of charity but mechanisms of justice: structural efforts to repair and redress harms rooted in colonialism, neocolonialism, and climate coloniality.[125] For Kelley, reparations mean redistributing wealth, remaking institutions, and fostering socio-economic arrangements that prioritise autonomy and equity.[126] For Táíwò, any "politically serious reparations project (…) must focus on climate justice," given the centrality of climate change to today's global order.[127]

The principles of reparations, however, remain contested. Current frameworks often rely on descriptive baselines of harm—recognising only those demonstrably worse off than before—rather than normative baselines of what could legitimately be

117 Amin (2009).
118 Malherbe & Oladejo (2025); Okoth (2023); Langan (2018); Wu et al. (2021).
119 Nsah (2023); Vasko (2022).
120 Sultana (2022).
121 Malherbe & Oladejo (2025).
122 Amin (2009).
123 Malherbe & Oladejo (2025); Ndlovu-Gatsheni et al. (2018: 127).
124 Amin (2009).
125 Malherbe & Oladejo (2025).
126 Kelley (2002).
127 Táíwò (2022: 157).

expected.[128] This risks excluding structural and intergenerational harms. Narrow accounts nonetheless find support in backwards-looking rationales (repairing moral disruption) and forward-looking rationales (deterring future violations, restoring victims' life chances).[129] Yet the most compelling accounts frame reparations not simply as restitution but as transformation.

Táíwò identifies three conceptualisations: reparations as reconciliation (relationship repair), as restitution or retribution (harm repair), and as transformation (worldmaking).[130] The latter, he argues, is most urgent in the climate context: reparations must reconfigure the global racial empire created by colonialism and slavery. This means cancelling illegitimate debts, transferring resources to marginalised communities, divesting from fossil fuels, restructuring global tax regimes, and creating decentralised, community-owned energy systems.[131] Reparations here are not backwards-looking compensation, but forward-looking world-making—projects of equity, solidarity, and planetary repair.

This worldmaking vision requires dismantling systems of unequal distribution, addressing what Achiume calls "global racial sacrifice zones"—lands and communities rendered uninhabitable through extraction and pollution.[132] It demands attention to long colonial histories and to future generations, insists on transnational approaches that transcend methodological nationalism, and embraces pluriversality—the idea of "a world in which many worlds can be embraced."[133]

The Cochabamba People's Agreement of 2010 provided an early expression of this vision, advancing demands related to climate debt, the decolonisation of the atmosphere, and the establishment of a Climate Justice Tribunal.[134] Importantly, it emphasised that reparations must not be limited to financial transfers but must also encompass restorative justice for soils, forests, water, and ecosystems.[135]

Monetary reparations remain essential, but structural reforms must accompany them.[136] From a social justice perspective, reparations confront the legacies of racism, slavery, and colonialism. From a climate justice perspective, they address ecological debt by compensating the Global South for the disproportionate harms it has suffered and enabling a just transition.[137] These claims have been further bolstered by the IPCC's findings, which underscore the uneven vulnerabilities and responsibilities within the global climate regime.[138] Small Island Developing States such as Barbados

128 Wenar (2006).
129 Ibid.
130 Taiwo (2022).
131 Ibid.
132 Ibid.: 74; Achiume (2022).
133 Fitz-Henry & Klein (2024: 7).
134 Ibid.
135 Ajl (2021).
136 Schmelzer (2022).
137 Sylla et al. (2024).
138 IPCC (2022).

have been particularly vocal, linking slavery's historical injustices with contemporary debt and climate vulnerability.[139]

These claims also resonate with earlier Pan-African initiatives. As early as 1992, the Organisation of African Unity (OAU), the AU's predecessor, established a Group of Eminent Persons to spearhead reparations, framing debt cancellation as partial compensation for the legacy of slavery and colonialism.[140] The Abuja Pan-African Conference on Reparations (1993) and the Truth Commission Conference in Accra (1999)[141] further linked reparations to processes of truth-telling and historical reckoning. Reparations in climate politics thus form part of a much deeper continuum of struggles for justice in the Global South.

Beyond these normative and instrumental justifications, some scholars highlight the strategic power of reparations claims. As Tan argues, "arguments about reparation can supplement arguments about global equality by providing additional motivation for compliance with the demands of egalitarian justice."[142] The principle of reparation appeals more directly to people's moral sensibilities than the abstract duty of justice to assist distant others, making it more effective at motivating both the public and policymakers to take action. However, as Engerman argues, regret and apology fall short without concrete redress.[143] Reparations extend beyond symbolic gestures; they are concrete mechanisms of redress, framed as debts that can be repaid through monetary payments, institutional reforms, or structural transformations. Conceptually, reparations differ from social reforms in that the latter entail ongoing responsibilities to restructure institutions until genuine equity is achieved. Lahiri and Darity concur, noting that development assistance in areas such as health, education, infrastructure, technology transfers, and preferential trade schemes is better understood as international economic support rather than "reparations."[144] Such measures address some visible consequences of inequality but do not systematically redress the historical injustices at its root. Nonetheless, they argue that these supply-side measures can deliver more sustainable outcomes—a potential "win-win"—compared to purely monetary payments, which risk being consumed without altering underlying structures and may be offset by substitution and price effects.[145]

Significantly, climate reparations should not be reduced to economic or financialised terms, as in climate aid, which strips them of their political content.[146] Reparations may include debt repudiation, halting the Global North's ongoing "atmospheric colonisation," and eco-industrialisation oriented towards meeting

139 Sylla et al. (2024).
140 Ibid.
141 Howard-Hassmann (2004).
142 Tan (2007).
143 Engerman (2009).
144 Lahiri & Darity Jr. (2024).
145 Ibid.
146 DuFord (2022).

people's needs rather than generating profit.[147] It also necessitates an end to environmentally destructive industrial expansion and militarism, much of which is driven by Global North states and corporations.[148]

Ultimately, reparations must be understood not as aid or charity, but as recognition of a social and ecological debt.[149] They demand structural change: the repudiation of illegitimate debt, the halting of atmospheric colonisation, and the creation of economies oriented toward life rather than profit. They also demand legislative transformation—remaking law itself to centre planetary repair and justice.[150] To call for reparations in the climate context is to reject the depoliticised logic of aid and to affirm an emancipatory politics in which soils, ecologies, and communities lie at the heart of global climate justice.

### 3.2. Restitution of cultural artefacts

"African heritage can no longer be the prisoner of European museums."[151] Today, it is estimated that up to 90% of Sub-Saharan Africa's cultural heritage is held outside the continent.[152] Germany's Berlin museums are among the most extensive repositories, holding about 75,000 objects of colonial provenance.[153] Paris and London also stand out: the Musée du Quai Branly houses roughly 70,000 items, and the British Museum houses about 69,000.[154] In Tervuren, near Brussels, the Royal Museum for Central Africa houses approximately 180,000 pieces from the Belgian colonial era.[155]

Seen in cultural-historical terms, the issue is larger than the number of custody counts. If we understand historical culture as the "practically effective articulation of historical consciousness in the life of a society," then debates over the restitution of objects taken under colonial rule touch every dimension of that culture.[156] These debates reveal that a society's historical culture is formed in—and altered by—its past and present interactions with others.[157] In contesting shared histories, a transnational historical culture emerges, one with tangible global effects. Yet it is not consensual by

147 Sultana (2022); Bond & Sharife (2009).
148 Bigger et al. (2023).
149 Hunt-Hendrix & Taylor (2024).
150 Malherbe & Oladejo (2025).
151 Hunt (2019: 1).
152 See https://africasacountry.com/2024/11/why-are-african-artifacts-everywhere-but-africa, accessed 22 September 2025.
153 Sandkühler et al. (2023: 22).
154 Ibid.
155 Ibid.
156 Ibid: 24.
157 Ibid.

default: the historical cultures of different societies shape one another asymmetrically, sometimes fostering mutual understanding and recognition, and sometimes not.[158]
At the UN General Assembly in 1973, for example, Zaire's president, Mobutu Sese Seko, advocated a UN resolution on restitution:

> During the colonial period, we suffered not only from colonialism, slavery, economic exploitation, but also and above all from the barbarous, systematic pillaging of all our works of art. In this way the rich countries appropriated our best, our unique works of art, and we are therefore poor not only economically but also culturally (...) I would also ask this General Assembly to adopt a resolution requesting the rich Powers which possess works of art of the poor countries to restore some of them so that we can teach our children and our grandchildren the history of their countries.[159]

The call for restitution has gained growing momentum over the past two decades. In 2007, the UN Declaration on the Rights of Indigenous Peoples (Article 11) urged states to restore "cultural, intellectual, religious and spiritual property" taken without the free, prior, and informed consent of indigenous peoples.[160] Concrete demands soon followed. In 2009, Egypt requested that the Louvre return fragments from the tomb of Tetaki.[161] In 2012, Nigeria sought the repatriation of 32 objects from the Museum of Fine Arts, Boston—artefacts looted during Britain's 1897 raid on the Royal Palaces of Abomey.[162] In 2017, Nigeria renewed its appeals to the British Museum for the celebrated Benin Bronzes, following Benin's formal petition to France the previous year.[163] At the heart of these claims lies a simple principle: people should be able to encounter their cultural heritage in its place of origin, to engage with it directly, and to transmit it to future generations.

In the capital of the West African country Burkina Faso, Ouagadougou, French President Emmanuel Macron declared on 28 November 2017, the eve of the Africa-Europe Summit at the University of Ouagadougou:

> I refuse to (...) refer back to [always] the same perceptions of the past (...) I am from a generation of French people for whom the crimes of European colonization cannot be disputed and are part of our history (...) The first remedy is culture. In this area, I cannot accept that a large share of several African countries' cultural heritage [is] kept in France (...) African heritage cannot solely exist in private collections and European museums (...) Within five years, I want the conditions to exist for temporary or permanent returns of African heritage to Africa.[164]

Among the treasures taken from Southern Africa are royal regalia, sacred objects, ceremonial masks, and ancestral remains—seized during military campaigns or obtained through exploitative means.[165] Though now housed abroad, these items

158 Ibid.
159 Ibid.: 19.
160 Among other international instruments, see Klesmith (2014).
161 Hunt (2019: 2).
162 Ibid
163 Ibid.
164 Sandkühler et al. (2023: 1).
165 See https://www.unesco.org/en/articles/reframing-return-and-restitution-cultural-property-southern-africa-healing-new-bold-step-toward, accessed 22 September 2025.

remain vital to cultural continuity and spiritual life. Their removal fractured identities and interrupted traditions, leaving wounds that endure:

> Above all else, we need to acknowledge that returning artefacts to their rightful owners is not just about the politics of value. It is a process that is meant to rehumanise what had been classified as objects. True justice lies in granting these communities the autonomy to determine how their artifacts are preserved, interpreted, and engaged with globally. This self-determination is not merely a right; it is the foundation of healing.[166]

The Benin Bronzes epitomise this struggle. Crafted by Edo artisans to symbolise royal authority, religion, and history, they were violently seized during the British punitive expedition of 1897 and dispersed to museums across Europe and North America.[167] Their absence marked a profound rupture in collective memory. Today, they remain in institutions such as the British Museum, the Metropolitan Museum of Art, and the Humboldt Forum. In such settings, scale is not neutral. The scale of a holding conditions its interpretation: with a few dozen objects, each piece can be encountered on its own terms; once a collection runs to several hundred, storage and rotation are unavoidable, and curatorial design begins to script the narrative—its themes, intended audiences and the meanings assigned to the works.[168] Flower Manase summed it up so aptly: "You have the objects, we have the knowledge."[169] Campaigns for their return, framed not as property recovery but as historical redress and cultural renewal.[170] As critics observe, "because they are in Europe rather than in their place of birth, misinterpretation is easy."[171] Misattribution, distortion, and the imposition of Western aesthetic categories have perpetuated a cultural enslavement that restitution seeks to undo.[172]

Thus, when it comes to the restitution of objects from colonial collections, it is more than a legal transaction; it is a matter of justice and moral reparation.[173] Cultural heritage—whether monuments, artworks, or ritual objects—matters not only as an educational resource or commodity but as a living bond between past and present.[174] For African nations, these bonds became especially urgent after decolonisation, with artefacts embraced as sources of pride, identity, and continuity.[175] Against this, cultural internationalism—the claim that heritage belongs to "all humanity" and can be stewarded anywhere—reveals its flaws.[176] Its proponents add that there was no historical legal obligation to restitution; that "universal" museums hold objects in trust

---

166 Ibid.
167 Idugie & Onochie (2025: 71).
168 Sandkühler et al. (2023: 43).
169 Habermas (2023: 111).
170 Idugie & Onochie (2025).
171 Agorsah (1977: 306).
172 Ibid.
173 Habermas (2023).
174 Klesmith (2014).
175 Ibid.
176 Ibid.

for world heritage rather than for any one nation; and that removal to Northern collections "saved" many items from neglect or destruction.[177] Yet visitors in London, Paris, or New York may learn something about African cultures, while citizens of the originating states are denied access to the very artefacts that embody their histories. The question is unavoidable: how can a people preserve their culture if they are deprived of its most tangible expressions?

The demand for restitution extends beyond artefacts to other enduring symbols of colonial extraction. South Africa has repeatedly called for the return of diamonds embedded in the British Crown Jewels. Chief among these are stones cut from the Cullinan diamond (the largest gem-quality rough diamond ever discovered), unearthed in 1905 and presented to King Edward VII two years later by the settler-dominated Transvaal government.[178] Britain insists the gift was voluntary. According to Savoy and Sarr, however, all African cultural property should ultimately be repatriated, albeit in phases; provenance—whether military seizure, market purchase, or scholarly collection—does not change the fact that dealings under stark power imbalances are inherently unjust.[179] The decision to "gift" the diamond was divisive even at the time. The Transvaal Legislative Assembly ultimately voted in favour of making the gift by a margin of 42 votes to 19. Still, opposition came not only from African communities, who were wholly excluded from political participation, but also from sections of the Afrikaner population bitter about Britain's role in the devastating South African War. As Lord Selborne later noted to the King, many had spoken and voted with "heavy hearts."[180] Read through that lens, assessing whether such transfers were "gifts" or acts of coercion demands more than labels: it requires a context-sensitive inquiry that scrutinises the scientific, legal, historical, and ethical frameworks—and the comparison practices—that shaped how legitimacy was defined at the time.[181] The Cullinan diamonds thus occupy a grey zone between gift and coercion, a contested legacy that remains at the heart of present debates.

Any credible approach must take into account the context. It is not acceptable to ignore the scale and character of colonial violence in a particular case simply because a given transfer was formally "non-violent."[182] Recognising that background, restitution can function as reparation—helping to make amends and to address colonial injustice—but only if it forms part of a comprehensive, trustworthy process backed by the descendants of those affected.[183] Such processes obligate states and engage entire societies, yet the institutions that hold colonial-era collections bear a special duty to

177 Habermas (2023).

178 See https://theconversation.com/south-african-diamonds-adorn-the-crown-of-king-charles-why-theyre-unlikely-to-be-returned-205597, accessed 22 September 2025.

179 Nietzel (2023: 161).

180 Guest (2007: 120).

181 Habermas (2023).

182 Hackmack & Kaleck (2023: 411).

183 Ibid.

act credibly.[184] They may face difficult choices and sometimes find restitution imperative. This, in turn, requires cooperation with societies of origin, non-bureaucratic access to information, and attention to remembrance and commemoration.[185]

Still, as regards other objects, momentum is shifting. More than 1,000 Benin Bronzes have now been repatriated to Nigeria.[186] In 2024, the UK announced the return of 32 treasures looted from the Asante King to Ghana.[187] French museums have restored El Hadj Oumar Tall's sabre to Senegal and 26 artefacts to Benin.[188] In 2021, the Dutch government committed to the unconditional return of objects removed from former colonies.[189] These gestures mark real progress, but countless artefacts remain scattered across the globe, withheld from the communities to which they belong.

Crucially, no museum currently operates under an automatic return policy.[190] In the absence of binding national laws, restitution has depended on piecemeal, often hesitant moral responses.[191] Institutions frequently propose long-term loans or co-curation arrangements rather than permanent return. These compromises are presented as a form of reconciliation, but in practice, they amount to bargaining over justice.[192] African states continue to insist that only permanent restitution is acceptable, and even some curators now acknowledge that piecemeal solutions are insufficient.[193] What is needed is a coherent framework for identification, resourcing, and safe return.

Decolonisation is not only about retrieving bronzes from museums or diamonds from crowns. It is also about reclaiming Africa's soil. Just as cultural treasures were removed, rebranded, and misrepresented, so too were Africa's soils alienated, depleted, and commodified under colonial regimes.[194] The looting of artefacts and the exhaustion of soils are inseparable: both reflect a worldview in which African value—material and spiritual—was uprooted and exported for imperial enrichment and must be reclaimed all the same. Mbembe's pointed question—"Do we really want to live in a world where everyone and everything has to go back home?"[195]—takes on a new layer of meaning when applied to the soil. Colonial powers have always insisted that Africans, as people, should 'stay home' or 'go back home', while simultaneously ensuring that the wealth of that 'home'—from artefacts to diamonds to the fertility of

184 Ibid.
185 Ibid.
186 See https://africasacountry.com/2024/11/why-are-african-artifacts-everywhere-but-africa, accessed 22 September 2025.
187 Ibid.
188 McAuliffe (2021: 680).
189 Ibid.
190 Ibid.: 679.
191 Ibid.
192 Ibid.
193 Ibid.
194 Makki (2018: 84); Wise (2021: 200-201).
195 Sandkühler et al. (2023: 31).

the soil itself—travels back to Europe. Decolonising the soil, therefore, is about reversing this flow. It is about insisting that the wealth generated from the soil must 'go back home' and remain there to nourish the communities from which it was taken. Read in this way, decolonising soil is not merely about participation or conservation, but about restitution in material form: reorienting soil governance away from extractive, export-oriented regimes and towards value retention, local benefit, and long-term stewardship within African communities.

### 3.3. Climate neutrality and just transitions

Abram et al have called for more "whole systems approaches" to decarbonisation—frameworks that move beyond policy silos to integrate all four dimensions of justice: distributive, procedural, recognition, and restorative.[196] Crucially, such approaches are not confined to managing socio-technical innovation efficiently; they also advance a transformational agenda to reshape the underlying structures of inequality and power. The urgency is stark. In 2022 alone, more than 110 million people across Africa were directly affected by weather-, climate-, and water-related hazards, with economic losses estimated at over USD 8.5 billion.[197] Official figures report around 5,000 fatalities, nearly half (48%) linked to drought and 43% to flooding, but the actual toll is likely much higher given chronic under-reporting in disaster monitoring systems.[198] Agriculture-based livelihoods are particularly exposed due to their reliance on climate-sensitive farming and low adaptive capacity, itself rooted in historical dispossession and structural poverty.[199] Current adaptation measures—whether existing, planned, or anticipated through mitigation benefits—remain inadequate to meet the unprecedented conditions ahead.[200]

Entrenched inequalities compound these vulnerabilities. Climate change threatens to reverse hard-won development gains by diverting resources from health, education, and infrastructure, reducing GDP in resource-dependent sectors, and destabilising fragile economies. Adaptation finance remains far below need. Even if commitments double to USD 40 billion annually by 2025, Africa will receive only around USD 180 billion by 2035.[201] Worse still, more than half of recent adaptation finance was delivered as debt, forcing states to repay funds intended to support their resilience rather than enabling adaptation; such financing risks deepening dependency and inequality.[202]

---

196 Abram et al. (2022).
197 African Climate Policy Center of the United Nations Economic Commission for Africa (2024: 15).
198 Ibid.
199 Mapfumo et al. (2025).
200 Ibid.
201 African Climate Policy Center of the United Nations Economic Commission for Africa (2024: 16).
202 Ibid.

These inadequacies are not incidental but structural. As the Independent Expert Group on Just Transition and Development underscores, three deficits—food sovereignty, energy sovereignty, and low-value-added exports—feed chronic trade gaps, weaken currencies, and push African states into foreign-currency debt, thereby shrinking their fiscal space for adaptation and mitigation.[203] A biased global trade–finance architecture then amplifies the squeeze: African sovereigns face perception-driven risk premia and borrow at multiples of the Organisation for Economic Co-operation and Development (OECD) rates (even when debt ratios are lower). At the same time, commodity dependence positions countries at the lowest rungs of value chains and exposes them to volatile flows.[204] The result is underinvestment where it matters most: energy investment has tilted toward fossil fuels, with only a thin slice allocated to renewables, and adaptation finance arrives largely as loans rather than grants—effectively asking vulnerable countries to repay resilience.[205]

Against this backdrop, the concept of a *just transition* has gained prominence. As Lane notes, "justice has been a major—perhaps the major—focus of political theorists working on climate change."[206] The transition to a low-carbon, climate-resilient economy is both inevitable and urgent, but it must be managed fairly.[207] A just transition seeks to protect vulnerable groups—especially workers, communities, and regions dependent on carbon-intensive or climate-sensitive sectors—while maximising the social and economic benefits of decarbonisation. It recalls core international principles, including the polluter-pays principle enshrined in the 1992 Rio Declaration, as well as the principle of equity and common but differentiated responsibilities outlined in the UNFCCC.[208]

The International Labour Organisation (ILO) has broadened the just transition concept to explicitly address environmental challenges, defining it as "greening the economy in a way that is as fair and inclusive as possible to everyone concerned, creating decent work opportunities and leaving no one behind."[209] This requires not only maximising opportunities, but also safeguarding fundamental labour rights and ensuring inclusive participation in decision-making. Similarly, the UNFCCC underscores equity as a guiding principle, affirming that parties must protect the climate system "for the benefit of present and future generations (…) on the basis of equity and in accordance with their common but differentiated responsibilities and respective capabilities."[210]

203 Sokona et al. (2023).
204 African Climate Policy Center of the United Nations Economic Commission for Africa (2024).
205 Ibid.
206 Lane (2016: 109).
207 Mapfumo et al. (2025).
208 Ibid.
209 Ruiz- Campillo (2025: 271).
210 Sardo (2023: 28).

Yet international frameworks remain cautious. The Paris Agreement (2015) mentions the just transition only once—in the preamble—narrowly framing it as the creation of "decent work and quality jobs in accordance with nationally defined development priorities."[211] Meeting the Paris goal of limiting the global temperature rise to well below 2°C requires a rapid transformation of the worldwide energy system. However, this shift is complicated by the fact that developmental priorities are still tied to carbon-intensive growth.[212] Early retirement of coal, for instance, promises enormous environmental and social benefits but also presents significant political and economic challenges.[213] Here, the lens of *energy justice* offers a helpful framework. Jenkins et al, Sovacool, and Dworkin emphasise three interrelated tenets:[214] Distributional justice—addressing how the benefits and burdens of energy transitions are shared. For example, coal-dependent communities face disproportionate costs from plant closures.[215] Recognition-based justice—asking which groups are excluded or misrepresented. Indigenous peoples, minorities, and older populations often lose both voice and recognition. Procedural justice—focusing on who participates in decision-making, under what conditions, and with what influence. Together, these principles frame *just transitions* not only as economic restructuring but also as projects of fairness, accountability, and participation.

The same dimensions apply to soils, but in ways that are structurally rooted in colonial land and agrarian regimes. Distributional injustices emerge when fertile soils continue to be channelled into extractive industries, large-scale carbon offset projects, or export-oriented monocultures, while smallholders and communal land users absorb the costs of erosion, contamination, and declining food security.[216] Recognition-based injustices persist when indigenous and local soil knowledge, developed through long-term stewardship and place-based practice, is marginalised in favour of technocratic, donor-driven models that prioritise yield, carbon metrics, or short-term restoration targets.[217] Procedural injustices arise when land-use planning, climate adaptation, and soil restoration programmes are designed without meaningful participation by those whose livelihoods and identities are bound to the land.[218] In this sense, decolonising soil governance is not merely adjacent to just transition agendas but constitutive of them. A transition cannot be just if it reproduces the colonial treatment of soils as extractable substrates or sacrifice zones for global environmental objectives. Integrating soils into just transition frameworks, therefore, requires concrete institutional shifts: securing communal and customary tenure as a foundation for soil

211 Fitz-Henry & Klein (2024: 1).
212 Spencer et al. (2018).
213 Hägele et al. (2024).
214 Jenkins et al. (2016); Sovacool & Dworkin (2015); McCauley & Heffron (2018).
215 Mapfumo et al. (2025).
216 Martinez-Alier (2018: 16); Chemhuru (2021: 232).
217 Molnár et al. (2023).
218 Effiong (2025).

stewardship; embedding free, prior, and informed consent in land and restoration projects; redirecting public finance toward agroecological and regenerative practices controlled by local communities; and recognising soil governance as a site of reparative justice rather than technical management. In this respect, arguments for the incorporation of indigenous jurisprudence do not advance a parallel normative agenda but rather identify legal and institutional mechanisms by which these just-transition commitments can be made operative, particularly in contexts where customary law continues to structure authority, compliance, and ecological knowledge.[219] Only through such mechanisms can transitions redistribute both the benefits and burdens of environmental change while breaking with the colonial logics that continue to shape soil use.

The international climate process has increasingly taken up this agenda. At COP24 in Katowice, 50 countries signed the Just Transition Silesia Declaration (2018), committing to protect workers and create decent jobs.[220] COP26 in Glasgow set a precedent with the launch of South Africa's Just Energy Transition Partnership (JETP), which combines finance and policy support to accelerate the phase-out of coal.[221] Most recently, the Just Transition Work Programme took centre stage at COP29 in Baku, reaffirming that net-zero pathways must safeguard workers, communities, and industries.[222]

Beyond the UNFCCC, according to ILO guidance,[223] national just-transition frameworks prioritise inclusive social dialogue, ex-ante employment/impact assessments, skills and active labour-market measures (including gender-responsive green job creation and support for workers in transition), strong social protection, and technology/knowledge cooperation with developing countries to enable responsible investment.

These measures reveal that just transitions are not only about managing technological change but also about restructuring economies and societies in democratic and equitable ways. The same imperative applies to soils: just as the energy transition cannot succeed without justice, soil governance cannot succeed without addressing colonial legacies, power imbalances, and exclusionary practices that continue to shape who benefits from Africa's most fundamental resource.

219 Anonymous. (forthcoming 2026). "From Fragility to Resilience: Indigenous Jurisprudence as an Institutional Technology for Hybrid Climate Governance in Sub-Saharan Africa". *Journal of Environmental Law* (manuscript under review).

220 Mapfumo et al. (2025).

221 Ibid.

222 Ibid.: 2.

223 ILO (2023).

## 4. Decolonising African soil

If colonial exploitation and climate injustice are interconnected, then so too must their remedies be. Meaningful reparations, whether through climate finance, the Loss and Damage Fund, or cultural restitution, are central to building trust and enabling cooperation in the pursuit of global sustainability. At the same time, forward-looking models of just transition must be grounded in fairness, reciprocity, and solidarity. Concepts such as *Ubuntu* offer guiding values rooted in mutual recognition and shared humanity rather than in exploitation.[224] Yet as Sarr and Savoy caution, healing remains incomplete if it relies only on the other side's acknowledgement of harm. Restitution must also be a process of self-rescue: a community-led reappraisal of its own history and renewal of the practices, institutions, and meanings that make repair durable.[225]

As Crosby's *Ecological Imperialism* reminds us, the expansion of the West relied on the domination of nature through force and fraud, generating crises that the Global South disproportionately bore.[226] These dynamics endure today. Historical land dispossession has been compounded by contemporary forms of "rent theft" and capital flight, which continue to drain African economies.[227] Between 1970 and 2018, illicit financial outflows and accumulated interest totalled USD 2.4 trillion—three times the amount of debt owed by the same countries.[228] These outflows weaken African states while fuelling metropolitan prosperity, sustaining property markets in London, Paris, New York, and Lisbon.[229] This ongoing ecological imperialism makes reparations not only a moral imperative but an economic necessity. Translated to soils, self-rescue means rebuilding endogenous capability—community tenure and guardianship, locally governed soil data and labs, extension that centres indigenous practice, and budget floors for restoration—so that external funds amplify, rather than substitute for, local stewardship.

From a European perspective, the territory of the colonised was cast as *terra nullius*—"no one's land"—awaiting appropriation.[230] Decolonisation, therefore, is not merely about political independence; it is about reclaiming the ground beneath people's feet. As Chitonge argues, Africa has yet to fully decolonise itself. The persistence of unresolved land and agrarian questions, coupled with the absence of profound structural transformation, underscores the incompleteness of the decolonial project.[231] Too often, decolonisation has been framed narrowly as the end of colonial

224 Oelofsen (2015: 137).
225 Habermas (2023).
226 Crosby (2009).
227 Obeng-Odoom (2021).
228 Obeng-Odoom (2022: 3).
229 Ibid.
230 Hackmack & Kaleck (2023: 413).
231 Chitonge (2018).

rule, while leaving intact the categories and legal structures through which colonial power was exercised.[232] Nowhere is this more evident than in the treatment of soil.

As the New Map Campaign underscores, inherited projections continue to shape Africa's relative size, centrality, and value; revising such mappings is closely tied to revising the legal categories that render soil invisible.[233] "It's not just a geography issue or just a map (...) It's a narrative issue about pride and identity (...) Ultimately, changing the map is about changing mindsets."[234] The same is true of soil.

> We now add another element to the teaching and learning and discussing of soils. Maps. Mapping in a cultural, traditional context are a key part of the soil discussion for it is the land that holds the laws. Maps are clearly part of storying domination and ownership.[235]

Colonialism became viable only after land was secured through conquest, dispossession, and exploitative treaties.[236] Yet in law, "land" was redefined in European terms, fusing soil, water, and air into a single object of private property. This collapsed the long-recognised distinctions in African thought between the soil (*solum*) and what grew upon it.[237] "Soil, perse, often was and remains shrouded in mystery and ritual, the subject of a vocabulary that made very little distinction between it and creatures which live upon it."[238] In many African customary systems, soil and land were not objects of absolute individual ownership but were held collectively under regimes of communal trusteeship.[239] While individuals and families enjoyed defined rights of use and cultivation, ultimate authority rested with the community, and chiefs or heads of families acted as custodians rather than proprietors, allocating access and safeguarding the land on behalf of both present and future generations.[240] Land was thus embedded in a temporal and spiritual continuum, linking ancestors, the living, and those yet to come, while remaining largely inalienable.[241]

Post-colonial governments dismissed customary tenure as backwards, reducing land reform to technical tenure regularisation and centralising administration in distant capitals.[242] As a result, soil remains mostly subsumed under "land" in law, with little recognition of its ecological specificity or cultural significance.[243] Historically, the dominant legal response to soil degradation took the form of soil conservation law, a body of legislation that emerged in the early twentieth century with a narrow focus on

232 Ndlovu-Gatsheni (2012).

233 See https://www.swp-berlin.org/publikation/mta-spotlight-59-africas-place-on-the-world-map, accessed 27 September 2025.

234 See https://www.aa.com.tr/en/africa/-correct-the-map-africa-takes-on-centuries-old-biggest-lie-in-world-geography/3689488, accessed 27 September 2025.

235 Poitras (2022: 4).

236 Chitonge (2018).

237 Okoth-Ogendo (1989).

238 Tafira & Ndlovu-Gatsheni (2017: 16).

239 Abdulai & Antwi (2005: 305).

240 van der Linden (2014: 41-47).

241 For a discussion, see Lentz (2013: 112).

242 Chitonge (2018: 31).

243 Fox (2024).

controlling wind and water erosion. These laws were primarily concerned with regulating land use rather than protecting soil as an ecological system in its own right, and they frequently used the term "land degradation" to capture problems arising from soil mismanagement.[244] Such conservation regimes were widely introduced across colonial Africa, Australia, New Zealand, the United States, and parts of Europe and Asia, reflecting a shared modernist and colonial legal logic that treated soil as an instrument of productivity rather than as a living resource requiring stewardship. By the late twentieth century, it became increasingly clear that erosion control alone was insufficient and that sustainable soil management could not be achieved through isolated conservation statutes.[245] Instead, it required a broader assemblage of legal, policy, and institutional measures—spanning national and local legislation, land-use planning, agricultural regulation, education, and incentive-based programmes. A review of national legal frameworks worldwide confirms this shift: rather than a single, coherent soil law, states have relied on a multiplicity of legal instruments—acts, regulations, codes, ordinances, by-laws, and administrative measures—addressing soil indirectly through planning, resource access, agricultural practices, nitrate controls, and restoration schemes.[246] In federal or multi-level systems, such as those of the United States, Australia, and China, this complexity is further amplified by overlapping federal and subnational regimes.[247] The cumulative result has not been integrated soil governance, but a dense yet fragmented legal landscape in which soil protection is dispersed across multiple sectors and scales. A comparative review of European legal systems illustrates that even jurisdictions with dense environmental regulation rarely govern soil as a distinct legal object. Across EU Member States, soil protection is typically addressed indirectly, through agricultural policy (CAP compliance, fertiliser and nitrate regulations), spatial planning and land-use controls, water and waste legislation, biodiversity frameworks, or remediation regimes for contaminated sites.[248] Detailed analysis of the United Kingdom's legal framework confirms this structural deficiency: despite extensive regulation of agriculture, water, waste, and pollution, soil is not governed through a comprehensive or coherent set of rules, and protection remains incidental to other regulatory objectives rather than an end in itself.[249] A similar review of soil governance in Uzbekistan identifies significant gaps in the legal framework, including the absence of dedicated regulations for biologically based soil surveys, quality control of soil laboratories, and explicit legal recognition of soil's carbon storage capacity and its role in climate change mitigation and adaptation. Despite multiple normative legal acts addressing land and natural resources, soil protection remains fragmented, technically under-specified, and

244 Hannam (2006: 225-226).
245 Ibid.
246 Ibid.
247 Ibid.
248 Ronchi et al. (2019); Leite (2025).
249 Demir (2021).

institutionally marginal, with limited integration of scientific data, climate objectives, and civil society participation.[250] Only a handful of states, most notably Germany and the Netherlands, have adopted soil-specific framework legislation, and even there, soil governance remains closely entangled with land-use planning, pollution control, and property regimes.[251] The prevailing pattern is fragmentation rather than integration: erosion is addressed through agricultural good-practice codes; contamination through waste or water laws; sealing through urban planning instruments; and biodiversity loss through nature conservation statutes. Soil thus appears not as a living system with its own functions and vulnerabilities, but as a residual concern, protected only insofar as it affects water quality, agricultural productivity, construction safety, or pollution control. In most cases, soil enters the legal field only once it has already been degraded—classified as "contaminated land," "waste," or "land requiring remediation"—rather than being governed proactively as a finite and non-renewable resource.[252]

Until soil is acknowledged as a distinct resource—requiring its own governance, standards, and stewardship—the decolonisation of Africa cannot be considered complete. The conflation of land and soil is not semantic but a structural barrier to genuine sovereignty, justice, and ecological resilience. As the New Map Campaign reminds us, representation itself has political effects: "It's the world's longest misinformation and disinformation campaign, and it just simply has to stop."[253] The same imperative applies to law's inherited categories—revising the map goes hand in hand with revising the legal frames that render soil invisible.

The Bété people of Côte d'Ivoire classify soils in ways that unsettle outside assumptions about what counts as "scientific." While these forest communities use just three colour classes—dark, light, and bright/red—they also listen to the soils to distinguish textures, discerning grittiness by the sound a handful makes when handled.[254] To understand such knowledge, we have to read it on its own terms and resist ethnocentrism: local classifications are embedded in place, practice, and purpose, not in outsider taxonomies.[255] Crucially, such classifications are not merely agronomic but are embedded in wider socio-cultural, spiritual, and cosmological orders. Across many African societies, land, soil, and earth are inseparable from moral authority and ancestral presence, giving rise to taboos and injunctions against environmental destruction, the pollution of sacred sites, or acts said to "offend" the soil.[256] Fertility is understood as contingent not only on technique, but on ritual

250 Kholdorov et al. (2023).
251 Ronchi et al. (2019).
252 Ibid.
253 See https://www.theguardian.com/world/2025/aug/15/african-union-true-size-world-map-replace-mercator-version, accessed 27 September 2025.
254 Showers (2006: 127).
255 Ibid.
256 Tafira & Ndlovu-Gatsheni (2017: 16–18).

observance, social conduct, and reciprocity with the living and the dead.[257] This epistemic humility should shape policy. Decolonising soil governance, therefore, requires more than the removal of colonial rulers; it demands transforming the inherited systems that commodify land, while reviving indigenous knowledge that sustained fertility through communal and diversified practices. Soil, in this sense, is both the material and cultural foundation of decolonisation: restoring it means restoring autonomy, identity, and ecological integrity—so that governance listens not only to instruments and indices, but also to the land and the people who know how to hear it.[258]

In practice, transnational governance must avoid reproducing colonial hierarchies. Partnerships between North and South should move beyond donor–recipient models and towards co-determination, ensuring that benefits and responsibilities are shared equitably. True decolonisation must address both backwards-looking demands for justice—such as compensation, restitution, and reparations—and forward-looking imperatives of just transitions, climate neutrality, and sustainability. Reclaiming agency in soil governance entails: integrating indigenous knowledge into soil management alongside modern science; revitalising cultural connections to land, recognising African traditions as assets in sustainable resource use; ensuring local participation in defining, monitoring, and addressing soil degradation, ending the exclusion of communities from decision-making; aligning development with African priorities, rather than donor-driven agendas.

Africa is too often depicted through external narratives of disease, poverty, and war. Yet in ecological terms, it remains one of the least degraded continents, rich in biodiversity, beauty, and soil resources, and home to resilient communities. Even our world maps have reinforced those narratives—hence the New Map Campaign, which contests cartographies that shrink Africa's ecological and geopolitical presence. With proper governance, Africa could become the "green lung of the world" and a vital global carbon sink, contributing not only to its own renewal but also to planetary sustainability.

## 4.1. Soil law and governance: pathways forward

The governance of soil in Africa stands at a crossroads. On one side is growing recognition of soil's central role in food security, livelihoods, and climate resilience. On the other hand, outdated legal frameworks, fragmented institutions, and extractive economic structures persist, undermining soil health by treating it either as part of or

257 Ibid.

258 Oelofsen (2015).

as a subset of "land". Moving forward requires building on Africa's existing strengths while addressing systemic weaknesses:[259]

### 4.1.1. Strengths

#### 4.1.1.1. Growing political recognition of soil's importance

Although there is an urgent need for decolonised legal frameworks, reform is not straightforward. Political resistance remains a major challenge. Powerful corporations, investors, and political actors who benefit from the existing system may resist reforms that threaten their control over resources or constrain profitable activities.[260] Meaningful transformation, therefore, requires political will and a genuine commitment to decolonisation.

Soil is increasingly recognised not merely as an environmental concern but as a strategic asset for development. Governments and regional bodies, such as the AU, now emphasise the importance of soil health for food security, climate change adaptation, and rural development. This political visibility lays the foundation for stronger legal and institutional frameworks.

#### 4.1.1.2. Deep cultural ties to land

Across Africa, soil is more than a productive resource—it is a vital anchor of identity, spirituality, and heritage. These ties make stewardship not merely a policy choice but a duty across generations, placing soil alongside other cultural artefacts that require restoration and protection for the future.

#### 4.1.1.3. Community-based knowledge of sustainable practices

African communities have long maintained soil fertility through practices such as mixed farming, terracing, crop rotation, and communal grazing. While often marginalised in formal law, this indigenous knowledge remains a living resource, offering context-specific strategies for sustainable soil governance.

259 Ruppel & Ginzky (2024).
260 Cordonier Segger & Olawuyi (2025: 663).

### 4.1.2. Weaknesses and gaps

#### 4.1.2.1. Outdated laws and conflicting tenure systems

Many states still rely on colonial-era land and agricultural laws that fail to integrate indigenous systems of stewardship. Conflicts between customary and statutory tenure regimes foster insecurity and discourage long-term investment in soil conservation.

#### 4.1.2.2. Fragmented governance responsibilities

Absent recognition of soil as a distinct policy field, responsibilities are scattered across multiple ministries—agriculture, environment, water, and mining—resulting in duplication, gaps, and diluted accountability. Lacking a central coordinator, the system defaults to piecemeal, crisis-driven responses.

#### 4.1.2.3. Weak or absent soil standards

Few countries have legal standards for soil health, monitoring, or remediation. Where such standards exist, enforcement is rare due to capacity constraints. This regulatory vacuum enables unchecked degradation, contamination, and overexploitation.

#### 4.1.2.4. Inadequate financing and unchecked foreign investments

Soil protection is chronically underfunded, while foreign investment regimes often prioritise extractive industries—such as mining, large-scale monoculture, and oil—over conservation. Without safeguards, these investments accelerate soil degradation and reinforce dependency on external interests.

#### 4.1.2.5. Exclusion of local communities

Despite their knowledge and reliance on soils, local communities are too often excluded from decision-making. Top-down governance models often overlook the voices of those they govern, resulting in policies that lack legitimacy and long-term sustainability.

## 4.2. Recommendations

A deeper problem with "return" is that it frames it as a mere transfer of title. Is it even possible to give African art "back" to its creators if the modern category of "art"—which separates objects from the practices that animate them—is not universal?[261] Masks, for instance, cannot simply be restituted into the ritual actions that once gave them meaning.[262] In this view, restitution is never only about objects: African art is a living practice that uses specific things but cannot be reduced to them. Communities know this; hope is less about seeing the exact items again than about restoring the conditions in which meaning is made.[263] Similarly, soil cannot be "returned" as a mere carbon metric or parcel. Soil health is a living practice—fallowing and rotations, grazing rules, water harvesting, composting, seed and knowledge exchange—embedded in tenure, culture, and local institutions. Decolonising soil governance, therefore, means restoring the conditions that make stewardship possible: secure and equitable tenure (including commons), community decision-making and guardianship, extension and research that centre on indigenous knowledge, locally governed soil data, enforceable soil-health standards, and budgets to sustain them.

Accordingly, building effective soil governance in Africa requires not only technical reforms but also bold legal and institutional innovation. The following recommendations outline pathways to strengthen soil protection, ensure justice, and align national and regional efforts with global sustainability goals.[264] Echoing civic movements across Europe and the Global South that decolonise public space by removing colonial-era monuments and street names to disrupt inherited racism,[265] soil governance must likewise decolonise its legal landscape—retiring extractive-era rules, correcting skewed tenure, and centring community stewardship and indigenous knowledge.

This transformation also resonates with broader calls for justice in an unsettled age. As Baroness Valerie Amos has argued, meaningful change begins with confronting the truth of history: colonialism and dispossession are not past events but enduring structures that continue to shape access to land and resources.[266] It further requires centring marginalised voices—particularly those of smallholder farmers, pastoralists, and indigenous communities—whose knowledge and practices have long sustained soil systems but remain undervalued in formal governance frameworks. Building effective soil governance will depend on forging coalitions across differences, bridging legal, scientific, and community perspectives, and resisting the fragmentation

261 Förster (2023: 192-193).
262 Ibid.
263 Ibid.
264 See Ruppel et al. (2025).
265 Sandkühler et al. (2023: 33).
266 See https://www.su.ac.za/en/news/stability-without-equity-fragile-baroness-valerie-amos-warns-7th-social-justice-lecture, accessed 22 March 2026.

that often undermines reform. It also demands a long-term commitment: soil restoration and governance reform are not short-term interventions but generational projects requiring sustained institutional and financial support. Finally, it calls for a form of grounded hope—not naïve optimism, but a deliberate commitment to act in the present, despite complexity and uncertainty, to secure the ecological foundations upon which future justice depends.[267]

#### 4.2.1. Adopt soil-specific policies and laws

Across Africa, neither national nor regional frameworks have historically provided dedicated legal protection for soils. Under the leadership of the Pan-African Parliament (PAP), an iterative process was undertaken to address this gap. The drafting of the Model Law on Soil Management proceeded in parallel with research and consultations across multiple African jurisdictions. Experts and stakeholders were engaged during studies conducted in Botswana, Burkina Faso, Cameroon, Kenya, Madagascar, Morocco, Mozambique, Namibia, South Africa, Uganda, and Zambia. Although these studies did not cover all 55 member states of the African Union (AU), they represent a substantial cross-section of the continent, spanning northern, southern, eastern, western, central, and island regions. Regional consultations further expanded participation and consistently confirmed similar governance gaps regarding soil protection and sustainable land use.

The Model Law emerging from this process provides a comprehensive framework to guide national soil governance. It establishes the objective of sustainable soil management, recognising that soils must be managed in the interest of people and ecosystems alike—supporting the eradication of poverty and hunger, ensuring food security, promoting economic prosperity, and contributing to climate change mitigation and adaptation. The Model Law introduces modern governance mechanisms, including permitting procedures, soil impact assessments, spatial and land-use planning tools, and environmental quality standards. It also addresses the full spectrum of soil degradation—from contamination, erosion, and compaction to soil sealing and salinisation—while integrating broader socio-economic considerations, including tenure security, gender equality, digitalisation, foreign investment, and social justice. Importantly, the framework promotes a collaborative governance model that engages public authorities, traditional leadership structures, scientific institutions, civil society, and economic actors.

This co-production with scientists, policymakers, and civil society ensured that the Model Law is both evidence-based and adaptable. The next and most critical step is domestication. African states are encouraged to translate the principles and

267 Ibid.

mechanisms of the Model Law into national legislation, policies, and institutional arrangements that reflect their specific legal systems, ecological conditions, and development priorities.

Moving beyond treating soil as a subsidiary concern within environmental or agricultural legislation is therefore essential. Dedicated soil legislation would explicitly regulate soil use and protection across sectors such as agriculture, urbanisation, mining, and infrastructure development. Such laws could establish clear standards for soil health, mandate monitoring and data collection systems, and create enforceable mechanisms to prevent degradation and restore damaged soils.

A national soil policy can serve as an important first step in this process. By setting out an overarching framework for the protection, restoration, and sustainable use of soils, such policies can guide legislative reform, coordinate institutions, and mobilise stakeholders. Governments alone cannot achieve soil health. Farmers, researchers, civil society organisations, and local institutions must all play active roles in collaborative action, coordinated governance, and continuous learning.

Domestication, therefore, represents the bridge between a shared continental vision and practical implementation. The Model Law provides a flexible legal toolbox through which countries can incorporate core duties—protect, prevent, restore, and report—into their national frameworks while adapting the instruments to their institutional capacities and policy priorities. Through this process, African states can progressively build coherent soil governance systems that safeguard soil resources for future generations.

### 4.2.2. Enshrine constitutional protections

To secure lasting safeguards, the right to a healthy environment—including healthy soils—should be recognised in constitutional frameworks. Constitutional guarantees strengthen the legal basis for citizens to demand accountability from governments and corporations, elevate soil governance beyond ordinary policy discretion, and align it with broader principles of human rights, intergenerational equity, and ecological integrity.

Article 60 of the Nicaraguan Constitution (1987 (rev. 2014)) attributes dignity to "Mother Earth" (*madre tierra*), recognising the Earth and its life-sustaining natural processes, including healthy soils, as living entities to be loved, protected, and regenerated. It imposes duties of responsible production and consumption grounded in solidarity, social equality, and ecological integrity. It explicitly aligns with the Universal Declaration of the Common Good of the Earth and Humanity.[268] This constitutional framing represents a profound ontological shift away from soil as mere

268 See https://www.humiliationstudics.org/documents/HoutartUniversalDeclarationoftheCommonGoodofHumanity.pdf, accessed 7 April 2026.

property or productive substrate toward soil as a living foundation of collective life. At the same time, Nicaragua also demonstrates the limits of constitutional recognition in the absence of legal and institutional translation. Despite its advanced constitutional language, soil protection remains poorly operationalised in ordinary law, dispersed across general environmental regulation, and triggered only after degradation has already occurred.[269] The lesson is therefore twofold: constitutional protection is a necessary foundation for decolonised soil governance, but it is not sufficient on its own. Without implementing legislation, dedicated institutions, enforceable standards, and community-centred stewardship mechanisms, even the most progressive constitutional commitments risk remaining aspirational.

#### 4.2.3. Integrate soils into climate and biodiversity law

Soils are critical carbon sinks and biodiversity reservoirs, yet they remain marginal in climate and biodiversity strategies. Explicitly incorporating soils into Nationally Determined Contributions (NDCs), climate change legislation, and biodiversity action plans would ensure that soils play a central role in both mitigation and adaptation.

#### 4.2.4. Strengthen governance frameworks

The fragmentation of responsibilities across ministries often undermines soil governance. Governments should establish centralised authorities or inter-ministerial bodies to coordinate soil policy, backed by adequate funding, technical expertise, and reliable monitoring systems. Without such institutional coherence, legal reforms risk remaining symbolic.

#### 4.2.5. Guarantee public participation

Capacity-building is also essential. Legal and institutional reform cannot succeed without strengthening the capacities of local governments, civil society organisations, and communities to participate effectively in governance processes.[270] In addition, reforms must often be harmonised carefully with existing international legal obligations, including trade and investment agreements. The challenge lies in balancing these commitments with the need to create fairer, more locally grounded, and ecologically sustainable legal orders. Ultimately, decolonising governance

269 Stubenrauch et al. (2018).
270 Cordonier Segger & Olawuyi (2025: 664–665).

structures requires a fundamental shift towards equity, participation, and plurality in decision-making. This includes moving beyond top-down centralised models inherited from colonial rule and embracing decentralisation, participatory governance, and context-sensitive institutional design.[271] Stronger local government, meaningful community participation, and capacity-building can help create governance systems that reflect local priorities and enable genuine collaboration.

Local communities and farmers are the frontline stewards of soils. Their participation must be a legal requirement in decision-making, not a discretionary consultation. Embedding participatory governance ensures legitimacy, harnesses indigenous knowledge, and empowers those most affected by degradation to shape sustainable solutions.

### 4.2.6. Harmonise at the regional level

Soil degradation transcends national borders and demands continental responses. The Pan-African Parliament (PAP) has adopted the Model Law on Soil Management.[272] The task has therefore shifted from designing a regional instrument to domesticating it: member states should adapt and enact the Model Law through national legislation, regulations, and programmes, with AU/PAP support to harmonise approaches, ensure public participation, and mobilise capacity and finance for soil restoration.

The PAP Model Law can contribute to the decolonisation of African soils, but not automatically. Its decolonial force depends less on the text alone than on how domestication is carried out—and, in particular, whether domestication is treated as translation into local constitutional, customary, and ecological realities, rather than as a copy-paste exercise into inherited statutory frameworks. In key respects, the Model Law marks a structural move away from colonial logics that reduced the earth to a platform for extraction. It defines "soil" in an explicitly ecological, social, and cultural register (Article 4(19)); recognises soil services that include cultural heritage and sacred and archaeological sites (Article 5(5)); and applies broadly to all forms of degradation and all activities that may harm soil (Article 3). Together, these provisions render soil legally visible as more than a productive input subsumed under "land". The Model Law also embeds justice-oriented governance principles that contest the colonial pattern of distant decision-making justified through "expert" authority. Its Guiding Principles include non-discrimination and social justice (Article 6(1)(d)),

271 Ibid.

272 See https://pap.au.int/en/news/press-releases/2025-11-06/african-parliamentarians-adopt-continents-first-model-law, accessed 19 March 2026; https://www.fao.org/partnerships/parliamentary-alliances/news/news-article/en/c/1754895/, accessed 19 March 2026; https://www.su.ac.za/en/news/pan-african-parliament-adopts-continents-first-model-law-sustainable-soil-management, accessed 19 March 2026.

subsidiarity (Article 6(1)(j)), and effective participation (Article 6(1)(b)). Read decolonially, these provisions shift communities from being objects of administration to being recognised, at least normatively, as subjects of soil governance. In a similar vein, the law treats indigenous knowledge as a valuable source for sustainable soil management. It requires the collection and dissemination of such knowledge, the funding of local research centres, and, critically, a payment/benefit system in which foreign investors intend to use such knowledge (Article 27(4)). This directly addresses an epistemic-colonial dynamic: extraction of local knowledge without consent, recognition, or return. The Model Law further confronts contemporary continuities of colonial concessionary rule by defining land grabbing robustly (Article 4(8)) and obliging competent authorities to ensure that large-scale acquisitions do not undermine soil health or local land rights (Article 13(2)). Finally, it internalises responsibility for harm through the degradation responsibility principle (Article 6(1)(i)) and guards against an anti-decolonial outcome—offloading repair costs onto the already dispossessed—by requiring support where smallholders and vulnerable communities cannot bear restoration or compensation burdens (Article 14(4)).

Accordingly, the Model Law provides a continental scaffold capable of unwinding key colonial afterlives in soil governance—soil invisibility, exclusion, investor dominance, and epistemic extraction. Yet the same framework can also be domesticated in ways that reinscribe state-centric, technocratic, and property-centric control, primarily where implementation relies on authorisation regimes, standards, and institutions that do not meaningfully redistribute decision-making power. Whether the Model Law decolonises African soils, therefore, turns on domestication as a political practice: not simply adopting rules, but reworking the inherited legal grammar so that soil governance is shaped by African norms, institutions, and lived relationships to land.

#### 4.2.7. Link neutrality and justice

Achieving land degradation neutrality must go hand in hand with social and environmental justice. Soil-related initiatives should ensure equitable benefit-sharing, fair financing, and restitution for communities that have been historically dispossessed. Without such safeguards, soil governance risks replicating extractive patterns rather than breaking from them.

Together, these recommendations chart a pathway from fragmented policies to a coherent framework that positions soils at the heart of Africa's development vision. By treating soil as both a legal and cultural foundation for food security, climate resilience, and identity, they lay the groundwork for national reforms and a Pan-African legal architecture that secures soils for future generations.

In this spirit, *ubuntu*—"I am because we are"—offers a normative anchor for soil governance: it frames soil not as a commodity but as the communal ground of life, memory, and livelihood.[273] It denotes a conception of humanness grounded in relationality. Although it resists easy translation within Western epistemological frameworks, it expresses the idea that personhood is realised through relationships with others.[274] Identity, on this view, is not autonomous but constituted through the well-being of the community as a whole. *Ubuntu*, therefore, articulates a relational ontology in which individual flourishing is inseparable from collective welfare. At its normative core lie values such as solidarity, mutual care, sharing, respect, compassion, and human dignity.[275] As a meta-concept rooted in African social and philosophical traditions, *ubuntu* affirms the interdependence of community members and, in contrast to individualist paradigms, accords priority to communal life and responsibility.[276] Beyond a worldview, *ubuntu* functions as a lived ethical practice and code of conduct, grounding justice, equality, and mutual responsibility as everyday obligations rather than abstract ideals.[277] While the term *ubuntu* comes from isiZulu and isiXhosa in South Africa, the idea is Pan-African. Many Sub-Saharan cultures use cognate words for the same ethic of shared personhood: Sesotho/Setswana speak of *botho*; Shona of Zimbabwe call it *hunhu* (often *unhu/hunhu*); in Kiswahili it is *utu*; and in the Great Lakes region, Kirundi (Burundi) and Kinyarwanda (Rwanda) use forms such as *ubuntu/ubumuntu*.[278] An *ubuntu*-aligned approach prioritises reciprocity and care: restoring degraded lands, securing communal and customary tenure, sharing benefits fairly, and ensuring that those most affected help shape decisions.[279] It links ecological stewardship to dignity and reparative justice, recognising that healing soils and healing communities are inseparable tasks. Practically, it calls for participatory institutions, culturally grounded safeguards, and intergenerational duties so that today's use of soil strengthens, rather than erodes, the collective well-being of tomorrow.

## 5. Conclusion: towards a just soil future

Soil is often cast as Nature preceding Culture: a dark, formless substrate on which human cultivation inscribes meaning.[280] It is at once origin and remainder—the humus from which we are made and the matter to which we return—"the basic kinaesthetic

273 Nxumalo (2025: 2 & 15).
274 Letseka (2012: 48).
275 Ibid.
276 Ibid.
277 Nussbaum (2003: 2).
278 Shange (2024: 1).
279 Nxumalo (2025: 2).
280 Tironi et al. (2020).

experience of having our feet planted on the earth".[281] In this register, soil appears as both essence and residue: what comes before exploitation and what remains after it.[282] Images of erosion make this stark, depicting depleted soil as the ultimate remainder of a civilisation's passing. Myths of autochthony link people directly to the soils from which they spring. At the same time, as Li shows, the axe, spade, plough, title deed, tax register, maps, graphs, satellite images, ancestral graves, and mango trees do not merely record land; they assemble it as a resource for different actors.[283] This is equally evident at the geopolitical scale. The New Map Campaign illustrates how Africa's position on the world map is not a neutral depiction, but a cartographic intervention that reorders relations of power and belonging.[284] Just as soil is constituted through implements and representations, so too is Africa's place in the global order reshaped by the lines, scales, and projections that render it visible. Both soil and maps remind us that what appears as background or substrate—the ground beneath our feet or the outline of a continent—is always being made, assembled, and contested through political and cultural practices.

Law is one of the most powerful of these "implements". The decolonisation of African soil is a legal challenge precisely because law itself is not neutral terrain. Modern African land and environmental law is inherited mainly from colonial legal orders designed to enable conquest, extraction, and control rather than stewardship, reciprocity, or care.[285] Colonial law transformed soil from a living commons into an object of administration, measurement, and commodification.[286] Through cadastral surveys, title deeds, concessions, and zoning regimes, soil was abstracted from its social, spiritual, and ecological relations and rendered legible primarily to the colonial state and external markets.[287] These legal architectures did not merely regulate land use; they reordered African relationships to territory, authority, and time. That inheritance persists, making decolonisation both historically urgent and institutionally difficult. Many postcolonial legal systems continue to rely on categories that subsume soil under "land" as a unit of property, reduce tenure to ownership or lease, and prioritise extractive productivity over regeneration. Customary systems of guardianship, intergenerational responsibility, and communal decision-making were marginalised or frozen into administrative caricatures, recognised only insofar as they did not disrupt state control or commercial interests.[288] As a result, soil governance remains fragmented, technocratic, and often hostile to the very practices that

281 Clark (2011).
282 Tironi et al. (2020).
283 Li (2014).
284 See https://www.swp-berlin.org/publikation/mta-spotlight-59-africas-place-on-the-world-map; https://correctthemap.org/, accessed 27 September 2025.
285 Kameri-Mbote & Cullet (1997).
286 Mauro & Sant (2020).
287 Braun (2008: 52).
288 Seutloali (2024: 9–24).

historically sustained fertility and resilience. Africa cannot be meaningfully "freed" while the legal strings of the past continue to structure the present: colonialism did not end with the lowering of flags; it sedimented itself into institutions, property regimes, investment laws, and environmental governance frameworks that still shape access to soil, exposure to degradation, and vulnerability to climate change. In this sense, soil becomes a material archive of colonialism. Its erosion, nutrient depletion, and contamination record centuries of extraction without repair, productivity without replenishment, and governance without consent.[289] To decolonise soil law is thus to interrupt durable causal chains between past dispossession and present insecurity, between historical enrichment elsewhere and contemporary vulnerability in Africa, so that sovereignty is not merely formal, but ecological, legal, and lived.

Against such reductions, soil emerges as a milieu in which the social becomes-with: an entangled, co-dependent field of relations. The fact that soil's internal dynamics are complex to perceive is itself an onto-political issue, not a barrier to politicisation.[290] Soils retain a creative, irreducible power that brings things, affects and relations into being; they are, in this sense, a force of their own.[291] In Meulemans's account of "living soils," their relational vitality animates otherwise inert minerals and calls forth practices of care and co-labouring.[292] Decolonising soil, then, means more than restoring parcels: it entails cultivating a sense of belonging to soils—being attuned to their radical autonomy—while recognising reciprocal responsibilities between soil worlds and social worlds.[293]

"The African continental surface is ancient, as is human experience on it."[294] The governance of Africa's soils is inextricably linked to the continent's broader struggles for justice, sovereignty, and sustainability. From colonial dispossession to contemporary forms of ecological imperialism, soils have been repeatedly commodified, depleted, and rendered invisible in law and policy. Yet they remain the foundation of food security, cultural identity, and ecological resilience. Read through the AU's own Africanization lens—"African solutions to African problems"—soil governance should be organised through continent-level norm-setting and enforcement, not by transplanting external models.[295]

This chapter has shown how global and regional frameworks increasingly recognise soils as vital to achieving sustainability goals, yet too often fall short in implementation. That shortfall mirrors a broader pattern the AU literature flags: rapid continental "legalization" and "judicialization" must be matched by credible enforcement and accountability—while remaining alert to continent-level parameters

289 Liboiron (2021).
290 Tironi et al. (2020).
291 Ibid.
292 Meulemans (2020).
293 Tironi et al. (2020).
294 Showers (2006: 133).
295 Wiebusch (2024).

that can unintentionally narrow domestic policy space.[296] Similarly, reparations debates—whether around climate finance, loss and damage, or cultural restitution—highlight that the legacies of extraction and exploitation are not merely historical but continue to structure present inequalities. An Africanized approach asks, at a minimum, what is to be remedied? Who benefits? Who loses?—and insists that problem-framing ("problematization") and solution design ("solutionization") be done in African terms, not through inherited categories.[297]

Decolonising soil governance, therefore, requires a double movement: confronting the backwards-looking demands of justice through restitution, reparations, and redress, while also advancing forward-looking imperatives of climate neutrality, just transitions, sustainable development, and new maps. Operationally, performance should be tracked beyond simple "compliance" through indicators that span norms (standards and distributive effects), actors (who are constituted and resourced), and processes (decision-making and implementation)—with explicit cautions about the politics and blind spots of these indicators.

This involves legal innovation—such as adopting soil-specific legislation, embedding constitutional protections, and integrating soils into climate and biodiversity regimes—as well as institutional reform to overcome fragmented governance and ensure meaningful community participation. Strategy-wise, a bottom-up/top-down ("guerrilla lawfare") pathway links community stewardship to AU-level mandates, keeping up constructive pressure to shift the dominant order.[298]

Beyond legal and institutional reform, capacity development is pivotal. FAO's Global Soil Partnership initiative, Capacity Development on Sustainable Soil Management in the Global South, launched in Zimbabwe in 2025, strengthens soil laboratories, mapping, and practitioner skills while fostering South–South learning and uptake of science-based practices—an approach that aligns with the AU's Africanisation lens and community-centred governance.[299] This kind of continental capacity infrastructure helps translate norms into implementable, locally led programmes.

It also requires shifting partnerships away from donor–recipient hierarchies towards genuine co-determination, guided by principles of equity, reciprocity, and *Ubuntu*. And because "Africa" is not a single essence but a contested construct, the continental frame must allow regional variation (Sahel, humid tropics; communal, freehold) rather than impose one-size-fits-all templates.[300]

Ultimately, reclaiming Africa's soils is not only an environmental task but also a reparatory act: restoring autonomy, dignity, and ecological integrity to communities

296 Ibid.
297 Ibid.
298 Ibid.
299 See https://www.fao.org/global-soil-partnership/resources/highlights/detail/en/c/1740896/, accessed 26 October 2025.
300 Wiebusch (2024).

that have been historically dispossessed of both land and livelihood. This also means acknowledging the epistemic conflict at the heart of soil governance: whose knowledge defines the value of soils, whose measurements set standards, and whose narratives render soils visible or invisible in law. How specific knowledge is privileged and other knowledge is obscured—this should be part of that repair. It requires not just technical solutions but also epistemic justice—valuing diverse knowledge systems and ensuring that a narrow set of actors does not monopolise the framing of problems and solutions. If pursued boldly, Africa can lead in articulating a new paradigm of soil governance—one that treats soil not as inert matter, but as living heritage, a source of sustenance, and a shared foundation for a just and sustainable future.

# Bibliography


Abdulai, A.-R., P.T. Quarshie, E. Duncan & E. Fraser, 2023, "Is Agricultural Digitization a Reality among Smallholder Farmers in Africa? Unpacking Farmers' Lived Realities of Engagement with Digital Tools and Services in Rural Northern Ghana". *Agriculture & Food Security* 12, 11.

Abdulai, R.T. & A. Antwi, 2005, "Traditional Landholding Institutions and Individual Ownership of Land Rights in Sub-Saharan Africa". *World Review of Science, Technology and Sustainable Development* 2(3/4) 302–319.

Abiri, G., 2025, "Public Constitutional AI". *Georgia Law Review* 59, 601–670.

Abram, S., E. Atkins, A. Dietzel, K. Jenkins, L. Kiamba, J. Kirshner, J. Kreienkamp, K. Parkhill, T. Pegram & L.M.S. Ayllón, 2022, "Just Transition: A Whole-Systems Approach to Decarbonization". *Climate Policy* 8, 1033–1049.

Academy of Science of South Africa, 2025, *POPIA Compliance Framework for Researchers and Research Institutions*. Pretoria.

Acemoglu, D., S. Johnson & J.A. Robinson, 2001, "The Colonial Origins of Comparative Development: An Empirical Investigation". *American Economic Review* 91(5), 1369–1401.

Achiume, T.E., 2022, *Report of the Special Rapporteur on Contemporary Forms of Racism, Racial Discrimination, Xenophobia and Related Intolerance on Ecological Crisis, Climate Justice and Racial Justice*, A/77/2990, General Assembly Resolution 43/36. New York, United Nations.

Adamu, A. & A. Peter, 2016, "Comparative Analysis of African Union (AU) and European Union (EU): Challenges and Prospects". *International Journal of Political and Cultural Studies* 3(1), 46–57.

Adeyemi, S., 2025, "From Data to AI: Inside Nigeria's Leading Blueprint for Africa's Digital Sovereignty". *Business Insider Africa*, 27 October. At https://africa.businessinsider.com/local/markets/from-data-to-ai-inside-nigerias-leading-blueprint-for-africas-digital-sovereignty/e6r7cxj, accessed 27 October 2025.

AEFJN, 2018. *Traités bilatéraux d'investissement: Une menace continue pour l'Afrique*.

African Land, 2020, "Africa's Land Ownership: Who Owns Most of the Land?". *African Land*, at https://african.land/blog/article/africas-land-ownership-who-owns-most-of-the-land-b91, accessed 22 September 2025.

African Parliamentary News, 2020, "PAP Maps First Steps for Model Legislation on Sustainable Soil Management in Africa". *African Parliamentary News*, at https://www.africanparliamentarynews.com/2020/03/pap-maps-first-steps-for-model.html?m=1, accessed 19 March 2026.

African Parliamentary News, 2025, "Pan-African Parliament Adopts Landmark Model Law on Sustainable Soil Management in Africa". *African Parliamentary News*, at https://www.africanparliamentarynews.com/2025/11/pan-african-parliament-adopts-landmark_7.html, accessed 28 March 2026.

African Union Commission, 2026, "African Union Commission and Google Sign Landmark Partnership to Advance Africa's Sovereign AI and Digital Capacity". *African Union*, at https://au.int/en/pressreleases/20260217/auc-google-sign-partnership-advance-africas-sovereign-ai-digital-capacity, accessed 20 March 2026.

African Union Development Agency, 2021, *AI for Africa: Artificial Intelligence for Africa's Socio-economic Development*.

Agorsah, E.K., 1977, "Restitution of Cultural Material to Africa". *Africa Spectrum* 12(3), 305–308.

Agwu, A.E., M. Suvedi, C. Chanza, K. Davis, A. Oywaya-Nkurumwa, M. Najjingo Mangheni & P.V.K. Sasidhar, 2023, *Agricultural Extension and Advisory Services in Nigeria, Malawi, South*

*Africa, Uganda, and Kenya* (Partnerships for Innovative Research in Africa (PIRA) Research Report). East Lansing, MI: Alliance for African Partnership, Michigan State University.

Ahmed, K., 2026, "'Invasive' AI-led mass surveillance in Africa violating freedoms, warn experts". *The Guardian*, at https://www.theguardian.com/global-development/2026/mar/12/invasive-ai-led-mass-surveillance-in-africa-violating-freedoms-warn-experts, accessed 20 March 2026.

Ahmed, N., M. Rahman, R. Karim & M. Hasanuzzaman, 2019, "Soil Management for Better Crop Production and Sustainable Agriculture". In: M. Hasanuzzaman (ed.), *Agronomic Crops*. Singapore: Springer, 83–121.

AI Verify Foundation / AI Verify Foundation, 2024, *Model AI Governance Framework for Generative AI*.

Ajjour-Charaï, A. 2004. *Investisseurs étrangers et offre créatrice: cas d'un pays émergent : le Maroc*.

Ajl, M., 2021, *A People's Green New Deal*. London: Verso Books.

Akana, C., & M. King'ori, 2024, "The African Union's Continental AI Strategy: Data Protection and Governance Laws Set to Play a Key Role in AI Regulation". *Future of Privacy Forum (blog)*, 18 November. At https://fpf.org/blog/global/the-african-unions-continental-ai-strategy-data-protection-and-governance-laws-set-to-play-a-key-role-in-ai-regulation/, accessed 27 October 2025.

Akhtar-Schuster, M., L.C. Stringer & N.N. Barger, 2024, "Fast-tracking Action on the Sustainable Development Goals by Enhancing National Institutional Arrangements". *PLOS ONE* 19(3), 1.

Ali, O., M. Aydin & S. Ali, 2024, "The African Continent: A Rich Land of Minerals and Energy Sources". *Inorganic Chemistry Communications* 169, 113123.

Allen, J.G., J. Loo & J. Luna, 2025, "Governing Intelligence: Singapore's Evolving AI Governance Framework". *Cambridge Forum on AI Law and Governance* 1, 1–20.

Alschner, W., & D. Skougarevskiy, 2016, Mapping the Universe of International Investment Agreements. *Journal of International Economic Law*, 19(3), 551–588.

ALT Advisory, 2022, *AI Governance in Africa: An Overview of Regulation and Policy Work on Artificial Intelligence in Africa*.

Amani Africa, 2022, *Special Research Report No. 12: Mapping of AU Decision-Making Actors and Processes*.

Amankwah, A., A. Ambel, S. Gourlay, T. Kilic, Y. Markhof & P. Wollburg, 2024, *Fertilizer Price Shocks in Smallholder Agriculture*. Washington, DC: World Bank.

Amanor, K., 2008, "The Changing Face of Customary Land Tenure". In: J.M. Ubink & K.S. Amanor (eds.) *Contesting Land and Custom in Ghana: State, Chief and the Citizen*. Leiden University Press, 55.

Amin, S., 2009, "Aid for Development". In: H. Abbas & Y. Niyiragira (eds.) *Aid to Africa: Redeemer or Coloniser?*. Nairobi: Pambazuka Press, 59–75.

Andere, B. & M. Kathure, 2024, *Strengthening Data Protection in Africa: Key Issues for Implementation*. Brussels: Access Now.

Andersson, E. & E. Isgren, 2021, "Gambling in the Garden: Pesticide Use and Risk Exposure in Ugandan Smallholder Farming". *Journal of Rural Studies* 82, 76–86.

Anonymous. Forthcoming 2026. "From Fragility to Resilience: Indigenous Jurisprudence as an Institutional Technology for Hybrid Climate Governance in Sub-Saharan Africa". *Journal of Environmental Law* (manuscript under review).

Anseeuw, W., L. Alden Wily, L. Cotula, & M. Taylor, 2012, *Land Rights and the Rush for Land: Findings of the Global Commercial Pressures on Land Research Project*. International Land Coalition.

Arakpogun, E.O., Z. Elsahn, F. Olan & F. Elsahn, 2021, “Artificial Intelligence in Africa: Challenges and Opportunities”. In: A. Hamdan, A.E. Hassanien, A. Razzaque, & B. Alareeni (eds.), *The Fourth Industrial Revolution: Implementation of Artificial Intelligence for Growing Business Success* Studies in Computational Intelligence Vol 935. Springer Nature Switzerland, 375–388.

Araújo, R. & L. Kössler, 2021, *The Rise of the Constitutional Protection of Future Generations*. LPP Working Paper Series No 7–2021.

Arredondo, P., 2023, “GPT-4 Passes the Bar Exam: What That Means for Artificial Intelligence Tools in the Legal Profession”. *Stanford Law School*, 19 April. At https://law.stanford.edu/2023/04/19/gpt-4-passes-the-bar-exam-what-that-means-for-artificial-intelligence-tools-in-the-legal-industry/, accessed 29 October 2025.

Ashukem, J.N. & C.C. Ngang, 2022, “Land Grabbing and the Implications for the Right to Development in Africa”. *African Human Rights Law Journal* 22(2), 403–425.

Aslam, M.F., B. Wang, S.Y.A. Zaidi & Z. Aslam, 2025, “The Legal Environment of Digital Trade: Inevitable for Sustainable Industrial Revolution”. *Preprints* 1–20.

Assemblée nationale du Burkina Faso. 2018. *Loi n°038-2018/AN portant Code des investissements au Burkina Faso*.

Assemblée nationale du Cameroun. 2013/2017. *Loi n°2013/004 telle que modifiée par la loi n°2017/015 relative à l'investissement privé au Cameroun*.

AU / African Union, 2018, *Migration Policy Framework for Africa and Plan of Action (2018–2030)*.

AU / African Union, 2019, *Africa Governance: Promoting African Union Shared Values*.

AU / African Union, 2020, *Digital Transformation Strategy for Africa (2020–2030)*.

AU / African Union, 2023a, *Digital Agriculture Strategy (DAS) and Implementation Plan 2024–2030*.

AU / African Union, 2023b, *Rapport annuel*.

AU / African Union, 2024a, *African Fertiliser and Soil Health Summit: Soil Initiative for Africa: Framework Document*, AFSHS/2(II), at https://au.int/en/AFSH-2024, accessed 22 September 2025.

AU / African Union, 2024b, *Continental Artificial Intelligence Strategy: Harnessing AI for Africa's Development and Prosperity*. Addis Ababa: African Union.

AU / African Union, 2024c, *Initiative en faveur des sols en Afrique: Document cadre*.

AU / African Union, 2024d, *Stratégie de l'Union Africaine et plan d'action pour la biodiversité (ABSAP)*.

AU / African Union, undated, “About Conflict Management”. *African Union*, at https://au.int/en/directorates/about-conflict-management, accessed 9 July 2025.

AU / African Union, undated, “Regional Economic Communities”. *African Union*, at https://au.int/en/recs, accessed 9 July 2025.

AU / African Union, OECD / Organisation for Economic Co-operation and Development, UNECA / United Nations Economic Commission for Africa & ADB / African Development Bank, 2022, *Africa's Urbanisation Dynamics 2022: The Economic Power of Africa's Cities (West African Studies)*. Paris: OECD Publishing.

AUDA-NEPAD / African Union Development Agency–NEPAD, 2022, *Second Continental Report on the Implementation of Agenda 2063*.

AUDA-NEPAD / African Union Development Agency–NEPAD, 2023, *Briefing Note: Addressing Africa's Soil Health Challenges through the Ten-year African Fertiliser and Soil Health Action Plan (2024–2034) and the Long-term Soil Initiative for Africa Framework*.

Audit, M., P. Calli, & S. Bollé, 2019, *Droit du commerce international et des investissements étrangers* (3rd ed.). LGDJ.

AU-IAPSC / African Union Inter-African Phytosanitary Council, 2012, "Harmonization of Pesticide Registration in Africa – 2012", 15 April. At https://auiapsc.org/2012/04/15/harmonization-of-pesticides-registration-in-africa-2012/, accessed 2 October 2025.

Australasian Institute of Judicial Administration Incorporated, 2022, *AI Decision-Making and the Courts: A Guide for Judges, Tribunal Members and Court Administrators*. Melbourne: AIJA.

Awais, M., S.M.Z.A. Naqvi, H. Zhang, L. Li, W. Zhang, F.A. Awwad, E.A.A. Ismail, M.I. Khan, V. Raghavan & J. Hu, 2023, "AI and Machine Learning for Soil Analysis: An Assessment of Sustainable Agricultural Practices". *Bioresources and Bioprocessing* 10(90), 1–16.

Azevedo, M. da F., 2024, *Navigating the AI Frontier in International Trade Law: The Role of the WTO's TBT Agreement*. WTI Working Paper No. 4/2024. Bern: World Trade Institute.

Baba, A. & B. Mngomezulu, 2021, "Implementing Accountability and Transparency in Supranational Organisations: A Comparison of the European Union and the African Union, 2001–2020". *Journal of African Union Studies* 10(2), 91–104.

Badillo, M., 2024, "Processing of Personal Data for AI Training in Brazil: Takeaways from ANPD's Preliminary Decisions in the Meta Case". *FPF*, at https://fpf.org/blog/processing-of-personal-data-for-ai-training-in-brazil-takeaways-from-anpds-preliminary-decisions-in-the-meta-case/, accessed 20 March 2026.

Baeyaert, J., 2025, "Beyond Personhood: The Evolution of Legal Personhood and Its Implications for AI Recognition". *Technology and Regulation*, 355–386.

Bakiner, O., 2023, "The Promises and Challenges of Addressing Artificial Intelligence with Human Rights". *Big Data & Society* 10(2).

Barfield, W., 2018, "Towards a Law of Artificial Intelligence". In: W. Barfield & U. Pagallo (eds.), *Research Handbook on the Law of Artificial Intelligence*. Cheltenham: Edward Elgar, 2–39.

Barratt, L., C. Gambarini, A. Witherspoon & A. Uteuova, 2025, "Revealed: Big Tech's New Datacentres Will Take Water from the World's Driest Areas". *The Guardian*, 9 April. At https://www.theguardian.com/environment/2025/apr/09/big-tech-datacentres-water, accessed 2 October 2025.

Barton, R., J. Burchard, V.E. Cabrera, D. Cook, W. Cooley, R. Cue, L. Fadul, J. Mattison & A. Saha, 2025, "Data Ownership and Privacy in Dairy Farming: Insights from U.S. and Global Perspectives". *Animals* 15, 524.

Basson, A., 2025, "Pan-African Parliament Adopts Continent's First Model Law on Sustainable Soil Management". *Stellenbosch University*, at https://www.su.ac.za/en/news/pan-african-parliament-adopts-continents-first-model-law-sustainable-soil-management, accessed 28 March 2026.

Bationo, A. & B.S. Wanswa, 2011, "New Challenges and Opportunities for Integrated Soil Fertility Management in Africa". In: A. Bationo et al. (eds.), *Innovations as Key to the Green Revolution in Africa*. Dordrecht: Springer, 3–18.

Bayer, C.-T., 2021, "Land Governance and Land Reform in Southern Africa". In: H. Chitonge & R. Harvey (eds.), *Land Tenure Challenges in Africa: Confronting the Land Governance Deficit*. Cham: Springer, 47–74.

Bedini, S.A., 1964, "The Role of Automata in the History of Technology". *Technology and Culture* 5, 24–42.

Behnke, R.H., I. Scoones & C. Kerven, 1993, *Rangeland Ecology at Disequilibrium: New Models of Natural Variability and Pastoral Adaptation in the African Savanna*. London: Overseas Development Institute.

Benamara, A., 2025, "Egypt Aims for AI Leadership in the Middle East and Africa with New National Strategy". *TechAfrica News*, 4 September. At https://techafricanews.com/2025/09/04/egypt-aims-for-ai-leadership-in-the-middle-east-and-africa-with-new-national-strategy/, accessed 27 October 2025.

Benhama, A. 2020. *Le régime d'investissements étrangers en Algérie: aspects juridiques.*

Bhagattjee, P. & S. Stephens, 2024, "The AI National Policy: South Africa's initial step to establish an AI policy and regulatory framework". *Werksmans Attorneys*, 10 April. At https://werksmans.com/the-ai-national-policy-south-africas-initial-step-to-establish-an-ai-policy-and-regulatory-framework/, accessed 29 October 2025.

Bhattacharyya, R., A. Bhatia, B.N. Ghosh, P. Santra, D. Mandal, G. Kumar, R.J. Singh, M. Madhu, A. Ghosh, A.K. Mandal, R. Paul, A. Datta, P.C. Sharma, U.K. Mandal, P. Jha, K.S. Anil, M. Lalitha, M. Kumar, N.R. Panwar, D. Sarkar, A.K. Patra, S. Kundu, M.A. Fullen, J. Poesen, B.S. Das, N.N. Reddy & S.K. Chaudhari, 2023, "Soil Degradation and Mitigation in Agricultural Lands in the Indian Anthropocene". *European Journal of Soil Science* 74, 1–23.

Bigger, P., N. Pearce, K. Rogaly & K. Zodgekar, 2023, "Less War, Less Warming: A Reparative Approach to US and UK Military Ecological Damages". *Common Wealth* 6 November, at https://www.common-wealth.org/publications/less-war-less-warming-a-reparative-approach-to-us-and-uk-military-ecological-damages, accessed 18 September 2025.

Binz, M., E. Akata, M. Bethge, F. Brändle, F. Callaway, J. Coda-Forno, P. Dayan, C. Demircan, M.K. Eckstein, N. Éltető, T.L. Griffiths, S. Haridi, A.K. Jagadish, L. Ji-An, A. Kipnis, S. Kumar, T. Ludwig, M. Mathony, M. Mattar, A. Modirshanechi, S.S. Nath, J.C. Peterson, M. Rmus, E.M. Russek, T. Saanum, J.A. Schubert, L.M. Schulze Buschoff, N. Singhi, X. Sui, M. Thalmann, F.J. Theis, V. Truong, V. Udandarao, K. Voudouris, R. Wilson, K. Witte, S. Wu, D.U. Wulff, H. Xiong & E. Schulz, 2025, "A Foundation Model to Predict and Capture Human Cognition". *Nature* 644, 1002–1009.

Birhane, A., 2020, "Algorithmic Colonization of Africa". *SCRIPTed* 17(2), 389–409.

Birkstedt, T., M. Minkkinen, A. Tandon & M. Mäntymäki, 2023, "AI Governance: Themes, Knowledge Gaps and Future Agendas". *Internet Research* 33(7), 133–167.

Boer, B.W., H. Ginzky & I. Heuser, 2016, "International Soil Law: History, Concepts and Latest Developments". In: Ginzky, H., I.L. Heuser, T. Qin, O.C. Ruppel & P. Wegerdt (eds), *International Yearbook of Soil Law and Policy*, Vol. 1. Cham: Springer International Publishing, 49–72.

Bond, P. & K. Sharife, 2009, "Africa Battles Aid and Development Finance". In: H. Abbas & Y. Niyiragira (eds.), *Aid to Africa: Redeemer or Coloniser?*. Nairobi: Pambazuka Press, 42–58.

Bonomo, S. 2012. *Les traités bilatéraux relatifs aux investissements entre protection des investissements étrangers et sauvegarde de la souveraineté des États.* Collection de l'Institut du droit des affaires, Centre de droit économique.

Booty, N., 2025, "Namibia Marks Colonial Genocide as Reparations Hang in the Balance". *BBC*, at https://www.bbc.com/news/articles/cy0jkynyln2o, accessed 22 September 2025.

Booyens, H., 2026, "Stability without equity is fragile, Baroness Valerie Amos warns in 7th Social Justice Lecture". *Stellenbosch University*, at https://www.su.ac.za/en/news/stability-without-equity-fragile-baroness-valerie-amos-warns-7th-social-justice-lecture, accessed 19 March 2026.

Bostoen, F., 2025, "Artificial Intelligence and Competition Law". In: N.A. Smuha (ed.), *The Cambridge Handbook of the Law, Ethics and Policy of Artificial Intelligence.* Cambridge Law Handbooks. Cambridge: Cambridge University Press, 174–191.

Bowman, S.R., 2024, "Eight Things to Know about Large Language Models". *Critical AI* 2(2).

Branca, G., T. Tennigkeit, W. Mann & L. Lipper, 2011, *Climate-smart Agriculture: A Synthesis of Empirical Evidence of Food Security and Mitigation Benefits from Improved Cropland Management.* Rome: FAO.

Brannon, K., 2024, "AI Sentencing Cut Jail Time for Low-Risk Offenders, but Study Finds Racial Bias Persisted". *Tulane University News*, 23 January 2024, at https://news.tulane.edu/pr/ai-sentencing-cut-jail-time-low-risk-offenders-study-finds-racial-bias-persisted, accessed 7 October 2025.

Braun, L.F., 2008, *The Cadastre and the Colony: Surveying, Territory, and Legibility in the Creation of South Africa, c.1860–1913*. PhD dissertation, Rutgers University.

Brunette, A., 2024, "Humanizing Justice: The Transformational Impact of AI in Courts, from Filing to Sentencing". *Thomson Reuters*, 25 October 2024, at https://www.thomsonreuters.com/en-us/posts/ai-in-courts/humanizing-justice/, accessed 7 October 2025.

Cabral, A., 1973, *Return to the Source*. New York, NY: Monthly Review Press.

Cabral, A., 1988, *Estudos Agrários de Amílcar Cabral*. Lisboa and Bissau: IICT.

Cajueiro, D.O. & V.R.R. Celestino, 2026, "A Comprehensive Review of Artificial Intelligence Regulation: Weighing Ethical Principles and Innovation". *Journal of Economy and Technology* 4, 77–91.

Canfield, M.C. & B. Ntamabirweki, 2024, "Datafying African Agriculture: From Data Governance to Farmers' Rights". *Development* 67(5–13), 1–13.

Carbonnier, J., 1976, *Flexible droit*. Paris: Librairie générale de droit et de jurisprudence.

Castro, J.P., C.K. Gasch & P. Flores, 2024, "Artificial Intelligence in Soil Science: Where Do We Go Now?". *Agricultural & Environmental Letters* 9, 1–5.

Césaire, S., 2012, *The Great Camouflage: Writings of Dissent (1941–1945)*. Middletown: Wesleyan University Press.

Chemhuru, M., 2021, "Land Reform and Redistribution as Environmental Justice Frameworks for Post-colonial Africa". In: E. Masitera (ed.), *Philosophical Perspectives on Land Reform in Southern Africa*. Cham: Springer Nature, 225–240.

Chen, B.M. & Z. Li, 2020, "How Will Technology Change the Face of Chinese Justice?". *Chinese Justice* 2020, 1–55.

Chevallier, A. D. N. 2020. *Droit de l'investissement internationaux* (3rd ed.). Collection Études International. Montchrestien.

Chevallier, J., 2015, *L'État de droit: Réflexion sur l'application des lois, la légitimité de la norme et les mécanismes institutionnels* (Coll. Clefs Politique). Paris: Montchrestien.

Chichaibelu, B.B., H. Baumüller & M.A. Matschuck, 2023, "Protecting the Data of African Agricultural Producers: A Review of National Laws, Compliance and Perceptions". *Law, Innovation and Technology* 15(2), 617–661.

Chigbu, U.E., E. Uwayezu & M. Katjuia, 2022, "Customary Versus Conventional Land Administration Systems in Sub-Saharan Africa". *African Journal on Land Policy and Geospatial Sciences* 5(4), 663–682.

Chimhowu, A., 2019, "The 'New' African Customary Land Tenure: Characteristic Features and Policy Implications of a New Paradigm". *Land Use Policy* 81, 897–903.

Chimuka, G., 2019, "Impact of Artificial Intelligence on Patent Law: Towards a New Analytical Framework". *World Patent Information* 59.

Chinnaiyan, B., S. Balasubaramanian, M. Jeyabalu & G.S. Warrier, 2024, "AI Applications – Computer Vision and Natural Language Processing". In: P.R. Chelliah, A.M. Rahmani, R. Colby, G. Nagasubramanian & S. Ranganath (eds.), *Model Optimization Methods for Efficient and Edge AI: Federated Learning Architectures, Frameworks and Applications*. Hoboken: Wiley-IEEE Press, Chapter 2.

Chitonge, H., 2018, "Trails of Incomplete Decolonisation in Africa: The Land Question and Economic Structural Transformation". *African Study Monographs. Supplementary Issue* 57, 21–43.

Chondros, T.G., 2017, "Natural Philosophy and the Development of Mechanics and Engineering from the 5th Century B.C. to the Middle Ages". *FME Transactions* 45, 603–619.

Chuhan-Pole, P., A.L. Dabalen, A. Kotsadam, A. Sanoh & A. Tolonen, 2017, *Mining in Africa: Are Local Communities Better Off?* Paris/Washington, DC: Agence Française de Développement & World Bank.

Clark, B. & J.B. Foster, 2012, "Guano". In: A. Hornborg, B. Clark & K. Hermele (eds.), *Ecology and Power*. London: Routledge, 68–82.

Clark, N., 2011, *Inhuman Nature: Sociable Life on a Dynamic Planet*. London: Sage.

Clarke, K., C. Jollah & V. Nmehielle, 2019, "Introduction: Origins and Issues of the African Court of Justice and Human Peoples' Rights". In: C. Jollah, K. Clarke & V. Nmehielle (eds.), *The African Court of Justice and Peoples' Rights in Context: Development and Challenges*. Cambridge: Cambridge University Press, 1–55.

CNN World, 2025, "African Union Urges Adoption of World Map Showing Continent's True Size". *CNN World*, at https://edition.cnn.com/2025/08/15/africa/africa-real-size-world-map-campaign-intl, accessed 22 September 2025.

Coetzee, J., 2024, "Cross-Border Data Flows and the Protection of Personal Information Act 4 of 2013 – Part I: The Territorial Scope Provision". *Potchefstroom Electronic Law Journal* 27, 1–25.

Combes, P.P., S. Magrini & M. Ndiaye, 2023, *An Anatomy of Urbanisation in Sub-Saharan Africa*. Washington, DC: World Bank, at https://documents1.worldbank.org/curated/en/0994153 11272320571/pdf/IDU0faef6c000aaba0485209f0e08928760d9a57.pdf, accessed 2 October 2025.

Cooper, D., B. Haley, D. Govender, A. Mokdad & M. Mkhize, 2025, "Kenya's AI Strategy 2025–2030: Signals for Global Companies Operating in Africa". *CovAfrica (Inside Africa Blog)*, 1 April, at https://www.covafrica.com/2025/04/kenyas-ai-strategy-2025-2030-signals-for-global-companies-operating-in-africa/, accessed 27 October 2025.

Cordonier Segger, M.-C. & D. Olawuyi, 2025, *Sustainable Development Law: Principles, Practices, and Prospects* (2 ed.). United Kingdom: Oxford University Press.

Cotula, L., 2007, *Changes in "Customary" Land Tenure Systems in Africa*. London: International Institute for Environment and Development (IIED).

Council of Europe, 2024, *Framework Convention on Artificial Intelligence and Human Rights, Democracy and the Rule of Law*. Council of Europe Treaty Series No. 225.

Council of the European Union, 2025, "Council Adopts New Rules for Healthier and More Resilient European Soils". *European Council*, at https://www.consilium.europa.eu/en/press/press-releases/2025/09/29/council-adopts-new-rules-for-healthier-and-more-resilient-european-soils/, accessed 3 March 2026.

Coursera, 2025, "AI vs. Generative AI: The Differences Explained". *Coursera*, at https://www.coursera.org/articles/ai-vs-generative-ai, accessed 2 October 2025.

Craswell, E., 2021, "Fertilizers and Nitrate Pollution of Surface and Groundwater: An Increasingly Pervasive Global Problem". *SN Applied Sciences* 3(4), 518.

Crosby, A., 2009. *Ecological Imperialism: The Biological Expansion of Europe, 900-1900*. Cambridge, United Kingdom: Cambridge University Press.

Cuatrecasas, undated, "New EU Directive on Soil Monitoring and Resilience". *Cuatrecasas*, at https://www.cuatrecasas.com/resources/new-eu-directive-on-soil-monitoring-and-resilience-694519fda4ab1032692762.pdf, accessed 3 March 2026.

Cuend, S. & B. Stern, 2017, *Droit des investissements internationaux: Perspective croisée*.

Dadashpoor, H. & G. Shahhossein, 2024, "Defining Urban Sprawl: A Systematic Review of 130 Definitions". *Habitat International* 146, 103039.

Daneliya, G., 2025, "Development of AI Regulations in Russia". *Law.asia*, at https://law.asia/russia-ai-regulations-legal-framework-ethics/, accessed 20 March 2026.

Danic, O. 2012. *L'émergence d'un droit international des investissements: Contributions des traités bilatéraux d'investissement et de la jurisprudence du CIRDI.*

Daniels, C., B. Erforth & C. Teevan, 2022, "Digitalisation for Transformation – New Frontiers for Africa–Europe Cooperation". In: C. Daniels, B. Erforth & C. Teevan (eds.), *Africa–Europe Cooperation and Digital Transformation*, 1–16.

Davidson, J.P.L., & F.C. da Silva, 2024, "Decolonising the Earth: Anticolonial Environmentalism and the Soil of Empire". *Theory, Culture & Society* 41(6), 3–19.

Davis, J.S., 2022, "Decolonising South African Agriculture – Bringing Dignity back to Small-scale Farming". *African Journal of Inter/Multidisciplinary Studies* 4(1), 195–204.

Davis, T. & W. Trott, 2024, "The Regulation of Artificial Intelligence Through Data Protection Laws: Insights from South Africa". *African Journal on Privacy & Data Protection* 1, 207–219.

Davis, T., M. Hunter, W. Trott & Z.A. Omar, 2022, *FA.I.LURE to Access: Testing Transparency in Data Protection and Artificial Intelligence in South Africa*. Johannesburg: ALT Advisory.

Davis, T., M. Hunter, Z.A. Omar & W. Trott, 2022, *AI Governance in Africa: An Overview of Regulation and Policy Work on Artificial Intelligence in Africa*. Johannesburg: ALT Advisory.

Dazzi, C. & G. Lo Papa, 2022, "A New Definition of Soil to Promote Soil Awareness, Sustainability, Security, and Governance". *International Soil and Water Conservation Research* 10(1), 99–108.

De Nanteuil, A., 2020, *Droit de l'investissement internationaux* (3rd ed.). Montchrestien.

De Vita, L. & C. Goschler, 2025, "Introduction Wassenaar, 1952: Redefining Reparations". In: L. De Vita & C. Goschler (eds.), *Redefining Reparations: Wassenaar 1952 and the Global Politics of Repair*. New York: Routledge, 1–26.

Demir, M., 2021, *A Critical Analysis of the Effectiveness of the United Kingdom Soil Protection Legislation from an Ecosystem Services Perspective*. PhD dissertation, Bournemouth University.

Desai, B.H. & M. Mandal, 2021, "Role of Climate Change in Exacerbating Sexual and Gender-Based Violence Against Women: A New Challenge for International Law". *Environmental Policy and Law* 51(3), 137–157.

Desai, B.H., 2023, "Land–Soil Sustainability: India's International Obligations". In: B.H. Desai (ed.), *Soil Law and Governance in India*. International Yearbook of Soil Law and Policy. Cham: Springer Nature Switzerland AG, 3–26.

Deutsche Bank, 2020, *Monthly Report: The EU Budget and its Financing: Looking Back and Ahead.*

Dimkpa, C., W. Adzawla, R. Pandey, W.K. Atakora, A.K. Kouame, M. Jemo & P.S. Bindraban, 2023, "Fertilizers for Food and Nutrition Security in Sub-Saharan Africa: An Overview of Soil Health Implications". *Frontiers in Soil Science* 3, 1123931.

Dingmanse, M., undated, "Talen van Afrika". *Stemmen van Afrika*, at https://stemmenvanafrika.nl/talen-van-afrika/, accessed 4 July 2025.

Dixon, J., A. Gulliver & D. Gibbon, 2001, *Global Farming Systems Study: Challenges and Priorities to 2030—System Synthesis and Global Overview*. Rome: FAO.

Dixon, J., D.P. Garrity, J.-M. Boffa, T.O. Williams, T. Amede, C. Auricht, R. Lott & G. Mburathi, 2020, *Farming Systems and Food Security in Africa: Priorities for Science and Policy under Global Change*. London/New York: Routledge, Taylor & Francis Group / ICRAF.

Dominic, C., 2025, "AI Laws: A Global Overview with a Focus on Africa". *Tech Culture Africa*, 9 April. At https://techcultureafrica.com/ai-laws-africa, accessed 27 October 2025.

Dosunmu, D., 2025, "Big Tech's 'AI for Good' Spending Increases in Africa. So does Skepticism". *Rest of World*, 18 August 2025, at https://restofworld.org/2025/africa-ai-for-good-big-tech/, accessed 7 October 2025.

DuFord, R., 2022, *Solidarity in Conflict: A Democratic Theory*. Redwood, CA: Stanford University Press.

Dunphy, K., 2025, "ChatGPT for Lawyers: Uses, Prompts, and Best Practices". *Spellbook Legal*, 21 October. At https://www.spellbook.legal/learn/chatgpt-for-lawyers, accessed 29 October 2025.

Eckersley, R., 2016, "Responsibility for Climate Change as a Structural Injustice". In: T. Gabrielson, C. Hall, J. Meyer & D. Schlosberg (eds.), *The Oxford Handbook of Environmental Political Theory*. Oxford: Oxford University Press, 346–361.

Effiong, C.J., 2025, "Climate Justice in Land Use Planning: Exploring the Potential and Challenges of Nature-Based Solutions Integration in Nigeria". *Journal of Environmental Management* 377, 1–12.

Ehlers, K., 2016, "Chances and Challenges in Using the Sustainable Development Goals as a New Instrument for Global Action against Soil Degradation". In: Ginzky, H., I.L. Heuser, T. Qin, O.C. Ruppel & P. Wegerdt (eds), *International Yearbook of Soil Law and Policy*, Vol. 1. Cham: Springer International Publishing, 73–84.

Eickhoff, K., 2025, "Africa's Place on the World Map". *SWP*, at https://www.swp-berlin.org/publikation/mta-spotlight-59-africas-place-on-the-world-map, accessed 27 September 2025.

EIP-AGRI / European Innovation Partnership for Agricultural Productivity and Sustainability, 2020, *Final Report: New Skills for Digital Farming*.

Ejims, O. 2019. The 2016 Morocco–Nigeria Bilateral Investment Treaty: More Practical Reality in Providing a Balanced Investment Treaty? *ICSID Review – Foreign Investment Law Journal*, 34(1), 62–84.

Ekhator, E., 2020, "Women's Access to Environmental Justice in Nigeria". *SSRN Working Paper*, at https://ssrn.com/abstract=3719831, accessed 2 October 2025.

Engerman, S.L., 2009, "Apologies, Regrets and Reparations". *European Review* 17(3–4), 593–610.

European Commission, 2021a, "EU Biodiversity Strategy for 2030: Bringing Nature Back into Our Lives". *European Commission*, at https://data.europa.eu/doi/10.2779/677548, accessed 11 March 2026.

European Commission, 2021b, "EU Soil Strategy for 2030: Reaping the Benefits of Healthy Soils for People, Food, Nature and Climate". *European Commission*, COM(2021) 699 final, at https://eur-lex.europa.eu/legal-content/EN/TXT/?uri=CELEX%3A52021DC0699, accessed 11 March 2026.

European Commission, 2021c, *Communication from the Commission to the European Parliament, the Council, the European Economic and Social Committee and the Committee of the Regions: EU Soil Strategy*, COM (2021) 699 final.

European Commission, 2023, "Proposal for a Directive of the European Parliament and of the Council on Soil Monitoring and Resilience (Soil Monitoring Law)". *European Commission*, COM(2023) 416 final, at https://eur-lex.europa.eu/legal-content/EN/TXT/?uri=CELEX:52023PC0416, accessed 11 March 2026.

European Commission, 2025, "The Soil Monitoring Law is Published in the EU Official Journal". *European Commission*, at https://mission-soil-platform.ec.europa.eu/news-events/latest-news/soil-monitoring-law-published-eu-official-journal, accessed 3 March 2026.

European Commission, undated, "AI Act". *European Commission*, at https://digital-strategy.ec.europa.eu/en/policies/regulatory-framework-ai, accessed 11 July 2025.

European Commission, undated, "EU Soil Observatory (EUSO)". *Joint Research Centre: EU Science Hub*, at https://joint-research-centre.ec.europa.eu/eu-soil-observatory-euso_en, accessed 3 August 2025.

European Commission, undated, "Horizon Europe". *EU Funding & Tenders Portal*, at https://ec.europa.eu/info/funding-tenders/opportunities/portal/screen/programmes/horizon, accessed 5 July 2025.

European Commission, undated, "Soil Monitoring Law". *European Commission*, at https://environment.ec.europa.eu/topics/soil-health/soil-monitoring-law_en#timeline, accessed 3 March 2026.

European Commission, undated, "Soil Strategy for 2030". *European Commission*, at https://environment.ec.europa.eu/topics/soil-health/soil-strategy-2030_en, accessed 9 July 2025.

European Commission High-Level Expert Group on Artificial Intelligence, 2018, *A Definition of AI: Main Capabilities and Scientific Disciplines*. Brussels: European Commission.

European Parliament, 2025, "EU AI Act: First Regulation on Artificial Intelligence". *European Parliament*, at https://www.europarl.europa.eu/topics/en/article/20230601STO93804/eu-ai-act-first-regulation-on-artificial-intelligence, accessed 2 October 2025.

European Parliament & Council of the European Union, 2025, "Directive (EU) 2025/2360 of the European Parliament and of the Council of 12 November 2025 on Soil Monitoring and Resilience (Soil Monitoring Law)". *Official Journal of the European Union* L series, at https://eur-lex.europa.eu/legal-content/EN/TXT/HTML/?uri=OJ:L_202502360, accessed 11 March 2026.

European Soil Partnership, 2025, "European Parliament Adopts First-Ever Soil Monitoring Law". *European Soil Partnership*, at https://www.europeansoilpartnership.org/news-page/european-parliament-adopts-first-ever-soil-monitoring-law, accessed 11 March 2026.

European Union, undated, "About Copernicus". *Copernicus Programme*, at https://www.copernicus.eu/en, accessed 3 August 2025.

FALL, C. L. 2018. *La protection juridique des investissements directs étrangers dans les pays en développement: l'exemple de l'Afrique de l'ouest.*

FAO / Food and Agriculture Organization. 2011. *La pratique de la gestion durable des terres: Directives et bonnes pratiques pour l'Afrique subsaharienne*.

FAO / Food and Agriculture Organization of the United Nations, 2013, *Children's Work in the Livestock Sector: Herding and Beyond.* Rome: Economic and Social Development Department, FAO.

FAO / Food and Agriculture Organization of the United Nations, 2015, *Healthy Soils are the Basis for Healthy Food Production.* International Year of Soils. Rome.

FAO / Food and Agriculture Organization of the United Nations, 2017, *Voluntary Guidelines for Sustainable Soil Management (VGSSM)*. Rome: FAO.

FAO / Food and Agriculture Organization of the United Nations, 2018, *Pastoralism in Africa's drylands: Reducing risks, addressing vulnerability and enhancing resilience*. Rome: FAO.

FAO / Food and Agriculture Organization of the United Nations, 2019, *Mainstreaming Gender for Sustainable Soil Management: Report of Activity No. 161, 23 September – 25 October 2019 (Global Forum on Food Security and Nutrition)*. Rome: FAO.

FAO / Food and Agriculture Organization of the United Nations, 2021, *Boosting Smallholder Resilience for Recovery: Restoring Soil Health and Productivity for Safe, Nutritious and Resilient Agri-Food Systems*. Rome: FAO.

FAO / Food and Agriculture Organization of the United Nations, 2023a, *Addressing Gender Equality in Sustainable Soil Management: A Technical Guide for Policymakers and Field Practitioners*. Rome: FAO.

FAO / Food and Agriculture Organization of the United Nations, 2023b, *Soils, Where Food Begins: How Can Soils Continue to Sustain the Growing Need for Food Production in the Current Fertiliser Crisis?* ITPS Soil Letter, Issue #6. Rome: FAO.

FAO / Food and Agriculture Organization of the United Nations, 2024, *The unjust climate: Measuring the impacts of climate change on the rural poor, women and youth.* Rome: FAO.

FAO / Food and Agriculture Organization of the United Nations, 2025a, "Pan-African Parliament Breaks New Ground with Landmark Soil and Gender Laws". *FAO*, at https://www.fao.org/policy-support/news/detail/pan-african-parliament-breaks-new-ground-with-landmark-soil-and-gender-laws/en, accessed 11 March 2026.

FAO / Food and Agriculture Organization, 2025b, "African Parliamentarians Adopt Landmark Model Laws on Soil Management and Gender Equality". *FAO*, at https://www.fao.org/partnerships/parliamentary-alliances/news/news-article/en/c/1754895/, accessed 19 March 2026.

FAO / Food and Agriculture Organization of the United Nations, 2025c, *Restoring Southern Africa's soils: The path to food security and sustainable agriculture.* Rome: FAO.

FAO / Food and Agriculture Organization of the United Nations, undated, *Women's Contributions to Agricultural Production and Food Security: Current Status and Perspectives.* Rome: FAO, at https://www.fao.org/4/X0198E/x0198e02.htm, accessed 2 October 2025.

FAO / Food and Agriculture Organization of the United Nations, undated, "Global Soil Partnership". *FAO*, at https://www.fao.org/global-soil-partnership/regional-partnerships/africa/en/, accessed 6 July 2025.

Fawad, A., 2025, "Prioritizing Gender Law and Policy Aspects of Climate Action". In: M.C. Cordonier-Segger & C. Voigt (eds.), *Routledge Handbook of Climate Law and Governance – Courage, Contributions and Compliance.* London/New York: Routledge, 367–380.

Ferencz, J., J. López-González & I. Oliván García, 2022, *Artificial Intelligence and International Trade: Some Preliminary Implications.* OECD Trade Policy Paper No. 260. Paris: OECD Publishing.

Filipova, I.A., 2024, "Legal Regulation of Artificial Intelligence: Experience of China". *Journal of Digital Technologies and Law* 2, 46–73.

Fischer, A.M. & S. Storm, 2023, "The Return of Debt Crisis in Developing Countries: Shifting or Maintaining Dominant Development Paradigms?". *Development and Change* 54(5), 954–993.

Fitz-Henry, E., & E. Klein, 2024, "From Just Transitions to Reparative Transformations". *Political Geography* 108, 1.

Fleming, S., 2025, "What is digital sovereignty and how are countries approaching it?". *World Economic Forum*, 10 January. At https://www.weforum.org/stories/2025/01/europe-digital-sovereignty/, accessed 27 October 2025.

Floridi, L., 2021, "The European Legislation on AI: A Brief Analysis of Its Philosophical Approach". *Philosophy & Technology* 34, 215–222.

Flowers, J.C., 2019, "Strong and Weak AI: Deweyan Considerations". *AAAI Spring Symposium: Towards Conscious AI Systems* 2019, 114.

Forrest, K.B., 2024, "The Ethics and Challenges of Legal Personhood for AI". *Yale Law Journal* 133.

Förster, T., 2023, "Alternatives to Restitution under Consideration. Local Perspectives on a Global Problem". In: T. Sandkühler, A. Epple & J. Zimmerer (eds.), *Historical Culture by Restitution? A Debate on Art, Museums, and Justice.* Leiden: Koninklijke Brill NV, 177–194.

Fox, S., 2024, "Soil Governance and Private Property". *Utah Law Review* 1, 1–56.

Freeman, K., 2016, "Algorithmic Injustice: How the Wisconsin Supreme Court Failed to Protect Due Process Rights in State v. Loomis". *North Carolina Journal of Law and Technology* 18, 75–106.

Fritzsche, K. & D. Spoiala, 2022, "The EU–AU Digital Partnership – Between Digital Geopolitics and Digital Sovereignty". In: C. Daniels, B. Erforth & C. Teevan (eds.), *Africa–Europe Cooperation and Digital Transformation*, 17–31.

From Lagos to the World (TTT Media), 2025, "Google's AI Forecasts Rain for Africa: A Game-Changer in Weather Prediction". *Medium*, 2 April 2025, at https://medium.com/@FromLagosto/googles-ai-forecasts-rain-for-africa-a-game-changer-in-weather-prediction-567b5c8f02eb, accessed 7 October 2025.

Gabor, D. & N.S. Sylla, 2023, "Derisking Developmentalism: A Tale of Green Hydrogen". *Development and Change* 54(5), 1169–1196.

Gardezi, M., B. Joshi, D.M. Rizzo, M. Ryan, E. Prutzer, S. Brugler & A. Dadkhah, 2024, "Artificial Intelligence in Farming: Challenges and Opportunities for Building Trust". *Agronomy Journal* 116, 1217–1228.

Gatla, T.R., 2024, "An Innovative Study Exploring Revolutionizing Healthcare with AI: Personalized Medicine, Predictive Diagnostic Techniques and Individualized Treatment". *International Journal of Advanced Research and Interdisciplinary Scientific Endeavours* 2, 61–70.

Gaur, A., A.K. Ray & S.J. Saxena, 2024, "Diabetes Prediction Using Supervised Machine Learning". In: M. Pandit, N. Paliwal, S.K. Rajput & T.P. Singh (eds.), *Smart Engineering Technology and Management (Proceedings of ISCMCTR–2023)*. New Delhi: Bharti Publications, 111–115.

Gedeon, J., 2025, "US Suspends Aid to South Africa After Trump Order". *The Guardian*, at https://www.theguardian.com/us-news/2025/mar/06/aid-trump-south-africa, accessed 27 September 2025.

Ghebretekle, T.B., 2017, "Traditional Natural Resource Conflict Resolution in East Africa: A Comparison of Formal Legal Systems in Ethiopia and Kenya". *African Journal on Conflict Resolution* 17(1).

Gilbert, P., 2025, "Google Commits $37M to Advancing AI in Africa". *Connecting Africa*, 24 July 2025, at https://www.connectingafrica.com/ai/google-commits-37m-to-advancing-ai-in-africa, accessed 7 October 2025.

Ginzky, H., 2021, "Soil Protection Governance in Germany". In: Ginzky, H., E. Dooley, I.L. Heuser, P. Kameri-Mbote, R. Kibugi, T. Markus & O.C. Ruppel (eds), *International Yearbook of Soil Law and Policy, Vol. 4*. Cham: Springer International Publishing, 295–333.

Ginzky, H., 2022, "Soil Governance: The Case of Implementation and Enforcement". *Soil Security*, Special Issue "Soil Governance", 6.

Ginzky, H., 2023, "Soil Governance at the International, Regional and National Level". In *Encyclopedia of Soils in the Environment* 3, 532–546.

Ginzky, H., 2024, "A New Soil Protection Legislation for Germany – Challenges, Conceptual Approaches and Next Steps". *Soil Security* (Special Issue II: Soil Governance).

Ginzky, H. & S. Pieper, 2025, "Soil Legislation by the European Union: An EU 'Soil Monitoring Law' on the Horizon?". In: Ginzky, H., O.C. Ruppel, I.L. Heuser, D. Grinlinton, A. Khatibi, P. Kameri-Mbote & N. Rodriguez-Eugenio (eds), *International Yearbook of Soil Law and Policy*, Vol. 7. Cham: Springer International Publishing, 411–433.

Ginzky, H. & O.C. Ruppel, 2025a, "Digitalisation, Artificial Intelligence and Sustainability in the Context of Sustainable Soil Management: The Future Role of Law and Governance?". In: H. Ginzky, O.C. Ruppel, I.L. Heuser, D. Grinlinton, A. Khatibi, P. Kameri-Mbote & N. Rodriguez-Eugenio (eds), *International Yearbook of Soil Law and Policy 2025*. Cham: Springer, 249–270.

Ginzky, H. & O.C. Ruppel, 2025b, "Executive Summary". In: Ruppel, O.C., H. Ginzky & R. Murray (eds), *Legal Pathways to Sustainable Soil Management in Africa: Insights from Botswana, Burkina*

*Faso, Cameroon, Kenya, Madagascar, Morocco, Mozambique, Namibia, South Africa, Uganda and Zambia.* Baden-Baden: Nomos, 19–42.

Ginzky, H., I.L. Heuser, T. Qin, O.C. Ruppel & P. Wegerdt (eds), 2017, *International Yearbook of Soil Law and Policy 2016.* Cham: Springer International Publishing.

Ginzky, H., E. Dooley, I.L. Heuser, E. Kasimbazi, T. Markus & T. Qin (eds), 2018, *International Yearbook of Soil Law and Policy 2017.* Cham: Springer International Publishing.

Ginzky, H., E. Dooley, I.L. Heuser, E. Kasimbazi, T. Markus & T. Qin (eds), 2019, *International Yearbook of Soil Law and Policy 2018.* Cham: Springer International Publishing.

Ginzky, H., E. Dooley, I.L. Heuser, E. Kasimbazi, R. Kibugi, T. Markus, T. Qin & O.C. Ruppel (eds), 2021a, *International Yearbook of Soil Law and Policy 2019.* Cham: Springer International Publishing.

Ginzky, H., P. Kameri-Mbote, C.F. Tamasang, T.P. Sambo & O.C. Ruppel, 2021b, "Mapping Out Options for Model Legislation for Sustainable Soil Management in Africa". In: *African Soil Protection Law – Mapping Out Options for a Model Legislation for Improved Sustainable Soil Management in Africa – A Comparative Legal Analysis from Cameroon, Kenya and Zambia.* Baden-Baden: Nomos, 379–454.

Ginzky, H., E. Dooley, I.L. Heuser, P. Kameri-Mbote, R. Kibugi, T. Markus & O.C. Ruppel (eds), 2022, *International Yearbook of Soil Law and Policy 2020/2021.* Cham: Springer International Publishing.

Ginzky, H., F. De Andrade Corrêa, E. Dooley, I.L. Heuser, P. Kameri-Mbote, R. Kibugi & O.C. Ruppel (eds), 2024, *International Yearbook of Soil Law and Policy 2022.* Cham: Springer International Publishing.

Ginzky, H., D. Grinlinton, I.L. Heuser, P. Kameri-Mbote, A. Khatibi, N. Rodriguez-Eugenio & O.C. Ruppel (eds), 2026, *International Yearbook of Soil Law and Policy 2025.* Cham: Springer International Publishing.

GIZ / Deutsche Gesellschaft für Internationale Zusammenarbeit, 2020, *The Renewable Energy Transition in Africa: Powering Access, Resilience and Prosperity.* Deutsche Gesellschaft für Internationale Zusammenarbeit (GIZ).

Gladwin, C.H., 2002, "Gender and Soil Fertility in Africa: Introduction". *African Studies Quarterly* 6(1&2).

Gooden, A., & D. Thaldar, 2024, "The Proposed Code of Conduct for Research in South Africa: Despite Good Progress, Unresolved Issues Remain". *Humanities and Social Sciences Communications* 11(251).

Graf, S., 2025, "Law, Time, and (in)justice After Empire: Germany's Objection to Colonial Reparations and the Chronopolitics of Deflection". *International Theory*, 1–28.

GRAIN, 2021, "Digital Control: How Big Tech Moves into Food and Farming (and What It Means)". *GRAIN*, 21 January 2021, at https://grain.org/en/article/6595-digital-control-how-big-tech-moves-into-food-and-farming-and-what-it-means, accessed 7 October 2025.

Gravett, W.H., 2022, "Digital Neocolonialism: The Chinese Surveillance State in Africa". *African Journal of International and Comparative Law* 30(1), 39–58.

Greenwood, J. & C. Roederer-Rynning, 2018, "The EU's Lawmaking Process in a Comparative Perspective". In: O. Costa (ed.), *The European Parliament in Times of Crisis: Dynamics and Transformations.* Cham: Palgrave Macmillan, 121–141.

Gret, 2024, "The Challenges of Land Governance in West Africa and Madagascar", March. At https://gret.org/en/the-challenges-of-land-governance-in-west-africa-and-madagascar/, accessed 2 October 2025.

Gualdi, F. & A. Cordella, 2021, *Artificial Intelligence and Decision-Making: The Question of Accountability*, Proceedings of the 54th Hawaii International Conference on System Sciences.

Guest, B., 2007, "The 'Row about the Great Diamond': The Presentation of the Cullinan Diamond to the British Crown, 1907". *Historia* 52(2), 112–124.

Guillermin, P., 2019, *L'élaboration et la mise en œuvre des politiques publiques: Approche structurée sur les dispositifs administratifs d'application des textes législatifs*. Paris: LGDJ.

Habermas, R., 2023, "Rescue Paradigm and Preservation Fetishism or: The Restitution Debate—Deep-Rooted in European Modernity?". In: T. Sandkühler, A. Epple & J. Zimmerer (eds.), *Historical Culture by Restitution? A Debate on Art, Museums, and Justice*. Leiden: Koninklijke Brill NV, 91-112.

Hacker, P., 2023, "Sustainable AI Regulation". SSRN https://papers.ssrn.com/sol3/papers.cfm?abstract_id=4467684.

Hackmack, J. & W. Kaleck, 2023, "Why Restitutions Matter: A Legal Reasoning". In: T. Sandkühler, A. Epple & J. Zimmerer (eds.), *Historical Culture by Restitution? A Debate on Art, Museums, and Justice*. Leiden: Koninklijke Brill NV, 399-424.

Hägele, R., G.I. Iacobuţă, & J. Tops, 2022, "Addressing Climate Goals and the SDGs Through a Just Energy Transition? Empirical Evidence from Germany and South Africa". *Journal of Integrative Environmental Sciences* 19(1), 85–120.

Hagos, T. & S. Dersso, 2025, "Is the AU Addressing the Challenges to Effective Enforcement of its Norm Banning Unconstitutional Changes of Government?". *Amani Africa*, at https://amaniafrica-et.org/is-the-au-addressing-the-challenges-to-effective-enforcement-of-its-norm-banning-unconstitutional-changes-of-government2/, accessed 9 July 2025.

Hall, C.M., 2019, "Constructing Sustainable Tourism Development: The 2030 Agenda and the Managerial Ecology of Sustainable Tourism". *Journal of Sustainable Tourism* 27(7), 1044–1060.

Hannam, I., 2006, "International and National Legal and Institutional Frameworks for Sustainable Use of Soil". *South African Journal of Environmental Law and Policy* 13, 223–232.

Harvey, F., 2025, "Energy Demands from AI Datacentres to Quadruple by 2030, Says Report". *The Guardian*, 10 April 2025, at https://www.theguardian.com/technology/2025/apr/10/energy-demands-from-ai-datacentres-to-quadruple-by-2030-says-report, accessed 7 October 2025.

Häusling, M., 2025, "Soil Monitoring and Resilience (Soil Monitoring Directive): The New – and First – EU Directive on Soil". *European Parliament*, at https://www.europarl.europa.eu/, accessed 11 March 2026.

Heinrich-Böll-Stiftung, 2024, *The Soil Atlas: Facts and Figures About a Vital Resource*.

Herder, J.G., 2004, *Another Philosophy of History and Selected Political Writings*. Indianapolis: Hackett Publishing.

Heuser, I., 2022, "Soil Governance in Current European Union Law and in the European Green Deal". *Soil Security* 6, 1–6.

Heuser, I.L. & I. Itey, 2021, "The European Green Deal: Progress for Soil Protection?". In: Ginzky, H., E. Dooley, I.L. Heuser, P. Kameri-Mbote, R. Kibugi, T. Markus & O.C. Ruppel (eds), *International Yearbook of Soil Law and Policy*, Vol. 5. Cham: Springer International Publishing, 263–304.

Hickel, J., 2020, *Less Is More: How Degrowth Will Save the World*. New York, NY: Random House.

Hilliard, A., 2023, "How is Brazil Leading South America's AI Legislation Efforts?". *Holistic AI*, at https://www.holisticai.com/blog/brazil-ai-legislation-proposals, accessed 20 March 2026.

Hilliard, A., A. Gulley, E. Kazim & A.S. Koshiyama, 2026, "Artificial Intelligence Policy Worldwide: A Comparative Analysis". *Royal Society Open Science* 13(2).

Hinz, M.O. & O.C. Ruppel (eds.), 2008, *Biodiversity and the Ancestors: Challenges to Customary and Environmental Law. Case Studies from Namibia.* Windhoek: Namibia Scientific Society.

Hinz, M.O., O.C. Ruppel & C. Mapaure (eds.), 2012, *Knowledge Lives in the Lake: Case Studies in Environmental and Customary Law from Southern Africa.* Windhoek: Namibia Scientific Society, 274 pp.

Holmes, G., 2012, "Biodiversity for Billionaires: Capitalism, Conservation and the Role of Philanthropy in Saving/selling Nature". *Development and Change* 43(1), 185–203.

Hooghe, L. & G. Marks, 2019, "Grand Theories of European Integration in the Twenty-first Century". *Journal of European Public Policy* 26(8), 1113–1133.

Hou, D., X. Jia, L. Wang, S.P. McGrath, Y.-G. Zhu, Q. Hu, F.-J. Zhao, M.S. Bank, D. O'Connor & J. Nriagu, 2025, "Global Soil Pollution by Toxic Metals Threatens Agriculture and Human Health". *Science* 388, 316–321.

Howard-Hassmann, R.E., 2004, "Reparations to Africa and the Group of Eminent Persons". *Cahiers d'études africaines* XLIV(1–2), 173–74.

Hu, B. & A. Au, 2025, "China Resets the Path to Comprehensive AI Governance". *East Asia Forum*, 25 December. Available at: https://eastasiaforum.org/2025/12/25/china-resets-the-path-to-comprehensive-ai-governance/.

Hughes, K.M., 2021, "Climate and Gender Justice in Sub-Saharan Africa: Emerging Trends Post-Paris 2015". *Wisconsin International Law Journal* 38, 197–230.

Hunt, T., 2019, "Should Museums Return their Colonial Artefacts?". *The Guardian*, at https://www.theguardian.com/culture/2019/jun/29/should-museums-return-their-colonial-artefacts, accessed 22 September 2025.

Hunter, Q., 2025, "Is South Africa 'Confiscating Land', Targeting some Groups as Trump Claims?". *Aljazeera*, at https://www.aljazeera.com/news/2025/2/5/is-south-africa-confiscating-land-targeting-some-groups-as-trump-claims, accessed 27 September 2025.

Hunt-Hendrix, L. & A. Taylor, 2024, *Solidarity: The Past, Present, and Future of a World-Changing Idea.* New York: Pantheon.

iAfrica, 2025, "Africa's First AI Factory Underway as Cassava and Nvidia Deploy 3,000 GPUs in South Africa". *iAfrica*, at https://iafrica.com/africas-first-ai-factory-underway-as-cassava-and-nvidia-deploy-3000-gpus-in-south-africa/, accessed 7 October 2025.

Ibbott, S., 2025, "A Weak Deal for Europe's Soils". *European Environmental Bureau*, at https://eeb.org/a-weak-deal-for-europes-soils, accessed 12 July 2025.

Ibrahim, I.M. & A.M. Abdulazeez, 2021, "The Role of Machine Learning Algorithms for Diagnosing Diseases". *Journal of Applied Science and Technology Trends* 2, 10–19.

Idugie, G.O. & A.U. Onochie, 2025, "Regulatory Frameworks and Challenges in the Repatriation of Benin Artefacts: A Postcolonial African Perspective on Cultural Heritage Preservation". *African Journal of Law and Human Rights (AJLHR)* 9(1), 70.

Ikram, I., 2025, "The Intersection of Environmental Law and Climate Justice in India: A Critical Analysis". *Indian Journal of Integrated Research in Law* 5(2), 1136–1147.

ILO / International Labour Organisation, 2023, *Just Transition Policy Brief.*

International Bar Association & Center for AI and Digital Policy, 2024, *The Future is Now: Artificial Intelligence and the Legal Profession.* September.

International Commission of Jurists, 2022, *Digital Technologies and Human Rights: A Legal Framework.* Briefing Paper, May.

IPCC / Intergovernmental Panel on Climate Change, 2019, *Climate Change and Land: An IPCC Special Report on Climate Change, Desertification, Land Degradation, Sustainable Land Management, Food Security, and Greenhouse Gas Fluxes in Terrestrial Ecosystems.*

IPCC / Intergovernmental Panel on Climate Change, 2022, "Summary for Policy Makers" in *Climate Change 2022: Impacts, Adaptation, and Vulnerability.* Working Group II to the Sixth Assessment Report.

ITPS / Intergovernmental Technical Panel on Soils, 2023, *Soil Letters #6: Soils, Where Food Begins – How Can Soils Continue to Sustain the Growing Need for Food Production in the Current Fertilizer Crisis?* Rome: Food and Agriculture Organization of the United Nations (FAO).

Jackson, I., D. Ivanov, A. Dolgui & J. Namdar, 2024, "Generative Artificial Intelligence in Supply Chain and Operations Management: A Capability-Based Framework for Analysis and Implementation". *International Journal of Production Research* 62, 6120–6145.

Jayaraman, S., M. Krishna, G.S. Yadav & R. Lal, 2023, "Sustainable Soil Management: Challenges, Prospects, and Benefits". In: S. Jayaraman, R.C. Dalal & R. Lal (eds.), *Sustainable Soil Management: Beyond Food Production.* Newcastle upon Tyne: Cambridge Scholars Publishing, 1–22.

Jenkins, K., D. McCauley, R. Heffron, H. Stephan & R. Rehner, 2016, "Energy Justice: A Conceptual Review". *Energy Research & Social Science* 11, 174–182.

Jensen, D. & S. Halle, 2015, *Natural Resources and Conflict: A Guide for Mediation Practitioners.* Nairobi: United Nations Environment Programme.

Johnson, K.B., W.-Q. Wei, D. Weeraratne, M.E. Frisse, K. Misulis, K. Rhee, J. Zhao & J.L. Snowdon, 2021, "Precision Medicine, AI, and the Future of Personalized Health Care". *Clinical and Translational Science* 14, 86–93.

Jones, K. & M. Buchser, 2022, "Challenges of AI". *Chatham House*, at https://www.chathamhouse.org/2022/03/challenges-ai, accessed 7 October 2025.

Judge, B., M. Nitzberg & S. Russell, 2025, "When Code Isn't Law: Rethinking Regulation for Artificial Intelligence". *Policy and Society* 44, 85–97.

Ka Mtuze, S.S. & M. Morige, 2024, "Towards Drafting Artificial Intelligence (AI) in South Africa". *Obiter* 161–180.

Kairouan, A. 2024. *Le Maroc et le droit international des investissements étrangers.* Legitech L.G.D.J., Collection Droit et Économie.

Kameoka, K. & M.A. Takahashi, 2025, "Social and Ecological Sustainability of Land Improvement and Soil Use in the Japanese Agricultural Sector: Focusing on Gender Equality and Biodiversity". In: Ginzky, H., O.C. Ruppel, I.L. Heuser, D. Grinlinton, A. Khatibi, P. Kameri-Mbote & N. Rodriguez-Eugenio (eds), *International Yearbook of Soil Law and Policy*, Vol. 7. Cham: Springer International Publishing, 477–490.

Kameri-Mbote, P. & P. Cullet, 1997, "Law, Colonialism and Environmental Management in Africa". *Review of European Community and International Environmental Law* 6(1), 23–31.

Kameri-Mbote, P., 2007, "Access, Control, and Ownership: Women and Sustainable Environmental Management in Africa". *Agenda: Empowering Women for Gender Equity* 72, 36–46.

Karpiuk-Wawryszuk, N. & K. Kasprowicz, 2025, "Legal Cultures and Strategies for Implementing Artificial Intelligence Regulations: Case Studies of the United States, People's Republic of China and European Union". *Teka Komisji Prawniczej PAN Oddział w Lublinie* 18(1), 131–147.

Kasimbazi, E., 2017, *Land Tenure and Rights for Improved Land Management and Sustainable Development (Global Land Outlook Working Paper).* Bonn: United Nations Convention to Combat Desertification.

Kassem, H.S., M.A. Hussein & H. Ismail, 2021, "Toward Fraudulent Pesticides in Rural Areas: Do Farmers' Recognition and Purchasing Behaviours Matter?" *Agronomy* 11(9), 1882.

Kassner, L. & O.C. Ruppel, 2025, "Soil Protection under African Union Law: Status Quo and Developmental Perspectives based on a Comparative Analysis with European Union Law". In: O. C. Ruppel, H. Ginzky & R. Murray (eds), *Legal Pathways to Sustainable Soil Management in Africa: Insights from Botswana, Burkina Faso, Cameroon, Kenya, Madagascar, Morocco, Mozambique, Namibia, South Africa, Uganda and Zambia.* Baden-Baden: Nomos, 749–803.

Kataray, T., R. Kumar & P. Saini, 2023, "Integration of Smart Grid with Renewable Energy Sources: Opportunities and Challenges – A Comprehensive Review". *Sustainable Energy Technologies and Assessments* 58, 103363.

Katzav, G., 2022, "Has POPIA Adequately Prepared People to Exercise Their Right Not to Be Subject to Automated Decision-Making?". *De Rebus*, 1 September 2022, at https://www.derebus.org.za/has-popia-adequately-prepared-people-to-exercise-their-right-not-to-be-subject-to-automated-decision-making/, accessed 7 October 2025.

Keet, A. & D. Rafaely, 2025, "'Beyond' Critique: Universities, Human Rights, Decolonisation, and the Sustainable Development Goals". *Comparative Education* 61(3), 461–479.

Kelley, R.D.G., 2002, *Freedom Dreams: The Black Radical Imagination.* Boston, MA: Beacon Press.

Kelly, A.M. & N.L. Nembot, 2025, "Understanding the Nexus: Economic Complexity and Environmental Degradation in Sub-Saharan Africa". *Clean Technologies and Environmental Policy* 27, 423–437.

Kholdorov, S., Z. Jabbarov & T. Shamsiddinov, 2023, "Soil Governance: A Review of the Current Legislative Framework for Managing Soil Resources in Uzbekistan". *Soil Security* 13, 100105.

Kidd, M., 2010, "Public Interest Environmental Litigation: Recent Cases Raise Possible Obstacles". *Potchefstroom Electronic Law Journal* 13(5), 27–45.

Kinhoh, H., 2023, "Why Aren't More African Union Decisions on Security Implemented". *Institute for Security Studies*, at https://issafrica.org/iss-today/why-arent-more-african-union-decisions-on-security-implemented, accessed 9 July 2025.

Klesmith, E.A., 2014, "Nigeria and Mali: The Case for Repatriation and Protection of Cultural Heritage in Post-Colonial Africa". *Notre Dame Journal of International & Comparative Law* 4(1), 45.

Klutse, A.R., A. Bationo & A. Mando, 2018, "Socioeconomic Determinants and Trends in Fertilizer Use in West Africa". In: *Improving the Profitability, Sustainability, and Efficiency of Nutrients through Site-specific Fertilizer Recommendations in West African Agro-ecosystems: Volume 1.* Cham: Springer, 253–274.

Kok-Chor, T. 2007. "Colonialism, Reparations and Global Justice". In: J. Miller & R. Kumar (eds.), *Reparations: Interdisciplinary Inquiries.* Oxford: Oxford University Press, 280–306.

Krauss, J.E., 2021, "Decolonizing Conviviality and Convivial Conservation: Towards a Convivial SDG 15, Life on Land?". *Journal of Political Ecology* 28(1), 945–967.

Kribek, B., I. Nyambe, O. Sracek, M. Mihaljevič, V. Majer & F. Veselovsky, 2023, "Impact of Mining and Ore Processing on Soil, Drainage, and Vegetation in the Zambian Copperbelt Mining Districts: A Review". *Minerals* 13(3), 384.

Krzywoszynska, A. & G. Marchesi, 2020, "Toward a Relational Materiality of Soils". *Environmental Humanities* 12(1), 190–204.

Kudama, G., M. Dangia, H. Wana & B. Tadese, 2021, "Will Digital Solutions Transform Sub-Saharan African Agriculture". *Artificial Intelligence in Agriculture* 5, 292–300.

Kumar, K., A. Palit, S. Sindhu, D. Divya, Yogita, R.L. Moharana, S. Hansda & A. Kumar, 2024, "Artificial Intelligence and Machine Learning in Soil Analysis Innovations for Sustainable Agriculture: A Review". *International Journal of Advanced Biochemistry Research* 8, 869–878.

Kuyoro, M. & U. Bagus, A. Bensrhir & Z. Bobat, 2025, "Leading, Not Lagging: Africa's Gen AI Opportunity". *McKinsey & Company*, 12 May 2025, at https://www.mckinsey.com/capabilities/quantumblack/our-insights/leading-not-lagging-africas-gen-ai-opportunity, accessed 7 October 2025.

Kuzelewska, E., 2014, "Unity in Diversity, the Language of the European Union". *Studies in Logic, Grammar and Rhetoric* 38(51), 151–165.

Kwarkye, T. G., 2025, "AI Policies in Africa: Lessons from Ghana and Rwanda". *The Conversation*, 25 April. At https://theconversation.com/ai-policies-in-africa-lessons-from-ghana-and-rwanda-253642, accessed 27 October 2025.

Kyere-Boateng, R. & M.V. Marek, 2021, "Analysis of the Social-Ecological Causes of Deforestation and Forest Degradation in Ghana: Application of the DPSIR Framework". *Forests* 12(4), 409.

Lahiri, B. & W.A. Darity Jr., 2024, "Global North–South Reparations: Demand-side and Supply-side Policies with a Dynamic View of International Trade and Finance". *Forum* 55(4), 1–21.

Laker, M.C., 2023, "Environmental Impacts of Gold Mining – With Special Reference to South Africa". *Mining* 3(2), 205–227.

Lamodiere, J. 1977. *L'évolution du droit des investissements étrangers au Maroc*. Centre de recherches et d'études sur les sociétés méditerranéennes.

Lane, M., 2016, "Political Theory on Climate Change". *Annual Review of Political Science* 19, 107–123.

Lang, M.K., 2017, "Land Disputes Between the Catholic Church and the Indigenes of Weh Fondom, 1957–1996". *Ghana Social Science Journal* 14(1), 109–138.

Langan, M., 2018, *Neo-colonialism and the Poverty of 'Development' in Africa*. Cham: Springer.

Laurens, N., 2023, "Institutional Adaptation in Slow Motion: Zooming in on Desertification Governance". *Global Environmental Politics* 23(2), 31.

Lavie, J. P., & Virally, M. 2015. *Protection et promotion des investissements étrangers: Étude de droit économique*.

Lawyers Hub, 2024, "Artificial Intelligence and Parliaments in Africa". *Lawyers Hub*, 15 October 2024, at https://www.lawyershub.org/news/post/artificial-intelligence-and-parliaments-in-africa, accessed 7 October 2025.

Lawyers Hub, 2024, *5 Years of AI Regulation in Africa*.

Leben, C. 2006. *Le contentieux arbitral transnational relatif à l'investissement*. Anthémis.

Leite, C.R.D.A.B. & C.G. Marreiros, 2026, "Critical Analysis of Portuguese and European Union Soil Legislation Based on Information Available in the SoiLEX Database". *Preprints* 1–37, doi:10.20944/preprints202502.0168.v2.

Lemma, A., P. Agarwal & D.W. te Velde, 2024, *Implementing the Digital Trade Protocol of the African Continental Free Trade Area: Expected Impacts, Early Experiences and Challenges Ahead*. London: ODI Global.

Lengoiboni, M., A.K. Bregt & P. Van der Molen, 2010, "Pastoralism within Land Administration in Kenya: The Missing Link". *Land Use Policy* 27(2), 579–588.

Lentz, C., 2013, *Land, Mobility, and Belonging in West Africa: Natives and Strangers*. Bloomington, IN: Indiana University Press.

Letseka, M., 2012, "In Defence of Ubuntu". *Studies in Philosophy and Education* 31, 47–60.

Li, T.M., 2014, "What Is Land? Assembling a Resource for Global Investment". *Transactions of the Institute of British Geographers* 39(4) 589–602.

Liboiron, M., 2021, *Pollution Is Colonialism*. Durham, NC: Duke University Press.

Lisinski, R., 2025, "Regulation of Artificial Intelligence in South Africa: Progress, Challenges and the Road Ahead". *Fluxmans*, at https://www.fluxmans.com/article/ai-regulation-south-africa, accessed 7 October 2025.

Long, J., 2024, "Reckoning Climate Apartheid". *Political Geography* 112, 1–9.

Lopez, I.P. 2016. *Le droit à un monde immuable: L'expropriation indirecte dans les accords internationaux d'investissement et la souveraineté des États.*

Lousqui, D., 2025, "AI Regulation and the New Geography of Influence". SSRN https://papers.ssrn.com/sol3/papers.cfm?abstract_id=5227415.

Lu, M., 2025, "Visualizing Global AI Investment by Country". *Visual Capitalist*, 21 April 2025, at https://www.visualcapitalist.com/visualizing-global-ai-investment-by-country/, accessed 7 October 2025.

Lynch, S., 2017, "Andrew Ng: Why AI Is the New Electricity". *Stanford Graduate School of Business (Insights)*, 11 March 2017, at https://www.gsb.stanford.edu/insights/andrew-ng-why-ai-new-electricity, accessed 7 October 2025.

Lyon, C.F., 2023, "Fake Cases, Real Consequences: Misuse of ChatGPT Leads to Sanctions". New York State Bar Association *NYLitigator* 28(2), 8–12.

MacDonnell, L.J., 1988, "Natural Resources Dispute Resolution: An Overview". *Natural Resources Journal* 28(1), 5–25.

Mack, E., 2014, "Elon Musk: 'We Are Summoning the Demon' with Artificial Intelligence". *CNET*, 26 October 2014, at https://www.cnet.com/science/elon-musk-we-are-summoning-the-demon-with-artificial-intelligence/, accessed 7 October 2025.

Mahlangu, J., 2025, *Comparing the Governance Models of the EU and the AU*. PhD thesis, *University of Pretoria*, at https://www.researchgate.net/publication/391444558_Comparing_the_governance_models_of_the_EU_and_the_AU, accessed 23 March 2026.

Makki, F., 2018, "The Political Ecology of Land Grabs in Ethiopia". In: R. Rozzi, R.H. May Jr., F.S. Chapin III, F. Massardo, M.C. Gavin, I.J. Klaver, A. Pauchard, M.A. Nuñez & D. Simberloff (eds.), *From Biocultural Homogenization to Biocultural Conservation*. Cham: Springer Nature Switzerland, 83–96.

Makulilo, A.B., 2024, "Data Privacy in Africa: Taking Stock of Its Development After Two Decades". In: L.A. Abdulrauf & H. Dube (eds.), *Data Privacy Law in Africa: Emerging Perspectives*. Pretoria: Pretoria University Law Press (PULP), 41–77.

Malherbe, N. & A.O. Oladejo, 2025, "Against Climate Aid Colonialism: The Case for Climate Reparations and South–South Solidarity". *Africa Spectrum* 60(1), 84–105.

Mamina, O. & E. Kobzeva, 2021, "Experimental Legal Regimes for Digital Innovation and a Special Regulation Mechanism: New Concepts of Russian Legislation and First Projects". *SHS Web of Conferences* 106, 02009.

Mandal, M., 2023, "Role of Women in Sustainable Soil Management: Some Legal Reflections". In: B.H. Desai (ed.), *Soil Law and Governance in India* (*International Yearbook of Soil Law and Policy*). Cham: Springer.

Mapfumo, P., J. Rurinda, L. Cramer, T.D. Mushore & G. Wamukoya, 2025, "Developing Just Transition Pathways for Africa's Agriculture towards Low Emission and Climate Resilient Development under a 1.5 °C Global Warming". *CABI Reviews* 20(1), 1.

Martinez, R., 2019, "Artificial Intelligence: Distinguishing Between Types & Definitions". *Nevada Law Journal* 19, 1015–1023.

Martinez-Alier, J., 2018, "Ecological Distribution Conflicts and the Vocabulary of Environmental Justice". In: V. Dayal, A. Duraiappah & N. Nawn (eds.), *Ecology, Economy and Society*. Singapore: Springer, 187–204.

Massey, K., R. Jyoti, D. Schubmehl, E. Elshewy, K. Ghildiyal, N. Guo, C. La Croce, T. Manabe, H. Roman & V. Venkatesh, 2024, *IDC's Worldwide AI and Generative AI Spending Guide Taxonomy: 2024, Release V1*.

Maxwell, S., 2025, "Farmland Abandonment Worldwide: The Detrimental Factor of Agricultural Crisis". *Science Insights* 46(2) 1741–1748.

Mazique, B., 2024, "Oleksandr Usyk vs. Tyson Fury 2 Results: Winner, Scorecards, Reaction". *Forbes*, 21 December. At https://www.forbes.com/sites/brianmazique/2024/12/21/oleksandr-usyk-vs-tyson-fury-2-results-winner-scorecards-reaction/, accessed 29 October 2025.

Mazwi, F. & G.T. Mudimu, 2021, "A Review of State-based Land Tenure: A Special Reference to Land Rights and Access to Rural Finance". In: H. Chitonge & R. Harvey (eds.), *Land Tenure Challenges in Africa: Confronting the Land Governance Deficit*. Cham: Springer, 225–245.

Mbonye, V., M. Moodley & F. Nyika, 2024, "Examining the Applicability of the Protection of Personal Information Act in AI-Driven Environments". *South African Journal of Information Management* 26(1), 1–9.

McAuliffe, P., 2021, "Complicity or Decolonization? Restitution of Heritage from 'Global Ethnographic Museums'". *International Journal of Transitional Justice* 15, 678–689.

McAuslan, P., 2006, "Legal Pluralism as a Policy Option: Is it Desirable? Is it Doable?" In: M. Mwangi & E. Patrick (eds.), *Land Rights for African Development – From Knowledge to Action*, 9–11, at https://landwise-production.s3.us-west-2.amazonaws.com/2022/03/UNDP_Land-rights-for-African-development-from-knowledge-to-action_2006.pdf, accessed 7 April 2026.

McCauley, D. & R. Heffron, 2018, "Just Transition: Integrating Climate, Energy and Environmental Justice". *Energy Policy*. 119, 1–7.

McLean, S., G.J.M. Read, J. Thompson, C. Baber, N.A. Stanton & P.M. Salmon, 2023, "The Risks Associated with Artificial General Intelligence: A Systematic Review". *Journal of Experimental & Theoretical Artificial Intelligence* 35, 649–663.

Media Institute of Southern Africa, 2025, "African Commission Study Charts Path for Ethical AI in Africa". *Press Council of South Africa*, 14 May. At https://presscouncil.org.za/2025/05/14/african-commission-study-charts-path-for-ethical-ai-in-africa/, accessed 27 October 2025.

Melber, H., 2024, "Colonialism, Genocide and Reparations: The German-Namibian Case". *Development and Change Forum* 55(4), 773–799.

Mesele, S.A., F. Tadesse & T.A. Liyew, 2025, "Current Problems Leading to Soil Degradation in Africa: Raising Awareness and Finding Potential Solutions". *European Journal of Soil Science* 76(1), e70069.

Meuck, M., C. Gaie & D. Gkikas, 2025, "Introduction to the European Artificial Intelligence Act". In: M. Meuck & C. Gaie (eds.), *European Digital Regulation*. Cham: Springer, 53–91.

Meuck, M., S. Du Boispean & C. Gaie, 2025, "Overview on European Digital Legislation". In: M. Meuck & C. Gaie (eds.), *European Digital Regulation*. Cham: Springer, 21–50.

Meulemans, G., 2020, "Wormy Collaborations in Practices of Soil Construction". *Theory, Culture & Society* 37(1), 93–112.

Middleton, C., 2025, "US AI Action Plan Part 1 – Beware of Its Local and Environmental Consequences, Warns the ACM". *Diginomica*, 29 August 2025, at https://diginomica.com/us-ai-action-plan-part-one-beware-its-local-and-environmental-consequences-warns-amc, accessed 8 October 2025.

Mienye, D.I., Y. Sun & E. Ileberi, 2024, "Artificial Intelligence and Sustainable Development in Africa: A Comprehensive Review". *Machine Learning with Applications* 16, 1–6.

Min, K., 2025, "South Korea's PIPC Flexes Its Muscles: What to Know about AI Model Deletion, Cross-Border Transfers and More". *IAPP*, at https://iapp.org/news/a/south-korea-s-pipc-flexes-its-muscles-what-to-know-about-ai-model-deletion-cross-border-transfers-and-more, accessed 20 March 2026.

Mishra, H. & D. Mishra, 2023, "Artificial Intelligence and Machine Learning in Agriculture: Transforming Farming Systems". In: *Research Trends in Agriculture Science*, Volume I. Pune: Bhumi Publishing, 1–16.

Molnár, Z., Á. Fernández-Llamazares, C. Schunko, I. Teixidor-Toneu, I. Jarić, I. Díaz-Reviriego, C. Ivascu, D. Babai, L. Sáfián, P. Karlsen, H. Dai & R. Hill, 2023, "Social Justice for Traditional Knowledge Holders Will Help Conserve Europe's Nature". *Biological Conservation* 285, 1-23.

Montaño-Lopez, F., M. Guevara & A. Biswas, 2021, "Soil Science Research and Development in Latin America and the Caribbean". In: A. Rakshit, S.K. Singh, P.C. Abhilash & A. Biswas (eds.), *Soil Science: Fundamentals to Recent Advances*. Singapore: Springer Nature Singapore Pte Ltd, 613–622.

Montgomery, D.R., 2018, *Growing a Revolution: Bringing our Soil back to Life*. New York, NY: W.W. Norton & Company.

Moodley, N., 2026, "AI Reshapes SA's Financial Sector, but the Rulebook Is Still Catching Up". *Daily Maverick*, at https://www.dailymaverick.co.za/article/2026-03-19-ai-reshapes-sas-financial-sector-but-the-rulebook-is-still-catching-up/, accessed 20 March 2026.

Moran, M.E., 2006, "Epochs in Endourology: The da Vinci Robot". *Journal of Endourology* 20, 986–990.

Morvaridi, B., 2012, "Capitalist Philanthropy and Hegemonic Partnerships". *Third World Quarterly* 33(7), 1191–1210.

Moseley, W.G., 2024, *Decolonizing African Agriculture: Food Security, Agroecology and the Need for Radical Transformation*. Newcastle upon Tyne: Agenda Publishing.

Müller, A., 2022, "Der Artificial Intelligence Act der EU: Ein risikobasierter Ansatz zur Regulierung von künstlicher Intelligenz". *Zeitschrift für Europarecht* (1), A1.

Munos, J., 2017, "Intercultural Europe: Cultural Diversity in the EU and the Debate on a Common European Cultural Identity". *Papeles de Europa* 30(2), 149–161.

Murray, R. & O.C. Ruppel, 2025, "Positioning the Pan-African Parliament: Origins, Legal Authority, and Its Role in Strengthening Africa's Soil Governance Framework". In: Ruppel, O.C., H. Ginzky & R. Murray (eds), *Legal Pathways to Sustainable Soil Management in Africa: Insights from Botswana, Burkina Faso, Cameroon, Kenya, Madagascar, Morocco, Mozambique, Namibia, South Africa, Uganda and Zambia*. Baden-Baden: Nomos, 749–801.

Mutingwende, B.A., 2025a, "Pan-African Parliament Committee Discusses Model Law on Soil: A Milestone for Climate and Agricultural Justice". *Spiked Media*, at https://spikedmedia.co.zw/pan-african-parliament-committee-discusses-model-law-on-soil-a-milestone-for-climate-and-agricultural-justice/, accessed 11 March 2026.

Mutingwende, B.A., 2025b, "PAP Adoption of Model Law on Sustainable Soil Management: Step Toward Food Security and Climate Resilience". *Spiked Media*, at https://spikedmedia.co.zw/pap-adoption-of-model-law-on-sustainable-soil-management-step-toward-food-security-and-climate-resilience/, accessed 11 March 2026.

Mwangi, J. & W. Njoroge, 2024, "AI-Driven Innovations in Financial Technology: A Review of Algorithmic Trading and Risk Management". *Artificial Intelligence and Machine Learning Review* 5, 1–9.

Nabuurs, G.-J., R. Mrabet, A. Abu Hatab, M. Bustamante, H. Clark, P. Havlík, J. House, C. Mbow, K.N. Ninan, A. Popp, S. Roe, B. Sohngen & S. Towprayoon, 2022, "Agriculture, Forestry, and Other Land Uses (AFOLU)". In: P.R. Shukla, J. Skea, R. Slade, A. Al Khourdajie, R. van Diemen, D. McCollum, M. Pathak, S. Some, P. Vyas, R. Fradera, J. Malley, M. Belkacemi & A. Hasija (eds.), *Climate Change 2022: Mitigation of Climate Change. Contribution of Working Group III to the Sixth Assessment Report of the Intergovernmental Panel on Climate Change*. Cambridge: Cambridge University Press.

Naidoo, V. & D. Plaatjies, 2026, "AI Regulation Progress in South Africa – A Further Step in the Right Direction". *Fasken*, at https://www.fasken.com/en/knowledge/2026/03/ai-regulation-progress-in-south-africa-a-further-step-in-the-right-direction, accessed 20 March 2026.

Nalwimba, N., 2024, *Working Paper No. 66: Digital Technology in Zambian Agriculture: A Scoping Report*.

Naré, R.W.A., P.W. Savadogo, Z. Gnankambary, H.B. Nacro & M.P. Sedogo, 2015, "Analysing Risks Related to the Use of Pesticides in Vegetable Gardens in Burkina Faso". *Agriculture, Forestry and Fisheries* 4(4) 165–172.

Nathaniel, S.P. & N. Adeleye, 2021, "Environmental Preservation Amidst Carbon Emissions, Energy Consumption, and Urbanization in Selected African Countries: Implications for Sustainability". *Journal of Cleaner Production* 285 124825.

Navshree, J., N. Wadhwa, M. Bhatia, P. Sharma, L. Khomdram, A. Mishra & S. Kaushik Love, 2025, "Impact of Pesticides on Soil Health of Agroecosystems and Plant Nutrition: Challenges and Sustainable Management". In: *CABI Books*, 44–73.

Ncube, S., 2020, "Human Rights Enforcement in Africa: Enhancing the Pan-African Parliament's Capacity to Promote and Protect Human Rights". *African Human Rights Law Journal* 20(1), 103–124.

Ndlovu-Gatsheni, S., 2012, "Fiftieth Anniversary of Decolonisation in Africa: A Moment of Celebration or Critical Reflection?". *Third World Quarterly* 33(1), 71–89.

Ndlovu-Gatsheni, S.J. & K. Tafira, 2018, "The Invention of the Global South and the Politics of South–south Solidarity". In: E. Fiddian-Qasmiyeh & P. Daley (eds.), *Routledge Handbook of South-South Relations*. London: Routledge, 127–140.

Négoce, N., N. Booty & J. Griffin, 2025, "Akon's Futuristic $6bn City Project in Senegal Abandoned, *BBC* Told". BBC News, at https://www.bbc.com/news/articles/c8xvrv21drjo, accessed 7 October 2025.

NEPAD / New Partnership for Africa's Development, undated, "Where are We? Agenda 2063 Progress Tracker". *Agenda 2063*, at https://www.nepad.org/agenda2063, accessed 25 September 2015.

Newell, P. & D. Mulvaney, 2013 "The Political Economy of the 'Just Transition'". *The Geographical Journal* 179, 132–140.

Niang, I., O.C. Ruppel, M.A. Abdrabo, A. Essel, C. Lennard, J. Padgham & P. Urquhart, 2014, "Africa". In: C.B. Field, V.R. Barros, K.J. Mach, M.D. Mastrandrea, K. Ebi, M. Chatterjee, Y. Estrada, R.C. Genova, B. Girma, E.S. Kissel, A.N. Levy, S. MacCracken, P.R. Mastrandrea, T.E. Bilir, D.J. Dokken & L.L. White (eds.), *Climate Change 2014: Impacts, Adaptation, and Vulnerability. Part B: Regional Aspects. Contribution of Working Group II to the Fifth Assessment Report of the Intergovernmental Panel on Climate Change*. Cambridge: Cambridge University Press, 1199–1265.

Nietzel, B., 2023, "Protection of Cultural Property in Europe since the 19th Century between Legalization and Colonial Practice". In: T. Sandkühler, A. Epple & J. Zimmerer (eds.), *Historical Culture by Restitution? A Debate on Art, Museums, and Justice*. Leiden: Koninklijke Brill NV, 161–176.

Njoroge, J., 2024, "Potential Role of African Union in Development of AI Governance Across the Continent". *European Journal of Science Studies* 1(10), 11.

Novak, M., 2024, "DoNotPay Has to Pay Up Over 'World's First Robot Lawyer'". *Gizmodo*, 25 September 2024, at https://gizmodo.com/donotpay-has-to-pay-up-over-worlds-first-robot-lawyer-2000503265, accessed 7 October 2025.

Nsah, K.T., 2023, "Conserving Africa's Eden? Green Colonialism, Neoliberal Capitalism, and Sustainable Development in Congo Basin literature". *Humanities* 12(3), 1–24.

Nussbaum, B., 2003, "African Culture and Ubuntu: Reflections of a South African in America". *World Business Academy: Rekindling the Human Spirit in Business* 17(1), 1–12.

Nxumalo, S.B., 2025, "Introducing Ubuntu to Property Law: A Case for Environmental Stewardship". *Edinburgh Student Law Review* 5(2), 1–23.

Nyst, A., 2024, "History of ChatGPT: A Timeline of the Meteoric Rise of Generative AI Chatbots". *Search Engine Journal*, 9 October. At https://www.searchenginejournal.com/history-of-chatgpt-timeline/488370/, accessed 2 October 2025.

Obeng-Odoom, F., 2021, "Oil Cities in Africa: Beyond Just Transition". *American Journal of Economics and Sociology* 80(2), 777.

Obeng-Odoom, F., 2022, *The Case for Ecological Reparations in Africa*. Nanyang Technological University – Singapore Business Federation Centre for African Studies.

OECD / Organisation for Economic Co-operation and Development, 2024a, *Assessing Potential Future Artificial Intelligence Risks, Benefits and Policy Imperatives*. Paris: OECD.

OECD / Organisation for Economic Co-operation and Development (Policy Network on Artificial Intelligence), 2024b, *Sub-group on AI Governance, Interoperability and Good Practices: Discussion Paper on AI Governance, Interoperability and Good Practices*.

OECD / Organisation for Economic Co-operation and Development, 2025a, *Africa's Urbanisation Dynamics 2025: Planning for Urban Expansion*. Paris: OECD.

OECD / Organisation for Economic Co-operation and Development, 2025b, *OECD Regulatory Policy Outlook 2025*. Paris: OECD.

OECD / Organisation for Economic Co-operation and Development & WTO / World Trade Organisation, 2025, *Economic Implications of Data Regulation: Balancing Openness and Trust*. Paris: OECD.

Oelofsen, R., 2015, "Decolonisation of the African Mind and Intellectual Landscape". *Phronimon* 16(2), 130.

Okolo, C.T., K. Aruleba & G. Obaido, 2023, "Responsible AI in Africa – Challenges and Opportunities". In: D.O. Eke, K. Wakunuma & S. Akintoye (eds.), *Artificial Intelligence in Africa: Challenges and Opportunities*. Cham: Springer.

Okoth, K.O., 2023, *Red Africa: Reclaiming Revolutionary Black Politics*. London: Verso.

Okoth-Ogendo, H.W.O., 1989, "Some Issues of Theory in the Study of Tenure Relations in African Agriculture". *Africa* 59(1), 6–17.

Olier, J., T.-Y. Seow & V. Lim, 2026, "AI Watch: Global Regulatory Tracker – Singapore". *White & Case Insights*, 4 March. Available at: https://www.whitecase.com/insight-our-thinking/ai-watch-global-regulatory-tracker-singapore.

Omasire, K.A., 2024, *Effects of Urban Sprawl on Agricultural Land Use in Peri-Urban Areas of Wote Town, Makueni County, Kenya*.

Ondanyo, M.A., M.M. Alhassan, C.M. Mugala & A. Omran, 2024, "Artisanal Gold Mining in Africa – Environmental Pollution and Human Health Implications". *Exposure and Health* 16(4) 1067–1095.

Ongoma V., Y. Brouziyne, E.H. Bouras & A. Chehbouni, 2025, "Closing yield gap for sustainable food security in sub-Saharan Africa – progress, challenges, and opportunities." *Front. Agron.* 7, 1572061. doi: 10.3389/fagro.2025.1572061.

Osborn, A., 2026, "Russia to Give Itself Sweeping Powers to Ban or Restrict Foreign AI Tools". *Reuters*, at https://www.reuters.com/business/russia-give-itself-sweeping-powers-ban-or-restrict-foreign-ai-tools-2026-03-20/, accessed 20 March 2026.

Osemuyi, O.C., 2024, "Cultural and Linguistic Diversity in Africa: The Impact of Colonial Imperialism on Economic Growth and Integration". *Journal of Contemporary Social and Economic Issues* 4(1), 20–31.

Osorio, C.P., A. Manuel & C. Irwin, 2025, "To What Extent Does Being Colonised Influence Climate Vulnerability?". *The Cambridge Journal of Climate Research* 2(1), 10.

Ost, F. & M. van de Kerchove, 2002, *De la pyramide au réseau?: Pour une théorie dialectique du droit.* Brussels: Publications des Facultés universitaires Saint-Louis.

Ostrom, E., 1990, *Governing the Commons: The Evolution of Institutions for Collective Action.* Cambridge: Cambridge University Press.

Oxford Insights, 2021, *Government AI Readiness Index 2021.*

Ozkan, M., 2025, "'Correct the Map': Africa takes on Centuries-old 'Biggest lie' in World Geography". *AA*, at https://www.aa.com.tr/en/africa/-correct-the-map-africa-takes-on-centuries-old-biggest-lie-in-world-geography/3689488, accessed 27 September 2025.

Pajuste, T. (ed.), 2025. *Human Rights in the Digital Domain: Core Questions – Part I: Adapting Human Rights to a Digital World.* Cambridge: Cambridge University Press.

Pan-African Parliament, 2025a, "African Parliamentarians Adopt the Continent's First Model Law on Sustainable Soil Management in Africa". *Pan-African Parliament*, at https://pap.au.int/en/news/press-releases/2025-11-06/african-parliamentarians-adopt-continents-first-model-law, accessed 11 March 2026.

Pan-African Parliament, 2025b, "Consultations with Central, Northern and Western African Regions on the Model Law on Sustainable Soil Management". *PAP Press Release*, at https://pap.au.int/en/news/press-releases/2025-10-19/consultations-central-northern-and-western-african-regions-model-la, accessed 19 March 2026.

Pan-African Parliament, 2025c, "PAP Analyses Draft Model Law on Sustainable Soil Management in Africa". *Pan-African Parliament*, at https://pap.au.int/en/news/press-releases/2025-09-26/pap-analyses-draft-model-law-sustainable-soil-management-africa, accessed 11 March 2026.

PAP / Pan-African Parliament & EP / European Parliament, 2025, *AU–EU Parliamentary Pre-Summit Meeting Joint Declaration under the theme "Renewing Africa-Europe Parliamentary Cooperation in a Changing Global Context".*

Patil, D., 2024, "Artificial Intelligence in Financial Services: Advancements in Fraud Detection, Risk Management, and Algorithmic Trading Optimization". SSRN https://papers.ssrn.com/sol3/papers.cfm?abstract_id=5057412.

Peña, P. & J. Varon, 2021, "Teenager Pregnancy Addressed Through Data Colonialism in a System Patriarchal by Design". *Not My AI*, 5 March 2021 (updated 26 April 2022), at https://notmy.ai/news/case-study-plataforma-tecnologica-de-intervencion-social-argentina-and-brazil/, accessed 7 October 2025.

Perumall, A. & F. Ismail, 2026, "South Africa: AI Policy Moves Towards Approval". *Fasken*, at https://www.fasken.com/en/knowledge/2026/02/south-africa-ai-policy-moves-towards-approval, accessed 20 March 2026.

Petse, I. & U. Phindelo, 2025, "The Influence of ChatGPT-generated Data on the Administration of Justice in South Africa". *Turf Law Journal* 5 1–14.

Pharatlhatlhe, K. & J. Vanheukelom, 2019, *Financing the African Union: On Mindset and Money.*

Pierce, L., 2024, "South Africa's Draft National AI Plan: Not Good Enough". *PPM Attorneys*, 6 April. At https://www.ppmattorneys.co.za/south-africas-draft-national-ai-plan/, accessed 29 October 2025.

Pirozolli, A., 2024, "The Human-Centric Perspective in the Regulation of Artificial Intelligence". *European Papers – European Forum*, at https://www.europeanpapers.eu/europeanforum/human-centric-perspective-regulation-artificial-intelligence, accessed 2 October 2025.

Poitras, M., 2022, "Soil Governance: Who is Governing Who? A North American Indigenous Perspective on Mother Earth". *Soil Security* 6, 1–5.

Poppiel, R.R., M.R. Cherubin, J.J.M. Novais & J.A.M. Demattê, 2025, "Soil Health in Latin America and the Caribbean". *Communications Earth & Environment* 6(141), 1–11.

Porter, S. & E. Cook, 2023, "Decolonisation as a Driver for the Sustainable Development Goals". *Times Higher Education*, 11 July, at https://www.timeshighereducation.com/campus/decolonisation-driver-sustainable-development-goals, accessed 7 January 2026.

Pring, G.R. & C.K. Pring, 2009, *Greening Justice: Creating and Improving Environmental Courts and Tribunals.*

Pring, G.R. & C.K. Pring, 2021, *Environmental Courts & Tribunals: A Guide for Policy Makers.* Nairobi: United Nations Environment Programme.

Randazzoa, M.S. & G. Hill, 2025, "Human Dignity in the Age of Artificial Intelligence: An Overview of Legal Issues and Regulatory Regimes". *Australian Journal of Human Rights*, 1–23.

Rashid, R., 2026, "South Korea's 'world-first' AI laws face pushback amid bid to become leading tech power". *The Guardian*, at https://www.theguardian.com/world/2026/jan/29/south-korea-world-first-ai-regulation-laws, accessed 20 March 2026.

Rautela, K.S. & M.K. Goyal, 2024, "Transforming Air Pollution Management in India with AI and Machine Learning Technologies". *Scientific Reports* 14.

Rawls, J., 1999, *A Theory of Justice*, rev. ed. Cambridge, Mass.: Harvard University Press.

Republic of Namibia, 2022, *Report of the First Ordinary Session of the Sixth Parliament of the Pan-African Parliament (PAP)*, Midrand, Johannesburg, South Africa, from 24 October to 12 November 2022, at https://www.parliament.na/wp-content/uploads/2023/02/Report-of-the-First-Ordinary-Session-of-the-6th-Paliament-of-PAP.pdf, accessed 14 April 2026.

Republic of The Gambia, 2022, *Report of the National Assembly delegation to the Pan-African Parliament*, Sixth Parliament, First Ordinary Session, Midrand, South Africa, October–November 2022, at https://www.assembly.gm/wp-content/uploads/2023/03/Report-on-the-First-Ordinary-Session-of-the-Sixth-Pan-African-Parliament.pdf, accessed 14 April 2026.

Rhim, D., 2026, "Understanding South Korea's New AI Law: Key Considerations for Multinational Employers". *Littler*, at https://www.littler.com/news-analysis/asap/understanding-south-koreas-new-ai-law-key-considerations-multinational-employers, accessed 20 March 2026.

Rhodes, C.J., 2014, "Soil Erosion, Climate Change and Global Food Security: Challenges and Strategies". *Science Progress* 97(2), 97–153.

Ritchie, O., M. Anderljung, & T. Rachman, 2025, "From Turing to Tomorrow: The UK's Approach to AI Regulation". Preprint of forthcoming book chapter.

Rodi, M., O.C. Ruppel & M.D. Leuzinger, 2025, "Bodenschutz und Landnutzung als Herausforderung für die Klimapolitik". *Zeitschrift für Klima und Recht (KlimR)* 10, 290–295.

Rodney, W., 1981, *How Europe Underdeveloped Africa.* Washington, DC: Howard University Press.

Rodrigues, R., 2020, "Legal and Human Rights Issues of AI: Gaps, Challenges and Vulnerabilities". *Journal of Responsible Technology* 4, 100005.

Roe, E., 1991, "Development Narratives, or Making the Best of Blueprint Development". *World Development* 19(4), 287–300.

Roe, E., 1995, "Except-Africa: Postscript to a Special Section on Development Narratives". *World Development* 23(6), 1065–1069.

Ronchi, S., S. Salata, A. Arcidiacono, E. Piroli & L. Montanarella, 2019, "Policy Instruments for Soil Protection among the EU Member States: A Comparative Analysis". *Land Use Policy* 82, 763–780.

Rosca, C.-M. & A. Stancu, 2025, "Emerging Trends in AI-Based Soil Contamination Monitoring and Prevention". *Agriculture* 15, 1–30.

Ruder, S.-L. & H. Wittman, 2025, "Agricultural Data Governance from the Ground Up: Exploring Data Justice with Agri-Food Movements". *Big Data & Society* 12(1).

Ruiz-Campillo, X., 2025, "Just Transitions in Climate and Sustainable Governance: A Perspective from the South". In: E. Domorenok, P. Graziano & K. Zimmermann (eds), *The Eco-social Polity? Theoretical, Conceptual and Empirical Issues*. Bristol: Policy Press, University of Bristol, 271.

Ruppel, O.C., 2022a, "Overview of International Soil Law". *Soil Security* 6.

Ruppel, O.C., 2022b, "Soil Protection and Legal Aspects of International Trade in Agriculture in Times of Climate Change: The WTO Dimension". *Soil Security* 6.

Ruppel, O.C., 2024, "Überblick über das internationale Bodenschutzrecht". In: Schnedl, G., O.C. Ruppel & M. Hofer (eds), *Bodenschutz im Zeichen der Klimakrise: Rechtliche Rahmenbedingungen, politische Herausforderungen und Konfliktpotentiale*. Wien: Verlag Österreich, 31–66.

Ruppel, O.C., 2025, "Bodenschutzrecht in Südafrika und der Afrikanischen Union". *Zeitschrift für Klima und Recht (KlimR)* 10, 303–310.

Ruppel, O.C. & H. Ginzky (eds.), 2021, *African Soil Protection Law – Mapping Out Options for a Model Legislation for Improved Sustainable Soil Management in Africa: A Comparative Legal Analysis from Cameroon, Kenya, and Zambia*. Baden-Baden: Nomos.

Ruppel, O.C. & H. Ginzky, 2024, *African Soils: The Foundation of Our Future: A Policy Report*. United Nations Environment Programme. Nairobi.

Ruppel, O. C., & A. Khatibi, 2025, "Assessing Namibia's Climate-related Laws and Policies: Applying the Human Rights Integration Framework for Climate Policy Evaluation". *Namibian Journal of Social Justice* 4, 2–40.

Ruppel, O.C. & R. Murray, 2024, "The Future of the SDGs: A Comparative Constitutional Rescue Plan?" *Journal of Environmental Policy and Law* 54, 155–187.

Ruppel, O.C. & R. Murray, 2025/2026, "Climate Change, Human Rights, and Soil Security: The Wider ICJ Advisory Opinion Nexus?". *Environmental Policy and Law* (Special Issue) 56(1-2), 1–16.

Ruppel, O.C. & P. Schweighofer, 2024, "Intergenerationelle Klimagerechtigkeit für das heutige Namibia: Lange Schatten des Kolonialismus im ehemaligen Deutsch-Südwestafrika?". In: D. Ennöckl, M. Hofer & V. Madner (eds.) *Festschrift für Eva Schulev-Steindl*. Verlag Österreich, 501–518.

Ruppel, O.C., H. Ginzky & R. Murray (eds), 2025, *Legal Pathways to Sustainable Soil Management in Africa: Insights from Botswana, Burkina Faso, Cameroon, Kenya, Madagascar, Morocco, Mozambique, Namibia, South Africa, Uganda and Zambia*. Baden-Baden: Nomos.

Ruthmann-Bloem, E., 2023, "Epistemic Justice and Dynamic AI Ethics in Africa". In: E.O. Arakpogun, Z. Elsahn, F. Olan & F. Elsahn (eds.), *Artificial Intelligence in Africa: Challenges and Opportunities*. Cham: Springer.

Salami, A.O., 2024, "Artificial Intelligence, Digital Colonialism, and the Implications for Africa's Future Development". *Data & Policy* 6, 1-12.

Samuel, S., 2019, "A New Study Finds a Potential Risk with Self-Driving Cars: Failure to Detect Dark-Skinned Pedestrians". *Vox* (Future Perfect), 6 March 2019, at https://www.vox.com/future-perfect/2019/3/5/18251924/self-driving-car-racial-bias-study-autonomous-vehicle-dark-skin, accessed 7 October 2025.

Sanchez, P.A., K.D. Shepherd, M.J. Soule, F.M. Place, R.J. Buresh, A.-M.N. Izac, U. Mokwunye, F.R. Kwesiga, C.G. Ndiritu & P.L. Woomer, 1997, "Soil Fertility Replenishment in Africa: An Investment in Natural Resource Capital". In: R.J. Buresh, P.A. Sanchez & F. Calhoun (eds.), *Replenishing Soil Fertility in Africa*. Madison: Soil Science Society of America, SSSA Special Publication No. 51, 1–46.

Sand Technologies, 2025, "AI for Environmental Monitoring: Benefits, Uses & Innovation". *Sand Technologies*, at https://www.sandtech.com/insight/ai-for-environmental-monitoring/, accessed 7 October 2025.

Sandkühler, T., A. Epple & J. Zimmerer, 2023, "Restitution and Historical Culture in the (Post)Colonial Context. Facets of a Challenging Debate". In: T. Sandkühler, A. Epple & J. Zimmerer (eds.), *Historical Culture by Restitution? A Debate on Art, Museums, and Justice*. Leiden: Koninklijke Brill NV, 15–48.

Sardo, M.C., 2023, "Responsibility for Climate Justice: Political not Moral". *European Journal of Political Theory* 22(1), 26–50.

Savela, N.J., R. Sairinen, M. Salkinoja & P. Kivimaa, 2020, "Rapid Urbanisation and Infrastructure Pressure: Comparing the Sustainability Transition Potential of Water and Energy Regimes in Namibia". *World* 1(2), 49–66.

Schipper, T., 2026, "Automation and Inequality: Social Safety Nets in the Age of AI". *GIGA Focus Global 3*, at https://www.giga-hamburg.de/en/publications/giga-focus/automation-and-inequality-social-safety-nets-in-the-age-of-ai, accessed 20 March 2026.

Schmelzer, M. 2022, "From Downscaling to Global Justice: On the Need to Integrate Climate Reparations into the Degrowth Agenda". Paper presented at the Dakar Conference on Facing Socio-ecological Crisis: Delinking and the Question of Global Reparations, Dakar (25–28 October).

Schnedl, G., 2025, "Soil Protection Law in Austria". In: Ginzky, H., O.C. Ruppel, I.L. Heuser, D. Grinlinton, A. Khatibi, P. Kameri-Mbote & N. Rodriguez-Eugenio (eds), *International Yearbook of Soil Law and Policy*, Vol. 7. Cham: Springer International Publishing, 377–409.

Schnedl, G., O.C. Ruppel & M. Hofer (eds), 2024, *Bodenschutz im Zeichen der Klimakrise: Rechtliche Rahmenbedingungen, politische Herausforderungen und Konfliktpotentiale*. Wien: Verlag Österreich.

Schwenga, S., L. Bernardini, K. Keiblinger, H.-P. Kaul, I. Fister Jr., N. Lukač, J. Del Ser & A. Holzinger, 2026, "What Can Artificial Intelligence Do for Soil Health in Agriculture?". *Computer Science Review* 59, 1–22.

Scoones, I., 2016, "Chinese engagement in African agriculture is not what it seems". *IIED (Insight)*, 6 April 2016, at https://www.iied.org/chinese-engagement-african-agriculture-not-what-it-seems, accessed 30 October 2025.

Selvakumar, P., Shabnam, A.H. Shah, S.G.B. Aradhya & T.C. Manjunath, 2025, "Applications of AI in Healthcare, Agriculture, Finance, and Other Industries". In: F.A. Shaik & M. Rahaman (eds.), *Innovative Approaches in Computational Systems and Smart Applications*. IGI Global Scientific Publishing, 43–70.

Seutloali, J., 2024, *Land of the Ancestors: Expropriation as a Necessity for Justice*. Ilanga BC Publishers.

Shange, N.T., 2024, "African Ubuntu Humanness Ontology and Ecological Connection". *Environmental Justice*, 1–4.

Shany, Y., 2025, "How Far Can You Go? Shoehorning Digital Rights into Existing Human Rights Treaties". *The Vienna Journal on International Constitutional Law* 19(4), 435–477.

Shirer, M., 2024, "Worldwide Spending on Artificial Intelligence Forecast to Reach $632 billion in 2028, According to a New IDC Spending Guide". *IDC*, at https://my.idc.com/getdoc.jsp?containerId=prUS52530724, accessed 2 October 2025.

Shivhare, S. & K.B. Park, 2025, "South Korea's New AI Framework Act: A Balancing Act Between Innovation and Regulation". *Future of Privacy Forum*, at https://fpf.org/blog/south-koreas-new-ai-framework-act-a-balancing-act-between-innovation-and-regulation/, accessed 20 March 2026.

Showers, K., 2006, "A History of African Soil: Perceptions, Use and Abuse". In: J.R. McNeill & V. Winiwarter (eds.), *Soils and Societies: Perspectives from Environmental History*. White Horse Press, 118–176.

Signé, L., 2025, "Leveraging AI and Emerging Technologies to Unlock Africa's Potential". In: *Foresight Africa: Top Priorities for the Continent 2025–2030*. Washington, D.C.: Brookings Institution, January, 138–149.

Silimina, D., 2019, "Case Study: Chinese Agricultural Firm Uses Drones to Fight Pests in Zambia". *China Global South*, 2 September 2019, at https://chinaglobalsouth.com/analysis/case-study-chinese-agricultural-firm-uses-drones-to-fight-pests-in-zambia/, accessed 30 October 2025.

Singh, M., 2020, "History of AI". *Journal of Emerging Technologies and Innovative Research* 7, 58–61.

Sinkner, J., 2024, "Why are African Artifacts Everywhere but Africa?". *Africa is a Country*, at https://africasacountry.com/2024/11/why-are-african-artifacts-everywhere-but-africa, accessed 22 September 2025.

Slow, O., 2023, "US Refuses Climate Reparations for Developing Nations". *BBC News* 14 July, at www.bbc.com/news/world-us-canada-66197366, accessed 18 September 2025.

Smit, W., 2021, "Urbanisation in the Global South". *Oxford Research Encyclopedia of Global Public Health*. Oxford University Press.

Smith, E., 2024, "Project Guacamaya Uses Daily Satellite Images, Amazon-Specific AI Models in Battle Against Deforestation". *Microsoft Source (LATAM)*, 25 September 2024, at https://news.microsoft.com/source/latam/features/ai/project-guacamaya-rainforest-deforestation/?lang=en, accessed 7 October 2025.

Smith, P., R.M. Poch, D.A. Lobb, R. Bhattacharyya, G. Alloush, G.D. Eudoxie, L.H.C. Anjos, M. Castellano, G.M. Ndzana, C. Chenu, R. Naidu, J. Vijayanathan, A.M. Muscolo, G.A. Studdert, N.R. Eugenio, M.C. Calzolari, N. Amuri & P. Hallett, 2024, "Status of the World's Soils". *Annual Review of Environment and Resources* 49, 73–104.

Smith, P., M. Bustamante, H. Ahammad, H. Clark, H. Dong, E.A. Elsiddig, H. Haberl, R. Harper, J. House, M. Jafari, O. Masera, C. Mbow, N.H. Ravindranath, C.W. Rice, C. Robledo Abad, A. Romanovskaya, F. Sperling & P. Tubiello, 2014, "Agriculture, Forestry, and Other Land Use (AFOLU)". In: O. Edenhofer, R. Pichs-Madruga, Y. Sokona, E. Farahani, S. Kadner, K. Seyboth, A. Adler, I. Baum, S. Brunner, P. Eickemeier, B. Kriemann, J. Savolainen, S. Schlömer, C. von Stechow, T. Zwickel & J.C. Minx (eds.), *Climate Change 2014: Mitigation of Climate Change. Contribution of Working Group III to the Fifth Assessment Report of the Intergovernmental Panel on Climate Change*. Cambridge: Cambridge University Press, Chapter 11.

Soils4Africa, undated, "The Project". *Soils4Africa*, at https://www.soils4africa-h2020.eu/the-project, accessed 4 July 2025.

Sokona, Y., Y. Mulugetta, M. Tesfamichael, F. Kaboub, N. Hällström, M. Stilwell, M. Adow & C. Besaans, 2023, *Just Transition: A Climate, Energy and Development Vision for Africa*. Independent Expert Group on Just Transition and Development.

Southall, R., 2023, "South African Diamonds Adorn the Crown of King Charles – Why they're Unlikely to be Returned". *The Conversation,* at https://theconversation.com/south-african-diamonds-adorn-the-crown-of-king-charles-why-theyre-unlikely-to-be-returned-205597, accessed 22 September 2025.

Sovacool, B.K. & M.H. Dworkin, 2015, "Energy Justice: Conceptual Insights and Practical Applications". *Applied Energy* 142, 435–444.

Spencer, P., P.E. Perkins & J.D. Erickson, 2018, "Re-establishing Justice as a Pillar of Ecological Economics through Feminist Perspectives". *Ecological Economics* 152, 191–198.

Spencer, T., M. Colombier, O. Sartor, A. Garg, V. Tiwari, J. Burton, T. Caetano, F. Green, F. Teng & J. Wiseman, 2018, "The 1.5 C Target and Coal Sector Transition: At the Limits of Societal Feasibility". *Climate Change* 18(3), 335–351.

Stanford HAI / Stanford Institute for Human-Centered Artificial Intelligence, 2025, *Artificial Intelligence Index Report 2025*. Stanford, CA: Stanford University.

Statista, 2023, "Urbanisation Rate in Africa in 2023, by Country". At https://www.statista.com/statistics/1223543/urbanisation-rate-in-africa-by-country/, accessed 2 October 2025.

Stone, K.E., 2025, "Trump's Funding Cuts Will Hurt South Africa and the Region". *ISS,* at https://issafrica.org/iss-today/trump-s-funding-cuts-will-hurt-south-africa-and-the-region, accessed 22 September 2025.

Stony, 2025, "Africa Rising or Africa Exploited? Big Tech's World Domination Plan". *Medium (Woza Business)*, 6 January 2025, at https://medium.com/woza-business/africa-rising-or-africa-exploited-big-techs-world-domination-plan-0c41dc1024ed, accessed 7 October 2025.

Stubenrauch, J., B. Garske & F. Ekardt, 2018, "Sustainable Land Use, Soil Protection and Phosphorus Management from a Cross-National Perspective". *Sustainability* 10(6), 1988.

Sulaiman, S. & D. Olën, 2024, "AI Regulation and Policy in Africa". *Dentons*, 13 June 2024, at https://www.dentons.com/en/insights/articles/2024/june/13/ai-regulation-and-policy-in-africa, accessed 7 October 2025.

Sultana, F., 2022, "The Unbearable Heaviness of Climate Coloniality". *Political Geography* 99, 1–16.

Sustainability Directory, 2025, "Algorithmic Bias in Soil Health Management Systems". *Prism (Sustainability Directory)*, 5 September 2025, at https://prism.sustainability-directory.com/scenario/algorithmic-bias-in-soil-health-management-systems/, accessed 7 October 2025.

Swift, J., 1988, *Major Issues in Pastoral Development, with Special Emphasis on Selected African Countries*. Rome: FAO.

Sylla, N., S. Fischer, A.M. Kaltenbrunner & S. Sathi, 2024, "Global Reparations within Capitalism: Aspirations and Tensions in Contemporary Movements for Reparatory Justice". *Development and Change* 55(4), 560–600.

Tafira, C.K. & S.J. Ndlovu-Gatsheni, 2017, "Beyond Coloniality of Markets: Exploring the Neglected Dimensions of the Land Question from Endogenous African Decolonial Epistemological Perspectives". *Africa Insight* 46(4), 9–22.

Tahura, U.S. & N. Selvadurai, 2022, "The Use of AI in Judicial Decision-Making: The Example of China". *International Journal of Law, Ethics, and Technology*, 1–20.

Táíwò, O., 2022, *Reconsidering Reparations,* Oxford University Press.

Táíwò, O., A. Saez de Tejada-Cuenca & T. Hin Tsoi, 2022, *Appendix B: Colonialism and Climate Vulnerability*. In O. Táíwò (ed.) *Reconsidering Reparations: Worldmaking in the Case of Climate Crisis,* Oxford University Press, 215–222.

Tan, K.C., 2007, "Colonialism, Reparations, and Global Justice". In: J. Miller & R. Kumar (eds.), *Reparations: Interdisciplinary Inquiries*. Oxford: Oxford University Press, 280–306.

Tandon, Y., 2011, "Kleptocratic Capitalism, Climate Finance, and the Green Economy in Africa". *Capitalism Nature Socialism* 22(4), 136–144.

Tanon, A.M.S. 2016. *Le droit des investissements internationaux vu par la CIJ et le CIRDI.*

Taylor, A., 2025, "Albania appoints world's first AI-made minister". *POLITICO*, 11 September. At https://www.politico.eu/article/albania-apppoints-worlds-first-virtual-minister-edi-rama-diella/, accessed 29 October 2025.

Teixeira, T.A., N.L. Vilaça, A.L. Printes, R.C.S. Gomes, I.G. Torné, T.-Y.A. Araújo & A.G. Dias e Dias, 2023, "Development of a Monitoring System against Illegal Deforestation in the Amazon Rainforest Using Artificial Intelligence Algorithms". *Engineering Proceedings* 58(1).

Telleria, J., 2022, "Diversity vs the 2030 Agenda: A Deconstructive Reading of the United Nations Agenda for Sustainable Development". *Critical Social Policy* 42(4), 607–625.

Tetteh, F.M., 2021, "Challenges to Soil Protection and Sustainable Management in Africa". In: H. Ginzky, E. Dooley, I.L. Heuser, E. Kasimbazi, R. Kibugi, T. Markus, T. Qin & O.C. Ruppel (eds.), *International Yearbook of Soil Law and Policy 2019*. Cham: Springer Nature Switzerland AG, 3.

Thaldar, D., 2025, "Ownership of Personal Information?". *The South African Law Journal* 142, 175–198.

Thaldar, D., 2025, "Who Owns Digital Data About You? South African Legal Scholar Weighs Up Property and Privacy Rights". *The Conversation*, at https://theconversation.com/who-owns-digital-data-about-you-south-african-legal-scholar-weighs-up-property-and-privacy-rights-249741, accessed 7 October 2025.

The Guardian, 2025, "African Union Joins Calls to End Use of Mercator Map that Shrinks Continent's Size". *The Guardian*, at https://www.theguardian.com/world/2025/aug/15/african-union-true-size-world-map-replace-mercator-version, accessed 27 September 2025.

Thomson Reuters Foundation, 2025, "Domestic AI governance". *TrustLaw*, 7 May 2025, at https://www.trust.org/toolkit/part-2-emerging-ai-governance-in-africa/domestic-ai-governance/, accessed 7 October 2025.

Thornton, I., 2023, "A Special Delivery by a Fork: Where Does Artificial Intelligence Come From?". *New Directions for Evaluation* (178–179), 23–32.

Timcke, S., Z. Schroeder & D. Haller, 2024, "Scaffolding for the South Africa National AI Policy Framework". *Tech Policy Press*, 29 November. At https://www.techpolicy.press/scaffolding-for-the-south-africa-national-ai-policy-framework/, accessed 27 October 2025.

Tinarwo, J. & S.C. Babu, 2023, "Chinese Artificial Intelligence in Africa: Digital Colonisation or Liberalisation?". Tayarisha Working Paper Series (African Governance in the Digital Age) 2023/012.

Tironi, M. & D.I. Rivera Lisboa, 2023, "Artificial Intelligence in the New Forms of Environmental Governance in the Chilean State: Towards an Eco-Algorithmic Governance". *Technology in Society* 74.

Tironi, M., M. Kearnes, A. Krzywoszynska, C. Granjou & J.F. Salazar, 2021, "Soil Theories: Relational, Decolonial, Inhuman". In: J.F. Salazar, C. Granjou, M. Kearnes, A. Krzywoszynska & M. Tironi (eds.), *Thinking with Soils: Material Politics and Social Theory*. London: Bloomsbury, 15–38.

Travers, L., 2024, "Algorithmic Coloniality? The Case of Chinese Artificial Intelligence Technology and Zimbabwean Surveillance". *Transcience* 15(2), 48–82.

Triki, A., 2022, "Decolonising Food Security in the UN SDGs: Challenging the Hegemonic Discourse". *LSE International Development Review* 2(2), 1–30.

Tuğrul, K.M., 2020, "Soil Management in Sustainable Agriculture". In: M. Hasanuzzaman, M.C.M.T. Filho, M. Fujita & T.A.R. Nogueira (eds.), *Sustainable Crop Production.* London: IntechOpen. https://www.intechopen.com/chapters/68683, accessed 2 October 2025.

Tulone, A., A. Galati, S. Pecoraro, A. Carroccio, D. Siggia, M. Virzì & M. Crescimanno, 2022, "Main intrinsic factors driving land grabbing in the African countries' agro-food industry". *Land Use Policy* 120, 1–9.

Turok, I. & G. McGranahan, 2013, "Urbanisation and Economic Growth: The Arguments and Evidence for Africa and Asia". *Environment and Urbanisation* 25(2), 465–482.

Ubink, J., 2008, *Traditional Authorities in Africa: Resurgence in an Era of Democratization.* Leiden: Leiden University Press.

Uddin, M., 2024, *Farm Data Ownership and Intellectual Property Laws.* CIGI Digital Policy Hub Working Paper. Waterloo, ON: Centre for International Governance Innovation.

UN / United Nations, 2002, *World Conference against Racism, Racial Discrimination, Xenophobia and Related Intolerance: Declaration and Programme of Action.* New York: United Nations Department of Public Information.

UN / United Nations, 2023a, *Our Common Agenda Policy Brief 5: A Global Digital Compact — an Open, Free and Secure Digital Future for All.* New York: United Nations, May.

UN / United Nations News, 2023b, "Guterres Calls for AI 'That Bridges Divides', Rather Than Pushing Us Apart". *UN News (Peace and Security),* 18 July 2023, at https://news.un.org/en/story/2023/07/1138827, accessed 7 October 2025.

UN / United Nations Office of the Special Adviser on Africa, 2025, *Africa Dialogue Series Concept Note: Justice for Africans and People of African Descent Through Reparations.* New York: United Nations.

UNCCD / United Nations Convention to Combat Desertification, 2019, *Creating an Enabling Environment for Land Degradation Neutrality and its Potential Contribution to Enhancing Well-being, Livelihoods and the Environment.* A Report of the Science-Policy Interface. Bonn, Germany.

UNCCD-SPI / United Nations Convention to Combat Desertification – Science-Policy Interface, 2017, Technical Series No. 01, *Scientific Conceptual Framework for Land Degradation Neutrality.* A Report of the Science-Policy Interface.

UNCTAD / United Nations Conference on Trade and Development, 2025, *Technology and Innovation Report 2025: Inclusive Artificial Intelligence for Development.* Geneva: UNCTAD.

UNEP / United Nations Environment Programme, 2021, *Legal Frameworks for Sustainable Land Use: A Comparative Analysis to Support Sustainable Soil Management (SSM).* Nairobi: UNEP.

UNESCO / United Nations Educational, Scientific and Cultural Organisation, 2021, *Recommendation on the Ethics of Artificial Intelligence.* Paris: UNESCO.

Unver, M.B. & S. Odusola-Stevenson, 2025, "UK AI Governance at a Crossroads: Charting the Path Ahead". *International Journal of Mass Communication* 3, 168–183.

*Urbanisation in Africa,* n.d., Africapolis, at https://africapolis.org/en?country=Angola&keyfigure=totalPop&type=abs&year=2015, accessed 2 October 2025.

Uyar, H., I. Karvelas, S. Rizou & S. Fountas, 2024, "Data Value Creation in Agriculture: A Review". *Computers and Electronics in Agriculture* 227, 1–12.

van der Linden, M., 2014, *The Acquisition of Africa (1870–1914): The Nature of Nineteenth-Century International Law.* Oisterwijk: Wolf Legal Publishers.

Van Eck, M., 2025, "What have the Courts Said About the Ethical Use of Artificial Intelligence in Legal Practice?". *De Rebus,* 1 May. At https://www.derebus.org.za/what-have-the-courts-said-about-the-ethical-use-of-artificial-intelligence-in-legal-practice/, accessed 29 October 2025.

Van Rickley, S., 2024, "The Disqualification of Expert Witness for Artificial Intelligence Use". *FreeReferral Blog*, 15 October 2024, at https://www.freereferral.com/blog/disqualification-of-expert-witness-for-artificial-intellegence-use, accessed 7 October 2025.

Vanlauwe, B., A. Bationo, J. Chianu, K.E. Giller, R. Merckx, U. Mokwunye & N. Sanginga, 2010, "Integrated Soil Fertility Management: Operational Definition and Consequences for Implementation and Dissemination". *Outlook on Agriculture* 39(1), 17–24.

Vasdani, T., 2020, "Robot Justice: China's Use of Internet Courts". *LexisNexis Canada (The Lawyer's Daily)*, at https://www.lexisnexis.ca/en-ca/ihc/2020-02/robot-justice-chinas-use-of-internet-courts.page, accessed 7 October 2025.

Vasko, T.B., 2022, "Nature and the Native". *Critical Research on Religion* 10(1), 7–23.

Venditto, B., N.J. Kamwanyah & C.H. Nekare, 2022, *Climate Change, Migration and Urbanisation in Contemporary Namibia* (SITES Working Paper No. 14).

von Carlowitz, P., S. Züfle & E. Schmid. 2025. "Die Rolle digitaler Technologien in Afrikas Landwirtschaftssektor". *GIGA Focus | Afrika* 6, 1–13.

von Eschenbach, W.J., 2021, "Transparency and the Black Box Problem: Why We Do Not Trust AI". *Philosophy & Technology* 34, 1607–1622.

Wachter, S., 2024, "Limitations and Loopholes in the EU AI Act and AI Liability Directives: What this Means for the European Union, the United States and Beyond". *Yale Journal of Law & Technology* 26(3), 671–718.

Walcott-Bryant, A. & Y. Matias, 2025, "5 Ways We're Bringing AI Innovations to People Across Africa". *Google Blog (The Keyword)*, 24 July 2025, at https://blog.google/intl/en-africa/company-news/outreach-and-initiatives/5-ways-were-bringing-ai-innovations-to-people-across-africa/, accessed 7 October 2025.

Wang, J., C. Xu, J. Zhang & R.Y. Zhong, 2021, "Big Data Analytics for Intelligent Manufacturing Systems: A Review". *Journal of Manufacturing Systems* 62, 738–752.

WBGU / German Advisory Council on Global Change, 2026, *Security – Sustainable and Integrated*. Situation Report No. 1.

WEF / World Economic Forum, 2024, *Community Paper: Scaling Technology Adoption for Soil Health: Focus on Africa*.

Wenar, L., 2006, "Reparations for the Future". *Journal of Social Philosophy* 37(3), 396–405.

Werner, J., 2024, "Navigating the New Frontier: How the EU AI Act Will Impact the Agriculture Industry". *Babl*, at https://babl.ai/navigating-the-new-frontier-how-the-eu-ai-act-will-impact-the-agriculture-industry/, accessed 12 July 2025.

White & Case, 2024, "AI Watch: Global Regulatory Tracker – African Union". *White & Case*, 4 December 2024, at https://www.whitecase.com/insight-our-thinking/ai-watch-global-regulatory-tracker-african-union, accessed 7 October 2025.

Wiebusch, M., 2024, *A Theory on Africanizing International Law*. Pretoria University Law Press.

Wilkinson, R., A. Krasodomski, I. Wilkinson & F.J. Varela Sandoval, 2026, *Breaking the Deadlock on AI Governance: How a Crisis Could Lead to Global Coordination*, Chatham House, London.

Williams, E., 1944, *Capitalism and Slavery*. Chapel Hill, NC: University of North Carolina Press.

Wily, L.A., 2011, "'The Law is to Blame': The Vulnerable Status of Common Property Rights in Sub-Saharan Africa". *Development and Change* 42(3), 733–757.

Wily, L.A., 2011, *Whose Land? The Status of Customary Land Tenure in Cameroon*. Yaoundé/London: Centre for Environment and Development, FERN & The Rainforest Foundation UK.

WIPO / World Intellectual Property Organisation, 2019, *WIPO Technology Trends 2019: Artificial Intelligence*. Geneva: World Intellectual Property Organisation.

Wise, L., 2021, "The Genocide–Ecocide Nexus in Sudan: Violent 'Development' and the Racial-Spatial Dynamics of (Neo)Colonial-Capitalist Extraction". *Journal of Genocide Research* 23(2), 189–211.

Wiseman, L., J. Sanderson, A. Zhang & E. Jakku, 2019, "Farmers and Their Data: An Examination of Farmers' Reluctance to Share Their Data Through the Lens of the Laws Impacting Smart Farming". *NJAS – Wageningen Journal of Life Sciences* 90–91, 1–10.

Woldeyes, Y. G. & T. Belachew, 2021, "Decolonising the Environment through African Epistemologies". *Gestión y Ambiente* 24(supl. 1), 61–81.

World Economic Forum, 2024, *Scaling Technology Adoption for Soil Health: A Focus on Africa.* Geneva: WEF.

World Economic Forum, 2024, *The Global Risks Report 2024* (19th ed.). Geneva: WEF.

Wörsdörfer, M., 2023, "The E.U.'s Artificial Intelligence Act: An Ordoliberal Assessment". SSRN https://papers.ssrn.com/sol3/papers.cfm?abstract_id=4544276.

WTO / World Trade Organisation, 2024, *Trading with Intelligence: How AI Shapes and is Shaped by International Trade*. Geneva: WTO.

WTO / World Trade Organisation, 2025, *World Trade Report 2025: Making Trade and AI Work Together to the Benefit of All.* Geneva: WTO.

Wu, X., A. Pan & Q. She, 2021, "Direct and Indirect Effects of Climate Aid on Carbon Emissions in Recipient Countries". *Journal of Cleaner Production* 290, 1–10.

Wyatt, A.M., 2008, "The Dirt on International Environmental Law Regarding Soils: Is the Existing Regime Adequate?". *Duke Environmental Law & Policy Forum* 19, 165–207.

Xu, H., K. Donovan, E.C. Franks, B.H. Lee & M. Wong, 2023, *China's New AI Regulation. Latham & Watkins*, at https://www.lw.com/en/admin/upload/SiteAttachments/Chinas-New-AI-Regulations.pdf, accessed 2 October 2025.

Yu, D., H. Rosenfeld & A. Gupta, 2023, "The 'AI Divide' Between the Global North and the Global South". *World Economic Forum*, 16 January 2023, at https://www.weforum.org/stories/2023/01/davos23-ai-divide-global-north-global-south/, accessed 7 October 2025.

Yu, Z., E. Hou, J. Pompeo, R. Huffaker, M. Wang & Y. Zhao, 2025, "Agriculture Technology Providers' Perspectives of Data Rights and Obligations in Agriculture Reflected by Farm Data Value Chain". *Sustainable Futures* 9, 1–10.

Yuen, A. & Y.L. Lee, 2026, "Understanding Singapore's New Model Framework for Agentic AI Governance". *Eversheds Sutherland Insights*, 2 February, at: https://www.eversheds-sutherland.com/en/global/insights/singapore-understanding-singapores-new-model-framework-for-agentic-ai-governance.

Zaballos, E., 2025, "DeepSeek Breach Opens Floodgates to Dark Web". *Dark Reading*, 22 April 2025, at https://www.darkreading.com/cyberattacks-data-breaches/deepseek-breach-opens-floodgates-dark-web, accessed 8 October 2025.

Zarcone, C., 2024, "Richtlijn Bodemmonitoring: EU op Weg naar Gezonde Bodems 2050". *Council of the European Union*, at https://www.consilium.europa.eu/nl/press/press-releases/2024/06/17/soil-monitoring-law-eu-on-the-pathway-to-healthy-soils-by-2050/, accessed 9 July 2025.

Zhan, H. & W. Liao, 2024, "Ways to Improve China's Ecological Governance Effectiveness through Artificial Intelligence". *Environment, Resource and Ecology Journal* 8, 160–169.

Zhang, Z., J. Zhang, X. Zhang & W. Mai, 2025, "A Comprehensive Overview of Generative AI (GAI): Technologies, Applications, and Challenges". *Neurocomputing* 632.

Zhelyazkova, A., E. Thomann, E. Ruffing & S. Princen, 2023, "Differentiated Policy Implementation in the European Union". *West European Politics* 47(3), 439–465.

Zhou, S., 2024, "Analyzing the Justification for Using Generative AI Technology to Generate Judgments Based on the Virtue Jurisprudence Theory". *Journal of Decision Systems*, 1–24.